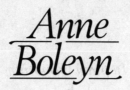

Anne
Boleyn

In piam memoriam
J. F. G.
magistri mei

Anne Boleyn

E. W. IVES

Basil Blackwell

First published 1986
Reprinted 1987
Reprinted and first paperback edition 1988

Basil Blackwell Ltd
108 Cowley Road, Oxford OX4 1JF, UK

Basil Blackwell Inc.
432 Park Avenue South, Suite 1503
New York, NY 10016, USA

British Library Cataloguing in Publication Data

Ives, E. W.
    Anne Boleyn.
    I. Anne Boleyn, *Queen, consort of Henry VIII,*
    King of England   2. Great Britain—Queens—
    Biography
    I. Title
    942.05′2′0924   DA333.B6

    ISBN 0–631–14745–4
    ISBN 0–631–16065–5 Pbk

Library of Congress Cataloging in Publication Data

Ives, E. W. (Eric William), 1931–
    Anne Boleyn.

    Includes index.
    I. Anne Boleyn, Queen, consort of Henry VIII,
    King of England, 1507–1536.   2. Great Britain—
    Queens—Biography.   3. Great Britain—History—
    Henry VIII, 1509–1547.   4. Henry VIII, King of England,
    1491–1547—Family.   I. Title.
    DA333.B6I84   1986   942.05′2′0924 [B]   86–6130

    ISBN 0-631-14745-4
    ISBN 0–631–16065–5 (pbk.)

Typeset by Freeman Graphic, Tonbridge, Kent
Printed in Great Britain

Contents

Contents

Preface

⟨decorative flourish⟩

THE STORY OF Anne Boleyn has inspired biography, drama, opera, film and television, to say nothing of historical fiction and semi-fiction. Why then another work about her? First, there is new material which was not available to the authoritative biography produced by Paul Friedmann as long ago as 1884. Not a great deal, it is true, but sufficient, and at points in the story significant enough to warrant a new assessment. Very much more important has been the advance in our understanding of England in the early sixteenth century – its culture, its society, its politics, indeed the whole context of Anne Boleyn's career. If the outline drawn by Friedmann remains, as it must, largely unchanged, the background is so substantially different as to offer almost a new picture. And this is guaranteed (if we may continue the metaphor) by the joint effect of detail and background on perspective. Anne stands out much more sharply, much more the mistress of her own destiny and much less an incidental appendage to the main story of Henry VIII and the English Reformation.

New detail, new background, new perspective – but the story of Anne Boleyn remains one of the great romantic tragedies of Europe, and the more so because acted out in flesh and blood, not in the artistic imagination. And this essential nature to the story poses a problem for the historian: as a younger colleague who heard that I was writing this book asked somewhat suspiciously, 'Is it scholarly?' I hope it is, but the story of Anne is too 'tuppence coloured' to be told entirely in the 'penny plain' of historical analysis. In any case, such an approach would mislead. We must finally be defeated in our attempt to penetrate to

Anne Boleyn's inner character or her private personality, but if
we are to have any hope of understanding what we can, we must
try to enter the extrovert world in which she lived and to allow
the apparent superficiality of parts of her life the importance
which they actually had for her and for the other denizens of the
Tudor court and country house. Aseptic dissection will leave a
cadaver. This point is especially important in the first part of the
book, which deals with Anne's origins and upbringing and tries
to explore the secret of her power and success. The second
section is more chronological and political, retelling a story
which has been attempted many times before, but putting Anne
in her rightful place at the centre and so discovering significances
and explanations that change the male-dominated interpretations
of traditional accounts. A similar approach is taken in the final
section, which continues the narrative to the tragedy of May
1536, showing how far from the reality is the usual tale of the
sordid end of a broken marriage.

   In the penultimate part of the book, something quite different
is attempted: an exploration of Anne Boleyn's lifestyle and, as far
as we can reach it, her mind. The marriage with Henry is looked
at as a marriage between real people, not merely a dimension of
kingship; Anne's approach to being queen is discussed; the
intellectual milieu surrounding her and her religious concerns,
likewise. The illustrations chosen are disposed to the same end,
not simply as visual relief to the text. They present a gallery of
many of those involved in Anne's story, but beyond this they
present a substantiated likeness of the queen to replace the many
supposititious images, and offer another way to reach out to her
through what she owned or experienced. Not all the material
associated with Anne is represented; in particular, a number of
manuscripts have been omitted, but the great bulk and variety of
genuine items is to be found here. At the end we still only see
through a glass darkly, but we do see.

Few works of history can come to birth in isolation, and certainly
not this or any other study of Anne Boleyn. Among the most
recent biographers, pride of place must go to M. L. Bruce,
whose book was published in 1972. Though broadly traditional
in her assessment, she did offer an imaginative interpretation of
Anne which was none the less well informed. And with such a
subject, the informed imagination will always have something to

tell us. At a more fundamental level there is, even after a century, the work of Paul Friedmann, whose book must be the groundwork for any study of Anne Boleyn. He offers our best access still to the invaluable Habsburg archive, and the need for renewed work on that collection so central to an understanding of events in the England of Henry VIII is second only to the need for a better entrée into the French diplomatic archive for the period, which, except for a few years, remains largely inaccessible. If this fresh study of Anne had identified important gaps in historical sources, it is precisely in these vital areas.

The difficulties of following characters and stories through the complexities of life at court are compounded by family names, promotions in rank and changes in office holding. I have therefore provided a brief list of titles and offices and three family trees, and indicated relationships in the index.

Titles of certain works cited frequently have been abbreviated, and a list of abbreviations provided at the end. Other works have been cited in full at first mention. Where the place of publication has not been included, it is London. Spelling has been modernised.

My thanks are due to many people for their kind assistance: to His Grace the Duke of Northumberland for generous access to his manuscripts, and to the archivist at Alnwick Castle, Dr Colin Shrimpton; to His Grace the Duke of Buccleuch and Queensberry for the use of the miniature of Anne Boleyn by John Hoskins, and to the staff of the Victoria and Albert Museum, particularly Miss Anne Buddy, for help in tracing this image; to the Trustees of the Chequers Estate and their secretary Mr Ken Taylor, for help over Queen Elizabeth's ring; to Mr Michael G. Taylor and to Mr Richard Allen of Sotheby's for information relating to the collection at Hever Castle. Many librarians, curators and their staffs have helped a great deal. I would name especially Miss Janet Backhouse of the British Library Department of Manuscripts; Miss Margaret Condon of the Public Record Office; Dr B. S. Benedikz, the Head of Special Collections, and Dr Susan Brock of the Shakespeare Institute Library and the staff of the Barber Institute Library, all of the University of Birmingham; the Department of Manuscripts of Trinity College, Dublin; the Bibliothèque Royale Albert Ier, Brussels; Dr Christiane Thomas of the Österreichisches Staatsarchiv, Vienna, and Dr R. J. Olney of the Royal Commission on Historical Manuscripts. As always, I owe much to many scholars and friends: Alan Davis, Marguerite Eve, Joan Glanville, John Guy, Gary Hill, Richard Hoyle, Robert Knecht, Virginia Murphy, and Margaret Midgley must be mentioned by name – the book is the richer for their kindness. It was in part written during study leave allowed me by the University of Birmingham, and the research has been supported by its Faculty of Arts. All this makes this book only partly my own, and that is most true of my debt to my wife, who has generously tolerated this 'other woman' in my life. Finally, the dedication is to the memory of the man who first showed me the richness in history.

The plates are to be found between page 206 and page 207.

Acknowledgements

The author and publishers are grateful to the following persons and institutions for permission to reproduce works of art.

1 National Portrait Gallery, London
2 Private Collection
3 In the collection of His Grace The Duke of Buccleuch and Queensberry, K.T.
4 Reproduced by courtesy of the Trustees of the British Museum (1975–6–21–22)
5 Copyright reserved. Reproduced by gracious permission of Her Majesty The Queen
6 Crown copyright. Reproduced with the permission of the Controller of Her Majesty's Stationery Office
7 Royal Ontario Museum, Toronto
8 Private Collection
9 National Portrait Gallery, London
10 Reproduced by courtesy of the Trustees of the British Museum (NI 34.22)
11 Copyright reserved. Reproduced by gracious permission of Her Majesty The Queen
12 Sudeley Castle
13, 14 Copyright reserved. Reproduced by gracious permission of Her Majesty The Queen
15 Patrimoine des Musées Royaux des Beaux-Arts, Brussels
16 Victoria and Albert Museum, London
17 Courtesy of the author
18 Reproduced by courtesy of the Trustees of the British Library (MS Harley 6205, folio 3r)
19 Courtesy of the author
20 Photographie Giraudon
21 Ashmolean Museum, Oxford
22 Biblioteca Vaticana
23 Crown copyright reserved

Titles and Offices

In the nearly forty years of Anne Boleyn's story, it is inevitable that office-holders and ranks altered. The following list sets out the principal identifications; for further details, see the index and the family trees.

Archbishop of Canterbury	to 1532	William Warham
	from 1533	Thomas Cranmer
Archbishop of York	to 1530	Thomas Wolsey
Boleyn		*see:* Ormonde, Pembroke, Rochford, Wiltshire
Brandon		*see:* Suffolk
Butler		*see:* Ormonde
Cardinal	to 1530	Thomas Wolsey
Chancellor	to 1529	Thomas Wolsey
	1529–32	Thomas More
	from 1533	Thomas Audley (keeper of the great seal, 1532–3)
Controller of the household	to 1519	Edward Ponynges
	1519/20–21/22	Thomas Boleyn
	1521/22–32	Henry Guildford
	from 1532	William Paulet
Howard		*see:* Norfolk, Surrey
Legate	1528–9	Cardinal Campeggio
The legates	1528–9	Cardinals Campeggio and Wolsey
Norfolk, dowager, duchess of		Agnes Howard, née Tylney, wife of Thomas Howard (d.1524)

Norfolk, duchess of		Elizabeth Howard, née Stafford, wife of Thomas Howard (d.1554)
Norfolk, duke of	1514–24 from 1524	Thomas Howard, d.1524 Thomas Howard, d.1554
Northumberland, countess of		Mary Percy, née Talbot, wife of Henry Percy
Northumberland, earl of	to 1527 from 1527	Henry Algernon Percy, d.1527 Henry Percy, d.1537
Ormonde, earl of	to 1515 from 1529	Thomas Butler Thomas Boleyn
Pembroke, marchioness of	1532–3	Anne Boleyn
Percy		*see:* Northumberland
Richmond, duchess of		Mary Fitzroy, née Howard, wife of Henry Fitzroy
Richmond, duke of	1525–36	Henry Fitzroy, bastard son of Henry VIII
Rochford, Lady Anne	1532–3	Anne Boleyn
Rochford, Jane Lady		Jane Boleyn, née Parker, wife of George Boleyn
Rochford, Viscount	1525–9 1529–36	Thomas Boleyn George Boleyn (courtesy title only to c.1530)
Secretary, king's	1529–34 from 1534	Stephen Gardiner Thomas Cromwell
Shrewsbury, earl of		George Talbot, d.1538
Suffolk, duchess of	1515–33 from 1533	Mary, sister of Henry VIII, wife of Charles Brandon Katherine Brandon, née Willoughby, wife of Charles Brandon
Suffolk, duke of	from 1514	Charles Brandon
Surrey, earl of	to 1514 1514–24 from 1524	Thomas Howard, d.1524 Thomas Howard, d.1554 Henry Howard
Talbot		*see:* Northumberland, Shrewsbury
Treasurer of the household	1519–21 1521/22–5 from 1525	Edward Ponynges Thomas Boleyn William Fitzwilliam
Wiltshire, earl of	from 1529	Thomas Boleyn

The Royal Houses of Europe.

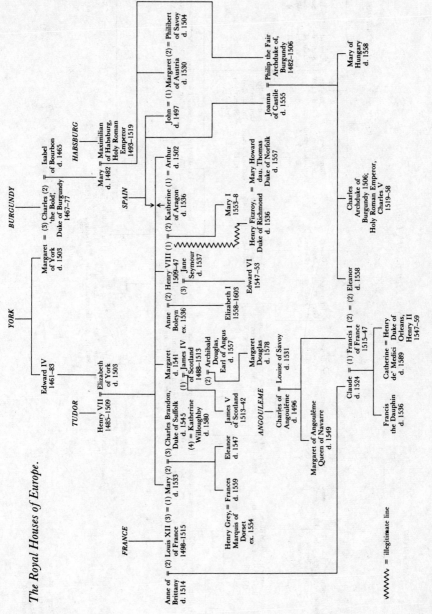

∿∿∿∿ = illegitimate line

The Nobility of Henry VIII's Court.

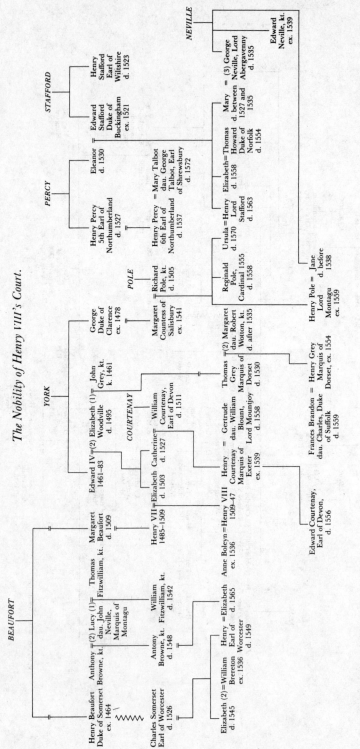

∿ = illegitimate line
k. = killed
kt. = knight
ex. = executed

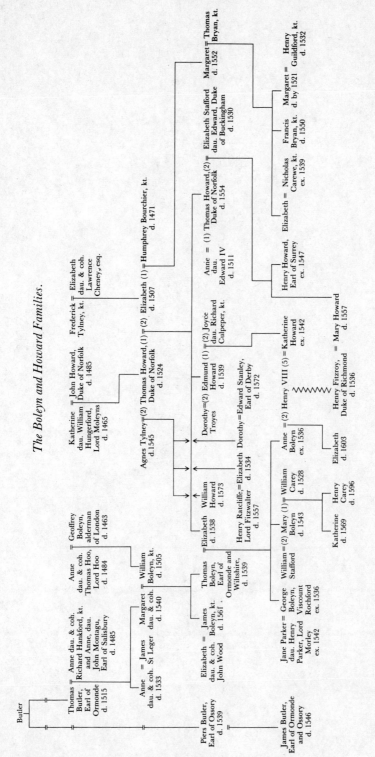

The Boleyn and Howard Families.

⋀⋀⋀ = illegitimate line
coh = co-heiress
ex. = executed
kt. = knight

I

Background and Beginnings

Prologue

IT WAS A long journey, the longest she would ever make. Through the hills of North Kent and its ancient towns, down to the sea at Dover and across the Channel. Like countless other girls of her age who would make a similar journey in later years, Anne Boleyn was going abroad to 'finishing school'.

We have no way of knowing what she made of the Flemish nobleman who was her escort, Claude Bouton, Seigneur de Courbaron. Nor can we know what Anne made of the sea, or of the crossing which could take anything from two or three hours to a day or more. But eventually she stepped ashore on the continent for the first time. It was 1513, and she was to stay for almost nine years.[1]

[1] Paget, in *BIHR*, 54, 65.

1

A Courtier's Daughter

⟨⟨⟨⟨≈⟩⟩⟩⟩

ANNE BOLEYN was born, so tradition goes, at the fairy-tale castle of Hever in the Weald of Kent. Reconstructed by the Astor family earlier this century, Hever remains a romantic shrine to Anne and her love affair with Henry VIII. Unfortunately for romance and tradition, Anne was in fact born in Norfolk, almost certainly at the Boleyn home at Blickling, fifteen miles north of Norwich. The church there still has brasses of the family. The Boleyns did own Hever, although it was less a castle than a comfortable manor house which her great-grandfather Geoffrey had built within an existing moat and curtain wall, and it did become the principal residence of her parents. But Matthew Parker, who became archbishop of Canterbury in 1559 and had earlier been one of Anne's private chaplains, was quite specific that she came, as he did, from Norfolk.[1]

Tradition also tells us that the Boleyns were a family of London merchants, and again tradition leads us astray. Anne Boleyn was born a great lady. Her father, Thomas, was the eldest son of Sir William Boleyn of Blickling, and her mother, Elizabeth, was the daughter of Thomas Howard, earl of Surrey, one of the premier noblemen in England. There was mercantile wealth in the family, but to get back to that we have to go to Geoffrey Boleyn, the builder of Hever. He had left Norfolk in the 1420s, made his fortune as a mercer in London, served as alderman and become lord mayor in 1457–8. Fifteenth-century

---

[1] Parker, *Correspondence*, p. 400. In calling himself Anne's 'poor countryman', Parker is using the term in its sixteenth-century local sense. For full information on all abbreviated titles, see Bibliographical Abbreviations, pp. 421–9.

England, however, was a society open to wealth and talent. After all, had not William de la Pole, the most powerful man in England, been created duke of Suffolk in 1448? And his great-grandfather was a merchant from Hull. It is no surprise, therefore, that Geoffrey Boleyn was able to secure as his second wife one of the daughters and co-heiresses of a nobleman, Thomas Lord Hoo. William, the eldest surviving son of that marriage, made an equally good match with Margaret Butler, daughter and co-heiress of the wealthy Anglo-Irish earl of Ormonde, so that when his eldest son, Anne's father, married a daughter of the earl of Surrey he was continuing a tradition into the third generation. As a result – and this should finally dispel all smell of the shop – Anne's great-grandparents were (apart from Geoffrey) a duke, an earl, the granddaughter of an earl, the daughter of one baron, the daughter of another, and an esquire and his wife.[2] Anne Boleyn came, in fact, from the same sort of background as the majority of the Tudor upper class. Indeed, she was better born than Henry VIII's three other English wives; marrying her did not, as has been unkindly said of Jane Seymour, give the king 'one brother-in-law who bore the name of Smith, and another whose grandfather was a blacksmith at Putney'.[3]

The Boleyns, thus, were not bourgeois, but Geoffrey's wealth had allowed his son William to establish himself as a leading Norfolk gentleman. Knighted in 1483, he became a JP and one of that elite of country gentlemen on whom the crown relied in time of crisis.[4] While he lived, however, his son Thomas was in an equivocal position. He was prospective heir to great wealth – the Boleyn and Hoo estates, half of the Ormonde fortune and half of the lands of the wealthy Hankford family inherited from his Butler grandmother – but in the meantime he had to exist on an annuity of £50 a year, the occupancy of Hever, and whatever his own wife had brought him.[5] That was probably not much, for the earl of Surrey had only just completed the expensive task of

---

[2] For the Boleyn pedigree see J.C. Wedgwood and A. Holt, *History of Parliament: Biographies* (1936), pp.90–1; *House of Commons*, i.456; G.E.C., *Peerage*, x.137–40.

[3] Strickland, *Queens of England*, ii.273.

[4] For William Boleyn see *Cal. Close Rolls, Henry VII* (1955–63), i.143; *Cal. Inquisitions Post Mortem, Henry VII* (1898–1955), i.322; Polydore Vergil, *Anglica Historia*, ed. D. Hay, Camden Society, 3rd series, 74 (1950), pp.52, 94.

[5] *LP*, xi.17.

buying back the Howard lands he had lost after his unfortunate support for Richard III at the Battle of Bosworth. The fifty pounds and his wife's portion meant that Thomas Boleyn was not penniless, but it was quite insufficient to sustain his pretensions, or that high profile which was necessary if he was to achieve his full promise – even, perhaps, the revival of the Ormonde earldom in his favour. The Howard marriage and the influence of his Butler grandfather did, though, offer one immediate prospect: entry to the traditional career of the ambitious English gentleman, service to the king.[6] In 1501 Boleyn graced the marriage of Katherine of Aragon to the king's eldest son, Arthur, and in 1503 helped to escort his eldest daughter, Margaret, to her marriage with the king of Scotland.[7] By the time Henry VII died, in the spring of 1509, Anne Boleyn's father had risen at court to the important rank of 'squire of the body', and as he walked in the king's funeral procession, clad in his newly issued black livery, he could reflect that since his father had died in 1505 and the old earl of Ormonde was about eighty-five, his private fortune now looked good also.[8]

Our appreciation of what it meant for Thomas Boleyn, and his daughter after him, to make a career at court is grievously impaired by knowledge of later times, of Fanny Burney's boredom and the insipid routine of the Victorian palace. Until very recently court life has been left by historians to the writers of fiction and the imagination of Hollywood. Yet there was one great difference between later courts and those of Tudor times. The court then was concerned with real power, real decisions and real wealth. Though display was highly important, to be a courtier was to be at the sharp end of politics, power and profit. And since Anne Boleyn, no less than her father, was first and last a phenomenon of the court, we need to explore the milieu to which she belonged.

The starting point is the commonplace that in the sixteenth century power was exercised by the ruler in person, or by direct delegation; this was the reality in England and in Europe alike. Policy was what he decided; advancement and honour was at his

---

[6] The earl of Ormonde was chamberlain to Henry VII's wife, Elizabeth of York.
[7] G.E.C., *Peerage*, x.137.
[8] *LP*, i.20 (p. 13).

gift; his person in fact personified the community. This is not to deny that all government was necessarily constitutionally and politically constrained – and in England limited by formal structures such as parliament and the due process of law – but in practical day-to-day terms it was a response to the will of one man. The ultimate demand on any subject was to be called to obey 'on your allegiance'.

The consequences which flowed from this personal monarchy determined the shape of Anne Boleyn's life. In the first place it meant that royal authority operated in terms of royal favour. There was no way in which men could challenge a policy when that policy was the king's will, other than themselves trying to gain the ear of the king so as to persuade him to will something different. This was precisely the dilemma of those like Thomas More who rejected both the king's objective and his methods, when Henry VIII put pressure on the pope and the English Church in his effort to break his marriage to Katherine of Aragon. To oppose openly would be treachery, but access to the king's mind and emotion was blocked by Anne Boleyn. Royal favour was just as vital in the exercise of power. The king gave executive authority to the men he trusted, and they acted so as to retain his trust. Thus Henry's interest in Anne had enormous implications for the government of the country at large. Favour was equally crucial in the matter of rewards. These were expressions of standing with the monarch, and it was thus of great significance when someone like Anne gained the influence which could ease her supporters into grants, offices and honours. A further consequence of personal monarchy was competition. The struggle for power was a struggle around the king's person, a battle for his favour; politics were thus court politics. Decisions, likewise, were court decisions, and promotion and advancement were things achieved at court. The court made Anne Boleyn, and it would be the court which destroyed her.

To say that Thomas Boleyn and his children after him set out to be courtiers is, therefore, to say a great deal; they were taking the road to power, prestige and profit. Whether, however, it was the road to honour is a different question, and most historians have felt that Anne's father personified all that was bad about the court. Friedmann's restrained comment that Boleyn 'mean and grasping was not beloved' echoed a contemporary opinion that 'he would sooner act from interest than from any other motive', while P. W. Sergeant's verdict that 'it is clearly hopeless to attempt a defence of Sir Thomas' may seem totally justified in the case of a man who, on his way to an earldom, slipped, or appears to have slipped, two daughters in succession into the king's bed.[9] Boleyn certainly had a lively sense of self-interest. When returning from an embassy in Spain in 1523 he brought with him an important messenger from Charles V, only to drop him when they reached London and leave the total stranger to find his own accommodation![10]

Courts and courtiers had, of course, existed throughout the history of Western Europe, and from the first a vigorous tradition of comment had condemned the courtier as a self-seeking sycophant and the court as a living hell.[11] Not only did the deadly sins of sloth, gluttony and lust flourish there, but all the rest – pride, avarice, envy, anger – were positively necessary to success as a courtier, along with falsehood, flattery and servility. The wealth, power and prestige which success at court could bring attracted countless young men and women to attempt their fortunes there. But the price was their integrity, their morality, their health, their spiritual safety and their self-respect. A telling instance is provided by the love notes which used to pass between Henry VIII and Anne Boleyn during morning mass in the royal chapel. They wrote them in an illuminated book of hours, and there is something gross in the king's scrawl below the miniature of the blood-stained Man of Sorrows:

If you remember my love in your prayers as strongly as I adore you, I shall hardly be forgotten, for I am yours.

Henry R. forever.

Anne replied:

By daily proof you shall me find
To be to you both loving and kind.

[9] Friedmann, *Anne Boleyn*, i.55; Brewer, *Henry VIII*, i.168 n.2; Sergeant, *Anne Boleyn*, p. 50.

[10] *LP*, iii.3386.

[11] For a perceptive essay on the following see S. Anglo, 'The Courtier', in *The Courts of Europe*, ed. A. G. Dickens (1977), pp. 33–53.

And, with deliberate promise, she wrote the couplet below the portrayal of the Annunciation.[12]

On this view, then, the court was a Moloch that sucked in good men, body and soul, and spewed out a noisome plague of parasites – Anne among them – corrupting the community in the process. On the other hand, to the landed elite from which courtiers ·came, even the servility required was intrinsically honourable. According to traditional chivalric values, still very much alive, the respect given to a task was determined by the rank of the person for whom it was performed, not by the nature of the task itself. To take an extreme example, the leading courtier was the man who held the post of 'groom of the stool' – by the time of Henry VIII's death he would be a knight and a member of the privy council – and his duty was to provide sanitary facilities for the king and attend the monarch when he relieved himself.

Apologists could also stress that the courtier bore a great moral responsibility. Precisely because of the potential to corruption it was imperative to surround a prince with good advice and men of honour. In 1536, in the Northern uprising which followed the political upheavals which took Anne's life, one of her enemies, Sir Thomas Tempest, reminded the rebels of the lessons of history:

> It is necessary that virtuous men that loveth the commonwealth should be of his council . . . such virtuous men as would regard the commonwealth above their prince's favour . . . In this noble realm, who[ever] reads the chronicles of Edward II [will see] what jeopardy he was in for Piers de Gaveston, [the] Spensers and such like counsellors and . . . Richard II was deposed for following the counsel of such like.[13]

Only the virtuous adviser could resist the potential of the court for corruption, and thereby help to make princely rule virtuous.

This line of thought appealed very much to the new, lay, intellectual fashion which we call Renaissance humanism. It was the service of the ruler, the embodiment of the community, that offered the supreme opportunity to apply the moral philosophy which the humanist study of classical literature taught. As

[12] BL, King's MS 9, ff. 66v, 231.
[13] Quoted in A. Fletcher, *Tudor Rebellions* (1983), p. 109.

Thomas More wrote in *Utopia*, 'You, if you be disposed and can find in your heart to follow some prince's court, shall with your good counsels greatly help and further the commonwealth. Wherefore there is nothing more appertaining to your duty, that is to say to the duty of a good man.'[14] The personal qualities that humanist education inculcated were important too: effective speech, impressive appearance and manner, personal achievement and *sprezzatura*, that unique 'something' which combined nonchalant ease with *savoir-faire*, these were exactly what was needed to command attention and allow the courtier to achieve his aim 'to become the prince's instructor'. More's own entry into public service was not, as is sometimes suggested, a turning-away from the ideals of humanism; it was their fulfilment.

Attitudes to the court and to courtiers were, thus, ambivalent. More himself was well aware that in the real world of the Renaissance court, the best that morality and honesty could hope to achieve was compromise.[15] How difficult that was, his own future career would show, but it is also explored at first hand in the poems of a courtier whose life was to be closely linked with that of Anne Boleyn, Sir Thomas Wyatt. Born about 1503, the son of a lifelong courtier, Thomas was at court in his early teens and, according to some stories, became Anne's lover in the 1520s. Thereafter, apart from several embassies abroad and a number of periods in the Tower or under house arrest, he spent the rest of his life in the royal household.[16] His satires are particularly revealing, two addressed to 'mine own John Poyntz', a minor courtier at one time in Anne's own service, and a third to one of the most prominent men at court, Anne's cousin, Francis Bryan. In the first, possibly written in 1536 soon after his release from the Tower after being arrested as one of Anne's supporters, Wyatt bitterly attacks the dishonesty, the prostitution and the denial of integrity necessary for success at court and, in particular, the moral reversal demanded of him:

> None of these points would ever frame in me –
> My wit is nought, I cannot learn the way.

[14] Thomas More, *Utopia*, trans. Ralph Robinson (1556), ed. E. Arber (1869), p. 55.

[15] Ibid., pp. 64–5.

[16] For Wyatt see P. Thomson, *Sir Thomas Wyatt and his Background* (Stanford, Calif., 1964); K. Muir, *The Life and Letters of Sir Thomas Wyatt* (Liverpool, 1963), and below, pp. 83–99.

And much the less of things that greater be,
That asken help of colours of device
To join the mean with each extremity:
With the nearest virtue to cloak alway the vice,
And as to purpose likewise it shall fall
To press the virtue that it may not rise,
As drunkenness, good fellowship to call . . .[17]

However, he was also well aware of the attraction of the royal court:

I grant sometime that of glory the fire
Doth touch my heart; me list not to report
Blame by honour, and honour to desire[18]

And the third satire is genuine in its approval of Bryan's rejection of the life of private self-indulgence:

'For swine so groins .
In sty and chaw the turds moulded on the ground,
And drivel on pearls, the head still in the manger,
Than of the harp the ass to hear the sound.
So sacks of dirt be filled up in the cloister
That serves for less than do these fatted swine.
Though I seem lean and dry, without moisture,
Yet will I serve my prince, my lord and thine,
And let them live to feed the paunch that list,
So I may feed to live both me and mine.'
By God, well said![19]

Yet Wyatt sees no escape from the courtier's dilemma, in this case how to afford to give this devoted service. Buy friends, maintain virtue only as a front, batten on the rich and elderly, marry for money and take your pleasure on the side; if a female

[17] Wyatt, *Poems*, CV, lines 56–64. Wyatt was reworking a recently published Provençal satire on court life. For this and Wyatt's modifications see *Collected Poems of Sir Thomas Wyatt*, ed. K. Muir & P. Thomson (Liverpool, 1969), pp. 347–50. 'colours of device' = deceptions; 'join the mean' etc. = accept outrageous behaviour as normal; 'as to purpose' etc. = and likewise as it shall be opportune.

[18] Ibid., CV, lines 14–16. 'me list' etc. = I do not wish to criticize honour and seek it at the same time.

[19] Ibid., CVII, lines 18–28.

relative 'be fair, if handsome by her middle', then sell her for a good price to 'thy better', and never let friendship get in the way of advantage – this is the only recipe.[20] It was one which Wyatt, Thomas Boleyn, his daughters, indeed every courtier at some time had to follow. Yet back to court Wyatt came, again and again, and it was on the way to meet the imperial ambassador and escort him to the king that the poet, as we would describe Wyatt, caught pneumonia and died at Sherborne. The parish register, however, calls him *regis consiliarius*, 'counsellor to the king'.[21]

There is no evidence that Anne's father shared Wyatt's qualms of conscience or that Anne, who did, learned them in the Boleyn household. Yet even if Thomas Boleyn typifies the self-seeking courtier, he did have many of the qualities which a ruler looked for. He was a man of some education, far and away the best speaker of French in the Tudor court, with Latin as well, and cultured enough to commission several items from Erasmus.[22] He was, as we shall see, careful to ensure that Anne had the best available education, and he was obviously also responsible for the education of her brother, George – possibly a product of Oxford and later a recognized court poet.[23] Thomas Boleyn was also adept at courtly entertainments, notably the tournament. He fought with the king himself at Greenwich in May 1510, and nine months later he was one of the 'answerers' at the great Westminster challenge of February 1511.[24] A tournament could be very much more than an occasion for tilting and other forms of combat, and by combining display, drama and symbolism could approach a major art form.[25] Thus on the second day of the 1511 tilt the leading answerer, Charles Brandon, entered the lists in dead silence, concealed beneath a moving tower; when

[20] For a discussion of this satire see D. R. Starkey, 'The Court: Castiglione's ideal and Tudor reality', in *Journal of the Warburg & Courtauld Institutes*, 45 (1982), 232–9.

[21] Muir, *Life and Letters of Wyatt*, p. 216.

[22] He probably had some legal training also: *LP*, i.438(3m.7). For his career generally see G.E.C., *Peerage* and *Dictionary of National Biography* (1885–1900), v.321. For Boleyn and Erasmus see below, p. 318. For his linguistic ability see *LP*, viii, p. 71.

[23] G.E.C., *Peerage*, x.140–2; *Tottel's Miscellany*, ed. H. E. Rollins (Cambridge, Mass., 1965), ii.83.

[24] *LP*, i.App.9; Anglo, *Great Tournament Roll*, p. 55.

[25] On tournaments and court festivals generally see ibid., pp. 19–40; Anglo, *Spectacle*, pp. 108–23.

the door was unlocked, he rode out in the costume of an old, bearded pilgrim, only to cast off this disguise and appear in polished armour once the queen, in whose honour the festivity was being held, had consented to his taking part.[26] Anne's father was third into the tiltyard, alongside the marquess of Dorset, and together they continued the theme:

> like two pilgrims from St. James [of Compostello], in tabards of black velvet, with palmers' hats on their helmets, with long Jacob's staves [pilgrim staffs] in their hands, their horse trappers of black velvet, their tabards, hats and trappers set with scallop shells of fine gold . . . their servants all in black satin, with scallop shells of gold in their breasts.[27]

There were also indoor festivities, and at Christmas 1514 Boleyn was joined by his son in a season which included a fancy-dress dance and an indoor mêlée.[28]

This experience and skill, and his knowledge of other things courtly – horses, hawks, bowls, shovelboard – allowed Boleyn to pass anywhere and gave him the final accolade of the humanist courtier, usefulness to his prince. A man of intelligence, gifts and capacity, with a loyalty only to himself (and so to the king) and a willingness to take on a heavy workload, was a courtier worth having. For example, in the period 1519–23 Thomas Boleyn was successively Henry VIII's ambassador to the court of France, one of those attending both the Field of Cloth of Gold and the subsequent meeting with the emperor Charles V at Gravelines, a participant in the Calais conference of 1521 (with a short mission to the emperor) and finally ambassador in Spain. He clearly had the flair for diplomacy as well as the languages; Henry was to say in 1530 that there was no skilled negotiator to equal him.[29] There is a revealing scene of Boleyn at Brussels on his first embassy in 1512, shaking hands on a bet with Margaret of Austria, regent of the Netherlands, about the speed of their negotiations – her Spanish courser against his hobby, that progress would be achieved in ten days.[30] One admires, too, his ability to handle Henry, the ease with which he slipped into one

[26] Anglo, *Great Tournament Roll*, p. 54.
[27] Hall, *Chronicle*, p. 518.
[28] *LP*, ii.pp. 1500–2; cf. ibid., ii.1490.
[29] *Cal. S. P. Span., 1529–30*, p. 422.
[30] *LP*, i.1448.

diplomatic report in October 1513 the remark that negotiating with Maximilian I was like tilting with a man whose horse was out of control: 'it will be long or they join well together' – just the pleasing, intimate metaphor to attract a king never fond of long epistles.[31]

Back in England, Boleyn was active on the king's council, that group of up to, perhaps, seventy individuals of varying importance and often fluctuating role, which was the nearest England then had to what might later be called 'the government'. He was, indeed, one of its most active members, whether policy and administration were on the agenda or judicial (star chamber) business.[32] And there were courtly chores too, such as a six-week assignment in 1517 looking after the king's sister, Margaret, during her visit from Scotland.[33] All this brought rewards – rank (knighthood in 1509), office, wardships, some grants of land – but rewards earned the hard way. Royal favour for the really ambitious did not come cheap.

Thomas Boleyn was not the only courtier on whom the young sun of Henry VIII's bounty shone, although all were eclipsed by Charles Brandon, who succeeded in marrying the king's younger sister Mary and founding the dukedom of Suffolk. Opportunities at court were, indeed, particularly good at this time. With the troubles of the mid-fifteenth century, royal service in England had lost some of its kudos, but the establishment of Edward IV in 1471 as the unchallenged king ushered in a period when first the Yorkists and then the Tudors used the royal court to draw together the upper classes in support of the throne.

Political exploitation of the court was, of course, hardly revolutionary, and the model for all this was the court of the duke of Burgundy, the ruler of what is today the Netherlands, Belgium, Luxemburg and sizeable parts of Northern France. There, in a deliberate attempt to unite these anything-but-coherent territories, the duke's household consciously cultivated magnificence in order to command prestige internationally as well as locally, and enrolled the arts in the service of the state. Edward IV (whose sister married the duke of Burgundy) set out to rival his brother-in-law, with results which can be seen today

[31] Ibid., i.1338.
[32] J. A. Guy, *The Cardinal's Court* (Hassocks, Sussex, 1977), pp. 28, 99.
[33] *LP*, ii.p. 1475.

in the architecture of St George's Chapel, Windsor, in the pages of the earliest books in the English royal library and in the reinvigoration of the Order of the Garter. Henry VII deliberately modelled his court on that of Burgundy, and his son followed suit.[34].

All this meant an increasing demand for able courtiers and a special premium on those with a European sophistication, something which, as we shall see, lies at the heart of Anne Boleyn's success. The need for a new breed of courtiers was also increased by more sober organizational changes in the English court, which created a distinctive pattern of court life for Henry VIII and his wives. For many generations kings (and great lords) had occupied that part of the 'household above stairs' known as the chamber, far away from the hustle of the kitchens and the rest of domestic life. In the fifteenth century, however the king began to desire greater privacy and to realize that the more private a monarch, the more impressive are his appearances. The result was that the chamber became divided into three parts: the privy chamber which was a suite strictly private to the king; the presence chamber which was open to courtiers except when the king was holding audience there; and the great or watching chamber which was regularly accessible to all entitled to attend the household above stairs.[35]

These changes would be of only technical interest were it not for the personnel changes which followed in their wake. First, a new and exclusive group of servants was established to serve in the new privy chamber; second, because Henry VIII wanted 'pastime with good company' as well as service, such posts began to be filled by men who were first and foremost his cronies. Some years were to pass before arrangements reached their final form, but by 1518 or 1519 we can see a small establishment of such men occupying posts as either 'gentleman' or 'groom of the privy chamber'. Over and above these was anyone who took the king's fancy and with whom he wished to pass the time. These might not have the pay of the official staff or the automatic right of entry to the privy chamber, but they were

---

[34] For the debt of the English court to Burgundy see Kipling, *Triumph of Honour*.

[35] For this and the following paragraph see A. R. Myers, *The Household of Edward IV* (Manchester, 1959); D. R. Starkey, 'The King's Privy Chamber, 1485–1547' (unpublished Ph.D. thesis, Cambridge, 1973).

part of the privy chamber circle, and everything depended, for salaried staff as for the rest, on the impression that could be made on the king. Never had a group of young men been in such a position of potential advantage since the hated minions of Richard II. Never, either, since that day, had there been men in such a position of potential power, especially given the highly persuadable man that Henry VIII was. They gave Cardinal Wolsey nightmares – his famous Eltham Ordinance which tried (in vain) to set privy chamber numbers at fifteen was only one of a series of attempts to keep the privy chamber circle at bay – and we shall see how strife within the privy chamber circle helped to destroy Anne Boleyn in May 1536.[36]

Thomas Boleyn was deeply involved in all this. He was close to the king in the early years of the reign as one of the aristocratic group which sympathized with the ambitions of the young, warlike Henry VIII against the more sober counsels of his father's churchmen and bureaucrats. All the while, however, the brilliant new administrator, Thomas Wolsey, was advancing in royal favour, and in 1515 and 1516 he came to grips with the courtiers. One of his targets was Thomas Boleyn, whom he was certainly trying to taint with disloyalty early in 1515, although nothing came of the insinuation.[37] For much of that year, indeed, Wolsey was very much on the defensive as the champion of the clergy, who were being heavily attacked following the notorious death in Church custody of a London merchant, Richard Hunne. One indication of his preoccupation was that about this time the king promised Boleyn the succession to the highly prized post of controller of the royal household when the existing occupant, Sir Edward Ponynges, was promoted to the senior post of treasurer.[38] Not until the autumn of 1516 did Wolsey finally triumph, or seem to triumph, though at the cost of the support of 'well nigh

---

[36] The ordinance promulgated at Eltham in 1526 was directed towards reform in the management of the royal household, but Wolsey used the opportunity to remove several courtiers from their privileged positions in the privy chamber: ibid., pp. 133–81. Dr Starkey has identified the importance of privy chamber office – it gave access to the king *ex officio* and promised predictability of contact with him; hence the constant and almost irresistible demand for places. Yet many privy chamber appointees made little mark, and space in any formulation about privy chamber influence must be left for royal cronies without formal posts.

[37] *LP*, ii.124, 125.

[38] Ibid., iii.223.

all' the magnates; 'the cardinal of York' was, so Sebastian
Giustinian said, 'the beginning, middle and end'.[39]

'Seemed to triumph' is an important qualification, for the
courtiers, defeated this time in the struggle to monopolize the
king, still occupied the citadel of royal favour, the privy chamber,
and continued to secure favours from the king under Wolsey's
disapproving nose. When the privy chamber staff was finally
organized, Boleyn had become neither a gentleman nor a groom
(these posts went to somewhat younger men), but he remained
in the privy chamber circle and his son George became the king's
page.[40] It was probably Wolsey's suspicion of this closeness to
the king, as much as his experience in diplomacy, which brought
Boleyn the posting to Paris in January 1519, and within weeks he
was showing anxiety about the promised controllership.[41] His
fears were well grounded, for in the second week in May, Wolsey
wrote to say that although Ponynges would move up to the post
of treasurer of the household after the 29th, Boleyn would not get
the succession this time; instead, he would succeed Ponynges in
due course. Boleyn's reply was an abject plea for Wolsey's
support; if the minister would favour him, neither he nor the
king would regret it.[42] A week later, the French king, Francis I
broke even more alarming news to him – Henry had expelled eight
or nine of the privy chamber circle.[43] Pastime in the privy
chamber between the king and his younger minions had been
pretty free, and Wolsey had seen his chance. Henry was told that
his 'minions were so familiar and homely with him, and played
such light touches with him that they forgot themselves.' He
reacted on cue to this slur on his dignity, and dispersed the young
men to posts remote from court.[44]

Wolsey left Boleyn to sweat for four months before sending a
message by word of mouth setting out his intentions about the
controllership, confirming that Sir Thomas would not get it, but
would become treasurer in due course. Boleyn took the hint and
wrote to say that he accepted the cardinal's decision and wholly

---

[39] Ibid., ii.2487, 2500; Giustinian, *Four Years at the Court of Henry VIII*, i.320,
326.
[40] *LP*, ii.4409.
[41] Ibid., iii.118.
[42] Ibid., iii.223.
[43] BL, Cott.MS Cal.D vii, f. 118 [*LP*, iii.246].
[44] Hall, *Chronicle*, p. 598; Giustinian, *Four Years at the Court of Henry VIII*,
ii.270–1.

resigned his claim to the controllership to the discretion of the king and Wolsey.[45] With his abject submission thus on file and a clear recognition that while the king might promise it was Wolsey who performed – and could refuse to perform – Boleyn got the job after all.[46] He held it for only a short time, for Ponynges died in the autumn of 1521, whereupon he succeeded as treasurer.[47] The lesson in the political facts of life remained with Thomas Boleyn for a decade; only when his daughter was there to shield him would he be prepared to challenge Wolsey again.

Such was the heated, some might say foetid, atmosphere of the court world into which Anne Boleyn was born, and such was her father. Her mother also was at court, in Katherine of Aragon's entourage, though we know less of her activities.[48] Also at court before 1520 was Anne's sister Mary, who in the February married William Carey of the privy chamber, with the king himself as the principal guest.[49] Her brother George had, as we have seen, played in a mummery at Christmas 1514–15 and gone on to become the royal page, but there were still some years to go before he would matter much at court.

Anne, Mary and George were the only children of Thomas Boleyn to survive to maturity, and there has been a long-running historical dispute about the date of Anne's birth and the relative ages of her brother and sister. Evidence from the later sixteenth century and the earlier seventeenth points to a date for Anne either of 1501 or thereabouts, or around 1507.[50] Modern scholars have been similarly divided, but the weight of opinion has favoured the later date.[51] The reality, however, is that around 1501 is correct. This has been demonstrated by the researches of the art historian Hugh Paget, which were published posthum-

---

[45] *LP*, iii.447.
[46] By Sept. 1520 (*St. Pap.*, ii.57).
[47] *LP*, iii.1712, 2481, g.2587. He was succeeded by Sir Henry Guildford.
[48] E.g. ibid., ii.3489; iii.491, 528.
[49] Ibid., iii.p. 1539.
[50] Herbert, *Henry VIII*, p. 399; Sander, *Schism*, p. 25; William Camden, *Annales* (1612), p. 2.
[51] J. H. Round, *The Early Life of Anne Boleyn* (1886), pp. 12–23; Brewer, *Henry VIII*, ii.170; J. Gairdner, 'Mary and Anne Boleyn', and 'The Age of Anne Boleyn', in *EHR*, 8(1893), 53–60; 10(1895), 104. Friedmann's conjecture of 1503 or 1504 [*Anne Boleyn*, ii.315] is based on a fallacious pictorial identification.

ously in 1981 and show that Anne Boleyn was twelve or thirteen years old when she left England in 1513.[52] She was thus significantly older than is usually imagined. The triangle which developed in 1527 was not between a thirty-six-year-old king and a wife over forty and a girl of nineteen or twenty, but rather a mature woman of twenty-six. Similarly, in the spring of 1536 Anne was not rejected by Henry when, as Catholic tradition has it, she was less than twenty-nine, but as a possibly ageing thirty-five, while her supplanter, Jane Seymour, was at twenty-seven marginally older than Anne had been when challenging Katherine for the first time.[53] The gossip that credited Henry with a taste for younger women was evidently ill informed.[54]

Dating the birth of Anne Boleyn to 1500–1 resolves one long-running dispute, but it does not tell us about her relationship with George and Mary Boleyn, and here the evidence is contra-dictory. As far as George is concerned, his appearance in court as a juvenile and the fact that he secured his first royal grant only in 1524 would suggest that he was the youngest of the three.[55] However, a poem by Cavendish (who had certainly known him) has George saying that he had obtained a place in the privy chamber 'or years thrice nine my life had past away', and Boleyn was retired from his place there by the Eltham Ordinance of January 1526.[56] Indeed, that is only an end date, and if Cavendish is referring to George's arrival as the king's page, that could have been several years earlier. Yet even for George Boleyn to have been in his twenty-seventh year at the latest by 1526, he would have to have been born by 1499 and thus would be older than Anne.

How reliable Cavendish is on this is, however, another question. He was writing thirty years after the event, and since the dictates of the verse made the next lowest number 'years thrice eight', he may have been trying to say no more than 'about twenty-five', thus indicating a birth-date of about 1500.[57] On the other hand, having lost the post of page in 1525, George was restored to a full adult place in the privy chamber by the end

[52] For the following see Paget, in *BIHR*, 54. 162–70 and below, pp. 22–3, 33–5.
[55] Clifford, *Dormer*, p. 80.
[54] *LP*, viii.567.
[55] Ibid., iv.546(2).
[56] Cavendish, *Metrical Visions*, p. 21; *LP*, iv.1939(14).
[57] See below, pp. 68–9.

of 1529, and it could be that Cavendish had this in mind.[58] In that case, 'or thrice nine' would, taken literally, indicate a date of 1503–4, while 'about twenty-five' would give 1504–5. What perhaps should clinch the acceptance of this last is a remark by Jean du Bellay in 1529 suggesting that he thought George too young to be sent as ambassador to France.[59]

For Mary Boleyn there is, again, no known date of birth, but her grandson Lord Hunsdon was quite specific in 1597 that she had been the elder sister.[60] Some historians have argued that he was mistaken, but the probability is remote. Hunsdon was agitating for Thomas Boleyn's earldom of Ormonde which should have descended through the elder daughter; if he was persisting despite the fact that Anne was the elder, it could only be by ignoring Queen Elizabeth's prior claim. On such a delicate matter he must have been doubly sure. Other pointers corroborate that Mary was the senior: the fact that after both daughters had gone to France in 1514–15, it was Anne who remained for further training and Mary who was brought back; the allegation that Mary was already active sexually while in France; the fact that she was launched at court before her sister and married in February 1520, while marriage plans for Anne were only seriously begun at the end of 1521.[61]

Mary Boleyn played much less of a part in Anne's life than did their brother, and she would have attracted little notice, except that she was for a time Henry VIII's mistress. Of this there can be no doubt, despite efforts to prove the contrary. It was most tellingly demonstrated when, later in life, the king himself was taxed with having slept with both Anne's sister and her mother. His naively revealing reply was: 'Never with the mother.'[62] The rumour of a relationship between Henry and Thomas Boleyn's wife did circulate widely, but nothing can be discovered to upset the king's denial; most probably there was a confusion of Elizabeth Boleyn with Elizabeth Blount, Henry's first mistress.[63] Later Catholic controversialists transmuted this into the claim

---

[58] *St. Pap.*, vii.219.
[59] Du Bellay, *Correspondance*, i.105. George was married by the end of 1525 and so must have been born no later than 1511 [*LP*, iv.1939(14)]. His part in the Christmas revels of 1514–15 [*LP*, ii.p. 1501] was obviously as a child.
[60] Gairdner, in *EHR*, 8. 58–9.
[61] Ibid., 8.55; *LP*, x.450.
[62] Ibid., xii(2), 952.
[63] Ibid., vi.923; viii.565(2), 567, 862; cf. ix.1123.

that Anne Boleyn was Henry VIII's daughter! One need hardly say that to achieve such a feat Henry would have had to have been astute enough to escape his father's well attested protectiveness, as well as somewhat precocious – he was ten years old in 1501.

Which Boleyn sister was the elder might be put beyond question if we were to know when Mary's relationship with Henry began. If this was before her marriage in 1520 it would argue that she must have been born soon after 1500; a girl born much after this could have been married in 1520 in her middle teens, but is hardly likely by then also to have had a prolonged relationship with the king. Unfortunately, however, it seems more probable that the affair postdated her marriage and therefore cannot be used to argue her approximate date of birth. Elizabeth Blount was the reigning mistress in or about 1519 when she bore the king a son, Henry Fitzroy, later duke of Richmond, and her marriage – an event that would normally mark the end of a royal amour – only took place about 1522. By contrast, the affair with Mary was alive in 1523 when one of the king's ships bore the name *Mary Boleyn*.[64] Perhaps Henry realized that it was much safer to risk begetting children whose paternity could be denied than bastards who only emphasized his lack of legitimate heirs. Faint corroboration of this is the long delay before Mary became pregnant early in June 1525. This would certainly coincide with what we would expect of a period when she was taken up with a man of such known low fertility as Henry VIII, and we may note that once she had begun to cohabit with William Carey her two children came in quick succession.[65] The spate of royal grants to her husband in 1522, 1523, 1524 and 1525 is also suggestive.

Henry VIII's affair with Mary Boleyn is not, therefore, the final corroboration that she was older than Anne, but there are the other indications that this probably was so. And here, perhaps, we can call in Sir Thomas Boleyn's own reflections in a letter to Thomas Cromwell in the summer of 1536, when his world had crashed around him, with George and Anne both dead, and most of the gains he had striven for, lost with the loss of royal favour. His early years of marriage, he recalled, had also been

---

[64] *House of Commons*, iii.419; *LP*, iii.3358.
[65] See below, pp. 236–7. The story that the first child, Henry Carey, was the king's son was spread about by supporters of Katherine: *LP*, viii.567.

financially straitened, not only because of the £50 a year, but because his wife brought him 'every year a child'.[66] He was certainly married by the summer of 1501 when Elizabeth Howard's jointure was settled on her, which suggests that they had not been married many years – not, say, before 1498.[67] If, then, we take Boleyn's memory literally, we may suppose a child in 1499, another in 1500, a third in 1501 and so on, although two children at least died before reaching adulthood.[68] Were Mary to be the eldest and born about 1499, this would make her fifteen-plus when going to France in 1514 and twenty-plus at marriage, with an affair with the king in her late teens or, more probably, early twenties. Anne would fit in at 1500–1, firmly dated by her journey abroad in 1513; then George at about 1504, so entering the privy chamber as an adult in 1529 at about the age of twenty-five. There are more assumptions in this than is good for any hypothesis, but it does satisfy the evidence.

Thus Anne Boleyn followed her sister into her teens and into the second decade of the sixteenth century, and in 1513 she went abroad. It was a journey that would have a decisive effect on the rest of her life. Ever after she would stand out from the women of the English court whom she was leaving, and always would leave, far behind.

[66] Ibid., xi.17.
[67] *Cal. Close Rolls, Henry VII* (1955–63), ii.179.
[68] See the brasses at Hever and Penshurst: M. Stephenson, *List of Monumental Brasses* (1926), ii.236, 251.

2

A European Education

〜〜〜

THE DESTINATION of the young Anne Boleyn in 1513 was the Habsburg court at Mechelen in Brabant. She was going to be a maid of honour to Margaret of Austria, who was ruling the Low Countries as regent for a thirteen-year-old nephew, Charles of Burgundy. Thomas Boleyn's decision to send his younger daughter to Margaret was inspired by a recognition of Anne's potential, but equally of the opportunities which a training at the premier court of Europe could open up.[1] True, the brilliance of the Burgundian ducal court was approaching its end. Through a series of vicissitudes, Burgundy was being drawn into a larger unit which would eventually bring also Austria, the Empire, Spain, Italy and the Americas under the Archduke Charles, by his better-known name of Charles V. Yet for the moment the regent had gathered around Charles and his younger sisters a court which was still the Mecca of aristocratic and princely behaviour. Also visiting from England in 1513 was William Sidney, one of Henry VIII's favourites, while another, Edward Guildford, would arrive as late as 1518, intent on learning what the king described as 'the right way of doing things'.[2]

The opportunity for training was there because Margaret of Austria was not bringing up her Habsburg nephew and nieces in isolation. The elite of Europe, indeed, were vying to place their

---

[1] For this chapter see T. Kren, 'Flemish Manuscript Illumination', and Janet Backhouse, 'French Manuscript Illumination' in *Renaissance Painting in Manuscript*, ed. T. Kren (1983), pp. 69–78, 147–92; de Boom, *Marguerite d'Autriche*; de Iongh, *Margaret of Austria*; Otto Pacht, *The Master of Mary of Burgundy* (1948); Sterling, *Master of Claude*; *The New Grove Dictionary of Music* (1980).

[2] De Boom, *Marguerite d'Autriche*, p. 118.

offspring as attendants on her and her charges in the knowledge that they would effectively be being educated alongside Europe's rulers of the next generation. Nowhere could a father find a better start for a future courtier. And Thomas Boleyn had something even more specific than this in mind. Henry VIII's wife, Katherine of Aragon, was sister-in-law to the regent; indeed, Margaret had taught her the French which the queen of England relied on to eke out her scanty English. If his daughter Anne could learn continental manners and good French, there was a future for her at Katherine's side, easing the way of the queen through the polite world of Northern Europe, where French was the language *de rigueur*. And, of course, she would be expected from time to time to put in a good word for the rest of the Boleyn family.

Thomas Boleyn was given the opportunity to realize this vision as a result of his first diplomatic posting in 1512, which was to the court of the Archduchess Margaret. As we have seen, he got on well with the regent, who agreed to take Anne as one of her eighteen *filles d'honneur*. Thus when Boleyn returned to England in the early summer of 1513 he immediately sent Anne to Margaret.[3] The regent's first impressions were good, and she wrote back to Sir Thomas:

> I have received your letter by the Esquire [Claude] Bouton who has presented your daughter to me, who is very welcome, and I am confident of being able to deal with her in a way which will give you satisfaction, so that on your return the two of us will need no intermediary other than she. I find her so bright and pleasant for her young age that I am more beholden to you for sending her to me than you are to me.[4]

Margaret was as good as her word. Anne was put to study under a tutor, one of the ducal household named Symonnet, and her

[3] Neither the copy of Margaret's letter reporting the arrival of Anne, nor Anne's own letter, is dated. She could not have gone before Boleyn had established himself at the Burgundian court, where he arrived in May 1512, and the letter recalling her to England is dated 14 Aug. 1514. The summer of 1513 looks the most likely date within this period, because Margaret's letter shows that Boleyn was then back in England, and he was in the Low Countries continuously from 26 June 1512 to early May 1513. Margaret was expecting Boleyn back, and thus another end-date is the arrival of new English ambassadors in February 1514: Paget, in *BIHR*, 54. 164–5; *LP*, i.2655.

[4] Paget, in *BIHR*, 54. 164–5.

first independent letter in French to her father (previous ones having been dictated by the tutor) survives in Corpus Christi College, Cambridge. Written from Margaret's summer residence at La Vure, now Terveuren, near Brussels, the letter shows that despite the charm that had won over the duchess, Anne had no illusions as to why she was there:

> Sir, I understand from your letter that you desire me to be a woman of good reputation [*toufs onette fame*] when I come to court, and you tell me that the queen will take the trouble to converse with me, and it gives me great joy to think of talking with such a wise and virtuous person. This will make me all the keener to persevere in speaking French well, and also especially because you have told me to, and have advised me for my own part to work at it as much as I can.[5]

Unfortunately, no intelligible English translation can give the flavour of the phonetic and idiosyncratic original; Anne did certainly need to work at her French!

Second to the intention of learning French was the determination to master the sophistication of polite society. A *fille* or *demoiselle d'honneur* had no specific duties, but was under the direction of *la dame d'honneur*, the head of the female establishment. She was expected to play her part as an attendant on the duchess and to share in the intimate society of the court, to make herself useful and perform tasks on request, and to join in the serious business of court entertainment. Without the women, a court was reckoned a poor place indeed.[6] There was, as we shall see, far more to entertainment than previous generations of historians have realized; confidence in the work ethic has obscured the fact that once leisure is plentiful, managing it becomes a serious business. The elaborate dances, hunts, tournaments and festivities which fill so many pages in contemporary accounts were not peripheral elements in a Renaissance court; they belonged to the core of princely rule – and of the success of his courtiers. Anne Boleyn's later achievements owed a very great deal to what she was now beginning to learn with Margaret of Austria.

[5] Ibid., 54. 166; Sergeant, *Anne Boleyn*, pp. 275–6.
[6] See below, p. 183.

The essential courtly skill was the dance. All the courts of Europe danced, and being there to take part was a principal obligation on Anne and the other maids of honour. The Mechelen books of dance music are well thumbed. The staple was the bass dance, a form of couple dance which was common to aristocratic circles throughout Western Europe, so called because 'to dance it, one moves tranquilly, without agitation, in the most gracious fashion one is capable of.'[7] Dancing was also integral to the indoor pageants and formal entertainments in which the Burgundian ducal court set the fashion for the rest of polite Europe. These were a composite art form, involving drama as well as music and dance, and organized on a single theme, very often of a debate between men and women, or an assault by the one on a castle garrisoned by the other. The language was the language of courtly love and the renewed chivalric fashions of the late middle ages – imprisoned maidens, noble knights, exotic foreigners, wildmen, vices personified, mythical beasts, mountains that moved, ships in full sail, castles making music – all the conceits of the *Roman de la Rose* and more.

Such courtly disguisings were not unknown on this side of the Channel, but they had usually been extremely simple affairs. The first in anything like the fashionable continental style would appear to have been celebrated for the marriage of Prince Arthur and Katherine of Aragon in November 1501, and the second, only weeks before Henry VII's death, to mark the betrothal of his younger daughter Mary to Charles of Burgundy. And although Henry VIII began to celebrate disguisings almost every year, the full elaboration of this Burgundian court form had still only been seen in England on seven or eight occasions in all.[8] In the Low Countries the tradition went back seventy or eighty years, and Margaret of Austria was an expert at it. When she had travelled in 1500 to meet her second husband, the duke of Savoy, one display prepared for her had been an assault by Venus and Cupid on the Castle of Love; in 1504, at the marriage of one Savoyard noble, she had herself appeared in the role of Queen of the Amazons, naked sword in hand, a silver cuirass studded with jewels, and a crimson head-dress topped by a great plume.[9] Anne Boleyn could have had no better mentor.

[7] De Boom, *Marguerite d'Autriche*, pp. 126–7.
[8] Anglo, *Spectacle*, pp. 102–3, 107, 116–19.
[9] De Boom, *Marguerite d'Autriche*, pp. 43, 52.

The Regent Margaret was a meticulous chaperone. Deportment and conversation had to be correct at all times, and Madame, as Margaret was called, kept a specially strict eye on the maids of honour, forbidding gossip and any by-play with the pages or gentlemen of the court. Adept as she was herself at the game of courtly love, in her household it was to be played according to the conventions. It was an attitude which Anne was to imitate when she had maids of honour of her own. As Margaret wrote:

> Trust in those who offer you service,
> And in the end, my maidens,
> You will find yourselves in the ranks of those
> Who have been deceived.
>
> They, for their sweet speeches, choose
> Words softer than the softest of virgins;
> Trust in them?
>
> In their hearts they nurture
> Much cunning in order to deceive,
> And once they have their way thus,
> Everything is forgotten.
> Trust in them![10]

Protection lay in a quick wit and a ready confidence:

> Fine words are the coin to pay back
> Those presumptuous minions
> Who ape the lover
> By fine looks and such like.

[10] Quoted in ibid., p. 123.

> Fiez-vous y en vos servans
> Dehure en avant, mes demoiselles,
> Et vous vous trouverés de celles
> Qui en ont eu des décepvans.
>
> Ils son en leurs ditz, observans
> Motz plus doulx que doulces pucelles,
> Fiés-vous-y.
>
> En leurs cueurs ils sont conservans,
> Pour decepvoir, maintes cautelles,
> Et puis que ils ont leurs fassons telles,
> Touts ainsi comme abavantz
> Fiés-vous-y

Not for a moment but instantly
Give to them their pay,
Fine words.

Word for word, that is justice,
One for one, two for two.

They are gracious so to converse,
Respond yourself graciously –
With fine words![11]

It was a lesson that Anne Boleyn learned quickly, and never forgot. It carried her to the heights of courtly success, only to betray her in the end, when faced by men to whom the measured conventions of Margaret of Austria meant nothing.

As well as French and the ways of the courtly world, the court of Margaret of Austria offered Anne Boleyn experience of a culture of which she could previously have perceived only pale reflections. Much though her countrymen might brag of their achievements, England was a cultural colony. Its principal debt was to Burgundy, and particularly Flanders – and for far more than the courtly expertise that she had come to absorb. For a century Flanders in particular and the lands adjacent had been the cultural heart of Europe north of the Alps. The prosperity of its cities had supported an artistic establishment which was the equal of anything in Italy. The market was threefold. First, the cities themselves: this was the era of the great cathedrals and civic buildings of the Low Countries, buildings that called for adornment, not just construction. Next, as we have seen, there was the magnificent society of the duke and his court which exploited art for princely prestige and married culture with chivalry as the beau ideal of every gentleman. Finally, there was the international market for painting, illumination, books and, of course,

[11] Quoted in ibid., pp. 123–4.

Belles paroles en paiement,
A ces mignons présumptieux
Qui contrefont les amoureux,
Par beau samblant et aultrement,

Sans nul credo, mais promptement,
Donnés pour récompense a eulx
Belles paroles.

Mot pour mot, c'est fait justement,
Ung pour ung, aussi deulx pour deulx,

Se devis ils font gracieulx,
Respondés gracieusement
Belles paroles.

music. When Henry VIII of England turned his hand to musical arrangement, it was the Low Countries which provided his material.

In comparison with the influence of the Low Countries, the direct impact of Italy upon early Tudor England was slight. The only influence which may to any degree have challenged Burgundy was that of France. This was often the closest Englishmen got to the new ideas of the Renaissance – second-hand from France if not third-hand from the Low Countries – and there was always the allure of Paris, its style and manners. The charge against Henry VIII's minions in 1519 of undue familiarity with him was the more credible because they had been in France recently (and two more actually lodging at the time with Thomas Boleyn in Paris fled back to London to demonstrate that they were at heart true Englishmen).[12] But in fact the contrast between Flanders and France is easily overstated. The two were parts of one cultural entity which some critics have labelled Franco-Flemish, and the doyen of that culture was Margaret of Austria.

At the age of three she had been sent to France, where for ten years she was brought up as the intended bride of the future Charles VIII. There French masters taught her to paint and draw, to sing and play the lute, to dance in the style of the French court and to appreciate the music of the royal chapel there. She learned to write French verse of considerable fluency, and French books would dominate her reading throughout life. Yet when she was jilted by Charles and returned to the Low Countries, there was no break in her education. The organist of the Burgundian ducal chapel now took over as music master; it was the art collections and illuminated manuscripts of her grandmother, Margaret of York, which now fed her taste. But it was essentially the same culture that she had always known, a contrast in no more than fashion or mood. Later experience would take her to Spain and then Savoy before she returned to Mechelen, but nothing disturbed the Franco-Flemish heart of her experience. And this was the woman who taught Anne Boleyn.

Anne's base in the Low Countries was Margaret's palace at Mechelen. The northern range, built in stone in Renaissance fashion, was only begun after she had left, but the southern face,

----

[12] *Cal. S. P. Ven., 1509–19*, 1235.

despite its nineteenth-century ill-treatment, is still much as she would have known it in 1513. Built, like all the older parts of the palace, of patterned local brick, with the occasional line of stone and a prominent string course along much of its length, it hardly seems unusual – Hampton Court near London springs at once to mind. Yet in 1513 the style was strikingly novel to the English visitor. It was less than twenty years since Henry VII had imported it for the first time for his new palace at Richmond.[13] And Anne's own palace, Whitehall, would be begun in the same style. To stand in the courtyard at Mechelen and face the southern range (see plate 19) – an open arcade at ground level, now enclosed by flattened arches supported on a row of columns, the bricks laid to form a diamond pattern, rectangular windows with mullions and transoms over the prominent string course, with quoins of stone at all the angles, and dormer windows above a brick parapet making a third storey into the steep pitched slate roof – this is to see much what Anne saw, a palace which would be recreated for her beside the Thames twenty years later.

The inventories of the household of Margaret of Austria give a vivid idea of the court which the young English girl had joined. The palace was resplendent with lavish fabrics of every kind. Even though the widowed duchess now regularly wore black, the material of her clothes was always of the finest, because appearances mattered. Particularly striking were the tapestries on the palace walls. Anne may well have seen some of the treasures that Henry VII had painfully assembled from the looms of the Low Countries. Now she could assess their real worth as she watched the court *tapissier*, Pierre van Aelst, who had produced a series in praise of the Tudor dynasty for the marriage between Arthur, prince of Wales, and Katherine of Aragon, turning his hand to five genealogical designs ordered by the Archduchess Margaret as a present for her father.[14]

We know that in later life Anne was excited by fabric and colour. We cannot, however, show that she was affected by another of Margaret's enthusiasms, painting, even though she would have experienced the work of Hieronymous Bosch and Jan van Eyck.[15] Not so with that other branch of pictorial art,

[13] Kipling, *Triumph of Honour*, pp. 3–10.
[14] Ibid., pp. 61, 68–71.
[15] Margaret owned two works by Bosch, one a 'Temptation of St Antony', and two by Jan van Eyck, 'The Virgin and Child by a Fountain' (Koninklijk Museum, Antwerp) and 'The Arnolfini Marriage' (National Gallery, London).

illumination: here we can say that 'the Court of Savoy', as it was called, did give Anne a taste that lasted for the rest of her life. The older masterpieces there included the *Très Riches Heures du Duc de Berry*, as well as many associated with Margaret of York. There were also brilliant examples of a new style in Flemish illumination which, instead of comprising a page of text with a patterned border, unified the whole page, often by directing the viewer's eyes through an almost tangible frame. Thus on one folio of a book of hours, over a window-sill littered with the paraphernalia of courtly life – illuminated manuscript, cloth-of-gold cushion, ring, necklaces, pomander, trinket box – we watch Christ being nailed to the cross, surrounded by a crowd, half curious, half hostile.[16] When, years later, Anne would exchange love notes with Henry in a book of hours, it would be one in this exact fashion.[17] (plate 27)

Anne Boleyn would have known Margaret's collection of illuminated manuscripts almost more as *objets d'art* than as books, but one sort which undoubtedly received considerable use was music books. Those that Margaret owned included masses, motets and chansons, by composers who determined at least half of Anne's later taste. One of the duchess's favourites was Pierre de la Rue, whose lifetime in Habsburg service had culminated in his becoming her court composer. Two others were from her brief time as duchess of Savoy – Antoine Brumel and Pierrequin de Therache. The most popular composer of all was Josquin Desprez, despite the fact that it now seems certain that he was never lured back from Paris to his native Picardy and, indeed, that he had no direct contact with the regent's court at all.

All these composers, and others, Anne certainly listened to in later years. The evidence for this is a manuscript in the Royal College of Music.[18] It carries on page 157 the words, 'M^{res} A.Bolleyne', and underneath her father's motto, 'nowe thus', followed by three short and one long note of music:– ◊◊◊ꞔ –.[19] Precisely what this signifies will concern us later, but the connection of the manuscript with Anne Boleyn seems clear. And of the thirty items so far identified, half are by the favourite composers heard at Margaret's court, especially early works by

---

[16] Osterreichische Nationalbibliothek, Vienna. Cod. 1857 f.43v.
[17] See above, pp. 7–8.
[18] See below, pp. 295–7.
[19] Lowinsky, in *Florilegium*, fig. 13.

Josquin, plus four items by Savoyard composers close to the duchess. The line of influence seems plain. One must assume, too, that this taste was shown in Anne's own music-making, for somewhere in her education she was able to develop considerable musical skill; this is evidenced in a number of sources and may well have been an interest in common with Henry VIII, who prided himself on his own musical abilities. The Archduchess Margaret would again have been the example, for she was famous for her music, especially as a keyboard performer. Her organist, Henri Bredemers, was also well known – he had visited England in 1506 – and he also taught music to Charles and his sisters. We do not know for sure that he took other pupils, but it seems reasonable to assume that he did teach Anne.

As well as absorbing the best education Europe could offer, Anne learned by observation, and learned quickly. People's memories of Anne as she was after some months at Mechelen were still vivid twenty years later – intelligent, self-possessed, wide awake, rapidly coming to grips with the French language and with the sophistication of European courts: 'la Boullant, who at an early age had come to court, listened carefully to honourable ladies, setting herself to bend all her endeavour to imitate them to perfection, and made such good use of her wits that in no time at all she had command of the language.'[20] Among those she could watch were the leaders of Europe who would so affect her later career. There was, for instance, the future Charles V. Whether he noticed the young English maid of honour is to be doubted, but she, undoubtedly, was familiar with the slight, reserved prince whose characteristic lift of the head accentuated the heavy jaw and open gaze of one born to command. It was probably also during her stay with Margaret of Austria that Anne first came to the notice of her future husband, the far more impressive Henry VIII. Not only did Henry's twenty-three years make the fourteen-year-old Charles seem a mere youth, but the slim six-foot two-inch extrovert who combined athletic prowess with intelligence, education, considerable musical skill and boundless energy was hard for anyone to match.

Henry was in Europe to press a joint Anglo-imperial attack on France which had been the prize of the negotiations between the

[20] De Carles, in Ascoli, *L'Opinion*, lines 43–8.

Archduchess Margaret and Thomas Boleyn. The war had opened successfully soon after Anne's journey to the Low Countries, and on 23 August the English captured Thérouanne, south of St Omer, after defeating a French relief force in a scrambling cavalry skirmish which became dignified by the title 'the Battle of the Spurs'. Henry then marched in company with Margaret's father, the Emperor Maximilian (characteristically, at Henry's expense), to the Burgundian town of Lille where the regent met him with her court in attendance. After three days of junketing, during which Henry made great show of his musical talents, the army moved off to besiege Tournai, which surrendered on 23 September. Maximilian sent for Margaret again to join the victors, and despite her complaint that it was not done for widows to trot about visiting armies, she came and brought her ladies with her.[21]

Even without the determination of the Habsburgs to make the greatest possible show, Anne would have been an obvious person to summon to Lille and Tournai, for her father was with the English army and French speakers were at a premium.[22] This fact comes out clearly in the story of the great scandal of the encounter, the flirtation between Margaret of Austria and Henry VIII's boon companion, Charles Brandon. The two of them played the game of courtly love with an enthusiasm which made up for the inability of either to speak the other's language, and eventually Henry egged Brandon on to propose to the duchess, which he did one evening, taking as a pledge one of the rings from her fingers. Margaret responded by calling him *un larron* (a thief), but he only got the point when one of the ladies in waiting offered the Flemish equivalent, *ein dief*. To finish the story, Brandon refused to return the ring and made such a fuss of his conquest that Margaret had to redeem the ring with another and issue vigorous denials of any agreement to marry.[23]

The probability that Anne Boleyn had been useful at the Lille and Tournai meetings is reinforced by what happened in the summer of the following year. On 14 August, Sir Thomas Boleyn wrote to the Archduchess Margaret from the court at Greenwich to ask her to release Anne and to return her in the care of the

---

[21] Scarisbrick, *Henry VIII*, pp. 36–7; de Iongh, *Margaret of Austria*, pp. 148–9.
[22] *LP*, i.2375.
[23] De Iongh, *Margaret of Austria*, pp. 150–1; Brewer, *Henry VIII*, i.5; de Boom, *Marguerite d'Autriche*, pp. 118–19; *LP*, i.2941; *Chronicle of Calais*, pp. 71–6.

escort he had sent. The reason for this sudden withdrawal, which to judge from his letter caused Sir Thomas acute embarrassment – as well it might – was a sudden turn-about by Henry, who had abandoned the marriage between his eighteen-year-old sister Mary and the Archduke Charles, which had been reconfirmed only the previous autumn at Lille. Instead she was to marry Louis XII of France, a very decrepit fifty-two. The affianced bride would need attendants who could speak French, and had not Sir Thomas a daughter who did? She must be sent for. And, as Sir Thomas wrote to his 'most redoubted lady', 'to this request I could not, nor did I know how to refuse.'[24]

In August 1514, therefore, Anne was on the list for France, but what happened then is not clear. Her sister Mary was also to go, and a list in the French archives shows that Mary Boleyn was one of the ladies in the household of the new queen of France, but it makes no mention of Anne.[25] The English sources concur. Mary Tudor left for France with a large escort and, after an appalling Channel crossing, arrived at Abbeville for the wedding.[26] There it was intended that the main party would return to England, leaving a group to remain with Mary Tudor, and the list of those included one, and only one, Mistress Boleyn. In the event Louis XII refused to put up with the interference of some of the older women and sent them packing the day after the wedding, but among those retained was yet again a single 'Madmoyselle Boleyne'.[27] The new queen stigmatized the survivors as 'such as never had experience nor knowledge how to advertise or give me counsel in any time of need', but these inexperienced young attendants evidently did not include Anne.[28]

Where then was Anne? Did she go to France at all in 1514? Some scholars have certainly questioned this, suggesting that she went to France some years later, at a time so far unknown.

---

[24] Paget, *BIHR*, 54. 167.
[25] The list of Mary Tudor's ladies paid for the period Oct. to Dec. 1514 includes Marie Boulonne, but not Anne [Paris, Bibliothèque Nationale MS fr.7853 f. 305b]. The list includes Anne de Boulogne and Magdaleine de Boulogne, but these had been paid from 1509 [ibid., ff. 311, 313]. I am indebted to R.J. Knecht for the references to this MS, which is of extracts from a lost original. The names agree with those in *LP*, i.3357, except for the payment to Mary Fiennes, which must argue for the reliability of the transcription.
[26] *LP*, i.3348(3).
[27] *LP*, i.3348(3), 3357.
[28] Ibid., i.3355, 3356.

The objection to this is the unambiguous statement in 1536 by de Carles, the French diplomat who reported her execution: 'My lord, I am well aware that you know and have known for a long time that Anne Boullant first came from this country when Mary [Tudor] left to go to join the king [Louis XII] in France to bring about the alliance of the two sovereigns.'[29] It could, of course, be argued that after such a time the two Boleyn sisters were being confused, but the French seem to have been well aware of their separate identities. Indeed, if a later report claiming to emanate from Francis I is to be believed (he was at that time the dauphin), Mary succumbed to the *gallant* atmosphere of the French court and acquired a name 'as a very great wanton with a most infamous reputation'.[30]

If, then, both sisters were in Mary Tudor's entourage, why was Anne not named? One hypothesis is that she was one of her sister's attendants and so does not figure on the establishment lists; perhaps she was too young to count. This seems unlikely in the light of the specific request to Sir Thomas to bring Anne back from Flanders to join Mary Tudor's party; it is sensible to suppose that Anne was needed as an interpreter, and it would be common Tudor practice to pay and list, or at least list, such a person, even if the pay was omitted. It is hard to resist the conclusion that Anne did not cross to France with the king's sister in the autumn of 1514. Again, where was she? The likely answer would seem to be 'somewhere in the Low Countries'. From the date of Sir Thomas's letter to the departure of the wedding party from England was exactly seven weeks, to the wedding a further seven days.[31] It would have been possible for Anne to make it, but there would have had to have been no hitch. One possible delay was that Margaret of Austria left Mechelen on 21 August to visit the islands of Zeeland, and the message from London dated 14 August may not have arrived in time to detach Anne from that expedition, or to allow her to say her goodbyes.[32] Another possible source of delay was that Margaret was personally affronted by the jilting of her nephew Charles and politically endangered by the *rapprochement* between

[29] De Carles, in Ascoli, *L'Opinion*, lines 37–42.

[30] *LP*, x.450: '*per una grandissima ribalda et infame sopre tutte*'.

[31] A journey partly by post and without hitches took, in 1531, six days inclusive, Brussels to London: *Cal. S. P. Ven. 1527–33*, 682.

[32] *LP*, i.3235.

England and her sworn enemy, France; she might take her time before giving permission for Anne to leave to assist in a marriage she so detested. We must, therefore, imagine Anne Boleyn catching up with Mary Tudor in Paris, where she was crowned on 5 November, and after the establishment lists which now survive had been drawn up; no doubt Anne would have appeared in later lists, but there were none. Louis lasted for eighty-two days with his young bride, and on 1 January 1515 Mary was a widow.

The situation of Mary and her attendants was not happy in a Paris where she was no longer queen. The new king, Francis I, probably did not force his attentions on the young widow, as A. F. Pollard believed, but he was determined to exploit his temporary prize, at least to prevent her marrying a prince hostile to himself.[33] Henry sent over Charles Brandon to negotiate relations with the new monarch and to arrange Mary's return, with as much of her dower and jewellery as was possible. Already in love with the beautiful *reine blanche,* as the French called a queen in mourning, Suffolk had neither the stamina to resist Mary's Tudor will nor the wit to see that Francis was playing him like a fish. Before he knew what was happening, he woke up in Mary's bed, secretly married to his sovereign's sister. Several abject weeks of grovelling and a series of humiliating bribes to Henry VIII were necessary before Wolsey could secure the king's forgiveness, and permission for the pair to return to England. The match with Brandon was resented by his rivals for Henry's favour, but it was also a flagrant instance of a princess marrying beneath her. Although we have no details, there certainly was talk among Mary's attendants at Brandon's undue familiarity, and one might guess that somewhere here is the root of the dislike which Mary Tudor had in later life for Anne Boleyn; the pert contempt of a fourteen-year-old product of the Habsburg nursery, well aware of Brandon's earlier and foolish behaviour with Margaret of Austria, might be hard to forgive and forget.[34]

Whatever the truth of this supposition, Anne Boleyn did not come back to England with Suffolk and Mary in April 1515, although her sister probably did. Neither, however, did she

[33] A. F. Pollard, *Henry VIII* (1951), p. 51; Knecht, *Francis I*, p. 38 n.4.
[34] *LP*, ii.80.

return to Mechelen and the Archduchess Margaret, but she entered instead the household of Francis I's wife, Queen Claude. Precisely how this was arranged is a mystery. Claude herself was only fifteen years old and had been married to Francis for less than a year, and there are no known links between the Boleyns and either. Claude, however, was the daughter of Louis XII, and it could be that she had taken a particular liking to Anne when she joined the entourage of her young stepmother Mary Tudor, so that at the end of Mary's brief time as queen of France Claude offered Anne a place in her household. Something of the kind was certainly the understanding of Lancelot de Carles, writing in 1536: 'After Mary had returned to this country, Anne was kept back by Claude, who later became queen.'[35] Once again the common-sense explanation is Anne's command of the language. Claude, whose appearance bordered on deformity, had a warm and gentle nature but could only have talked to her stepmother and to the magnificent English visitors she had to entertain at the time of the coronation by means of some interpreter. Anne perhaps?

Anne Boleyn was to stay with Claude for nearly seven years, a period about which there is no direct evidence. No doubt she visited her father when he became ambassador to the French court, and tradition has it that she had some sort of base at Briare on the Loire above Orleans.[36] This is by no means impossible, for the town was well placed in relation to the movements of the court of Queen Claude, where Anne's duties kept her much of the time. Although only of an age with Anne, Claude's short life (she was to die in 1524) was a succession of almost annual pregnancies spent very largely in the Upper Loire at Amboise and at Blois which, although the queen's own palace, was the site of the first major building scheme of her husband, Francis I.[37] Waiting on the queen of France could not have been markedly different from waiting on the regent of the Low Countries, and it is clear that Anne continued to soak in the sophisticated atmosphere around her. De Carles particularly emphasized her musical ability – 'she knew perfectly how to sing

[35] De Carles, in Ascoli, *L'Opinion*, lines 49–51; Herbert, *Henry VIII*, pp. 161, 218.
[36] Jan. 1519 to Mar. 1520, see above, p. 12; Sander *Schism*, p. 25; Friedmann, *Anne Boleyn*, ii.320. But cf. Gairdner, in *EHR*, 8. 56.
[37] Knecht, *Francis I*, pp. 88, 103.

and dance . . . to play the lute and other instruments' – and her skill was such as to be remembered even in hostile reminiscences.[38] Nicholas Sander, the Elizabethan recusant exile, said that Anne could play 'on the lute and was a good dancer', while another and possibly earlier Roman Catholic source referred to her 'plausible qualities, for such as one to delight in, for she could play upon instruments, dance &c.'[39] Some confirmation, if not of her skill in performance, at least of her developing musical taste in France, is to be found in the items in the Royal College of Music manuscript mentioned earlier, which are closely connected with the French court: for example, two motets by Antoine de Févin who had recently died at Blois, and nine by Jean Mouton of Samer, then at the height of his career under Louis XII and Francis I.[40]

It was, of course, at Cloux, just outside Amboise, that Leonardo da Vinci came to settle in 1516 as a pensioner of the French king.[41] That Anne saw him seems probable; whether it meant anything to her we cannot know. One area of painting where we can show a response on Anne's part is book illumination. Claude of France was a noteworthy patroness of the miniature, a taste inherited from her mother, Anne of Brittany, who undoubtedly commissioned for her daughter the primer now in the Fitzwilliam Museum, Cambridge.[42] The Kraus Collection in New York includes two later works for Claude, a book of prayers which was in the queen's hands before Anne Boleyn arrived in France (it probably dates from 1511–14) and a book of hours which Anne may well have seen arrive from the studio in 1517.[43] What was unusual about the latter (and so effective that Claude had five illuminations of a similar style inserted in the book of prayers) was the introduction of borders in Renaissance style, a fashion which had entered France ten years earlier.[44] Two types of border are known, pilasters or columns and candelabra (though there are combinations of the two), and the effect is quite different from the *trompe-l'oeil*

---

[38] De Carles, in Ascoli, *L'Opinion*, lines 55–8.
[39] Sander, *Schism*, p. 25; BL, Sloane MS 2495 f. 2v. The author claimed to know eyewitnesses of Henry VIII's funeral.
[40] Lowinsky, in *Florilegium*, pp. 206–17.
[41] Knecht, *Francis I*, p. 99.
[42] J. Harthan, *Books of Hours* (1977), pp. 134–7.
[43] Sterling, *Master of Claude*, pp. 16–17.
[44] Ibid., pp. 11–15.

decoration that Anne had experienced at Mechelen. When, a queen herself, she had her own illuminated treasures, these would include books decorated in the new fashion, with Renaissance-style borders.

Experience at the court of Queen Claude thus built on the brief time that Anne Boleyn had spent with Margaret of Austria, but there was one obvious difference: life with Claude was much less public. Political power, and all the concomitants of decision-making, rivalry and faction, travelled with the king who, although not an unaffectionate or absentee husband, certainly did not believe in companionate marriage. Thus, commentators who have been tempted to picture Anne in regular contact with the blatant sexuality of Francis I's household and his 'privy band of ladies' are in error; in any case, the latter seems more a feature of the king's life after Claude's death and the trauma of his capture and imprisonment by Charles V between 1525 and 1526.[45] One event which Anne probably did take part in was the queen's personal triumph when she was crowned at St Denis in May 1516 before making her state entry into Paris, a magnificent affair which the English government saw fit to ignore.[46]

Claude and her ladies did, however, appear on two great occasions which involved the English, when Anne would also have been in demand as an interpreter. The first began on 22 December 1518, when a state banquet was given at the Bastille in honour of the English mission which had come to negotiate for the marriage between Henry VIII's daughter Mary and the dauphin, born to Claude and Francis the previous February.[47] The courtyard of the fortress was covered with an awning of waxed blue canvas painted with the heavenly bodies, the floor was carpeted with white and orange cloth, and the whole was lit from sconces and chandeliers everywhere, reflecting on the mass of gold and silver plate on tables and cupboards. The English and French delegations were seated alternately with the ladies of the court who, after some hours of dancing later in the evening, served supper at midnight, dressed in the latest Italian costumes, all under the eyes of the queen and her mother-in-law, Louise of Savoy. No sooner had the guests gone than the setting was

[45] Knecht, *Francis I*, pp. 427–9.
[46] Ibid., p. 88.
[47] *LP*, ii.4674, 4675. According to Hall, *Chronicle*, p. 596, her father was also present.

reconstructed to allow a tournament to take place, apparently a mêlée on foot, twenty-four a side with Francis leading one of the teams. That over, the set was reconstructed yet again for another evening of dancing and feasting.

The second great occasion was the Field of Cloth of Gold, the famous meeting between Henry VIII and Francis I outside Calais from 7 to 23 June 1520. This was something of a family affair for the Boleyns, with both Sir Thomas and Lady Elizabeth there, possibly the newly wedded Mary Carey and, one must assume, brother George among his father's allocation of eleven attendants (or one of the three gentlemen allowed his mother).[48] Called in the name of peace and friendship, the Field of Cloth of Gold was an occasion for international one-upmanship on a vast scale, no less deadly in intent for being (usually) polite. Richard Wingfield, who had taken over from Thomas Boleyn as ambassador to France four months previously, had written to Henry soon after his arrival to warn that the French royal ladies were as intent on gaining the day as their menfolk:

> Your Grace shall also understand that the Queen here, with the King's mother [Louise of Savoy], make all the search possible to bring at the assembly the fairest ladies and demoiselles that may be found. The daughters of Navarre be sent for; the Duke of Lorraine's daughters or sisters in like manner. I hope at the least, Sir, that the Queen's Grace shall bring such in her band, that the visage of England, which hath always had the praise, shall not at this time lose the same.[49]

Claude and her attendants made their first appearance at the Field of Cloth of Gold on Sunday 10 June when the royal ladies of both nations made their debut at separate banquets, although Claude, being thirty-one weeks pregnant as well as naturally retiring did leave the more active parts of the ensuing fortnight of festivity to Louise the queen mother and Marguerite d'Angoulême, the king's sister.[50] Queen Claude was, however,

---

[48] Russell, *Cloth of Gold*, pp. 195, 202, quoting Oxford, Bodleian MS Ashmole 1116. This gives [p. 204]: 'Cary Lord Fitzwater's daughter', but *Rutland Papers*, ed. W. Jerdan, Camden Soc., 21 (1842), p. 38 divides this entry into two, and *Chronicle of Calais*, p. 25 lists 'mistres Carie' and later 'mistres Margery, Lord Fitzwaren's dowghter'.

[49] *St. Pap.*, vi.56.

[50] Russell, *Cloth of Gold*, pp. 159–61; Knecht, *Francis I*, p. 88.

the star of the French contingent when the ladies made their first appearance in public at the joust on the following Monday.[51] She wore cloth of silver over an underskirt of cloth of gold, and rode in her coronation litter of cloth of silver decorated with friars' knots in gold, a device which she had taken over from her mother.[52] Her ladies rode in three carriages similarly draped in silver and, no doubt were dressed to match the queen. Claude was also the hostess on the French side when, on several evenings, the kings, attended by ladies and gentlemen of their respective courts (usually in masque costume), changed places. Where Anne was in all this we do not know. Beside Queen Claude, one would assume. What seems unthinkable is that she was not present at all or that she did not meet Henry VIII there for a second time.[53]

Anne Boleyn's long service at the French court was interpreted in the later sixteenth century to mean that she must have had close relations with Marguerite d'Angoulême as well as Queen Claude.[54] Marguerite became a noted – if somewhat eclectic – supporter of religious reform, and it was easy for men like Sander to conclude that Anne, the embodiment of heresy, had been first subverted by the duchess. Was not the web of unbelief without seam? Soon even careful scholars like Herbert of Cherbury took it as a fact that Anne served in the household of 'the Duchess of Alençon, sister to Francis'.[55] That, however, is wrong; Anne was almost certainly never a member of Marguerite's household. When reporting Francis I's complaint in January 1522 about Anne leaving France, the imperial ambassadors described her quite unequivocally as one of the queen's ladies, the same as she had been in 1515.[56] On the other hand, Anne does seem to have known Marguerite. True, Marguerite might have encountered her only as one of her sister-in-law's waiting-women. Something to that effect can be read into the efforts which the English made to get Marguerite (by then queen of Navarre) to accompany her brother to Calais in 1532 to meet

[51] Russell, *Cloth of Gold*, pp. 124–5.
[52] Sterling, *Master of Claude*, pp. 8–9.
[53] For language problems among the ladies see Russell, *Cloth of Gold*, p. 125.
[54] Sander, *Schism*, p. 56; George Wyatt, *Papers*, p. 143; Dowling, in *JEH*, 35.32, referring to *Extracts from the Life of the virtuous . . . Queen Anne Boleigne*, ed. R. Triphook (1817), pp. 14–15.
[55] Herbert, *Henry VIII*, p. 399.
[56] *Cal. S. P. Span.*, *Suppl. 1513–42*, p. 30; *LP*, iii.1994.

Henry and Anne.[57] Francis came alone, and Pierre Jourda concluded from this that contemporary imperial diplomats were right to say that Marguerite was bitterly hostile to the projected marriage.[58] Yet the French refusal to nominate ladies to the official Calais delegation could have a different explanation. Francis was just then angling for a match between his son Henry and the pope's niece Catherine de Medici – hardly the moment to appear to give public endorsement to Anne's position.[59]

Anne Boleyn's later behaviour certainly implies that she knew Marguerite well. A message from her to Marguerite in September 1535 was 'that her greatest wish, next to having a son, was to see you again', and the year before Anne had assured her that while at the 1532 meeting there had been 'everything proceeding between both kings to the queen's grace's singular comfort, there was no one thing which her grace so much desired . . . as the want of the said queen of Navarre's company, with whom to have conference, for more causes than were meet to be expressed, her grace is most desirous.'[60] Such could be the remarks of someone trying to turn mere acquaintance into a bosom friendship, but there are other indications that Marguerite was at least by this time favourable to England, and to Anne. The duke of Norfolk had two five-hour consultations with her in 1533 which convinced him that she was 'as affectionate to your highness as if she were your own sister, and likewise to the queen . . . My opinion is that she is your good and assured friend.'[61] In July 1534 Anne's intimacy with Francis's sister was exploited to conceal Henry's wish to withdraw from an agreed meeting with Francis. Anne was, she confided to Marguerite, expecting a child and so prevented from travelling, but she was very anxious to come to any meeting and, what was more, she needed Henry with her at the time of her confinement – so could the meeting be postponed until April 1535?[62] The true reason seems to have been Henry's fear of trouble at home, but why he should have felt the need for this roundabout way of postponing something as notoriously

[57] Cal. S. P. Span., 1531–33, pp. 257, 990; LP, v.1187.
[58] Pierre Jourda, Marguerite d'Angoulême (Paris, 1930), p. 172; Cal. S. P. Span., 1531–33, p. 588.
[59] See below, p. 196.
[60] LP, ix.378; St. Pap., vii.566 [LP, vii.958].
[61] LP, vi.692.
[62] St. Pap., vii.565–9 [LP, vii.958]; Cal. S. P. Span., 1534–5, p. 229; Lisle Letters, ii.240 (LP, vii.1014).

chancy as a royal summit meeting is not obvious. Whatever the motive, Anne's brother, who took the message to Marguerite, was told to insist that Henry was so determined to meet Francis as arranged that:

> Her Grace is now driven to her sheet anchor in this behalf, that is, to the only help of the said Queen of Navarre, and the goodness of the good King her brother, for Her Grace's sake, and at this Her Grace's suit and contemplation, to stay the King's Highness her husband, and to prorogue their interview till a more commodious and convenient time for all parties.

Nor was this the only occasion when the English used Marguerite as a stepping-stone to Francis; they did the same in November 1535, though without the 'woman to woman' touch.[63]

Yet if later evidence does suggest a more than accidental link between Anne Boleyn and Marguerite d'Angoulême, it does not follow that she was the source of any reformed religious opinions Anne may have shown later. First, the simple confessional patterns of later generations do not apply to the chaos of religious opinion in the early sixteenth century. Christian humanism was then well established in France, as it was in England, with men like Jacques Lefèvre d'Etaples mirroring the role of John Colet or Thomas More, and like Colet and More, recognizing the primacy of that Christian humanist *sans frontières*, Erasmus of Rotterdam.[64] Yet active reform within the French Church only began with the formation of the famous Cercle de Meaux in 1518, in the diocese of that name east of Paris, and it was not until the papal condemnation of Luther in 1520, and his response in pamphlets which denied the authority of the pope, that any but arch conservatives in France became aware of a challenge to the unity and orthodoxy of the Church. Thus, for most of Anne Boleyn's time in France, there was no ideological position to absorb. She could have caught and probably did catch something of the fervour of the Christian humanists who were to be found at court, but hardly from Marguerite, who gave few indications in these years of the personal religious disquiet which would make her in and after the 1520s the patron of the Cercle de Meaux and its ideas. Her famous correspondence with

[63] *LP*, ix.838.
[64] Knecht, *Francis I*, pp. 132–43.

Guillaume Briçonnet, bishop of Meaux, which introduced her to the ideas of Lefèvre, did not begin until June 1521.

Anne Boleyn's career at the French court came to a somewhat abrupt halt towards the end of 1521 when she was recalled to England.[65] Francis took this as one more sign of the growing *rapprochement* between his alleged friend Henry and his perpetual enemy, Charles V, although war between England and France did not break out until the following May. But, as Wolsey explained, Anne had been recalled for an entirely different reason. For this we have to go back to 1515 and the death in his nineties of Anne's grandfather, Thomas Butler, earl of Ormonde, leaving the Boleyns and the St Legers jointly as his heirs general. Given Sir Thomas's closeness to the king, it is no surprise that livery of his wife's new estates was granted in four months, but to be granted and to occupy were two very different things, at least in Ireland, where the rights of the heirs general were obstructed by the heir male, Piers Butler, who had been acting for years as the representative of the absentee earl.[66] Ireland was rarely high on the early Tudor agenda, but the rights of the Boleyns were the one topic there in ten years in which Henry VIII did show an interest, no doubt prompted by Sir Thomas. Letters to the Irish lord deputy, the earl of Kildare, produced a hearing on 18 November 1516 at which the Boleyns and St Legers were able to prove their case, but as the archbishop of Dublin explained to Wolsey three weeks later, legal right was not enough.[67] Piers Butler, styling himself 'earl of Ormonde', had mustered the support of the most powerful Irish lords, including Kildare himself, and was calling for trial before a common law jury where, of course, Sir Thomas Boleyn would have had no chance. What was more, the English interest in Ireland needed Butler. No settlement was reached, and when in the spring of 1520 a second burst of royal interest selected the earl of Surrey, Thomas Howard, to go to Ireland as lord lieutenant, Surrey

[65] *Cal. S. P. Span., Suppl. 1513–42*, p. 30, quoting a report which can be dated 12–14 Jan. 1522; *LP*, iii.1994, dated 11–23 Jan. 1522. But the ambassador with the original complaint had left France before 6 Jan. [*LP*, iii.1946], possibly before 26 Dec. 1521 [ibid., iii.1947], making it certain that Anne left France in 1521.

[66] Ibid., ii.1277.

[67] Ibid., ii. 1230, 1269.

suggested to Wolsey that James Butler, Sir Piers' son, should marry Anne Boleyn and unite the warring claims.

Where Surrey got the idea is not clear. It was certainly from neither Wolsey nor Henry. Since Surrey was Boleyn's brother-in-law one might be inclined to suspect Boleyn (appearing reasonable might well suit the book of a man only recently restored to Wolsey's favour), were it not for the fact that he later took no initiative in the scheme. It may rather be that we have here another example of Thomas Howard's skill in taking care of Thomas Howard. The young James Butler was available: he was being brought up – or kept as a hostage – in Wolsey's household. Surrey's niece Anne was of an age to marry and could easily be recalled from France; the earl loathed the Irish appointment and knew that the king would soon tire of a problem which he did not have the resources or interest to solve.[68] What better escape for Surrey than a scheme which would make respectable the abandonment of Ireland to Piers Butler as earl of Ormonde, with Anne and James Butler sealing his loyalty to and dependence on Henry (as long as Henry was looking)? No sooner had Surrey arrived in Ireland than Piers was his right-hand man, his title as earl taken for granted, his sterling virtues and commitment to the English cause trumpeted in letter after letter.[69] By early September 1520 Surrey had got the Irish council to propose the match to Henry VIII, and a letter of 6 October jogging Wolsey's memory about the proposal crossed with a reply giving the king's reactions:

> And like as ye desire us to endeavour ourself that a marriage may be had and made betwixt the earl of Ormonde's son and the daughter of Sir Thomas Boleyn Kt., controller of our household; so we will ye be [a] mean[s] to the said earl for his agreeable consent and mind thereunto, and to advertise us, by your next letters, of what towardness ye shall find the said earl in that behalf. Signifying unto you, that in the mean time, we shall advance the said matter with our controller, and certify you how we shall find him inclined thereunto accordingly.[70]

---

[68] *St. Pap.*, ii.49 [*LP*, iii.1628]; D. B. Quinn, 'Henry VIII and Ireland, 1509–34' in *Irish Historical Studies*, 12 (1961), 331; the letter of 6 Oct. 1520 could be taken to hint that Butler favoured the scheme at an early stage, which would explain his support for Surrey: *St. Pap.*, ii.50–1 [*LP*, iii.1011].

[69] Ibid., ii.35, 58 [*LP*, iii.924, 1034].

[70] Ibid., ii.50–1 [*LP*, iii.1011].

Surrey kept up the campaign, sending over in December the draft of an act for the Irish parliament recognizing Butler as head of his family.[71] And then, nine months' silence.

The Boleyn–Butler marriage resurfaced in October 1521 after Surrey, already pressing for a recall, had fallen seriously ill. He appealed for approval of the act in Butler's favour, asked for the return of James to help his father and sent a personal messenger to press his own problems.[72] Butler, meanwhile, sensed victory and started to haggle for the return of his son and the completion of the marriage with Anne.[73] Wolsey, who all this while was tied up in a European peace conference at Calais, advised Henry in mid-November that James Butler was too valuable a hostage to be surrendered, but

> I shall, at my return to your presence, devise with Your Grace how the marriage betwixt him and Sir Thomas Boleyn['s] daughter may be brought to pass, which shall be a reasonable cause to tract [delay] the time for sending his said son over to him; for the perfecting of which marriage I shall endeavour myself at my return, with all effect.[74]

Wolsey left Calais on 28 November, and it was soon after that Anne must have received her recall to England.[75]

Yet Wolsey, for the first but not for the last time, did not 'perfect' marriage for Anne Boleyn. Why is not clear. Butler's arch-rival in Ireland, the earl of Kildare, reported that Sir Piers had by May 1523 decided that he would have to defend his claim by force.[76] According to Kildare's new wife, formerly Elizabeth Grey, a woman with a decade of court experience reaching back as far as her attendance on Mary Tudor in France in 1514, Butler was trying to bind nobles to support him against the Boleyn claim, and the Kildares, fresh from England, knew that Henry would not approve.[77] If we are to take seriously these

---

[71] Ibid., ii.63 [*LP*, iii.1099]; *LP*, iii.1926.
[72] Ibid., i.69; ii.49, 84, 91 (*LP*, iii.1646, 1628, 1583, 1830].
[73] Ibid., i.69–70, 72–3, 76–7, 81–2; ii.88–91 [*LP*, iii.1646, 1675, 1709, 1718]; *LP*, iii.1719.
[74] *St. Pap.*, i.92 [*LP*, iii.1762].
[75] *LP*, iii.1817.
[76] *St. Pap.*, ii.100 [*LP*, iii.3048].
[77] Ibid., ii.101 [*LP*, iii.3049]. Kildare had supported Boleyn and St Leger in 1516; see above, p. 43.

straws in the wind, then it was Butler who gave up hope of a settlement by marriage, presumably because Boleyn made difficulties – and the man who in 1521 had been promoted treasurer of the household was in a position to be obstructive. What, on this construction, Sir Thomas was standing out for was the earldom of Ormonde. The compromise which was ultimately agreed with the Butlers in February 1528 virtually gave them the land in dispute on long lease at very moderate rents, but saw them surrender the title into the king's hand, receiving instead, five days later, the earldom of Ossory.[78] The logic was then for Boleyn to become earl of Ormonde, but this did not take place until December 1529, after Wolsey's fall. It may well be that the cardinal was none too pleased at the way events had gone against him. By then Henry's interest in Anne was obvious, and Wolsey may well have rued the day when he had been unable to pack her off to Ireland. Boleyn won, Wolsey lost.

Against this, it does seem curious that Wolsey should have taken it upon himself to 'perfect' Anne's marriage in 1521 without first consulting her father, for Sir Thomas was then at Calais with him. Perhaps Wolsey never intended the possibility of a match between James and Anne to be anything other than a long-term inducement to the Butlers to behave. If this alternative scenario is the correct one, we must see the period after Anne's return from France as a time of semi-engagement to James – and separation, for he returned to Ireland in the summer of 1526. Certainly he was not the only suitor she had.[79] Yet when he returned to England in the summer of 1528 it was to find even competition a thing of the past. The king had declared himself, and Anne was no longer on the marriage market.[80]

---

[78] *LP*, iv.3937, 3950.
[79] Quinn, in *Irish Historical Studies*, 12. 333. James was at court until at least 27 Aug. 1526 [*LP*, iii.1628; iv.1279, 2433]. For Anne's other suitors see below, pp. 77–99.
[80] James Butler was in Ireland from at least 27 Dec. 1527 to 20 May 1528, at court on 26 June 1528 and in Ireland again by 18 Sept. 1528 [*LP*, iv.3698, 3922, 3952, 4283, 4422, 4748]. For a convincing identification of the Windsor Holbein 'Ormond' [Parker, *Drawings*, no. 23] as James Butler, see D. R Starkey, 'Holbein's Irish sitter?' in *Burlington Magazine*, 123 (1981), 300–3.

3

Debut at the English Court

<hr style="width:30%" />

ANNE BOLEYN a courtier's daughter, Anne Boleyn being educated abroad, Anne Boleyn a prospective bride. But the first direct glimpse we get of Anne on her return from France is at a court pageant in March 1522 – doing precisely what she had been trained for over all these years, and doing it before the eyes of experts from the Habsburg court at Brussels. A new chapter had opened in the interminable saga of the Italian Wars, and England, despite the protestations at the Field of Cloth of Gold, had decided to back Charles V rather than Francis I. Negotiations for a joint attack on France, a visit by the emperor to England and his betrothal to the Princess Mary were nearing completion, and the English court, to honour the ambassadors of the new ally, laid on specially magnificent pre-Lent festivities.

The theme of the opening tournament on 1 March was the cruelty of unrequited love, and this was continued when festivities reached a climax on the evening of Shrove Tuesday with a characteristically Burgundian pageant, the assault on 'the *Château Vert*'.[1] There were eight court ladies involved, each cast as one of the qualities of the perfect mistress of chivalric tradition – Beauty, Honour, Perseverance, Kindness, Constancy, Bounty, Mercy and Pity – with Anne playing Perseverance and her sister Mary, Kindness (roles of historic appropriateness). The king's sister Mary led as Beauty, with the countess of Devonshire as Honour – two women who would be among Anne's most

---

[1] *LP*, iii.p. 1559; *Cal. S. P. Span., Suppl. 1513–42*, pp. 69–73; Hall, *Chronicle*, p. 631.

implacable opponents – while of the other characters, Constancy was played by Jane Parker, soon to become Anne's sister-in-law. They wore white satin, each with her character or 'reason' picked out twenty-four times in yellow satin, and the head-dresses were cauls of Venetian gold set off by Milan bonnets. Opposite them were the eight male virtues of the ideal courtier – 'Amoress[ness]', Nobleness, Youth, Attendance, Loyalty, Pleasure, Gentleness and Liberty – with the king playing the lead. The men were dressed in caps and coats of cloth of gold and tinsel, with blue velvet buskins and 'great mantle cloaks of blue satin', each of which had forty-two scrolls of yellow damask on which were pasted, in blue letters, the name of the character and appropriate 'poems'. This was a wise precaution, as matters had got out of hand on a previous occasion when the character names had been made of actual gold, and the costumes had been stripped by spectators – one London seaman getting away with gold worth £3 14*s*. 8*d*., almost two ounces.[2]

The performance was put on at York Place, Wolsey's episcopal palace in Westminster which was later to become Whitehall Palace, with Anne the first queen to live there. It began after supper, with the audience being led into a large chamber, hung with arras and brilliantly lit, and at one end the glittering *Château Vert* itself. This was an elaborate wooden construction with three towers, painted green and with the battlements covered in hundreds of pieces of green tinfoil. It contained hidden musicians, and standing on the towers were the eight ladies. Anne was probably in the main tower, which had a burning cresset and, like the other two, a banner – three hearts torn to pieces, a woman's hand gripping a man's heart and a woman's hand turning a man's heart upside down. The ladies were protected from assault by eight choristers of the royal chapel manning the lower walls and dressed as Indian women, each depicting one of the contrary feminine vices (or virtues) – Danger, Disdain, Jealousy, Unkindness, Scorn, 'Malebouche' (Sharp Tongue) and Strangeness (Off-handedness). The men entered, led by Ardent Desire dressed in crimson satin embroidered with burning flames in gold, a role almost certainly played by William Cornish, master of the Children (choristers) of the Chapel Royal and very probably author, designer and

[2] Ibid., p 519.

producer of the whole affair.[3] Then Desire begged the ladies to come down, but when Scorn and Disdain announced that they would resist, he called on the courtiers to take the ladies by force. To a peal of cannon, synchronized from outside, Henry led the attack, bombarding the castle and its garrison with dates, oranges and 'other fruits made for pleasure' to which the 'ladies', genuine or choristers, replied with a barrage of sweetmeats and rose water until Lady Scorn and the rest of the boys retreated, keeping up a defensive fire 'with bows and balls'. Female coldness having fled before masculine ardour, the warm and soft qualities were taken prisoner and brought out of the castle to dance. When the dancing was over, masks were removed and 'all were known'; then they went off with the audience to 'a costly banquet'. The whole performance had cost over £20, including three hats which the boys had lost in the course of their retreat.[4] Edward Hall tells us that the strangers were 'much pleased', at least by the dance, but Charles V's secretary apologized to his master: 'I have written very little about the reception accorded us by the king, the queen, and the cardinal, but Anthoine, your usher, saw most of the festivities and can recount them to you.' They were much more interested in the six-year-old Princess Mary.[5]

Anne Boleyn thus made her debut on an occasion which allowed her to show off all she had learned in her years abroad. But what was she like? Unfortunately the first descriptions of her only date from six years after the *Château Vert*, and already by then opinions were being coloured by the controversy surrounding her relationship with the king. By the time of her coronation in 1533, one hostile observer would be reporting to the court at Brussels that Anne's crown did not fit, that she was badly disfigured by a wart, and that she wore a violet velvet mantle with a high ruff to conceal a swelling in the neck, possibly a goitre.[6] Some writers have seriously repeated this, although much of it has an obvious explanation. The crown was removed

---

[3] Anglo, *Spectacle*, pp. 121, 179–80. It is clear from Hall's account that Henry was not Ardent Desire [*pace* Anglo, ibid., p. 121]. Since Ardent Desire was a speaking role in dialogue with the Children, he was probably not a courtier at all. Cornish had played similar roles in other entertainments [ibid., pp. 119–20].

[4] *LP*, iii.p. 1559.

[5] *Cal. S. P. Span., Suppl. 1513–42*, p. 86. For Hall, see p. 69.

[6] RO, PRO 31/8 f. 51 [*LP*, vi.485].

and replaced immediately after the actual coronation but this was because the traditional crowns were too heavy; the imperial crown, for example, weighed seven pounds, whereas the one made for Anne to wear instead weighed only three.[7] The practice was so sensible that it was followed for Edward VI, Mary and Elizabeth, each of whom actually wore a crown personally made for them (as did Elizabeth II at her coronation in 1953). As for the high collar, Anne wore the required surcoat with a mantle of ermine, although the material seems to have been purple velvet and not white cloth of gold. If the style was the same as the surcoat and mantle her daughter wore at her coronation in 1559, then the neck was high.[8] The need to conceal a goitre is malevolent embroidery.

The most extreme exponent of this 'monster legend' was the Elizabethan recusant activist, Nicholas Sander. According to his account:

> Anne Boleyn was rather tall of stature, with black hair and an oval face of sallow complexion, as if troubled with jaundice. She had a projecting tooth under the upper lip, and on her right hand, six fingers. There was a large wen under her chin, and therefore to hide its ugliness, she wore a high dress covering her throat. In this she was followed by the ladies of the court, who also wore high dresses, having before been in the habit of leaving their necks and the upper portion of their persons uncovered. She was handsome to look at, with a pretty mouth.[9]

Apart from the evident self-contradiction of the last sentence, Sander, born 1527 and in exile from 1561, was hardly a contemporary witness of the events of Anne's life, or an expert on the vagaries of female fashions of earlier generations – high necks came into fashion after Anne's death. The fact that he records well established tradition, but tradition that was current among recusant exiles, also cuts both ways. Nevertheless, although we may dismiss the tooth, there may be some truth in the sixth finger and the wart. George Wyatt, writing at the end of the century to contradict Sander, and having access to some genuine

---

[7] See the accounts cited below, p. 216[5]. For Anne's and the other Tudor royal crowns and the ceremony, see J. Arnold, 'The coronation portrait of Queen Elizabeth I', in *Burlington Magazine*, 120 (1978), 731–2.

[8] NPG, no. 5175; cf. ibid., 120. 727–41.

[9] Sander, *Schism*, p. 25.

family traditions of his own about Anne, was compelled not only to accept her 'beauty not so whitely as clear and fresh, above all we may esteem', but to admit that

> there was found, indeed, upon the side of her nail, upon one of her fingers, some little show of a nail, which yet was so small, by the report of those that have seen her, as the work master seemed to leave it an occasion of greater grace to her hand, which, with the tip of one of her other fingers might be, and was usually by her hidden without any blemish to it. Likewise there were said to be upon some parts of her body, certain small moles incident to the clearest complexions.[10]

A minor malformation of one finger-tip thus seems very probable, and so too one or two moles, possibly on the chin, but never the disaster Sander imagined; one man's beauty-spot is hardly another man's 'wen'.

What makes the more horrific stories about Anne implausible is the undoubted impact that she made. Not that she was ever a ravishing beauty. Lancelot de Carles did call her 'beautiful and with an elegant figure', and a Venetian reporting what was known of her in Paris in 1528 described her as 'very beautiful'.[11] Yet John Barlow, one of her favourite clerics, when asked to compare Anne to Elizabeth Blount, the duke of Richmond's mother, replied that Elizabeth 'was more beautiful', although Anne 'was very eloquent and gracious, and reasonably good looking [*competement belle*]'.[12] Simon Grynée, a professor of Greek at Basle whom Henry VIII employed to canvas Swiss opinion as to the validity of his marriage to Katherine, was similarly cautious (and also not entirely persuaded as to her morals): 'young and good-looking' was his verdict.[13] The Venetian diplomat, Francesco Sanuto, was even less certain though he clearly knew of no goitres or 'large wens': 'Not one of the

---

[10] George Wyatt, in *Wolsey*, ed. Singer, p. 424.

[11] De Carles, in Ascoli, *L'Opinion*, line 61; *Cal. S. P. Ven., 1527–33*, 236.

[12] *Cal. S. P. Span., 1531–33*, p. 473. Contradictory versions have been published of what Barlow said, muddling the terms used: '*ladite dame*' and '*ladite fille*'. The context makes clear that the former is Anne, and the BL text reads in the original: '*Ledit doyen* [Barlow] *respondit qu'il avoit connaisance tant de ladite dame que de ladite fille, et que ladite fille estoit plus belle que ladite dame mais ladite dame estoit bien eloquente et gracieux et competement belle et de bonne maison*' [Addit. MS 28585, f. 45].

[13] *Original Letters*, ii.553.

handsomest women in the world; she is of middling stature,
swarthy complexion, long neck, wide mouth, a bosom not much
raised and eyes which are black and beautiful.'[14] Henry, as we
shall see, saw nothing wrong with Anne's breasts, but the overall
evidence of these less prejudiced observers hardly suggests
compelling physical attractiveness.

That Anne did have fine eyes was noticed by others than
Sanuto. De Carles waxed lyrical about them. She had

> . . . eyes always most attractive
> Which she knew well how to use with effect,
> Sometimes leaving them at rest,
> And at others, sending a message
> To carry the secret witness of the heart.
> And, truth to tell, such was their power
> That many surrendered to their obedience.[15]

All agreed, too, that Anne was dark. As well as Sanuto's
'swarthy', Thomas Wyatt gave her the poetic name, 'Brunet'.[16]
Simon Grynée described her complexion as 'rather dark', while
when her daughter Elizabeth was born it was remarked how fair
she was, taking after her father rather than her mother.[17] A
feature of which Anne herself was clearly proud was her hair. A
good deal of comment was caused by her wearing her hair down
for the coronation procession through London, but this was only
in accordance with established etiquette. Anne, however, had
also worn her hair down for the entirely unprecedented ceremony
where she was created marchioness of Pembroke.[18]

Looks only tolerable, but a splendid head of dark hair and fine
eyes – this then was the impression that Anne Boleyn made on
her contemporaries, but it would be good also to have some
direct visual evidence to judge by. Here the past has not been
kind. The painter coming into prominence at the English court
was, of course, Hans Holbein the younger, but no painting of
Anne by Holbein is known to have been made, and certainly

[14] *Cal. S. P. Ven., 1527–33*, 824.
[15] De Carles, in Ascoli, *L'Opinion*, lines 62–8.
[16] See below, p. 91.
[17] *Original Letters*, ii.553; *Cal. S. P. Ven., 1527–33*, 824; de Carles, in Ascoli,
L'Opinion, lines 170–1.
[18] *Ordinances for the Household*, pp. 123–4. For the creation as marchioness, see
below, p. 198.

none has survived.[19] Two of his drawings are alleged to be of her: one in the set of his drawings in the royal collection at Windsor (plate 5), and the other now in the British Museum and formerly at Weston Park (plate 4).[20] The Windsor drawing carries the legend 'Anna Bollein Queen', in eighteenth-century lettering which is said to have derived originally from Sir John Cheke, Edward VI's tutor, and since Cheke had known Anne the identification might appear to have authority.[21] There is, however, no certainty that the story about Cheke is true – by no means all the Holbeins at Windsor are correctly labelled – and there is evidence on the 'Anna Bollein' to link it with the Wyatt family.[22] The British Museum drawing also has an inscription (in Latin), 'Anne Bullen was beheaded, London 19 May, 1536', but the writing dates only from the first half of the seventeenth century. Certainly when both it and the Windsor drawing were owned by the earl of Arundel in the 1640s it was the British Museum Holbein which was engraved as Anne, but on what authority is not clear.[23]

Thus neither of the Holbein drawings claimed to be Anne Boleyn has real authority. The one firm contemporary identification is the medal of Anne struck in 1534 (plate 10); it carries her motto, 'The Moost Happi' and the initials 'A.R.' – Anna Regina.[24] Unfortunately the nose has been badly, perhaps deliberately, damaged in the only specimen known, so that its value as a likeness is seriously impaired. The shape of the face,

[19] NPG, *Portraits*, i.7. Seventeenth-century inventories reveal that other portraits of Anne did exist, e.g. Historical Manuscripts Commission, *Manuscripts of the Marquess of Ormonde*, new series (1902–20), vii.507.
[20] HM the Queen, Windsor [Parker, *Drawings*, no. 63]. BM, Dept. of Prints and Drawings, 'Portrait of a Lady', 1975–6–21–22.
[21] For the vicissitudes of the Holbein drawings, see Parker, *Drawings*, pp. 7–20; J. Rowlands, 'A portrait drawing by Hans Holbein the younger', in *British Museum Yearbook*, 2 (1977), 231–7.
[22] J. Rowlands & D. R. Starkey, 'An old tradition reasserted: Holbein's portrait of Queen Anne Boleyn', in *Burlington Magazine*, 125 (1983), 88–92, argue for the identification of the Windsor drawing as that of Anne, on the basis of Cheke's authority and on circumstantial grounds. However, the fact that Margaret Gigges, More's foster daughter, is called 'Mother Iak', i.e. Mrs Jackson, Edward VI's nurse, whom Cheke as the king's tutor must have known, must cast doubt on the story about the identifications being made by him. More's daughter-in-law Elizabeth Dauncey, called 'The Lady Barkley', is similarly worrying; Parker, *Drawings*, p. 53 no. 63.
[23] Rowlands, in *British Museum Yearbook*, 2. 233–4.
[24] BM, Dept. of Coins and Medals. G. Hill, *Medals of the Renaissance*, rev. edn J. G. Pollard (1978), p. 145.

however, can be clearly seen – long and oval with high cheek-bones, much the sort of face that her daughter Elizabeth was to have, according to some painters. Given the condition of the medal it is impossible to go further than that, but it cannot be said to inspire confidence in the identification of either of the Holbein drawings as Anne Boleyn.

A number of paintings from the later sixteenth century claim to be of Anne, but none of the surviving examples is earlier than fifty or sixty years after her death. There are two images for Anne, showing quite different costume and head-dress and so clearly representing different traditions. The better-known pattern (of which the example in the best condition is in the National Portrait Gallery and reproduced in plate 1) shows Anne in a French hood picked out with two rows of pearls, and wearing a pair of pearl carcanets (necklaces), one loose and one choker, with a gold letter 'B' hanging from the choker, and a somewhat curious gold chain acting as a halter.[25] The alternative or 'Nidd Hall' pattern (plate 2) has Anne in a gable hood with carcanets of alternate rubies and clusters of pearls, and a matching pendant of three rubies and a drop pearl.[26] The monogram, this time 'AB', is pinned to the front of the bodice and has a single drop pearl. The paintings of each pattern are survivors from the sets of 'Kings and Queens of England' which Elizabethan and Jacobean gentry liked to have in their houses to demonstrate loyalty, and are thus far removed from a first-hand likeness. Everything depends upon one – or both – deriving from an authoritative original. Neither could have derived from the portrait medal, nor does the medal derive from an ancestor which is common to either. The Nidd Hall image does have the same sort of head-dress, yet neither it nor the National Portrait Gallery pattern has the medal's striking lift of the head.

An authoritative original image can, however, now be produced, resolving once and for all this pictorial game of 'find the lady'. The key is a ring which is in the collection belonging to the Trustees of Chequers, the prime minister's country residence

----

[25] NPG, no. 668.

[26] Private Collection. NPG, *Portraits*, ii.pl. 10. A version of this type, without the monogram and with a single pearl carcanet and a cross decorated with rectangular stones (presumably rubies) in place of the pendant, was engraved by Richard Elstrack and published in Thomas Holland, *Baziliwlogia* (1618), the only queen consort to appear in this series of English monarchs.

(reproduced as plate 6). It was previously in the possession of the Home family, having been given, it is said, from the English royal treasures by James I to the then Lord Home.[27] The shank is set with rubies and the bezel carries the monogram 'E' in diamonds which, with the provenance, establishes the link with Elizabeth I. The head of the ring is hinged and opens to reveal two enamel portraits, one of Elizabeth and one of a woman in the costume of Henry VIII's reign, wearing a French hood. The portrait is minute – the shank itself is only 175 mm across – but the image is quite clearly of the same sitter as the National Portrait Gallery painting. The face-mask of Elizabeth indicates a date for the ring of about 1575, which therefore pushes back this image of Anne by some twenty years. Far more important, it authenticates the image by showing that it was accepted in Elizabeth's court as a likeness of the queen's mother. Elizabeth herself could obviously have had no clear recollection of Anne's face, but others around her had known Henry's second wife well. Direct confirmation of the Chequers likeness is given by a comparison with the 1534 medal. The facial type is clearly the same.

There is thus now a sequence for an authenticated image of Anne Boleyn, comprising the medal, the Chequers enamel and the National Portrait Gallery pattern. Between the last two there is a suspicion of some degradation – a prettying up and a loss of character – but as the ring is tiny, it is very hard to tell.[28] Fortunately the sequence also has the effect of corroborating a seventeenth-century miniature in the collection of the duke of

[27] P. Somerset Fry, *Chequers, the Country Home of Britain's Prime Ministers* (1977), p. 52; *Catalogue of the Principal Works of Art at Chequers* (HMSO, 1923), no. 507; *Princely Magnificence, Court Jewels of the Renaissance* (Victoria & Albert Museum, London, 1980–1), no. 37 and p. 26. A. G. Somers Cocks has suggested that the appearance of an enamel phoenix arising from a flaming crown beneath the bezel of the ring indicates a connection with Edward Seymour, earl of Hertford, who campaigned ceaselessly to get Elizabeth I to recognise his marriage with Jane Grey's sister, Katherine. The Seymour device, however, would serve a double reference, since Elizabeth both used the phoenix symbol and had risen miraculously from the flames of the destruction of her mother, the only one of Henry VIII's later wives to wear a crown. The ring is not mentioned in the inventories of Elizabeth's jewels, but must have been made for her, or as an elaborate gesture of loyalty to her, and the association of the image is secure either way.

[28] The apparently inferior version of the National Portrait Gallery pattern owned (1969) by Mrs. K. Radclyffe may give the truer impression: NPG, *Portraits*, ii.pl. 9. Cf. also the example at Hever Castle, Kent.

Buccleuch and Queensberry which was copied for Charles I 'from an ancient original' as 'Anne Boleyn' (plate 3).[29] The artist was John Hoskins the elder (*c.*1590–1664/5), so that the piece preserves what a highly talented seventeenth-century miniaturist made of the Chequers image, and though again softened, is the best depiction of Anne we are likely ever to have, failing the discovery of new material. Medal – Chequers ring – National Portrait Gallery pattern – Hoskins miniature: the chain is complete. We have the real Anne Boleyn at last.

Of the other alleged likenesses, opinion must be left to judge. There is little to be said for either Holbein drawing, but the Nidd Hall painting is not impossible to reconcile with the authoritative image, especially as the sitter appears somewhat older. What does seem improbable is the latest candidate as a likeness of Anne Boleyn, a portrait miniature assigned to the Flemish artist Lucas Hornebolt and found in two versions, in the Royal Ontario Museum and in the Buccleuch collection (plate 7).[30] The costume is certainly in line with the Nidd Hall painting, yet the appearance of the sitter is quite different from the Chequers image. There is also a difficulty about the date. The Toronto miniature gives the age of the sitter as twenty-five, which, if Anne Boleyn, would put the piece in 1526. Since it is argued that miniature portraits at this date were a distinctively princely art form, Anne would hardly yet seem to qualify.

Establishing a reliable image for Anne Boleyn only accentuates the evidence of contemporaries that her attraction was not outstanding natural beauty. What, then, explains her power? In the first place she radiated sex. A son of the earl of Northumberland would try to break a six-year-old engagement for her; Sir Thomas Wyatt would become passionately involved, and it was the inability of a Flemish musician to stand the heady atmosphere around her that would help to bring Anne to destruction. As for Henry, the king's own letters show how explicit was his desire:

---

[29] Duke of Buccleuch and Queensberry. H. A. Kennedy, *Early Portrait Miniatures in the Collection of the Duke of Buccleuch*, ed. C. Holmes (1917), no. C8: 'From an ancient original' is written on the back of the mounting.
[30] *Artists of the Tudor Court*, ed. R. Strong (Victoria & Albert Museum, 1983), no. 14 and pp. 39–40; R. Strong, *The English Renaissance Miniature* (2nd edn 1984), no. 22 and pp. 36, 189.

Mine own sweetheart, this shall be to advertise you of the great loneliness that I find here since your departing – for I assure you methinketh the time longer since your departing now last, than I was wont to do a whole fortnight. I think your kindness and my fervencies of love causeth it; for otherwise I would not have thought it possible that for so little a while it should have grieved me . . . wishing myself (especially of an evening) in my sweetheart's arms, whose pretty dugs I trust shortly to kiss.[31]

We may feel too that, while the licentiousness of Francis I's court has been exaggerated (in particular by that purveyor of soft porn, the Abbé de Brantôme), Anne's attendance on Claude during visits to the court which was much more explicitly erotic than those at London or Brussels must have made her aware of her power.

Yet sexuality was only a part of Anne Boleyn's attraction. What made her stand out was sophistication, elegance and independence, in fact the continental experience and upbringing which we have explored. De Carles wrote:

> To France, which brought her such fortune,
> Ah! what honour. What a debt
> She owed to the skill
> Of those from whom she had learned such accomplishments,
> Which have since made her queen of her own people.
> She was happy, but how more happy
> If she had trodden the way of virtue,
> And had kept to the direction of the way
> Which her honourable mistress had shown her.[32]

France and Queen Claude, and, one might add, Margaret of Austria: these had made the difference. There were foreign ladies at the English court. Some, now ageing, had come over with Katherine of Aragon, but among the English there was nobody with a tithe of the continental polish of Anne Boleyn. One of Wolsey's servants who had known her remembered how she stood out among the other women at court 'for her excellent grace and behaviour'.[33] A less than enthusiastic Protestant writer of the next generation told how 'albeit in beauty she was

---

[31] *Love Letters*, p. 47 [*LP*, iv.4597].
[32] De Carles, in Ascoli, *L'Opinion*, lines 75–84.
[33] Cavendish, *Wolsey*, p. 29.

to many inferior, but for behaviour, manners, attire and tongue she excelled them all, for she had been brought up in France.'[34] A Catholic account of the same period stressed that 'she was in the prime of her youth', and as well as her musical abilities 'had her Latin and French tongue'.[35] True, one of her chaplains recalled that she used to lament her ignorance of Latin, but the two memories are not incompatible; it was polite convention to plead inadequacy – her daughter did, and she was an excellent Latinist.[36] Even the recusant tradition remembered her elegance and gave her credit for it, if for nothing else: 'She was the model and the mirror of those who were at court, for she was always well dressed, and every day made some change in the fashion of her garments. But as to the disposition of her mind . . .'[37]

Anne Boleyn had style, and continental style at that. George Wyatt might look back and write of 'the graces of nature graced by gracious education', but de Carles declared at the time: 'no one would ever have taken her to be English by her manners, but a native-born Frenchwoman.'[38] And she took the English court by storm.

[34] George Wyatt, *Papers*, p. 143.
[35] BL, Sloane MS 2495 f. 2v.
[36] Oxford, Bodleian MS C. Don. 42 f. 32.
[37] Sander, *Schism*, p. 25.
[38] George Wyatt, in *Wolsey*, ed. Singer, p. 423; de Carles, in Ascoli, *L'Opinion*, lines 53–4.

4

The Sources

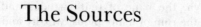

ANNE BOLEYN is the most controversial woman ever to have
been queen consort of England. Disagreement among
historians in more recent times only continues a controversy
which began as soon as her name was seriously linked with that of
Henry VIII, and persisted until subsumed in the adulation or
vituperation which came to surround her daughter. The result is
that, as we have seen, from the first there are partisan versions
even on simple points of fact.

To Roman Catholics it was not just that Henry had displaced
his rightful wife in favour of Anne Boleyn, and in order to satisfy
his lust had broken with the true Church. Anne herself was soon
being blamed for what had happened. George Cavendish, in the
confidence that God had restored right rule to England with the
accession of Mary, produced a series of *Metrical Visions* in which
over forty victims of political disaster, from Wolsey onwards,
lament their ill fortune; Anne declares:

> I may be compared in every circumstance
> To Athalia who destroyed David's line,
> Spared not the blood by cruel vengeance
> Of God's prophets, but brought them to ruin:
> Murder asketh murder, by murder she did find,
> So in like wise resisting my quarrel
> How many have died and ended pareil [the same].[1]

By the accession of James I, an analysis preserved in the papers
of those incorrigible recusants the Treshams of Rushton could

[1] Cavendish, *Metrical Visions*, pp. 41–2.

attribute all the sufferings of Roman Catholics under Elizabeth's
penal laws to the fact that Anne 'did beget a settled hatred of
them against her and hers':

> Anne Boleyn, the bane of that virtuous and religious Queen
> Katherine, the ruin of many pious, worthy and famous men who
> favoured not that unlawful marriage, the first giver of entrance to
> the Protestant religion and the principal cause of her husband's
> dissolving of religious houses and slaughtering multitudes of
> religious people as not favouring her marriage with Henry VIII in
> the lifetime of his first wife.

Anne had been 'of bad parentage, of bad fame afore her
marriage, and afterwards executed for adultery'.[2]

The descendants of Thomas More had a particularly nice line
in insult, quite understandably. Sir Thomas, so we are told,
dismissed wordly status as vanity, but we cannot assume that his
family was as sanctified; one blow of the axe had put an end to
their bright prospects and undone the patient social climbing of
three generations. William Roper, the chancellor's son-in-law,
claimed that Anne's personal hostility to More drove Henry to
demand that he conform.[3] It was William Rastell, More's
nephew, religious exile and (briefly) judge of the court of
queen's bench, who gave currency in his lost *Life* of his uncle to
the lie that Henry VIII was Anne Boleyn's father.[4] He also
alleged – with obvious echoes of Herodias, Salome and Herod –
that Anne put on a great banquet for Henry at Hanworth, where
she 'allured there the king with her dalliance and pastime to
grant unto her this request, to put the bishop [Fisher] and Sir
Thomas More to death.'[5] In his edition of More's English works,
Rastell even edited out remarks by Sir Thomas which were
favourable to the queen. In a letter to Thomas Cromwell in
March 1534, More had written:

> So am I he that among other his Grace's faithful subjects, his
> Highness being in possession of his marriage and this noble

---

[2] Hist. Mss. Comm., *Various Collections* (1901–14), iii.131.
[3] William Roper, *The life, arraignement and death of . . . Syr Thomas More*, ed.
E. V. Hitchcock. Early English Text Society, 197 (1935), p. 74.
[4] Sander, *Schism*, p. 23 n.2.
[5] Nicholas Harpsfield, *The life and death of Sir Thomas More*, ed. E. V.
Hitchcock & R. W. Chambers. Early English Text Society, 186 (1932), p. 235.

woman really anointed queen, neither murmur at it nor dispute upon it, nor never did nor will, but without any other manner meddling of the matter among his other faithful subjects, faithfully pray to God for his Grace and hers both long to live and well, and their noble issue too, in such wise as may be to the pleasure of God, honour and surety to themselves, rest, peace, wealth and profit unto this noble realm.

In the published edition this became:

So am I he that among his Grace's faithful subjects, his Highness being in possession of his marriage, will most heartily pray for the prosperous estate of his Grace long to continue to the pleasure 'of God.[6]

That More should have recognized Anne as queen was unthinkable; worse still, saints cannot be allowed to praise whores. To Catholics, the deaths of Anne and those accused with her and, later, that of Cromwell, 'and most of all those who procured his death', were blood sacrifices to expiate More's murder, and the drops which fell from their bodies on to his grave at the door of the Tower chapel, 'peace offerings, or rather, confessions of the wrong they had done him'.[7]

Protestant hagiography told the opposite story. John Foxe staunchly defended both the queen's morals and her religious commitment. He hints at the involvement of the papists in her fall and cannot resist assigning responsibility to his *bête noire*, the conservative champion, Stephen Gardiner: 'neither is it unlike, but that Stephen bishop of Winchester, being then abroad in an embassy was not altogether asleep.'[8] And Foxe had the clinching proof of Anne's virtue:

to all other sinister judgements and opinions, whatsoever can be conceived of man against that virtuous queen, I object and oppose again (as instead of answer) the evident demonstration of God's favour, in maintaining, preserving, and advancing the offspring of her body, the lady Elizabeth, now queen.[9]

---

[6] *LP*, vii.289 at pp. 123–4.
[7] BL, Sloane MS 2495, f. 27.
[8] Foxe, *Acts and Monuments*, v.136–7; see below, pp. 372–3.
[9] Ibid., v.137.

Protestant writers are not, however, always unanimous in their praise of Anne Boleyn. William Thomas, that pseudo-intellectual hustler who was to be Northumberland's clerk of the privy council, and executed for plotting Mary's assassination, firmly maintained the official version of Anne's guilt, even after Henry VIII's death:

> [Anne's] liberal life were so shameful to rehearse. Once she was as wise a woman endued with as many outward good qualities in playing on instruments, singing and such other courtly graces as few women of her time, with such a certain outward profession of gravity as was to be marvelled at. But inward she was all another dame than she seemed to be; for in satisfying of her carnal appetite she fled not so much as the company of her own natural brother besides the company of three or four others of the gallantest gentlemen that were near about the king's proper person – drawn by her own devilish devices that it should seem she was always well occupied.[10]

A school of puritan opinion was prepared to accept that passion might explain Henry's second marriage, just as much as principle:

> Whether he did it of an upright conscience or to serve his lusts I will not judge for in the burrows of man's heart be many secret corners and it cannot be denied but that he was a very fleshly man, and no marvel for albeit his father brought him up in good learning yet after ... he fell into all riot and overmuch love of women.

As for Anne herself:

> This gentlewoman in proportion of body might compare with the rest of the ladies and gentlewomen of the court, albeit in beauty she was to many inferior, but for behaviour, manners, attire and tongue she excelled them all ... But howsoever she outwardly appeared, she was indeed a very wilful woman which perhaps might seem no fault because seldom women do lack it, but yet that and other things cost her after dear.[11]

[10] William Thomas, *The Pilgrim*, ed. J. A. Froude (1861), p. 70.
[11] George Wyatt, *Papers*, pp. 141, 143.

It is indeed noticeable that a number of writers seem almost reluctant to write about Anne Boleyn in any detail. Thus Holinshed remarked:

> Because I might rather say much than sufficiently enough in praise of this noble queen as well for her singular wit and other excellent qualities of mind as also for her favouring of learned men, zeal of religion and liberality in distributing alms in relief of the poor, I will refer the reader unto that which Mr. Foxe says . . .[12]

Foxe, however, had already himself referred to better-informed reports still to appear:

> because touching the memorable virtues of this worthy queen, partly we have said something before, partly because more also is promised to be declared of her virtuous life (the Lord so permitting) by others who were then about her, I will cease in this matter further to proceed.[13]

No vindication of Anne Boleyn was ever published. Her chaplain, William Latimer, presented to her daughter an encomium on her religious activities, and the Scottish Lutheran Alexander Ales wrote an account of her fall, placing all the blame on the enemies of the Reformation, but both men had an evidently partisan intent, while Ales included an address for any financial contributions Elizabeth would like to send.[14] The reason for silence elsewhere is not far to seek. Few defences of Anne Boleyn have been entirely happy. Any vindication of the wife was an implicit criticism of the husband; if Anne was 'noble', 'virtuous' and 'worthy', Henry had been either a monster or a gull.

One of those who may have been concerned with a project for an official Elizabethan account of 'the mother of our blessed Queen' was George Wyatt of Boxley Abbey in Kent (1554–1624).[15] One of the most assiduous of Anne's defenders, Wyatt claimed that he had begun work at the request of an official biographer who had asked him to set down what he knew of

---

[12] Raphael Holinshed, *Chronicles* (1577), 1565.

[13] Foxe, *Acts and Monuments*, v.136.

[14] Oxford, Bodl. MS C. Don.42, ff. 20–33; RO, SP70/7, ff. 1–11 [*Cal. S. P. For., 1558–9*, 1303].

[15] George Wyatt, *Papers*, pp. 20–1.

Anne Boleyn's early years, and had continued it under the encouragement of the archbishop of Canterbury. With the accession of James, interest, so he implies, had waned, leaving him to carry on alone. George had a strong personal interest in vindicating the English Reformation in general and Anne Boleyn in particular; he was the youngest son (but heir) of Thomas Wyatt, the leader of the 1554 rebellion against Katherine of Aragon's daughter Mary I, and grandson of Thomas Wyatt the poet who had been imprisoned in the Tower in 1536 as one of those suspected of involvement with the queen. So George devoted the latter part of his life not only to her biography but, as we have seen over the business of her alleged deformity, to an effort to reply specifically to the Catholic propagandist, Nicholas Sander. Sander was no original authority, but his *Origins and Progress of the English Schism* (posthumously published in Cologne in 1585) had broadcast very effectively the allegations against Anne which were current in recusant circles.[16] In the end Wyatt was no more successful than others had been in publishing a defence of the queen, but this was not for want of effort – rather, indeed, because of the grandiose nature of his plans. Two, or possibly three, of his preparatory pieces have survived: the earliest, a brief but completed 'Life of Queen Anne Boleigne', then a vindication of the relations between Anne and Thomas Wyatt the elder which may not be by, but is certainly after, George Wyatt, and finally (and after 1603) the opening section of a massive 'History of the English Reformation'.[17]

The purpose of what George does have to say about Anne is naively obvious. 'Elect of God', 'heroical spirit', 'princely lady' – the adjectives abound. Henry VIII, so the 'Defence of Sir Thomas Wyatt' has it:

> joined himself unto her [Anne] as the oak to the vine, he sustaining her, she adoring him, both embracing and clasping one another with that most straight and sacred knot, that heaven and earth were consenting to knit not to be loosed ever without the impiety of those that envied so incomparable felicity, like to

[16] *Nicolai Sanderi, De origine ac progressu Schismatis Anglicani liber,* ed. Edward Rishton (Cologne, 1585); see above, pp. 50–1.
[17] 'The Life' was edited in *The Life of Cardinal Wolsey by George Cavendish,* ed. S. W. Singer (2nd edn, 1827), pp. 417–49; 'The History' in George Wyatt, *Papers,* ed. D. M. Loades. Camden Soc., 4th series, 5 (1968), pp. 19–30; 'A Defence of Sir Thomas Wyatt the elder, etc' in ibid., pp. 181–205.

grow to this noble realm thereby ... Thus they lived tokens of
increasing love perpetually increasing. Her mind brought him
forth the rich treasures of love of piety, love of truth, love of
learning. Her body yielded him the fruit of marriage inestimable
pledges of faithful and loyal love.

And what put a period to this idyll?

She had a king, he not his like, ever liked and loved, and to be
liked and loved of her, (alas), too much liked of others that were
practised to draw his liking from her, thereby to have him not like
himself, whereby they wrought her end.

Which, despite the attempted concealment of the play on words,
is to say that the incomparable Henry was a dupe.[18]
Propaganda is not, however, entirely valueless to the historian.
We have seen how contemporary gossip about the king's relations
with the women of the Boleyn family gave rise to the Catholic
story that he was Anne's father. Much, of course, depends upon
whether writers had access to real sources of information. The
line from Sander back to William Rastell is direct, but if we are
to believe More, he never discussed Anne with Rastell or anyone
else, and the personal recollections of the members of his family
were confined to his life outside the council and the court. They
certainly breathe no word of More's dangerous and deeply
buried management of the opposition to the king's divorce.
On the other hand, even the author of a Catholic account as full
of picaresque invention as the mid-century *Cronica del Rey Enrico
Otavo de Inglaterra* had from time to time access to genuine
recollections – for example, his report that Thomas Wyatt
watched the execution of Anne's alleged lovers in 1536, which
was only confirmed in 1959 when a manuscript containing
hitherto unknown Wyatt material was identified in Trinity
College, Dublin.[19] George Wyatt certainly collected material
about Anne, and he claimed that he had three particular sources
in addition: 'some helps' left by his grandfather the poet, the
recollections of his mother Jane who had married in 1537 and
lived to the end of the century, and the memories of Anne

[18] Ibid., pp. 24, 29, 185–6.
[19] *Cronica del Rey Enrico Otavo de Inglaterra*, ed. Marquis de Molins (Madrid,
1874), p. 88; trans. M. A. S. Hume (London, 1889) (hereafter, *Chronicle*, ed.
Hume), at p. 68; Muir, *Life and Letters of Wyatt*, p. 221; Wyatt, *Poems*, CXLIII.

Gainsford, later the wife of George Zouche, gentleman pensioner and a target for Catholic investigation in Mary's reign. Given such links, the volume of material Wyatt recorded is disappointing, but at least one important episode has independent warranty in other sources.[20]

Historians are always likely to differ over the level of credence to be given to different strands in these traditions. They cannot, however, be ignored, and for two reasons. First, they are a primary, sometimes the only, source for the personal and psychological element which is at the heart of the story of Anne Boleyn and Henry VIII. In the second place, information about Anne is not so plentiful that we can set aside what we do have. Material is particularly scarce among the administrative records of government which historians so much prefer. Anne Boleyn did not become important until her mid-twenties. Until then we have no more glimpses of her life than of the lives of other ladies of her age and class, nor should we expect any. Furthermore, even when she did become prominent, even when she was queen, we continue to know almost as little of her day-to-day life as we do of the other women in Henry VIII's life. One exception to this general lack of information is the single surviving account for this period of Henry's private expenses.[21] These provide a vivid picture of the king's disbursements on Anne's behalf from November 1529 to December 1532, the crucial period during which Anne moved from being a recognized rival to Queen Katherine to being queen herself in all but name. The loss of these particular accounts for later years has probably not deprived us of much information since Anne was, from the autumn of 1532, in receipt of a regular direct income – first as marchioness of Pembroke and then as queen – and would have put many of these costs through her own accounts (now, unfortunately, also lost). But the disappearance of earlier volumes of Henry's private expenses does deny us valuable confirmation as to the date when he first began to pay marked attentions to 'the lady Anne'.

Judicial records supply important information about Anne Boleyn, as is so often the case for individuals in the sixteenth century. The material covering her indictment and trial and that

---

[20] George Wyatt, *Papers*, p.27; in *Wolsey*, ed. Singer, p. 422; see below, pp. 161–3.
[21] *Privy Purse Expenses of King Henry the Eighth*, ed. N. H. Nicolas (1827), from BL, Addit. MS 20030.

of her alleged accomplices was put in the Tudor equivalent of the file marked 'Top Secret' – the *Baga de Secretis* – and survives virtually intact.[22] Even more interest attaches to a number of depositions relating to Anne, most giving clear indication of her general lack of popularity and the gossip which circulated about her, but one in particular which sheds light on the execution of her supposed lovers. This was submitted by the reformer George Constantine to Thomas Cromwell in the autumn of 1539 in an effort to fight off allegations that he had broken the Act of Six Articles, enacted earlier in the year, and in the course of it he set down his memories of the events of 1536 with which he was directly connected.[23] As in all evidence of this kind it must be remembered that the deponent is telling a story to produce the effect he wants – in this case, to gloss a conversation so as to remove all hint of criticism of the crown – but as a confession was subject to factual scrutiny, variation is likely to be more in the manner of presentation than in content.

Another obvious target for the biographer might appear to be correspondence. Anne's own letters are disappointing. Few have survived and most are strictly concerned with practicalities – for instance, announcing the birth of Elizabeth. There is, admittedly, the remarkable letter which she is supposed to have written to Henry VIII on 6 May 1536, after her committal to the Tower. It exists in many copies, but none is contemporary, and although the tradition is that it was originally discovered among the papers of Thomas Cromwell, its 'elegance' (to use Herbert of Cherbury's word) has always inspired suspicion. It would also appear to be quite out of character (and totally counterproductive) for a Tudor prisoner in the Tower to warn the king, as 'Anne's' letter does, that he is in imminent danger of the judgement seat of God.[24] This shortage of letters is nothing to wonder at, either. Except in diplomacy or matters of exceptional importance, people at this period did not normally keep copies of the letters they sent. Letters are known, therefore, only where the original has survived in the papers of the recipient. Letters to the

[22] Edited in Charles Wriothesley, *A Chronicle of England, 1485–1559*, ed. W. D. Hamilton. Camden Soc., 2nd series, 11 & 20 (1875, 1877), i.189–226.

[23] T. Amyot (ed.), 'A memorial from George Constantine', in *Archaeologia*, 23 (1831), 50–78.

[24] Burnet, *History*, iv.291–2; vii.239–40; *LP*, x.808; Herbert, *Henry VIII*, pp. 569–70. Cf. the genuine letter from Katherine of Aragon: Mattingly, *Catherine of Aragon*, p. 308.

queen are somewhat more plentiful and more revealing, in
particular the seventeen love-letters from Henry himself, ten in
French and the rest in English, which have ended up – of all
places – in the Vatican. These letters have no dates; although
some belong to the summer and autumn of 1528 there is, as with
Shakespeare's *Sonnets,* no firm agreement about the order in
which they were written.[25] Letters by third parties are also
valuable, particularly to and from correspondents within court
circles such as the governor of Calais, Lord Lisle, and his wife,
but with one proviso: communicating political information or
gossip could get people into serious trouble, so that sensitive
material was normally conveyed by word of mouth.[26]

On-the-spot reporting of news had no place in sixteenth-
century life, but a number of eyewitness accounts have survived
of several of the episodes in Anne Boleyn's career, including a
number by foreigners. These are, of course, confined to the more
public events, from the creation of Anne as marchioness of
Pembroke in September 1532 to her execution in the Tower
three years and nine months later. They are also limited by the
prejudices of the various eyewitnesses. Carping descriptions of,
say, Anne's coronation procession contrast with the initial
neutrality of Justice John Spelman, the warmer recollection of
Thomas Cranmer, and the semi-official propaganda of Wynkyn
de Worde's pamphlet, *The noble tryumphant coronacyon of quene Anne,
wyfe unto the most noble kynge Henry the VIII.* And in such a range of
reporting there lies, of course, safety.[27]

An additional complication arises when first-hand reports
have been worked into consciously produced pieces of literature.
One example we have already encountered is the poetry of
George Cavendish.[28] From about 1522 until the cardinal's death
in 1530, Cavendish was one of his gentlemen ushers and so
splendidly placed to collect first-hand information about Wolsey
and the court, but he wrote only in Mary's reign. What is more

---

[25] *The Love Letters of Henry VIII,* ed. H. Savage (1949), pp. 27–48; *LP,*
iv.3218–21, 3325–6, 3990, 4383, 4403, 4410, 4477, 4537, 4539, 4597, 4648, 4742,
4894. The Savage edition must take priority because it contains photographs
of the letters, but readings below usually follow *The Private Lives of the Tudor
Monarchs,* ed. C. Falkus (1974), whose translations are normally to be preferred.
[26] *The Lisle Letters,* ed. M. St. Clare Byrne (1981).
[27] See below, p. 216[5].
[28] Cavendish, *Metrical Visions,* pp. 20–47.

the intention of his poems to deal with the mutability of Fortune makes his verses heavy on lamentation and light on information; although there are some nuggets of value, the 365 lines covering Anne and each of her alleged lovers in turn contain fewer than twenty points of substance. Cavendish's better-known 'Life and Death of Cardinal Wolsey' is far more informative, but this work, also, was written from the hindsight of Mary's reign, long after the event.[29] It, too, is concerned with the fickleness of Fortune, so that Anne Boleyn is cast as the agent of 'Venus the insatiate goddess', called in by Fortune to 'abate' Wolsey's 'high port' and humble him to the dust.

Another important source that has been processed as literature is Edward Hall's *The Union of the Two Noble and Illustre Famelies of York and Lancaster*. Better known as Hall's *Chronicle*, this is the work of a Londoner who did see much of what he described and tried to investigate more. Yet his theme is 'The triumphant reign of King Henry the VIII', and his finished narrative (to 1532) has only three isolated sentences about Anne, and a short paragraph about her dancing with Francis I at Calais. The rest of the book, worked up posthumously from Hall's notes and drafts, has two sentences about Anne's marriage, another about her pregnancy, a long description of her coronation and the birth and christening of Elizabeth, terse reports of Anne's reaction to Katherine of Aragon's death and of her own subsequent miscarriage, six final sentences on her condemnation and a brief version of her speech on the scaffold! Perhaps if Hall had lived to write the material in final form himself we would have had more, but a hint in one passage suggests that he intended to gloss over Anne's marriage as something on which 'the king was not well counselled'.[30] Anything else would be quite out of character for Hall's hero–king.

A similar difficulty arises with the *Histoire de Anne Boleyn Jadis Royne d'Angleterre*, the French metrical account of Anne's trial and execution by Lancelot de Carles which we have already encountered. It was published at Lyons in 1545 by the author, now described as '*Charles aulmosnier de M. le Dauphin*', but a

---

[29] *The Life and Death of Cardinal Wolsey by George Cavendish*, ed. R. S. Sylvester. Early English Text Soc., 243 (1959). The completion date of the MS containing both the *Metrical Visions* and the *Life* was 24 June 1558.

[30] Edward Hall, *The Union of the Two Noble and Illustre Famelies of York and Lancaster*, ed. H. Ellis (1809), pp. 789–90, 793–6, 798–806, 818–19.

number of manuscript versions exist in London, in a number of repositories in France and at Brussels.[31] The author of the poem was in London at the time as secretary to the French ambassador, and although he did not himself witness the trial of Anne and her brother he may have attended the trial of the other accused and, in any case, had contacts with well informed eyewitnesses.[32] Most important of all, his account was completed on 2 June 1536, a bare fortnight after Anne's execution. What is uncertain, however, is the extent to which his desire to write in the tragic mode affected the story he had to tell, a point of particular relevance to his long and unique accounts of the confidential speech by an unnamed lord reporting Anne's misdeeds to Henry (which must be fabricated) and the queen's own response to being found guilty by the jury of peers (which is clearly right in tone but may elaborate on the occasion). Her scaffold speech, too, may be somewhat coloured; she seems to have said, 'I am come hither to accuse no man of my death, neither my judges nor any other', or something of the kind, but the *Histoire* has her say: 'The judge of all the world, in whom abounds justice and truth knows all, and through his love I beseech that he will have compassion on those who have condemned me to this death.'[33] Clearly, one of those remarks which ought to be made and are not.[34]

In the absence of any regular reporting of news by Englishmen – and, indeed, given the conviction of the Tudors that it was safer for people to know only what the government wished them to

---

[31] BL, Addit. MS 40662; Brussels, Bibliothèque Royale Albert Ier, MS 19378 ff. 1–19v. For an edition of Paris, Bibliothèque Nationale f.fr. no. 12795 collated with six versions in France see G. Ascoli, *La Grande-Bretagne Devant L'Opinion Française* (Paris, 1927). The poem, printed as *Epistre contenant le proces criminel faict a l'encontre de la royne Anne Boullant d'Angleterre*, by Carles, aulmosnier de Monsieur le Dauphin (Lyons, 1545), was reprinted in *Lettres de Henri VIII à Anne Boleyn*, ed. G. A. Crapelet (Paris, 1826), pp. 167–214. It is probably the Brussels MS '*Traictie pour feue dame Anne de Boulant, jadis Royne d'Angleterre, l'an Quinzecem trent trois*' that de Meteren used for his account of Anne's fall, which was taken up by Burnet, *History*, iii.222–5.

[32] De Carles cannot have seen the trial in the Tower as he reverses the order, placing Rochford's first, but the Westminster Hall trial account shows a good acquaintance with English criminal procedure.

[33] Comparing Hall, *Chronicle*, p. 819; Wriothesley, *Chronicle*, i.41–2; Friedmann, *Anne Boleyn*, ii.295 n.2, with de Carles, in Ascoli, *L'Opinion*, lines 1235–9.

[34] Another French MS poem tells the story of Rochford in the first person: in ibid., pp. 273–8.

know – the one thing that approaches any regular commentary on English affairs is the reports of foreign ambassadors resident here. The resident ambassador was a new breed in Northern Europe. Only in the sixteenth century had it been recognized that a country needed to keep a representative at the court of an important neighbour to watch over its own interests and to send back a steady flow of news. Older-style envoys continued to be sent to handle special negotiations, but there were now men stationed abroad and, according to the manuals, reporting back every few days, with monthly situation reports and, on their return, a *relation* or written debriefing. Theory did not turn out quite like that in practice, but a series of letters to the home government updating the situation every ten or twelve days – which is what survives from the best-organized embassies – is an outside commentary on affairs of immense value to the historian.[35]

The three principal embassies in England during Anne Boleyn's career were from Venice, from France and from the Empire. Venetian ambassadors tended to have short tours of duty (less than five years), until 1535 when representation lapsed to secretary level, and they were primarily concerned with trade questions and international relations.[36] The French had a greater interest in English domestic affairs, and for much of the time they had the chance to try to exploit Anne Boleyn in order to detach Henry VIII from Charles V. Anne, indeed, was sometimes wholly identified with French interests, almost another ambassador in residence. Yet the reports of Francis I's representatives in London are frequently disappointing. Various reasons can be put forward for this. The French diplomatic service, if that term is not an anachronism, was still (like the English) in its infancy, and it has not received the editorial attention from modern historians which its reports need and deserve. What is more, the relative ease of communication between the French and the English courts may have encouraged the use of messengers, rather than lengthy letters, for the more difficult matters.

Relations may, in any case, have been mainly at an official level, with the French ambassadors, representatives of the old enemy, finding it difficult to penetrate to non-government sources;

[35] G. Mattingly, *Renaissance Diplomacy* (Boston, 1955).
[36] *Cal. S. P. Ven.*, *1534–54*, 31, 242.

in February 1535 when English suspicions of French treachery were running high, apparently even Anne Boleyn herself felt it unwise to talk freely with Francis's envoy, Gontier.[37] There was also a sense in which the French took Anne Boleyn for granted. She was there by Henry's will and they would use her, but policy was not determined by the need to support her position. Even more important, perhaps, was the brevity of French ambassadorial tours – the 1533 resident was complaining after six months![38] This did not impede the ambassador's representative duties, but it did limit his usefulness as a news-gatherer. Ambassadors tended to get better the longer they stayed. As a result, for example, in 1532, the year most critical for the English Reformation and for Anne herself, we have very little first-hand evidence from French sources. The ambassador, Giles de la Pommeraye, was new to the job but was gone within the year, and from 5 May to 21 June he was away in Brittany 'consulting with his government'.[39] He was a strong supporter of Henry's wish for a divorce; he worked hand in glove with the king and his ministers, even helping them to put out the official explanation for the antipapal statute conditionally ending the payment of annates to Rome; above all, he was close to Anne. Yet all of this we know from other sources, not from de la Pommeraye.[40]

No contrast could be more marked than with the last of the principal foreign embassies resident in England, that of the emperor, Charles v. The Habsburg–Burgundian diplomatic service was the oldest in Northern Europe and the best-organized – essential in view of the extent of the territories the ruler had to govern and the issues he had to cope with. Furthermore, Charles v had a deep interest in affairs in England, not simply because of the possible impact Henry VIII might have on the emperor's continuous rivalry with Francis I, but because his interests were personalized in the fate of his aunt, Katherine of Aragon, and the legitimacy of his cousin Mary. Thus when it was suggested that the reports he received might have too much in them about Henry's divorce, the emperor requested even more information.[41]

---

[37] *LP*, viii.174.
[38] Ibid., vi.614.
[39] He arrived 24 Dec. 1531 [ibid., v.614] and was replaced Nov. 1532 [ibid., v.1531, 1579]; in Brittany: ibid., v.1013, 1110.
[40] *Cal. S. P. Span.*, *1531-33*, pp. 378, 417, 463-4, 475-7, 525, 561; *LP*, v.614.
[41] *Cal. S. P. Span.*, *1531-33*, p. 466 (*LP*, v.1109].

Not that Charles was thereby allowing sentiment to rule; as long as Katherine was queen or Mary the acknowledged heir, there would be powerful interests in England keeping the country to the traditional alliance with the Burgundian Low Countries. Yet sophistication of diplomatic technique and depth of interest go only part way to explain the fullness and value to historians of reports from the imperial embassy in England. It was the ambassador who made the difference – Eustace Chapuys, a lawyer from Annecy in Savoy who arrived in England in 1529 and remained here until almost the end of Henry VIII's life, only retiring in 1545 at the age of fifty-six.[42]

Chapuys was first a highly efficient and assiduous envoy, writing between thirty and forty reports a year to the emperor, plus letters to his officers. Next, the length of time he spent in England allowed him to overcome many of the obstacles in the way of an ambassador seeking news.[43] How, in the first place, was a stranger speaking no English to find informants? It took time to discover sensitively placed individuals who would supply information, or servants who could go out freely enough to be able to verify reports. But funds were limited and the real secrets were at court. How was an ambassador to succeed there? The answer Chapuys adopted was the answer of the diplomatic manuals: speak French, make yourself *persona grata* with the elite, and news and contacts will come to you. And this is where his training and experience came in, and especially his standing as a humanist and friend of Erasmus. Clearly a man of address, he was worth conversing with and very soon passed everywhere; even in the difficult times of Anglo-imperial tension when an envoy might be expected to be cold-shouldered, Chapuys continued to be welcomed as an individual, even by Henry VIII, who clearly enjoyed his relationship with this shrewd, brilliant, cynical cosmopolitan. And Chapuys soon discovered something else as he committed himself wholly to the cause of Katherine and Mary, refusing ever to treat Anne Boleyn as anything but Henry's mistress: he became the focus for all those who disliked what was going on, who believed as he did. Here was a ready-made set of contacts more anxious to give him news, even, than he was to collect it. His house became almost the confessional for

[42] For this and the following see G. Mattingly, 'A humanist ambassador', in *Journal of Modern History*, 4 (1932), 175–85.

[43] *Cal. S. P. Span., 1531–33*, p. xxvii; ibid., *1536–38*, p. xviii.

the king's critics, and Chapuys dabbled a good deal more deeply in English politics than the emperor either knew or would have sanctioned.[44] As a result, Chapuys' diplomatic reports are the most important continuous source for the understanding of politics and court life in England in the lifetime of Anne Boleyn.

The professionalism of Charles V's envoys, and especially the personality of Eustace Chapuys, come clearly to us over the centuries, and it is easy to succumb to their authority: 'The agents of Charles V . . . spoke the truth, or what they believed to be the truth. Now and then they took a little too much credit for ability and energy; but they never gave an essentially false idea of the events they had to report.'[45] We must remember, however, that there were pitfalls waiting for even the ablest ambassador, and disadvantages as well as advantages in the total acceptance of Chapuys by English society, and especially by Anne's opponents. In the first place, his reports of what is going on at court tend to derive from individuals who share a single point of view and, what is more, pass news on with the gloss which that view gave. Thus, when Chapuys reports bad feeling between Anne and Henry he is relying on informants who wanted to believe that Anne was falling out of royal favour and were ready to see hopeful signs in almost anything. There is also the certainty that many of those he met would attempt to convey a particular impression to serve their own purpose. When Henry or one of his ministers tried to 'feed' Chapuys in this way, the envoy was usually on his guard, but private individuals may have been more successful. For example, the expression of loyalty to Mary which courtiers regularly made to him could have been inspired by everything from genuine affection, through a desire to hedge bets or disguise true feelings, to a wish to stand well with a popular court figure or merely be polite to his known prejudices. The matter was more serious in the early 1530s as certain conservatives tried to precipitate Charles V's intervention in England, by claiming that the country was a powder-keg of resentment against Henry and Anne which only awaited the spark of an imperial invasion. Chapuys' reports of unrest can be especially misleading because this was exactly what

---

[44] Ibid., *Suppl. 1513–42*, pp. xxxviii, 452.
[45] Friedmann, *Anne Boleyn*, i. p. viii. To be fair to Friedmann, he was contrasting this with English duplicity, and he later made points qualifying this encomium: ibid., i. p. xiv.

he himself wished to believe, and exactly what he wanted his home government to act on. Ambassadors with Chapuys' level of commitment can easily find themselves in the business of self-fulfilling prophecy. It is true, also, that however long he remained in England, Chapuys continued to see things loyally in Habsburg terms – even when these were misleading. Thus his continual description of Anne Boleyn as 'the concubine', although understandable, completely missed the point that to appreciate the situation in England as it actually was, it was vital to recognize that to Henry his marriage with Katherine had been, and would always be, a nullity. As it was, the imperial ambassador's failure to see this cost Mary Tudor dear in the summer of 1536.[46]

History is always more than the aggregation of source material, but the sources determine the limits of history – what can be explored, what cannot be explored. Though a truism, this must always be the text on the wall of a historical biographer, at least of a figure such as Anne Boleyn. Putting what the sources reveal in the context of what we know about the period, its events, its ethos, its ambience, is one thing; imaginative projection is another. We do not need to be as pessimistic as Paul Friedmann, who closed his magisterial two-volume study, *Anne Boleyn: A Chapter of English History, 1527–1536*, with the depressing comment: 'my object has been to show that very little is known of the events of those times, and that the history of Henry's first divorce and of the rise and fall of Anne Boleyn has still to be written.'[47] The bits and pieces, despite their distortions and irregularities, do add up to a great deal. Yet the sources stop short of that level of inner documentation which real biography requires.

Only at a handful of points in the story do we know anything of what Anne thought. Only in Henry's love-letters and in remarks scrawled on that book of hours do we know for certain what they said to each other. All the rest is of the order of what somebody said somebody else thought or said – and according to tradition it was Henry VIII who remarked, 'if I thought my cap knew my counsel, I would cast it into the fire and burn it.'[48] The limitations are galling, given the fascination that Anne Boleyn

[46] See below, pp. 412–13.
[47] Friedmann, *Anne Boleyn*, ii.312.
[48] L. B. Smith, *Henry VIII: the Mask of Royalty* (1971), p. 36.

and her story still exercise over the intervening centuries, and many have concluded that only artistic imagination will bring us to the truth. There is a place for Donizetti's *Anna Bolena,* for *The Private Life of Henry VIII,* for *Anna of the Thousand Days,* for the many literary attempts at biographical *actualité,* provided we recognize them for what they are: statements about ourselves. They explore our values, they tell us how we feel men and women would react, might react, should react in an imagined situation. What they can never tell us is how Henry VIII and Anne Boleyn did react.

5

Passion and Courtly Love

PROBLEMS IN assessing the sources are particularly relevant to our pursuit of Anne Boleyn in the years that lie between March 1522 and the end of 1527. At the first date she was newly come from France, the most glamorous of the ladies freed from the *Château Vert*, although in reality on passage to exile in Ireland. By the latter date, her name was beginning to pass along the diplomatic grapevine as Henry VIII's mistress, his *inamorata*, even his next wife. In England her stock was soaring and Anne could 'look very haughty and stout [self-confident], having all manner of jewels or rich apparel that might be gotten with money'.[1] The events of these five years see Anne involved first with Henry Percy, heir to the earldom of Northumberland, then with Thomas Wyatt the elder, and finally with Henry VIII and the problem of his childless marriage to Katherine of Aragon.

The principal source for the Percy story, and the only one which gives any detail, is Cavendish's biography of Cardinal Wolsey. According to Cavendish – and he writes as though he were an eyewitness – Percy was a young man being brought up in Wolsey's household while Anne was a maid of honour to Queen Katherine.[2] When accompanying his master to court, Percy gravitated to the queen's chamber: 'And there would fall in dalliance among the queen's maidens, being at the last more conversant with Mistress Anne Boleyn than with any other, so that there grew such a secret love between them that at length

[1] Cavendish, *Wolsey*, p. 35.
[2] Ibid., pp. 29–34.

they were ensured together intending to marry.' Henry, however, was himself taken with Anne, who 'for her excellent gesture and behaviour did excel all other', and ordered the cardinal to put a stop to these plans. So when Wolsey got back to York Place, he called Percy to the gallery there and told him off in no uncertain terms:

> I marvel not a little of thy peevish folly that thou wouldest tangle and ensure thyself with a foolish girl yonder in the court. I mean Anne Boleyn. Dost thou not consider the state that God hath called thee unto in this world, for after the death of thy noble father thou art most like to inherit and possess one of the most worthiest earldoms of this realm? Therefore it had been most meet and convenient for thee to have sued for the consent of thy father in that behalf, and to have also made the king's highness privy thereto, requiring then his princely favour.

The king would have found him a far better match and formed a much better impression of his worth, but now he had offended both father and monarch at once. Wolsey would send for the earl to discipline his son and the king would insist on the end of the relationship because he had planned another match for Anne (unknown to her) and 'was almost at a point with the same person'.

This reduced Percy to tears, but he defended his right to choose and also Anne's suitability, beseeching the cardinal to persuade the king 'on my behalf for his princely benevolence in this matter the which I cannot deny or forsake'.[3] At this Wolsey addressed some bitter comments to Cavendish and others of his household about the wilfulness of youth, but Percy insisted that 'in this matter I have gone so far before so many worthy witnesses that I know not how to avoid myself nor to discharge my conscience.' The worldly-wise cardinal saw no problem, sent for the earl and, in the meantime, forbade Percy to see Anne.

When the father arrived, he and Wolsey planned what to do. Then, as Cavendish and his fellows were escorting Northumberland to his barge, Henry Percy was sent for and given a public dressing down by his formidable parent: 'Son, thou hast always been a proud, presumptuous, disdainful, and

---

[3] Friedmann, *Anne Boleyn*, i.44 interpreted this as a request to break his earlier betrothal to Mary Talbot, but such a construction is clearly wrong.

very unthrifty waster, and even so hast thou now declared thyself.' Threats of the king's displeasure, the horrible prospect that he would be the last Percy, earl of Northumberland, unfavourable comparison with his brothers and a threat of disinheritance followed in quick succession, and the earl swept out with a dire prophecy to those around that they would see it all come true. At this Lord Percy crumbled, and 'after long debating and consultation' (presumably with the canon lawyers), a way was found to invalidate the young lord's commitment to Anne, who had, in the meantime, been sent away from court to her father's country house. To make assurance sure, Percy was married off to a daughter of the earl of Shrewsbury (George Talbot), and Anne thereafter nursed an implacable hatred for Wolsey, even uttering threats that 'if it lay ever in her power, she would work the cardinal as much [similar] displeasure.'

Such is the story Cavendish tells, and the final act of the romantic tragedy was the ruin of Henry Percy.[4] He did succeed his father as sixth earl of Northumberland in 1527, but his marriage to Mary Talbot disintegrated and his personality collapsed. He disposed of power and property to spite his family, and in February 1535, accepting that he had no chance of begetting a legitimate son and rejecting the king's wish that he groom one of his hated brothers to succeed him, he made the king his heir.[5] When in 1536 his brothers earned glory and martyrdom as leaders of the Pilgrimage of Grace, the head of the Percy family skulked in Wressle Castle, a broken reed to both king and rebels. By June 1537 he was dead.

How much are we to credit Cavendish's story of Percy's one attempt at independence and personal happiness? That it has some foundation in fact is clear. When in 1527 Henry VIII secured from the pope a dispensation to marry when free to do so, the bull was drafted to cover a woman 'who has already contracted marriage with some other person, provided she has not consummated it'.[6] In 1532 Mary Percy claimed that her husband had admitted that before he had married her he had promised himself to Anne.[7] The earl was known as a supporter of

---

[4] J. M. W. Bean, *The Estates of the Percy Family, 1416–1537* (Oxford, 1958), pp. 144–57; cf. M. E. James, *Change and Continuity in the Tudor North* (York, 1965), pp. 13–15.

[5] *LP*, viii.166.

[6] Ibid., v.3986; Pocock, *Records*, i.22; Herbert, *Henry VIII*, p. 394.

[7] See below, p. 207.

Anne Boleyn (he became physically ill after having to serve on the jury which found her guilty), and the story of the precontract was, Chapuys said, common knowledge – *manifeste a pluseurs*.[8] And it would not go away. Chapuys picked it up again in 1536 and Charles Wriothesley, another contemporary, categorically stated that Anne was divorced prior to her execution because of a precontract with the earl.[9] Cavendish is in good company.

What we cannot be sure about is the nature of the commitment between Anne Boleyn and Henry Percy. The two denied Mary Percy's story, but Chapuys believed that the earl had been got at, or was impelled by fear. He certainly was frightened when he had to repeat his denials at the time of Anne's fall. Chapuys' later information was that their marriage had even been consummated. This seems improbable, for such a relationship no one could have overturned, not even a combination of Henry VIII, Wolsey and the fifth earl of Northumberland! What is more, given the interest of king and minister at that time in the alternative match between Anne and James Butler, it is surprising that the existence of so insuperable a contract had not already come out. Chapuys' sources were, in any case, less reliable than they might have been, for the alleged marriage was claimed to have taken place in 1527! Whatever Henry Percy felt bound by, it seems clear that it was less than marriage, and fell short of a contract capable of resisting a persistent canon lawyer. One possibility is that he had tied himself to both Mary Talbot and Anne; another is that he had felt himself more deeply committed to Anne than she had been to him, hardly a novel situation.

If a consummated marriage is the most extreme possibility, the minimum is some sort of understanding between Anne and Henry Percy which had force in affection and honour, but not in law. This, by contrast, makes too little of the evidence. After all, the Boleyn–Butler marriage plan did founder, and a legal entanglement of Anne with Henry Percy could help to explain why Piers Butler lost patience in 1523.[10] The detailed wording of the dispensations which Henry sought or secured to cover his proposed second marriage certainly suggest that Anne's marital

---

[8] *Cal. S. P. Span.*, *1534–35*, p. 33 [*LP*, vii.171]. For the phrase see below, p. 207[84].

[9] See below, pp. 404–5.

[10] See above, pp. 45–6.

situation was less than straightforward.[11] Their object seems to have been to cover two situations: an earlier betrothal of Anne to a third party, and a non-consummated marriage between Anne and either that same third party or another man. It may be that these dispensations are referring to abortive marriage proposals of which we know nothing, for it is strange that Anne was still unmarried in 1527. They can be read, however, as an indication that she had been betrothed and then contracted to Percy or, more probably perhaps, betrothed to Butler and then contracted to Percy.[12] Dispensations however, had to provide for the worst case, and we can only assume from them that negotiations and agreements had gone far enough to make it advisable to cover objections which might arise in the future, not that betrothal and marriage had formally taken place.[13] Yet there may have been something. When her marriage to Henry was annulled in 1536, the supporting statute described the grounds as 'certain just true, and lawful impediments, unknown at the making' of the previous act in support of the Boleyn marriage, and now 'confessed by the said Lady Anne before the . . . archbishop of Canterbury, sitting judicially'. Various suggestions have been made as to the nature of this novel information – if, indeed, there was any – but one possibility would be that Anne, while not admitting any marriage to Percy, had explained her relations with him in terms which allowed Cranmer the excuse that he, or rather, Henry, was looking for.[14]

Where Cavendish cannot be correct is in telling his readers that Henry VIII removed Percy in order to take his place with Anne. The episode must be dated between Anne's return to England late in 1521, and the marriage of Henry Percy to Mary Talbot. That had been in the air ever since the respective fathers had first explored the possibility in 1516, but nothing was finalized until the autumn of 1523, with the actual marriage probably between 14 January and 8 February 1524.[15] Gossip

[11] Kelly, *Matrimonial Trials*, pp. 35–53.
[12] Ibid., p. 53.
[13] This sets aside Kelly's more extreme hypothesis of marriage to a person unknown.
[14] 28 Henry VIII, c.7; Kelly, *Matrimonial Trials*, pp. 245–59; see below, pp. 404–7.
[15] *Illustrations of British History*, ed. E. Lodge (1838), i.20–1; *LP*, ii.1893, 1935, 1969–70, 3819, 3820; E. B. de Fonblanque, *Annals of the House of Percy* (1887), i.385.

circulated from the autumn of 1522 about Percy being sent to the north to take up his family's traditional duty on the Marches, but there is no clear evidence of when he took post permanently which would date any romance with Anne Boleyn more precisely within the period from the spring of 1522 to the summer of 1523. This is long before the king's first known involvement with Anne – indeed, he was probably busy with her sister – and the plans which it threatened to upset were clearly those of the Butler– Boleyn settlement. Further, if this is so, then one may wonder whether it was Henry who was incensed so much as Wolsey, who had committed himself to 'perfect' that marriage: the cardinal was adept at threatening royal wrath when he was the one who was really annoyed![16] Given the probability that Boleyn was dragging his feet over the deal with the Butlers, it could even be that Anne's encouragement of Percy was calculated and had her father's approval. And if Wolsey was facing resistance which was hard to deal with and was determined to get his own way, this would also explain the panic-stricken reaction Cavendish saw in the earl of Northumberland, who had learned to his great cost in 1516 the lengths to which the cardinal would go.[17]

There must be doubts, too, about the detail of the conver- sations recorded by Cavendish. The eyewitness irrelevancies confirm the outline of the events – Wolsey calling for wine when conversing with the earl, the earl berating his son while sitting on the bench where the gentlemen-in-waiting sat, his departure by barge – but after thirty-five years Cavendish could only have retained an impression of what was said. Hindsight clearly plays a part in the script he writes for his actors – very noticeably in the earl's prophecy that his son will be 'a wasteful prodigal' and 'the last earl of our house'. Not that Cavendish's remembered impression is wholly without conviction. It is significant that the reconstruction is built upon Wolsey's rejection of Anne as no fit wife for a Percy and his emphasis on the king's alternative plans, and upon Henry Percy's detailed defence of Anne's suitability and his insistence on the depth of his commitment to her. These points could well have stuck in the mind. What is less credible is

---

[16] The Boleyn–Butler match had not been initiated by the king and he was not committed to it unreservedly.

[17] J. A. Guy, *The Cardinal's Court* (Hassocks, Sussex, 1977), pp. 27, 31, 122, 163.

what Cavendish says about Anne herself. To go about making threats against the cardinal was both unwise and childish, and Anne was neither of these. When we have some first-hand evidence of her relationship with Wolsey some six or seven years later, it is far more subtle than would fit with a long-held grudge.

How long Anne Boleyn was away from court after the Percy episode – indeed, if she was away at all – is not known. The next evidence we have concerns her friendship with Thomas Wyatt. This is, second to her relationship with Henry VIII, the episode in Anne's life which has commanded the greatest attention from subsequent generations: Anne Boleyn and the first great Tudor poet.

The Wyatts moved in the same court circles as the Boleyns and they had become neighbours when Sir Thomas took up residence at Hever in Kent, some twenty miles away from Sir Henry Wyatt's home at Allington Castle, near Maidstone. Despite this, family tradition has it that Sir Henry's son, Thomas, first met Anne at court on her return from France, which may well be true, given that Thomas was barely ten years old when she had left for Brussels. But when they did meet, he was bowled over. His grandson George has it thus:

> The knight, in the beginning, coming to behold the sudden appearance of this new beauty, came to be holden and surprised somewhat with the sight thereof; after much more with her witty and graceful speech, his ear also had him chained unto her, so as finally his heart seemed to say, *I could gladly yield to be tied for ever with the knot of her love*, as somewhere in his verses hath been thought his meaning was to express.[18]

As for Anne's response, we can assume that the attentions of so notable a suitor as Wyatt were not unwelcome to a newcomer at court. Percy's was the greater scalp, but even at nineteen Wyatt had the enviable combination of physique and good looks, intelligence, an articulate personality, spontaneity and good humour, which already promised a glittering career at court.

What we cannot assume is the nature of the relationship between Anne Boleyn and Thomas Wyatt. Ever since the sixteenth century there has been disagreement over this, and

[18] George Wyatt, in *Wolsey*, ed. Singer, pp. 424–5.

even sedate scholars of the later twentieth century seem strangely committed in their attempts at demonstrating that Anne did or did not share Thomas Wyatt's bed. The crucial evidence is Wyatt's own poetry, and the age-old problem of interpretation – how 'autobiographical' is great poetry? A number, particularly of Wyatt's later or supposed poems, clearly do arise from specific situations: the execution of Anne Boleyn's alleged lovers, the execution of Cromwell in 1540, a number of his own misfortunes and imprisonments. But poems which arise not from an event but from a relationship are much more difficult to pin down. One, however, combines both an event and a relationship and can serve as a datum line. It was written in 1532 when Wyatt was in the entourage accompanying Henry VIII and Anne Boleyn to Calais for their meeting with Francis I.

> Sometime I fled the fire that me brent
> By sea, by land, by water and by wind;
> And now I follow the coals that be quent
> From Dover to Calais against my mind.
> Lo how desire is both sprung and spent!
> And he may see that whilom was so blind,
> And all his labour now he laugh to scorn
> Meshed in the briars that erst was all to-torn.[19]

Taken literally, this suggests that Wyatt had been seriously in love with Anne, had had to struggle not to become too deeply involved with her and now, cured of his passion, ruefully contemplated what a fool he had been. But are we to take this literally? Wyatt was writing within the often complex and baffling convention of courtly love, whose nature resembles nothing so much as an onion, where to peel away one layer is only to reveal yet a further layer underneath.

Courtly love was an integral element in chivalry, the complex of attitudes and institutions which was central to the life of the Tudor court and elite. To modern eyes this may appear a tissue of artificialities which fails to disguise the ephemeral nature and conspicuous waste of tournaments, pageants, dances and masques.

---

[19] Wyatt, *Poems*, LIX. 'quent' = quenched; 'erst' = erstwhile; lines 7–8 = 'And he who was once torn to pieces when he was entangled in the briars, can now laugh contemptuously at all the effort he expended.'

In fact, chivalry was an idiom through which society managed to say many important things and regulate many important relationships. At a tournament, for example, the focus of action was always the king – even if someone else actually won. Participation enabled men to draw attention to their own honour and prowess but also, in particular, to express the idea of service to their sovereign; the attendance of the rest of the court elite as spectators was a public demonstration that they were loyal and dependent too. The fancy dress and role-playing of tournaments and indoor festivities could also make a powerful and specific statement about the royal person, as when Henry VIII appeared at the Field of Cloth of Gold in the guise of Hercules. There was also the element of international prestige and one-upmanship. The forms of display were common throughout Europe, and a country was judged by its spectacles – a criterion which was encouraged as the traffic of diplomacy and polite communication between the various courts of the West increased. There was as nice and as subtle a gradation in chivalric ballyhoo as in the cordiality (or otherwise) of the welcome accorded by a modern government to a visiting statesman.

At a very basic level, chivalry was also a defence against boredom and vice. The mark of gentility was, in the well known words of Sir Thomas Smith, Elizabeth I's secretary of state, being able to 'live idly and without manual labour', but there were still twenty-four hours in the day to fill. Chivalric convention therefore created as busy a lifestyle as ever would be experienced by later generations of the upper ten thousand worn out by the exigencies of the Season. The serious pursuit of entertainment was the only alternative to demoralization, as Henry VIII pointed out in his most famous song, 'Pastime with good company':

> Youth must have some dalliance,
> Of good or ill some pastance.
> Company methinks then best
> All thoughts and fancies to digest.
>   For idleness
>   Is chief mistress
>   Of vices all;
>   Then who can say
>   But pass-the-day
>   Is best of all?[20]

Out of doors, when not engaged in war, training for war or the pseudo-war of the tournament, the gentleman was busy with its substitute, hunting. Indoors – dancing, music, poetry, good conversation and the game of courtly love.

The notion that the chivalric cult of courtly love was an antidote to boredom when the weather was bad or hunting out of season is hardly romantic. Nor is the idea that another of its functions was to place the personal relationships of men and women, and especially emotional ones, within the straitjacket of convention. It is a simplification to say so, but among the Tudor elite, property considerations were accorded more importance than emotional satisfaction when it came to making a marriage. As we have seen, when Anne Boleyn was proposed as the bride of James Butler, personal feelings were not consulted, and when they did surface, as in the case of Henry Percy, material considerations allowed them short shrift. In some cases, perhaps many, husbands and wives found that a relationship which began in property could grow into passion, but there were others who were left to seek emotional or personal fulfilment with someone other than their spouse; not to mention the needs of those who were not yet, or who might in fact never be, economically free to marry. The problem was at its most acute at court. Here was a highly masculine environment with many men away from their families, but not a monastic one; the queen and the other women of the royal family and their attendant ladies were very much an integral part. That made a volatile mixture and it was the function of courtly love to stabilize it.

The heart of the conventions of courtly love was the same ideal which disposed men to attend the king: service. The ideal courtier, the 'perfect knight' was supposed to sublimate his relations with the ladies of the court by choosing a 'mistress' and serving her faithfully and exclusively. The lady was understood to be far above him in status and unattainable in virtue, and the role of the knight was unselfish and unswerving devotion. He formed part of her court, wooed her with poems, songs and gifts, and if she was gracious enough to recognize the link he could wear her favour and joust in her honour. In return he must look for one thing only, 'kindness' – an understanding and platonic

---

[20] John Stevens, *Music and Poetry in the Early Tudor Court* (Cambridge, 1979), pp. 344, 388–9. I have omitted the first and third stanzas and utilized readings from both the Ritson and the Henry VIII MSS.

friendship of the sort we today might expect of an older woman towards a younger man. Many a lady might, in fact, be older than her 'lover', and in practical terms she would then act as his patroness and launch him into court society. But at a deeper level, courtly love was important psychologically. It met the need we have seen for warm emotional ties and, although to twentieth-century eyes, conditioned to see the only normal relationship between man and woman as the sexually active one, such a phenomenon may appear nonsensical, the convention regulated relations between the sexes in an acceptable fashion. We must not, on the other hand, imagine that courtly love was asexual. It had the inner ambivalence that while the lady was expected not to give her favours, they were there to gain, and while the lover offered service, he also threatened possession. The manly virtues might conquer the feminine ones; at the fall of the *Château Vert* Perseverance did yield at least her hand in the dance to Amoressness, Nobleness or whoever it was had captured her. And herein lay the possibility. The conventions of courtly love could be the channel for real passion; the love lyric may be autobiographical, not merely artful; the 'mistress' may become the mistress. Yet after four hundred years, how is the historian to know? And that is the problem with Anne and Wyatt.

A good example is presented by the so-called 'Devonshire MS', once at Chatsworth and now among the Additional Manuscripts of the British Library, which has for the last seventy years been claimed as direct evidence linking Wyatt with Anne Boleyn.[21] It is certainly an anthology associated with Anne's Howard relations and with one of her own waiting-women, Madge Shelton. It was, apparently, lent quite widely at court, and borrowers would repay the loan by inscribing a poem to which they had access, and the manuscript now includes almost two hundred items in a variety of hands. Some pieces are undoubtedly autobiographical. The Devonshire MS appears to have belonged to Mary Howard who married Henry Fitzroy, duke of Richmond, in 1534 and whose initials are on the original binding; as well as Madge Shelton, it was shared by Margaret

[21] For the following, see R. Southall, *The Courtly Maker* (Oxford, 1964); R. C. Harrier, *The Canon of Sir Thomas Wyatt's Poetry* (Cambridge, Mass., 1975), pp. 23–54; *Collected Poems of Sir Thomas Wyatt*, ed. K. Muir & P. Thomson (Liverpool, 1963), pp. xiii–xv.

Douglas, the king's niece (on one page there is an inscription to Margaret and Mary Fitzroy). Many of the poems are connected with, or were older pieces selected for their relevance to, the secret marriage between Margaret and Lord Thomas Howard, for which he was imprisoned in the Tower from 1536. Indeed, about a dozen of the items are by Thomas or Margaret. There seems every possibility, therefore, that Anne Boleyn and Wyatt might be here too.

The manuscript certainly includes some 125 pieces attributed to Wyatt or assigned to him by later scholars. Anne's own participation has been seen on a number of folios, with a signature ('an'), an expression of good wishes ('amer ann i'), and a riddle:

> am el men
> an em e
> as I haue dese
> I ama yowrs an,

which is supposedly solved by the transposition of the second and fourth letters of each line:

> a lemmen
> amene
> ah I saue dese
> I ama yowrs an.[22]

The circle seems completed by one of Wyatt's stanzas:

> That time that mirth did steer my ship
> Which now is fraught with heaviness,
> And fortune bit not then the lip
> But was defence of my distress,
> Then in my book wrote my mistress:
> 'I am yours, you may well be sure,
> And shall be while my life doth dure.'[23]

The poem goes on to lament that now his erstwhile mistress is 'mine extreme enemy' – Wyatt rejected by Anne.

[22] BL, Addit. MS. 17492, ff. 56, 67v, 69. 'amer ann i' = (supposedly) 'love Ann'.

[23] Wyatt, *Poems*, CXLII.

Unfortunately for romance, very little of this stands up to close scrutiny. There is no evidence that the volume ever belonged to Wyatt or that he ever handled it, and the poems in the manuscript which are his indicate the collecting taste of Mary Fitzroy and her circle. The jottings are not in the handwriting of Anne Boleyn; the 'signature' is a couple of letters written to test a pen; the expression of good wishes is a mere doodle; the 'riddle' is hardly intelligible in solution, and is better understood as a series of random exercises, the last two of which are clearly part-versions of phrases such as 'as I have deserved' and 'I am yours and ever will be' – expressions of courtly love as stock as the greetings on any Valentine card. In addition, 'That time that mirth did steer my ship' is a poem assignable to Wyatt in the opinion of only some modern editors, and it is very probably by another author. So the Wyatt–Boleyn connection in the Devonshire MS collapses.[24]

If a text as closely associated with the ladies of Anne Boleyn's entourage as the Devonshire MS tells us nothing of Anne and Wyatt, it is small wonder that many attempts to interpret isolated poems by (or perhaps by) Sir Thomas carry little conviction.[25] Apart from the conventional poses of courtly love, Wyatt had been very active sexually in his younger days; as he later admitted, 'I grant I do not profess chastity, but yet I use

---

[24] Harrier, *Canon*, pp. 31–2, 41–5; see also R. C. Harrier, 'Notes on Wyatt and Anne Boleyn', in *Journal of English and German Philology*, 53 (1954), 581–2. The hand that wrote the jottings and 'signature' occurs elsewhere in the MS [Harrier, *Canon*, pp. 28–9]; since the poem 'That time that mirth' concludes by imagining the relationship of poet and mistress restored, it cannot be directed to the supposed loss of Anne to Henry VIII [Muir, *Life and Letters of Wyatt*, pp. 16–17; Thomson, *Wyatt and his Background*, p. 22].

[25] G. F. Nott, *The Works of . . . Surrey and of Sir Thomas Wyatt* (1815–16), suggested 'Alas poor man, what hap have I', which Harrier and Muir agree not to assign to Wyatt; Strickland, *Queens of England*, ii.219 and M. A. S. Hume (ed.), in *Chronicle* p. 69, offer 'Forget not yet', a Wyatt probable, but concerned with reminder rather than renunciation. S. W. Singer (ed.), *Wolsey*, p. 425, suggested 'A face that should content me', but the addressee had blonde hair! A. K. Foxwell, *The Poems of Sir Thomas Wiat* (1913) proposed 'Now must I learn to live at rest', but this concerns hurt pride at being conned by a woman who pressed her attentions but then failed to deliver. Raymond Southall argues for 'Ye know my heart' on the slim ground that the phrase 'I and mine' echoes a motto attributed to Anne, 'Me and Mine' [*Courtly Maker*, p. 174]. His argument [ibid., 174–5] for 'Lux, my fair falcon' as referring to Anne's falcon badge cannot be accepted, since the imagery is of flight as freedom and there is nothing to associate it with any particular of the badge.

not abhomination.'[26] There are, therefore, no grounds for assuming that any of his poems of desire, rivalry, possession, rejection or retreat refer to Anne, unless there is clear corroboration. And corroboration does not include allusions to Wyatt losing out to the higher bidder. Even in a private poem (and poems were rarely entirely private) it was ill advised to write

> I quit the enterprise of that that I have lost
> To whomsoever lust [likes] for to proffer most

if the higher 'bidder' was Henry VIII![27]

A proper historical scepticism leaves only four poems by Wyatt where there can be reasonable confidence that he is referring to his relationship with Anne Boleyn. One of the pseudo-Wyatts does seem a defence of the defiant motto which she adopted for a brief period in 1530 – '*Ainsi sera groigne qui groigne*' ('Let them grumble; that is how it is going to be') – but if it were to be by Wyatt, the poem could only suggest that in 1530 he was one of the future queen's entourage, which we might guess anyway.[28] The 1532 poem about the journey to Calais we have already noted, with its suggestion of a real but burnt-out commitment. Much less helpful is an earlier poem (again genuine) which takes the form of a riddle to which the solution is the name 'Anna':

> What word is that, that changeth not?
> Though it be turned and made in twain?
> It is mine answer, God it wot,
> And eke the causer of my pain.
> A love rewardeth with disdain,
> Yet it is loved. What would ye more?
> It is my health eke and my sore.[29]

Of course, even here it is only a matter of probabilities – the poem would fit any woman named Anna – but Anne Boleyn is the likeliest subject. At the immediate level this is a neat courtly

---

[26] Muir, *Life and Letters of Wyatt*, p. 206; cf. Wyatt, *Poems*, CXXVI.
[27] Ibid., V, and the editor's comment on line 24.
[28] For the motto, see below, pp. 173–5. R. L. Greene, 'A Carol of Anne Boleyn by Wyatt', in *Review of English Studies*, n.s. 25 (1974), 437–9; but Harrier, *Canon*, p. 54, rejects Wyatt's authorship. For the text see below, p. 174.
[29] Wyatt, *Poems*, L. 'answer' = 'An'er' = Anna.

conceit, a teasing trifle ornamented with conventional emotions, but it is quite impossible to say if there was more behind the verse than that. We are back with the problem of the Calais poem.

We are on better ground again with the verse mentioning 'Brunet'. Again definitely by Wyatt, 'If waker care, if sudden pale colour' tells of the poet falling in love again:

> If thou ask whom, sure since I did refrain
> Brunet that set my wealth in such a roar
> The unfeigned cheer of Phyllis hath the place
> That Brunet had: she hath and ever shall.[30]

That Brunet was Anne Boleyn is beyond doubt, since Wyatt originally wrote:

> . . . since I did refrain
> Her that did set our country in a roar
> The unfeigned cheer of Phyllis hath the place
> That Brunet had . . .[31]

This must indicate at least that Wyatt had the admitted courtly relationship with Anne of servant and mistress, and may mean more if we take literally both the sentence, 'Phyllis hath the place that Brunet had', and the description which follows:

> She from myself now hath me in her grace:
> She hath in hand my wit, my will, and all.
> My heart alone well worthy she doth stay
> Without whose help scant do I live a day.

Wyatt, however, could not have written the original version when Anne was still alive, and if we take Phyllis to be Elizabeth Darell his final mistress, with whom the poet had a stable relationship from, it seems, at least 1536–7, the comparison of the sentiments he expresses for her with those he had for Anne may be confused by time as well as poetic licence.[32]

That a caution about the depth of their relationship is wise, is

---

[30] Ibid., XCVII.
[31] Harrier, *Canon*, pp. 204–5.
[32] Muir, *Life and Letters of Wyatt*, pp. 37, 85.

indicated by the final poem to link Wyatt and Anne Boleyn, and the only one which makes a clear allusion to the king himself. It is, admittedly, inspired by a poem of Petrarch (and perhaps by other Italian sources), but as usual Wyatt twists 'Petrarch's meaning to suit his own more urgent and worldly interest in the business of wooing'.[33]

> Whoso list to hunt: I know where is a hind.
> But as for me, alas I may no more:
> The vain travail hath wearied me so sore,
> I am of them that farthest cometh behind.
> Yet may I by no means my wearied mind
> Draw from the deer, but as she fleeth afore
> Fainting I follow. I leave off therefore,
> Sithens in a net I seek to hold the wind.
> Who list to hunt, I put him out of doubt,
> As well as I may spend his time in vain,
> And graven with diamonds in letters plain
> There is written her fair neck round about:
> '*Noli me tangere*, for Caesar's I am,
> And wild for to hold, though I seem tame.'[34]

What Wyatt appears to be claiming here is a powerful fascination with Anne, 'the hind', which he has to break by deliberately drawing back from her crowd of admirers, something which is very close to the sentiment of the Calais poem. He adds this time, however that he had been only part of that crowd, and by no means near to Anne's favours – 'I am of them that farthest cometh behind.' The final sextet is a warning to others. Anne belongs to Henry; though 'tame', approachable, she will shy away from any attempt at possession by another; the collar, which in Petrarch tells of Laura's devotion to God, becomes a slave collar. If this is autobiographical, it suggests that the relationship of Wyatt and Anne was wholly one-sided.

No doubt the search for contemporary allusions in the poetry associated with Thomas Wyatt will continue, but the reliable references certainly add up to less than some writers have claimed. If we discount the 'Anna' riddle as a mere triviality, we

---

[33] Thomson, *Wyatt and his Background*, pp. 194, 196–200.
[34] Wyatt, *Poems*, VII. 'sithens' = seeing that; George Wyatt implies that Anne adopted the motto 'I am Caesar's all, let none else touch me', no doubt on the authority of this poem by his grandfather: George Wyatt, *Papers*, p. 185.

find that all the three remaining pieces tell of a deep commitment on Wyatt's part, but one clearly implies no response from Anne, another gives no guidance, and only the poem written to his mistress after Anne's death has anything that might be read to suggest she had reciprocated his affection. And this is certainly not enough to support the hypothesis that Anne and Thomas were lovers. The more likely interpretation of the poems is that Wyatt became one of a number of Anne's acknowledged suitors according to the convention of courtly love, then found himself becoming emotionally involved but with no response from the lady. And one can see why. Wyatt was already married, and although separated from his wife because of her adultery, was in no position to offer Anne anything but a place as his mistress. From what we know of Anne's sister Mary, she would have counted 'all lost for love', but as Anne's conduct with the king was to show, she thought otherwise.

Against the autobiographical material of the poems there is, of course, the strident voice of recusant sources that Wyatt did have an illicit sexual liaison with Anne Boleyn. The earliest version is recorded by Nicholas Harpsfield, archdeacon of Canterbury and a former religious exile, writing in the reign of Mary. Commenting on the bull to allow Henry to marry Anne despite any unconsummated pre-contract, Harpsfield added that the king was so bewitched that he would even 'marry her whom himself credibly understood to have lived loosely and incontinently before'.[35] The lover in question was Thomas Wyatt who, on hearing that Anne was to marry Henry, had gone to the king and said:

> Sir, I am credibly informed that your grace intendeth to take to your wife the Lady Anne Boleyn, wherein I beseech your grace to be well advised what you do, for she is not meet to be coupled with your grace, her conversation [way of life] hath been so loose and base; which thing I know not so much by hear-say as by my own experience as one that have had my carnal pleasure with her.

At this, Harpsfield says, the king was – as one might imagine – 'for a while something astonied', but then said, 'Wyatt, thou hast done like an honest man, yet I charge thee to make no more

[35] Harpsfield, *Pretended Divorce*, p. 253.

words of this matter to any man living.' And of course, the marriage went ahead.

Harpsfield himself was less than ten years old at the time, but he tells us that he had the tale from 'the right worshipful merchant Mr. Anthony Bonvise ... which thing he heard of them that were men very likely to know the truth thereof', and since we know that Antonio Bonvisi left England for Louvain without permission in September 1549, with or soon to be followed by Harpsfield, Thomas More's nephew William Rastell, and his adopted daughter and her husband, Margaret and John Clement, it is clear when and where Nicholas got his story.[36] What he says of Bonvisi's connections is true.[37] A merchant from Lucca, he was a banker with close and friendly ties with the English government and its ministers, both traditionalists and innovators; as well as with Wolsey and More, he was intimate with Cromwell (who was close to Wyatt) and, through Stephen Gardiner's chaplain, knew Wyatt himself and another mutual friend. This might suggest that Bonvisi had the sources of information and the neutrality expected of an international banker, and thus gain credence for the report about Wyatt. As Harpsfield himself wrote, 'This worthy merchant would oft talk of [More] and also of Sir Thomas Cromwell, with whom he was many years familiarly acquainted, and would report many notable and as yet commonly unknown things, and of their far [much] squaring, unlike and disagreeable natures, dispositions, sayings and doings, whereof there is now no place to talk.'[38]

On the other hand, there is no doubt that Bonvisi's real sympathies lay with Thomas More, who called him 'the apple of his eye' and who had been supported by him while in the Tower.[39] One may suspect, indeed, that the survival of More's circle owed a good deal to Bonvisi, and Nicholas Sander is specific that it was Antonio who supported the exiles at Louvain.[40] Not only, therefore, was Bonvisi not disinterested but he was telling his stories among the same coterie which produced the claim that Anne Boleyn had been fathered by Henry VIII! There are, also, inherent improbabilities in the story. With

[36] Harpsfield, *More*, pp. clxxvii, clxxx; Sander, *Schism*, p. 201.
[37] Harpsfield, *More*, p. 341.
[38] Ibid., p. 138.
[39] Ibid., p. 138.
[40] Sander, *Schism*, p. 201.

Wyatt sworn to secrecy, how did Bonvisi's informants get their knowledge? After Wyatt's involvement in Anne's exposure in 1536, could be the answer, but the government's case that she was an adulterous wife would have been seriously weakened by any hint of a premarital reputation. Furthermore, any revelation that Anne had slept with Wyatt at a time when she was refusing to sleep with Henry must have triggered the king's phobia about loyalty.

By the time the next generation of recusants told the same story, it has become modified and embellished. According to Sander, Wyatt first told the council, not the king.[41] When the king was informed, his reaction was to dismiss the stories as calumny and to affirm his belief in Anne's virtue, whereupon Wyatt was very angry that his word was doubted and offered to give the king visible proof of Anne's affection for him. The duke of Suffolk passed the message to Henry, who 'answered that he had no wish to see anything of the kind – Wyatt was a bold villain, not to be trusted.' The story has clearly been influenced by the events of the later Katherine Howard affair, where the initial complaint was made to certain counsellors (but secretly), and where Henry did dismiss the report as slander and did affirm his wife's innocence.

Refuting Sander's story took many lines of George Wyatt's heavy prose – even his summary of the case for his grandfather contains six points – and all to labour the obvious implausibilities and the improbability of a character such as Henry's responding in such a way.[42] It is fortunate, however that George did not know of a third version of the story in the *Cronica del Rey Enrico*.[43] Here Henry angrily refuses to hear Wyatt's evidence for his claim that Anne is 'a bad woman' and no fit wife for the king. Instead Thomas is rusticated from court for two years and arrested again in 1536, though Cromwell's favour and his earlier attempt to warn the king save him from execution. He thereupon writes to Henry, setting out the evidence that he had not been allowed to present earlier. On a night when her parents

[41] Ibid., pp. 28–30.

[42] George Wyatt, in *Wolsey*, ed. Singer, pp. 430–1 implies a doublet with Francis Bryan, who told Henry of his relationship with a lady (not Anne) whom the king was pursuing, who thereupon broke off his suit; see also *Papers*, pp. 182–5.

[43] *Cronica del Rey Enrico*, pp. 88–91; trans. in Muir, *Life and Letters of Wyatt*, pp. 22–3.

were at court, Wyatt had, he says, arrived at Hever (presumably) and gone up to Anne Boleyn's chamber, where she was already in bed.[44] 'Lord, Master Wyatt,' she said, 'What are you doing here at such a late hour?' Thomas – one is tempted to say Sir Jasper – explained that he had come for 'consolation': 'And I went up to her as she lay in bed and kissed her, and she lay still and said nothing. I touched her breasts, and she lay still, and even when I took liberties lower down she likewise said nothing.' Nothing discouraged, Wyatt began to undress, when a great stamping was heard in the room above. Anne got up, put on a skirt and disappeared upstairs for an hour. When she came down she would not let Wyatt come near her, although within a week he did have his way with her. And the explanation for Anne's curious conduct? Wyatt has one pat, straight from *The Decameron*: she obviously had a lover waiting in the room above – a groom, probably, if Boccaccio is to be trusted!

The only interest for the historian in this farrago of rubbish is that it represents a separate tradition from that of the recusant writers. The details may be dismissed as the reworking of a well known novella, but the merchants of the Spanish community in London, who supplied the author of the *Cronica* with some of his information, may have kept alive a genuine tradition about the relationship between Anne and Thomas, their interest in his doings (also reflected elsewhere in the text) being easily explained by his subsequent career as the English ambassador in Spain. Yet even if this was so, the tradition cannot have been an informed one; how could outsiders know which relationships in courtly love were real and which not? The event which would have been known is Wyatt's arrest in 1536 along with Anne's lovers, her well publicized sexual appetite and yet, surprisingly, his survival. The *Cronica* story, in other words, is unlikely to preserve a true memory of Anne and Thomas in the 1520s, but rather to extrapolate from the events surrounding Anne's fall in order to explain the contradiction Wyatt himself used to joke about grimly – 'God's blood! Was not that a pretty sending of me

---

[44] The Spanish may be confused and should read: 'the Lady Anne's father and mother were in the court at Greenwich, eight miles from where, as everybody knows, they had taken up residence', not 'in the court eight miles from Greenwich, where . . .'. Alternatively, the author may suppose that the Boleyns resided at Greenwich and had gone to join the court at, say, Richmond. Hever is twenty-eight miles from Greenwich.

ambassador to the emperor, first to put me into the Tower, and then forthwith to send me hither?'[45]

One major Catholic sympathizer who displays a significant ignorance of Wyatt and of Anne's premarital misbehaviour is George Cavendish. *The Life and Death of Cardinal Wolsey* makes Anne Boleyn's pride very clear; the *Metrical Visions* accept entirely the story of her adultery:

> My epitaph shall be: – 'The vicious queen
> Lieth here, of late that justly lost her head,
> Because that she did spot the king's bed.'[46]

Yet Cavendish almost goes out of his way to make the point that Anne was still a virgin when she married:

> The noblest prince that reigned on the ground
> I had to my husband, he took me to his wife;
> At home with my father a maiden he me found,
> And for my sake, of princely prerogative,
> To an earl he advanced my father in his life,
> And preferred all them that were of my blood;
> The most willingest prince to do them all good.

It was, in fact, difficult to traduce Anne Boleyn both for promiscuity before marriage and promiscuity after marriage; if she had always been as lecherous as some conservatives wanted to believe, Henry was more stupid than wronged.

So analysis of the traditions hostile to Anne does not disturb the conclusion suggested by the poems, that she and Thomas flirted together with increasing seriousness on his part but with little more than courtly convention on hers. That conclusion does, moreover, tally with the one story about the relationship that comes from Anne's former attendant, Anne Gainsford, although by the time she told it to George Wyatt she had long been a widow following the death of her husband George Zouche.[47] Thomas Wyatt, she recalled:

---

[45] Muir, *Life and Letters of Wyatt*, pp. 66, 200–2.

[46] Cavendish, *Metrical Visions*, pp. 39–46; NB the pun: 'queen'/'quean'.

[47] George Wyatt, in *Wolsey*, ed. Singer, pp. 426–7. The courtly setting suggests Anne Zouche as the source rather than Jane Wyatt, who was a girl at this date: *Narratives of the Reformation*, p. 52.

entertaining talk with [Anne Boleyn] as she was earnest at work, in sporting wise caught from her a certain small jewel hanging by a lace out of her pocket, or otherwise loose, which he thrust into his bosom, neither with any earnest request could she obtain it of him again. He kept it, therefore, and wore it after about his neck, under his cassock, promising himself either to have it with her favour or as an occasion to have talk with her, wherein he had singular delight, and she after seemed not to make much reckoning of it, either the thing not being much worth, or not worth much striving for.

George Wyatt, and no doubt Anne Zouche, was determined to vindicate Anne Boleyn's reputation, but the occasion rings very true to what we know of courtly dalliance.[48] As for the theft of the jewel and its subsequent exploitation, we have only to recall Brandon and Margaret of Austria's ring, and Anne's reaction is very much that of Margaret, refusing at first to take such a male display routine with any seriousness.

The attentions paid to Anne Boleyn by such a popular courtier as Thomas Wyatt had, or so his grandson's tortured prose seems to want to tell us, the effect of whetting the king's interest. Henry first tested Anne's 'regard of her honour' by 'those things his kingly majesty and means could bring to the battery', and then set out 'to win her by treaty of marriage', 'and in this talk took from her a ring, and that wore upon his little finger; and yet all this with such secrecy was carried, and on her part so wisely, as none or very few esteemed this other than an ordinary course of dalliance.' A few days after this, the king made an óccasion to warn Wyatt off. Playing bowls with Thomas and some other courtiers, Henry claimed that his wood held shot when it clearly did not; pointing with his little finger with the ring on it, 'he said, "Wyatt, I tell thee it is mine", smiling upon him withal.' The point was taken, but Wyatt, 'pausing a little, and finding the king bent to pleasure', decided on a bold response. He produced Anne's jewel and proceeded to use the ribbon to measure the distances, remarking, 'If it may like your majesty to give me leave to measure it, I hope it will be mine.' The king's good humour vanished – 'It may be so, but then am I deceived' – and he stalked off to see Anne. She, discovering what was wrong, explained the business of the jewel to Henry, and sunlight was restored.

[48] Wyatt, *Poems*, LVI.

George Wyatt probably wrote his biography of Anne Boleyn in the later 1590s, in which case he was retelling here what he remembered of a conversation ten or twenty years previously, when Anne Zouche, a woman in her sixties or seventies, had recalled events of fifty or more years before that.[49] It is not surprising, therefore, to find inconsistencies. Wyatt implies that Henry's affair with Anne went from initial interest to agreement to marry in rapid time, whereas it was actually spread over more than a year, as we shall see; he suggests that the king's interest in Anne was secret, whereas the story requires Thomas Wyatt to perceive instantly both the identity and the significance of Anne's ring; Wyatt is then portrayed as recognizing that the king was 'bent on pleasure' – engaging in courtly competition over a lady – when the story next requires the king to be in earnest; Anne's response, however, is still in the language of courtly love, explaining to one favoured gallant that a rival has not also been given a token by her. The way to remove these inconsistencies is to place the story earlier in time, and to see Henry, Wyatt and, probably, other courtiers vying with one another for Anne's attention. We may also note on this reading that while the king's reaction might suggest that he was getting more deeply involved, Wyatt's implies that he has already decided that he is not going to succeed with Anne. And in such circumstances he favoured, he said, what might today be called the laid-back style.[50]

The arrival of the king on the scene in Anne Zouche's story as a competitor for Anne Boleyn's courtly favours is an important indication of the way his interest in her began, but it is useful, first, to attempt to chart the chronology of it all. There were, in fact, two processes at work – the move to divorce Katherine of Aragon, and Henry's growing involvement with Anne – and initially and for a long time they were quite separate. The rejection of Katherine had begun in 1524 when Henry gave up sleeping with her, although he had clearly been drifting away from her for some years.[51] She was thirty-nine and had not

[49] She must have been born not later than *c.*1510; George Wyatt was born 1554. He implies [in *Wolsey*, ed. Singer, p. 422] that his mother was dead, and she was probably alive in 1595 [George Wyatt, *Papers*, p. 10]. Wyatt's 'Life' certainly postdated Sander, *Schism* (1585).

[50] Wyatt, *Poems*, CXXXIV.

[51] Brewer, *Henry VIII*, ii.162; Scarisbrick, *Henry VIII*, p. 152.

conceived in the previous seven years. Moreover, time had cruelly destroyed both her petite beauty and her gentle good spirits – she was thick of body and dull of appearance, and apart from passionate concern for Mary, her one child, it was only duty which drew Katherine from religious observances to the frivolities of court life. With no hope of children if he had intercourse with her there was nothing else to make Henry want to.[52] This situation was, of course, hardly novel, and although there is reason to doubt the king's famed sexual prowess, he had, in the manner of monarchs of his day, solaced himself from time to time with a mistress – most recently Mary Carey, née Boleyn. But with the final recognition that he would have no son by Katherine, Henry's position changed. Occasional adultery was now no longer enough; if Henry – and the country – was to have a son to succeed him, he had to marry again. Already he was over thirty.

When it was that Henry VIII reached this conclusion we do not know. There are stories that he was thinking of a divorce as early as 1522, but the actual date was probably after June 1525, when he brought his one illegitimate child, Henry Fitzroy, out of obscurity and created him duke of Richmond (a title resonant of his own father, Henry VII) with precedence over every nobleman in the land, except any legitimate son the king might have.[53] This was widely recognized as a portent for the future, and the Venetian ambassador – who reported that Richmond had actually been legitimated – was quick to observe that Queen Katherine had been deeply offended and that three of her ladies had been dismissed from the court for supporting her in this.[54]

To attempt to oust the legitimate Mary from the succession in favour of the illegitimate Richmond was a policy of high risk, and within the next eighteen months Henry turned to a more conventional answer: he would seek a decree of nullity from the pope. Popes were always sensitive to the special matrimonial problems of monarchs, provided some plausible rationalization could be offered, and Henry had discovered what he thought was irrefutable proof that his marriage with Katherine was defective and invalid in canon law. Not even her European connections gave him pause; England was already in process of breaking

---

[52] He occasionally shared her bed for appearance's sake.
[53] Scarisbrick, *Henry VIII*, p. 154.
[54] *Cal. S. P. Ven., 1520–26*, 1037, 1053.

with the emperor, and when Charles' ambassador reached London late in December 1526 he found the queen hopelessly isolated – indeed, it took him over two months to engineer a private meeting with her.[55] Various reports associated the decision to divorce Katherine with the diplomatic situation in 1526–7, but the discovery of a way to divorce her was probably Henry's own.[56] It depended for its compelling force on the direct relevance to his position of a threat in the Bible – Leviticus 20, verse 21: 'If a man shall take his brother's wife, it is an unclean thing ... they shall be childless.' Henry *had* married the wife of his brother Arthur, who had died after twenty weeks of marriage to Katherine, when Henry had been eleven. Henry and Katherine had had sons, but all of them had died; they *were* childless (Mary did not count). The sense of appropriateness was psychologically overwhelming and never, thereafter, did it desert the king. God had spoken directly to his condition; Henry had no option as a devout Christian but to obey, to contract a legal (indeed, his first) marriage, and a son would be the reward. Post-Freudian scepticism may smile, but the vital historical point is that Henry believed. Armed with his certainty he consulted Wolsey and his lawyers, and on 17 May 1527 took the first and secret steps to divorce his wife.[57]

Where did Anne Boleyn fit in? The one certain date we have is September 1527, when the king applied to the pope for the dispensation to allow him to marry Anne. She is not identified by name, but in addition to the reference to a woman previously contracted in marriage (that is, possibly to Percy), the draft also covered a woman who was related to the king in the 'first degree of affinity ... from ... forbidden wedlock' (that is, the sister of a previous mistress, in this case Mary Boleyn).[58]

As for the time before this, there are two possibilities. It may

---

[55] *Cal. S. P. Span.*, *1527–29*, 17, 110, 116.

[56] Henry told different stories about the origin of his doubts [Scarisbrick, *Henry VIII*, pp. 152–4]. The two versions differ in detail, but the claim that the French raised the question of Mary's status during the marriage negotiations was never denied. English attempts to keep the knowledge of French objections from the emperor strongly suggest that Paris had raised the matter. Charles was concerned lest a divorce would permit Henry to contract a menacing marriage with a French princess.

[57] See below, p. 113.

[58] J. Gairdner, 'New light on the divorce of Henry VIII', in *EHR*, 11 (1896), 685; Herbert, *Henry VIII*, p. 393.

be that J. J. Scarisbrick is correct to suggest 'that by 1525–6 what had probably hitherto been light dalliance . . . had begun to grow into something deeper and more dangerous.'[59] In that case, the importance of Henry's courtly flirtation with Anne was that it so subverted him that he seized with enthusiasm on the monstrous notion that his devoted wife of sixteen years was nothing but his accomplice in fornication; passion for Anne triggered Henry's wish-fulfilment. This scenario would certainly help to explain why it was that Anne did not herself marry after the loss of Henry Percy to Mary Talbot in 1524: growing royal interest could well account for a sudden dearth of other suitors.

On the other hand, the probabilities are more in favour of a relationship which became serious only after the decision to divorce Katherine. In the first place, it is clear that Wolsey, despite his careful monitoring of the court, was not aware how committed Henry was to Anne Boleyn until the autumn of 1527.[60] In the second, no hint of Anne's involvement with the king has been discovered in any records before that date – an unlikely thing if the affair was already two years old; it is significant that the imperial ambassador identified Anne in August 1527.[61] Earlier in the year her public position was what it had always been, that of a court lady with valuable links with France. Thus in May, when the French envoys who had successfully negotiated a marriage between Henry VIII's daughter Mary and Francis I himself, or his second son the duc d'Orléans, were guests of honour at a splendid evening at Greenwich, they merely reported: 'we were in the queen's apartments where there was dancing and M. de Turaine, on the king's command, danced with Madame the Princess, and the king with Mistress Boulan who was brought up in France with the late queen.'[62] The normally hawk-eyed Venetians did not become aware of Anne until February 1528.[63]

The one direct and personal piece of evidence for the growing relationship between Henry and Anne is the king's seventeen

[59] Scarisbrick, *Henry VIII*, p. 149.
[60] *Cal. S. P. Span.*, *1527–29*, p. 432.
[61] Ibid., p. 327.
[62] Quoted in J. Lingard, *History of England* (1855), iv.237 n.3. The temporary banqueting house erected for the occasion was decorated with 'H' and 'K': Hall, *Chronicle*, p. 722.
[63] *Cal. S. P. Ven.*, *1527–33*, 236.

letters to her.[64] They fall into four groups which clearly correspond to the progress of the affair. The first three letters belong to the period when the conventions of courtly romance began to change to something more serious. The earliest accompanied the gift of a buck which the king had killed the evening before, and chides his 'mistress' for neither keeping her promise to write nor replying to his earlier letter; it concludes: 'Written with the hand of your servant, who oft and again wisheth you [were here] instead of your brother – H.R.'[65] The next letter is more serious:

> Although it doth not appertain to a gentleman to take his lady in place of a servant, nevertheless, in compliance with your desires, I willingly grant it to you, if thereby you can find yourself less unthankfully bestowed in the place by you chosen than you have been in the place given by me. Thanking you right heartily for that it pleaseth you still to hold me in some remembrance.
>
> Henry R.[66]

Clearly, Anne was being chary of the king's attentions and in particular refusing to accept the public relationship of courtly mistress and servant. It was her place to be the servant, and the king had to capitulate in the hope that the relationship could continue at least on that basis.

The next letter was written after an interval, and is the most important of the three.[67] It shows a Henry who has accepted that Anne would not be 'his mistress', but is nevertheless confused by his continued feelings and by the signals he was receiving from her:

> Debating with myself the contents of your letter, I have put myself in great distress, not knowing how to interpret them, whether to my disadvantage, as in some places is shown, or to advantage, as in others I understand them; praying you with all my heart that you will expressly certify me of your whole mind concerning the love between us two. For of necessity I must ensure me of this answer having been now above one whole year

---

[64] See above, p. 68.

[65] *Love Letters*, pp. 40–1 [*LP*, iv.3220].

[66] Ibid., pp. 38–9 [*LP*, iv.3219]. The letter ends with a cryptogram which appears to be: O N R I de R O M V E Z. The significance of this is not known, but may be connected with some courtly charade.

[67] Ibid., pp. 32–4 [*LP*, iv.3218].

struck with the dart of love, not being assured either of failure or
of finding place in your heart and grounded affection. Which last
point has kept me for some little time from calling you my
mistress, since if you do not love me in a way which is beyond
common affection that name in no wise belongs to you, for it
denotes a singular love, far removed from the common.

After more than a year, Henry now insisted on a straight answer:

> If it shall please you to do me the office of a true, loyal mistress
> and friend and to give yourself up, body and soul, to me who will
> be and have been your loyal servant (if by your severity you do
> not forbid me), I promise you that not only shall the name be
> given you, but that also I will take you for my only mistress,
> rejecting from thought and affection all others save yourself, to
> serve you only.

What was Henry asking and offering? Surely something more
than convention. He appears to be offering a recognized permanent liaison, perhaps like the French '*maîtresse en titre*'. Francis I,
after all, had had Françoise de Foix and was even at that
moment (though Henry probably had yet to hear of it) fixing his
interest with the woman who was to be his companion for the
rest of his life, Anne d'Heilly, later duchesse d'Etampes.[68] Why
should Henry VIII not have his Anne Boleyn?

In the next four letters the relationship has moved on, yet not
quite in the direction Henry proposed. He had asked for an
answer to his offer either in writing or in person, but when they
met something in Anne's response had caused him to rush
matters and deeply offend her. Whether he became too ardent or
whether he shocked her by demanding unconditional acceptance
of a place in his bed is not known. Writers hostile to Anne tell a
story in which she refuses the king (something which George
Wyatt also hints at), although, predictably, they turn it to her
discredit by suggesting that she, 'having had crafty counsel, did
thus overreach the king with show of modesty'.[69] When pro-
positioned:

> she fell down upon her knees saying, 'I think your majesty, most
> noble and worthy king, speaketh these words in mirth to prove

[68] Knecht, *Francis I*, p. 192.
[69] George Wyatt, in *Wolsey*, ed. Singer, p. 426; BL, Sloane MS 2495, f. 3.

me, without intent of defiling your princely self, who I find thinks nothing less than of such wickedness which would justly procure the hatred of God and of your good queen against us . . . I have already given my maidenhead into my husband's hands.

Whatever the truth of this, Henry thought he had patched matters up before Anne retired to her parents' home, but a subsequent silence drove the king to write again:

Since I parted with you I have been advised that the opinion in which I left you is now altogether changed, and that you will not come to court, neither with my lady your mother, and if you could, nor yet by any other way [the proprieties have suddenly begun to matter] the which report being true I cannot enough marvel at, seeing that I am well assured I have never since that time committed fault.

And if he knew Anne was, in fact, staying away deliberately: 'I could do none other than lament me of my ill fortune, abating by little and little my so great folly.'[70]

'My so great folly' is a highly perceptive remark from a man not given to much self-analysis. Moralists have frowned on such letters from a man already married (and on Anne for entertaining them), and even implied something gross in middle age so obviously losing its head. But charity demands that we recognize the genuineness of the king's passion; from a person who hated writing as much as Henry did, such letters are in themselves a remarkable testimony. For the first time in his life he was having to build a relationship with a woman who had not been provided by the diplomatic marriage agency or whistled up by the *droit de seigneur*. What is less easy to interpret is Anne's position. Again moralists are clear – she should have had no truck with a man already married. But if, as seems certain, she did refuse to sleep with Henry at this time and instead kept away from court, why did she not break with him entirely? The relationship did not develop into an auction, so Anne cannot be accused of standing out for a better price; instead it moved towards respectability. Only one thing could explain this: the king's decision to divorce Katherine. We cannot know how Anne would have responded in different circumstances, but her distinctly muted encouragement

[70] *Love Letters*, pp. 29–30 [*LP*, iv.3326].

of the king reflected the opportunity opened up by his growing breach with Katherine. And we cannot, in fairness, discount emotion on Anne's side. It was a heady experience to have at your feet someone as magnificent as Henry VIII still was, and it was not just that: we must not forget that she kept his letters.

It was perhaps in response to Henry's evident misery that Anne decided to order one of those symbolic trinkets that Tudor people loved – a ship with a woman on board and with a (presumably) pendant diamond. The meaning was clear. For centuries the ship had been a symbol of safety – the ark which rescued Noah from the destroying deluge; the diamond – as the *Roman de la Rose* had said – spoke of a 'heart as hard as diamond, steadfast and nothing pliant'.[71] The king reacted with delight to this confirmation that Anne was eternally committed to him and would rely on him to protect her from the storms that would come:

> For so beautiful a gift, and so exceeding (taking it in all), I thank you right cordially; not alone for the fair diamond and the ship in which the solitary damsel is tossed about, but chiefly for the good intent and too-humble submission vouchsafed in this by your kindness; considering well that by occasion to merit it would not a little perplex me, if I were not aided therein by your great benevolence and goodwill, for the which I have sought, do seek, and shall always seek by all services to me possible there to remain, in the which my hope hath set up his everlasting rest, saying *aut illic aut nullibi* [either here or nowhere].
>
> The proofs of your affection are such, the fine poesies of the letters so warmly couched, that they constrain me ever truly to honour, love and serve you, praying that you will continue in this same firm and constant purpose, ensuring you, for my part, that I will the rather go beyond than make *reciproque* [equivalent response], if loyalty or heart, the desire to do you pleasure, even with my whole heart root, may serve to advance it.

And the king makes clear, for the first time, the basis of this new relationship between them. He wants Anne no longer as a mistress, but as a wife:

> Praying you also that if ever before I have in any way done you offence, that you will give me the same absolution that you ask

[71] Chaucer, *Roman de la Rose*, line 4385.

[no doubt for appearing cold], ensuring you that henceforth my heart shall be dedicate to you alone, greatly desirous that so my body could be as well, as God can bring to pass if it pleaseth Him, whom I entreat once each day for the accomplishment thereof, trusting that at length my prayer will be heard, wishing the time brief, and thinking it but long until we shall see each other again.

Written with the hand of that secretary who in heart, body and will is

Your loyal and most ensured servant

H. aultre A B ne cherse R.[72]

His next letter starts, 'My Mistress and Friend', and laments the prospect of more and more time spent apart (as propriety now dictated); it included a trinket for Anne to remind her of him, 'my picture set in a bracelet, with the whole device which you already know' – unfortunately a secret not revealed to us.[73] Then we find Henry telling Anne to urge her father to bring her back to court earlier than planned, and again the inscription is 'H. *aultre ne cherse* R.', with a heart surrounding the initials 'A.B.'.[74] Henry was engaged!

Such, it may be suggested, is the story of the start of Henry VIII's love affair with Anne Boleyn, as revealed in the king's own early letters. The rest can all be dated after negotiations for the divorce had begun in Rome in December 1527, and belong to the next stage in the story, but this of itself suggests something about the dating of the earlier letters.[75] Almost certainly, they once had formed a single bundle, and since the ten final letters can be dated between December 1527 and October 1528, it is likely that the earlier items belong not earlier than the previous year, 1527. The alternative explanation would be that the letters are random survivals from over a longer period, but since they must have been kept by Anne herself it would then be necessary to explain why only early and late letters were preserved when she was put to death, and nothing for the period in between; in any case, the emotional tone of the letters is hardly that of a long-drawn-out courtship. If this assessment is correct, it follows that Henry was

---

[72] *Love Letters*, pp. 34–6 [*LP*, iv.3325]: last line = 'looks for no other'.
[73] Ibid., pp. 27–8 [*LP*, iv.3221].
[74] Ibid., pp. 41–3 [*LP*, iv.4537].
[75] See below, pp. 116, 120.

'struck with the dart of love' sometime in 1526, and since it is
clear that Henry's emotion grew out of a courtly-love pose we
may tentatively identify his first sign of interest in Anne with the
Shrovetide joust in February of that year, when he appeared
displaying the device of 'a man's heart in a press, with flames
about it', and the motto 'Declare I dare not.'[76] And we may risk
another conclusion. 'Above one whole year' would date Henry's
offer to Anne of the position of *maîtresse en titre* at after Easter
1527, despite the fact that at the same time he was beginning
moves to divorce Katherine.[77] It was not, therefore, until Anne's
bleak response had been sorted out – say, in mid-summer – that
the king realized that she could solve both his sexual and his
matrimonial frustrations, which explains why in August he
began sudden moves (behind Wolsey's back) to appeal to the
pope for a dispensation to cover Anne's canonical disabilities. As
for the business with Wyatt, we must date it before, probably
immediately before, Sir Thomas left for Italy on 7 January
1527.[78]

If we put all these indications together with the dates of
Henry's disintegrating marriage with Katherine, the following
chronology emerges:

1524	Henry and Katherine cease to have sexual relations
1525 (summer)	Attempt to build up Richmond as the alternative heir
1526 (Shrovetide)	Henry begins the courtly pursuit of Anne
1526–7 (winter)	Henry decides on divorce
1526 (December)	Friction between Henry and Wyatt over Anne
1527 (Easter)	Henry presses Anne to become his mistress
1527 (May)	Secret divorce proceedings attempted
1527 (June)	Henry tells Katherine of his divorce plans

[76] Hall, *Chronicle*, p. 707. This could suggest that Henry began his pursuit of
Anne soon after finishing with her sister.
[77] The buck mentioned in the first letter could imply a date before the
breeding season.
[78] See below, pp. 171–2.

| 1527 (summer) | Henry and Anne agree to marry after the divorce |
| 1527 (August) | Decision to ask the pope for a dispensation |

Given the difficulty in charting any emotional history, and the inadequacies of the sources in this particular case, this timetable must be somewhat speculative. Nevertheless it does fit the context as we understand it, and it is psychologically credible. There is also independent corroboration. Among the papers in the Public Record Office is a statement of jewels and other costly items delivered to the king in a period described as 'since 1 August in the yeare aforesaid' until the following May.[79] Obviously part of a larger list, it includes items for the king himself such as three walking staves equipped with one- or two-foot measures, compasses and dividers, but many of the pieces are 'for Mistress Anne'. What was 'the yeare aforesaid'? The latest possible date for the list is August 1531 to May 1532, for by May 1533 Mistress Anne was queen. It includes, however the gift to Anne of an emerald ring at Beaulieu on 3 August and the only year between 1525 and 1531 when Henry was at Beaulieu in early August was 1527.[80] What we have here, therefore, is a record of the torrent of gifts which the king had begun to shower on Anne by the summer of that year: rings, bracelets, brooches, diamonds for a head-dress, diamonds set in true-lover's-knots, diamonds and rubies set in roses and hearts, gilt and silver bindings for books, velvet bindings, repairs to a book 'garnished in France' – the list goes on for page after page. Such a torrent can mean only one thing: Henry and Anne had an understanding – they were betrothed.

The timetable suggested brings to the fore an obvious, frequently overlooked, but crucial fact in the relationship of Anne Boleyn and Henry VIII: they were expecting to marry within months.[81] The delay would certainly be longer than the king had hoped when he had sought her for his mistress – the requirement

---

[79] RO, SP1/66, ff. 39–45 [*LP*, v.276].

[80] Confirmation of the year is provided by the reference to 29 Feb. [f. 42v] which dates the document either to 1527–8 or 1531–2. There is a reference to Henry at Hampton Court on 3 Dec. which might suggest 1531, but the Beaulieu coincidence seems conclusive.

[81] *Love Letters*, pp. 36–7 [*LP*, iv.4742].

for various papal dispensations saw to that. Yet the couple were certainly thinking in terms of current convention where, after the details of a possible marriage settlement had been hammered out, a quick decision was taken one way or the other, and any wedding followed promptly. English society was not equipped to handle a long engagement between two adults passionately in love and in regular contact with each other; after all, in canon law if not in Church discipline, only sexual intercourse was lacking to turn that engagement into lawful marriage – provided there was no impediment. If Katherine's imperial nephew had not been in a position to compel the pope to drag his feet, and if Mary had not already been heir to the throne, Henry could have had the courage of his convictions, imitated his brother-in-law Suffolk, and married again immediately: a first union which was null and void left a man quite free to contract another.[82] Thus the need to wait for a decision from Rome created a highly unnatural situation, and the strain is evident in the king's letters.[83] With hindsight we can know that technicalities at Rome and manoeuvres in England were only the initial moves in what would prove a long-drawn-out and ultimately abortive attempt to secure an annulment. To Henry and Anne they were only tedious preliminaries to the wedding that they were planning.[84]

[82] For Suffolk's complicated exploitation of matrimonial law, see Brewer, *Henry VIII*, i.95 n.3.

[83] *Love Letters*, pp. 27–8, 46, 39–40, 48 [*LP*, iv.3221, 3990, 4410, 4894].

[84] *LP*, iv.4206: *Love Letters*, p. 48 [*LP*, iv.4894]; *Cal. S. P. Span., 1527–29*, p. 789.

II

A Difficult Engagement

6

A Marriage Arranged

◦━━◦◦◦━━◦

THE STORY of the struggle over Henry VIII's divorce has been told many times and in great detail, and here is not the place to rehearse it at length.[1] The king's conviction that his marriage with Katherine had brought down the wrath of God was one thing, but satisfying the proper Church authorities was another, and this, despite six years of continuous effort, a massive expenditure of funds and the mobilizing of all the resources of the English hierarchy plus the brains of a good part of Europe too, the king was never able to do – with momentous consequences for England, and for Anne Boleyn.

The first steps taken in May 1527 towards a divorce would have revealed to a less egocentric man than Henry that his was not an open and shut case. On the face of it those steps were routine – Wolsey called Henry to answer the charge that he was living in sin with his brother's widow – but because Katherine was carefully kept in the dark it was suspected at the time, and has often been suggested since, that Wolsey and the king were trying to achieve a divorce by stealth. Yet since nothing could have extinguished Katherine's right to appeal to the pope, it is more likely that they were testing the water, seeing if support could be mustered for the king's case. If so, they found the water very cold indeed; the lawyers shrank from deciding without advice from the senior bishops, and at least some of the latter felt that canon law was not in the king's favour.[2] That marriage between a man and his former sister-in-law was incestuous was accepted throughout Western Europe at the time, and Henry and

[1] In general, for the following see Scarisbrick, *Henry VIII*, pp. 147–228.
[2] *LP*, iv.3148, 3232.

Katherine had only been able to marry in the first place after a dispensation from the pope had allowed them to ignore that objection. Thus, if Henry's divine revelation was genuine, the pope had exceeded his powers and must now eat his words.

The international situation, too, was anything but favourable. For over thirty years the French and a succession of enemies (most recently the Habsburgs) had been fighting for the mastery of Italy. In May 1527 this had reached a climax in the Sack of Rome by troops loyal to the emperor Charles V, which reduced the pope for some months to being a prisoner in his own citadel and then a pauper refugee – a situation made far worse for him by a concurrent uprising in Florence which expelled his family, the Medici. For some months Pope Clement VII looked for help to a French relieving force (backed by Henry VIII), but he never forgot that if this failed he would ultimately have to deal with the emperor. It did fail; by September 1528 the French were pinned back to a few garrisons in Milan, and a further effort in 1529 ended in final defeat in June at the Battle of Landriano. The consequence of all this was that only in the immediate aftermath of the Sack, when he was desperate for friends, did the pope have any incentive to accommodate Henry's wish for an annulment of his marriage to Katherine. Otherwise, although whenever the French made gains in Italy Clement VII became more amenable, he never committed himself to anything – such as annulling the marriage of the emperor's aunt – which would prevent an accommodation with Charles and the recovery of Florence, should the emperor win, as looked increasingly likely.

Divorce from Katherine, therefore, was difficult in law and impossible politically. Rome's answer was to make a series of deceptive concessions to Henry's demand that the case should be settled in England by Wolsey and a visiting papal legate, acting with full authority delegated from the pope. Even when the legate, Cardinal Campeggio, did arrive in the autumn of 1528, his powers were not complete, necessitating further wearisome and unsatisfactory negotiation with the papal Curia, while Katherine added her contribution to frustration by producing a new and different dispensation which meant that all the progress so far was threatened. Eventually Campeggio, who knew that the pope expected him to stall as much as possible, was forced to start proceedings on 31 May 1529, but it was not until 21 June that the famous public confrontation between Katherine and

Henry took place in the parliament chamber at Blackfriars, with the queen's plea to her husband which has re-echoed ever since on the Shakespearean stage. When Henry sat in embarrassed silence, Katherine appealed from the partiality of Blackfriars to the justice of God, turned her back on husband and legates alike and walked out, never to return. Her counsel, however, continued, tying the trial up in technicalities, and Campeggio announced that, in conformity with the practices of the Curia, a summer recess would start on 31 July. By that time, in far-away Italy, the pope had bowed to imperial pressure and issued orders recalling the case to Rome and, by the Treaty of Barcelona, announced that, as Clement himself put it, he 'had made up his mind to become an imperialist, and live and die as such'.

In all this Anne Boleyn had no place – or not officially. The public line was always that the king's conscience was troubled. With the prospect of Campeggio's imminent arrival, Henry had sent Anne in September 1528 to Hever to stay with her mother, and he ostentatiously continued to live with Katherine.[3] In November 1528 he became seriously concerned about the rising level of popular support for the queen, and on Sunday the 8th called a meeting of his courtiers and counsellors and the leading citizens of London to insist that there was no result he would like better from the suit than the confirmation that Katherine was his wife.[4] And on the principle that a lie might as well be a good one, he said (so Edward Hall recollected):

> I assure you all, that beside her noble parentage of the which she is descended (as you all know), she is a woman of most gentleness, of most humility and buxomness, yea and of all good qualities appertaining to nobility, she is without comparison, as I this twenty years almost have had true experiment, so that if I were to marry again, if the marriage might be good, I would surely choose her above all other women.

Of course, in Henry's mind there was no 'if' about the marriage being valid. When Campeggio arrived he found the king impervious to reason: 'I believe that an angel descending from Heaven would be unable to persuade him otherwise.'[5]

---

[3] *Cal. S. P. Span., 1527–29*, pp. 789, 831; *LP*, iv. App.206.
[4] Ibid., iv.4942; *Cal. S. P. Span., 1527–29*, p. 845; Hall, *Chronicle*, p. 754.
[5] *LP*, iv.4858.

But if Anne was out of sight – at least when convenient – she was not out of mind. The king's letters in 1528 show how significant was the pressure she exerted towards a divorce. When in February Stephen Gardiner, the up-and-coming man in the Church, and Edward Fox, beginning to make a name as an expert on the king's 'great matter', were sent to Rome with the latest bright new proposal, they were ordered to call in at Hever, first, to report to Anne. 'Darling,' the king wrote, 'these [words] shall be only to advertise you that this bearer and his fellow be dispatched with as many things to compass our matter and to bring it to pass as our wits could imagine or devise.' He warned her that it would take time, 'yet I will ensure you there shall be no time lost that may be won, and further can not be done; for *ultra posse non est esse* [anything more is quite impossible]. Keep him not too long with you, but desire him, for your sake, to make the more speed.'[6] In a later letter, full of the misery of absence, Henry is careful to tell Anne that he has given himself a headache after four hours' work on the divorce; in another he sends her brother to break bad news tactfully.[7] When Campeggio at last reached Paris, he writes with the good news; when the legate, having at last arrived, failed to visit Anne, thus driving her into an outburst of fear and suspicion, he manages to calm her, and then writes to welcome her promise to behave sensibly in future:

> what joy it is to me to understand of your conformableness to reason, and of the suppressing of your inutile and vain thoughts and fantasies with the bridle of reason. Wherefore, good sweetheart, continue the same, not only in this, but in all your doings hereafter; for thereby shall come, both to you and me, the greatest quietness that may be in this world.

And he very tactfully went on to mention the wedding preparations![8]

The importance of Anne as a spur in the divorce is well illustrated in Edward Fox's letter to Stephen Gardiner, reporting

---

[6] *Love Letters*, p. 46. [*LP*, iv.3990].

[7] Ibid., p. 47 [*LP*, iv.4597, a dating which assumes that the 'book' he was working on was not the one taken to Rome by Fox and Gardiner: ibid., iv.4120]; ibid., pp. 46–7 [*LP*, 4539].

[8] Ibid., pp. 36–7, 48 [*LP*, iv.4742, 4894].

his reception when in May 1528 he returned to England. The ambassadors had written ahead to announce that the pope had conceded almost everything Henry had asked for, and when Fox arrived at Greenwich at 5.00 pm only to find that Wolsey had already departed, Henry seized the chance to surprise Anne.[9] The envoy was told not to come to the king, but to go at once to Anne's chamber in the Tiltyard Gallery and break the news to her first. She was overcome with joy – so delighted, in fact, that she forgot Fox's name and insisted on calling him 'Master Stevens' (that is, Stephen Gardiner)! Then the king came in to enjoy his little surprise and, after Anne had left, to get down to detailed discussion with Fox. But Henry could not be without her at such a moment and he called her back for an intense barrage of questions to Fox – was the pope favourable, what had the lawyers said, what about the items that had not been conceded? Whereupon Henry sent Fox, then and there, on to London to see Wolsey. The poor man, who had not reached Sandwich until eleven the night before and had already that day ridden fifty-five miles, with several brushes with inquisitive local officials to delay him and then this excited interview, eventually got the cardinal out of bed at his London residence, well past ten o'clock.

Six months later the story was no longer of Henry wanting to demonstrate to Anne his success with the pope, but of Anne standing between the king and a total loss of nerve. The support for Katherine and the poor reception of his speech by the notables on 8 November so shook him that he rushed off to see Anne (despite his intention to keep his distance from her while the divorce was going through).[10] The imperial ambassador, believing Anne to be already Henry's mistress, interpreted this as a decision to pursue the amour with more privacy.[11] But it is more likely, one may hazard, that Henry was in despair at the difficulties, and making a frantic plea that Anne face the realities and accept the position of *maîtresse en titre* after all. Instead of that she stiffened his nerve and insisted that he return to London at once to press the divorce.[12] She seems also to have insisted on

[9] Pocock, *Records*, i.120–35, 141–55.
[10] For the mixed reaction to Henry's speech, see Hall's eyewitness comment: *Chronicle*, p. 755.
[11] *Cal. S. P. Span.*, *1527–29*, pp. 845–6.
[12] It may be at this time that Henry made an attempt to have renewed sexual relations with Katherine: *LP*, iv.4981.

being allowed back to court herself; if Henry's resolve could crack like this, she needed to be on the spot. Given the need to preserve the dictates of modesty, and the presence of Katherine at court, this was not easy, but Henry was soon able to write to Anne that Wolsey had come up with the answer: 'As touching a lodging for you, we have gotten one by my lord cardinal's means, the like whereof could not have been found hereabouts for all causes, as this bearer shall more show you.'[13] Du Bellay, the French ambassador, was quick to notice, and report on 9 December, that Anne was at last back at court and lodged grandly near to the king.[14] Where that was is not clear. One tradition suggests Durham House where Wolsey had been staying while his palace York Place was being rebuilt, or the nearby Suffolk Place, but the most likely reading of Henry's letter suggests a suite at the king's palace at Bridewell, secured by Wolsey sweeping out the existing occupants.[15] Certainly when the court moved to Greenwich for Christmas, Anne had her own separate suite in the palace.

As the French ambassador pointed out, there was some delicacy in the king housing his current wife and her intended successor under the same roof, and he may have been right to suggest that Anne took care to meet Katherine as little as possible. Or perhaps the reverse was the case.[16] Hall's account of Christmas 1528 does not suggest much enthusiastic participation by the queen:

> The more to quicken his spirits and for recreation, the king kept his Christmas at Greenwich, with much solemnity and great plenty of viands, and thither came the two legates, who were received by two dukes, and divers earls, barons and gentlemen, to whom the king showed great pleasures, both of jousts, tourney, banquets, masques and disguisings, and on the Twelfth Day he made the lawful son of Cardinal Campeius [Campeggio] born in wedlock, a knight, and gave him a collar of esses of gold. But the queen showed to them no matter of countenance, and made no joy of nothing, her mind was so troubled.[17]

[13] *Love Letters*, p. 37 [*LP*, iv.4648].
[14] *Ambassades de du Bellay*, 171 at p. 481 [*LP*, iv.5016].
[15] Strickland, *Queens of England*, ii.205.
[16] *Ambassades de du Bellay*, 178 at p. 518 [*LP*, iv.5063].
[17] Hall, *Chronicle*, p. 756. Campeggio had been a widower when he entered the Church.

Almost nothing has survived to reveal the personal relations of Anne and Katherine once the king's intentions were out in the open, or, indeed, before that. Cavendish would have it that Katherine behaved impeccably and 'shewed [neither] (to Mistress Anne, ne to the king) any spark or kind of grudge or displeasure'; indeed, she 'dissembled the same, having Mistress Anne in more estimation for the king's sake'.[18] This, Cavendish says, showed her to be a true patient Griselda, as in the Boccaccio/Chaucer story, and other writers made the same identification.[19] One may suggest, however, that Katherine was keeping her nerve. Kings had mistresses, Henry had had mistresses. So long as the wife tolerated the other woman she should present no danger; the only error was to treat her as a real threat and so elevate her to the status of queen in waiting. Katherine's mistake – and though she would have been a saint not to make it, a mistake that was fatal for her handling of Henry – was not to recognize the depth of Henry's self-deception. George Wyatt (and he is supported by some Catholic sources) claims that Anne was loyal to the queen and that Katherine tried to help her to resist the king's advances, which could be true of the stage of his 'courtly love' attack.[20] He spoils the story, however, by suggesting that Katherine did this by engaging Anne in frequent games of cards which were intended to make it impossible for her to keep her deformed finger out of sight, which only makes sense if the games were intended to disgust the king rather than give Anne an excuse to keep away from him. The muddle is probably Wyatt's, embroidering a family story about one card game (unidentified) in which Anne frequently turned up a king, and Katherine remarked, 'My lady Anne, you have good hap to stop at a king, but you are not like others, you will have all or none.' Whether, as is often suggested, Katherine was delivering a warning and a prophecy 'under game', or whether a chance remark in gaming subsequently assumed an unintended significance, it is impossible to say.[21]

---

[18] Cavendish, *Wolsey*, p. 35.

[19] Ibid., pp. 259–62; cf. W. Forrest, *The History of Griselda the Second*, ed. W. D. Macray, Roxburghe Club (1875).

[20] BL, Sloane MS 2495, f. 2v. The Latin MS edited by C. Bémont under the title *Le premier divorce de Henri VIII*, *fragment d'une chronique* (Paris, 1917) agrees, but is not independent of the Sloane MS.

[21] George Wyatt, in *Wolsey*, ed. Singer, p. 428. He does not mention Anne Zouche as the source; cf. ibid., p. 429.

As 'the other woman' in a difficult, public and unpopular divorce case, Anne Boleyn was in no enviable position. Despite Henry's promise to marry her, she had nothing but his affection to rely on. For the moment that was a powerful resource, and all the evidence is of an increasing commitment by the king. Du Bellay, the French ambassador, wondered whether the relationship would survive a sudden separation in June 1528 when one of Anne's ladies went down with an attack of the sweating sickness.[22] 'The sweat' was a highly contagious and frequently fatal disease (probably a virus infection akin to the Spanish flu of 1918 which would kill more people in Europe than would die in the Great War). Now, Henry took off on a flight from safe house to safe house at a speed which demonstrated his paranoia about infection.[23] Accompanied by Katherine he began a most meticulous round of religious observances. Yet the king still wrote to Anne, in quarantine at Hever, to tell her he was safe and to reassure her that 'few women or none have this malady.'[24] When this proved a false hope and Anne did go down with the sweat, Henry reacted with real anxiety. Off went Butts, his second-best doctor – 'the physician in whom I put most trust is now at this time absent when he could most do me pleasure' – carrying a letter of sympathy and support from Henry, once more signed with the initials 'H' and 'R' flanking a heart and 'AB'.[25] Care and sympathy worked, and by 23 June Anne had recovered, while Henry was wallowing in the excitement of danger at a safe distance, averted by his own prompt response. As Brian Tuke, one of the counsellors in attendance, read Wolsey's letter advising the king on precautions to take as the epidemic ran its course,

> [Henry] thanked your grace: and showing me, first, a great process of the manner of that infection; how folks were taken; how little danger was in it, if good order be observed; how few were dead of it; how Mistress Anne, and my lord of Rochford, both have had it; what jeopardy they have been in, by returning in of the sweat before the time; of the endeavour of Mr. Butts, who hath been with them, and is returned; with many other things touching those matters, and, finally, of their perfect recovery.[26]

22 *Ambassades de du Bellay*, 101 at p. 304 [*LP*, iv.4391].
23 Ibid., 114 at p. 320 [*LP*, iv.4440]; 124 at pp. 339–40 [*LP*, iv.4542].
24 *Love Letters*, pp. 30–2 [*LP*, iv.4403].
25 Ibid., pp. 43–4 [*LP*, iv.4383].
26 *St. Pap.*, i.298–9 [*LP*, iv.4409].

When, perhaps a month later, Anne was able to return to court, du Bellay noted that separation had made no difference: 'the king is in so deeply that God alone can get him out of it.'[27]

Despite this, Anne faced powerful opposition. Katherine of Aragon had much support in England; apart from her general popularity, many powerful courtiers and nobles held her in great affection. Beyond them was the Emperor Charles V, and the traditional English sentiment in favour of an alliance with the Low Countries rather than the old enemy, France. Even among those who supported the need for a divorce there were some who looked for a more suitable second queen: most probably a foreign princess who could do what royal brides were expected to do – cement international alliances, not satisfy royal passions. A different woman might have ignored the critics and trusted to her own attractions and her ability to nag or persuade the king into marriage, but not Anne Boleyn. Instead she entered politics.

The first evidence of this is her growing exploitation of her influence over Henry. Given the realities of personal monarchy, the public manifestation of royal favour was the ability to secure benefits, and since the hot money of courtly support flowed to where the interest rate was greatest, to demonstrate favour was to attract support. George Cavendish remarked of Anne that it was 'judged by and by, through all the court, of every man, that she, being in such favour with the king, might work mysteries [wonders] with the king and obtain any suit of him for her friend.'[28] How near he was to the truth was made apparent when in April 1528 Cecily Willoughby, abbess of Wilton, died.

The nunnery of St Edith at Wilton was a large Benedictine house with a number of aristocratic connections which were not always conducive to a life of prayer and domestic duties.[29] It was, to be blunt, the sort of community where a well born woman who could not be found a suitable husband could retire to live the genteel life to which she was accustomed and without too irksome a religious routine. The obvious successor to Cecily was the second-in-command, Prioress Isabel Jordayn, whose sister was head of the even more prestigious nunnery at Syon. Wilton, however, contained two nuns who were the sisters of William Carey of the privy chamber, husband to Mary Boleyn

---

[27] *Ambassades de du Bellay*, 132 at p. 363 [*LP*, iv.4649].
[28] Cavendish, *Wolsey*, p. 35.
[29] D. Knowles, 'The matter of Wilton', in *BIHR*, 31(1958), 92–6.

and thus brother-in-law to Anne, and William was determined to secure the promotion for the younger of the two, Eleanor, and to block the advancement of the elder, or of anyone else.[30] He secured the support of Wolsey and then went for the bigger prize of the king's approval, which was given as a favour to Anne. Everything was going well, but at this point Eleanor Carey's past caught up with her. She had been the mistress of and had children by two priests, and more recently had lived with one of the entourage of the Willoughby family. It is not known whether this was before becoming a nun, in which case the late abbess was, by accepting her, helping to resolve a family scandal, or whether it was afterwards, in which case one might suspect some aiding and abetting, but the fact was clear enough.[31] When faced with it, Henry wrote to Anne that Eleanor Carey was quite impossible as a candidate and asked her to drop her support, but adding that 'to do you pleasure' he had given instructions that neither Isabel Jordayn nor the elder Carey sister should be appointed, 'but that some other good and well-disposed woman shall have it'. In the event Wolsey slipped up and nominated Isabel Jordayn, which precipitated one of those rare and terrifying letters in the king's own hand, and a display of grovelling submission by Wolsey. It was clearly a bad thing to cross Lady Anne, even if you were the king's chief minister and had right on your side.

Anne Boleyn's hand thus begins to be seen in the key political area of patronage, control of which was essential if a minister was to maintain his prestige and command the support of the court. Cavendish also tells us that she began to play a part in that other key activity, faction. The passage is crucial to an understanding of Tudor politics:

> The king waxed so far in amours with this gentlewoman that he knew not how much he might advance her. This perceiving, the great lords of the council, bearing a secret grudge against the cardinal because that they could not rule in the commonweal (for [because of] him) as they would, who kept them low and ruled them as well as other mean subjects, whereat they caught an

[30] Eleanor seems also to have been supported by those nuns opposed to any tightening of discipline.
[31] *LP*, iv.4477; cf. ibid., vi.285; *House of Commons*, iii.627.

occasion to invent a mean[s] to bring him out of the king's high favour and them into more authority of rule and civil governance, after long and secret consultation among themselves how to bring their malice to effect against the cardinal. They knew right well that it was very difficult for them to do anything directly of themselves, wherefore they perceiving the great affection that the king bare lovingly unto Mistress Anne Boleyn, fantasying in their heads that she should be for them a sufficient and an apt instrument to bring their malicious purpose to pass; with whom they often consulted in this matter. And she having both a very good wit, and also an inward desire to be revenged of the cardinal, was agreeable to their requests as they were themselves, wherefore there was no more to do but only to imagine some pretended circumstance to induce their malicious accusation, in so much that there was imagined and invented among them divers imaginations and subtle devices how this matter should be brought about.[32]

Belling the cat was, however, difficult so long as Henry kept his confidence in Wolsey, and Wolsey his 'wonder wit'.

Faction in Tudor England is a phenomenon frequently misunderstood but one which was crucial to Tudor politics and to the career of Anne Boleyn in particular.[33] It is easy to dismiss it as mere backbiting and self-advantage, but faction was more than that. It was, indeed, the distinctive form of politics appropriate to an era of personal monarchy, the means by which competition for profit and for power could take place when the will of one man was final and decisive. Direct challenge to the king was impossible. Only the rebel attempted to force policies on the crown; only the conspirator attempted to force himself into place and profit. The loyal way was to seek to gain the king's goodwill, to achieve what men recognized Anne Boleyn had achieved – royal favour. Then the way was open to securing grants and honours, then the way was open to advancing alternative suggestions on policy, courses which, if accepted by the king, he would look to you to execute. This principle applied throughout the country, down to very minor matters, but only a

[32] Cavendish, *Wolsey*, pp. 35–6.
[33] For faction generally, see E. W. Ives, *Faction in Tudor England* (1979) and the bibliography cited there; also D. R. Starkey, 'Representation through intimacy', in *Symbols and Sentiments*, ed. I. M. Lewis (1977), pp. 187–224; 'The age of the household', in *The Later Middle Ages*, ed. S. Medcalf (1981) pp. 225–90; 'From feud to faction', in *History Today*, 32 (1982), 16–22.

very few people were in a position to compete directly for royal favour. They, therefore, were pressed to solicit favour for third parties, which they did partly in return for material rewards and partly for status and prestige; and third parties could lead to fourth and fourth to fifth until the resulting pattern of clientage resembled nothing so much as a root system. By the nature of things, too, those who were in direct contact with the king were not of equal importance, and thus also had their own pattern of relationships. The result was that these wider systems came together at court into a limited number of groups for mutual support and advantage, the test of sufficiency being the ability to persuade the king.

Such was faction, which permeated and structured Tudor society and was the medium of Tudor politics. Two further points need to be stressed. Even though a faction might have a policy dimension – a preference, say, for the Empire or for France, or, later, for religious change or traditional forms – it did not put forward an ideological programme as a political party does today; instead, policy was subsumed in the individual. Thus as Henry's pursuit of a divorce went on to produce increasing tension between Church and state in England and between England and Rome, support for traditional religion came to be expressed as support for Katherine and Mary; likewise, acceptance of Anne meant hostility to Rome and (eventually) acceptance of royal supremacy over the Church. In the second place, neither factions, nor the relationships between them, were fixed. Admittedly, it would be too much to use the word 'fluid'; some groupings, some antagonisms, lasted for many years. Factions, too, were not merely the creation of private calculation, but could express the permanences of friendship, family, locality or upbringing. Yet the system did, nevertheless, exist to promote objectives which were seen in primarily personal terms, and the calculations could and did alter. As we shall see, Anne Boleyn's fall in 1536 was a consequence of precisely such a recalculation among some of her supporters.

In 1527, of course, Anne Boleyn had very few. Katherine, by contrast, had the support of one of the most enduring factions of the time. Its origins went back to the reign of Henry VII, and although it is sometimes referred to as 'the Aragonese faction' it is better described as 'the Stafford–Neville', later 'the Neville–Courtenay', connection, after the principal families involved. In the early years of Henry VIII's reign its members were among the most prominent courtiers, with Edward Stafford, duke of Buckingham, his brother Henry (later earl of Wiltshire), George Neville, Lord Abergavenny, and his brother Sir Edward Neville, always around the king and his young wife.[34] Towards the end of the second decade of the century George married Buckingham's daughter Mary, a former waiting-woman to the queen, and at the same time both families contracted alliances with another important group, the Pole family. The matriarch of that family, Margaret Pole, countess of Salisbury, was a close friend to Katherine of Aragon; her second son, Reginald, was being groomed at the king's expense for high office in the English Church; her cousin, Henry Courtenay, earl of Devon, was one of the king's intimates, having 'been brought up of a child with his grace in his chamber', and his wife, Gertrude (also one of Katherine's ladies), was daughter to William Blount, Lord Mountjoy, chamberlain to the queen, by his wife Inez, one of the attendants who had come with her from Spain.[35] The faction had lost ground to Wolsey after 1514 and in 1521 had suffered a massive blow when Buckingham was executed and Abergavenny, Edward Neville, the countess of Salisbury and her eldest son, Henry, Lord Montagu, all fell into disfavour. But the faction survived and recovered somewhat as the 1520s progressed; the countess became governess to Princess Mary, while Henry Courtenay was raised to the rank of marquis of Exeter and appointed a nobleman to serve in the privy chamber.[36] As Katherine came under threat the Neville–Courtenay connection was in a position to give her very powerful support, and Exeter and Montagu would live to be among the peers who condemned Anne to death.

What had Anne Boleyn to set against the queen, backed by the weight of canon law, popular sentiment and the support of a powerful faction at court? At first sight, perhaps, less than she would have had two years earlier. In June 1525 Sir Thomas Boleyn had at last achieved his ambition of a peerage, but this had meant his leaving the vital court post of treasurer of the household. Seven months later, Anne's brother George lost his

---

[34] See above, p. 15; Mattingly, *Catherine of Aragon*, pp. 160–1, 288; J. E. Paul, *Catherine of Aragon and her Friends* (1966).
[35] *Ordinances for the Household*, p. 154.
[36] *LP*, iii.2955; *Ordinances for the Household*, p. 154.

formal position in the privy chamber as a result of the Eltham reorganization.[37] Both men, however, remained part of the king's intimate circle, and although the earl of Northumberland carried little weight and was, in any case, usually on duty in the north, another former admirer, Wyatt, was in high favour with the king.[38] Yet three men, however much in the king's graces, were not enough, and Anne set out to gain more. She did everything she could to secure the support of her brother-in-law, William Carey – hence the business of the appointment to Wilton. Another of the gentlemen of the privy chamber was Sir Thomas Cheney, whom Anne may already have encountered as a fellow resident in Kent, and she first intervened on his behalf in March 1528 when he was in disgrace with Wolsey.[39]

A more serious problem over Cheney arose some months later, when the sweat carried off the stepson of another privy chamber gentleman, Sir John Russell. The young man, John Broughton, had been in service to Wolsey and had left £700 in chattels and substantial lands in Bedfordshire, so that his two sisters were considerable heiresses.[40] The younger, Katherine, was under age, and already her wardship had been granted to Wolsey, but Russell's wife was frantic to keep her daughter, and Sir John went to work at once to get Wolsey to sell the wardship to the family. He had good hopes – he was very much a Wolsey man and the cardinal had liked Broughton – but Cheney and another gentleman of the privy chamber, Sir John Wallop, were pressing the king and Anne Boleyn for support in securing both girls. Russell, therefore, mobilized Wolsey's contact man in the privy chamber, Thomas Heneage, and one of the minister's closest aides, Thomas Arundel, to intercede on his behalf and secure from the cardinal the wardship of Katherine Broughton, as well as confirmation that her elder sister, Anne, was now of age. Cheney and Wallop, however, were successful (after, apparently, insinuating that both girls were under age and in the king's gift), and Henry promised Anne Broughton to Sir Thomas and Katherine to Sir John. This put Wolsey in great difficulty – he was already in the king's bad books over the Wilton affair – but

---

[37] See above, p. 15.
[38] *LP*, iv.5497 shows Percy in trouble with Wolsey, apparently for making overtures to the court; cf. ibid., iv.3748.
[39] Ibid., iv.4081.
[40] For the following see ibid., iv.3216, 4436–7; 4452; 4456; 4710; 6748(15).

when a blazing row broke out between Cheney and Russell, the
king felt that his candidate had gone too far.[41] Richard Page,
another of the gentlemen of the privy chamber, wrote to Wolsey:

> His grace answered that he [Cheney] was proud and full of
> opprobrious words, little esteeming his friends that did most for
> him, and did the best he could to put them to dishonesty that
> were most glad to do him pleasure and in such wise handled
> himself that he should never come in his Chamber until he had
> humbled himself and confessed his fault and were agreed with
> Mr. Russell.[42]

What part Anne played in all this is not known, but she was
active on Cheney's behalf when the matter erupted again in
January 1529 in a confrontation between him and Wolsey. No
doubt insisting that the king's promise of Anne Broughton
should be honoured, Cheney offended the minister and was
rusticated, only to be brought to court by Anne, with many
harsh words against the cardinal.[43] In May Wolsey gave up his
effort to direct Anne Broughton's marriage, and she apparently
passed into Cheney's control, eventually becoming his wife.[44]
The cardinal did retain the wardship of the younger sister
Katherine, and the king paid Wallop £400 in compensation.[45]
Yet if this was the compromise it appears to be, it did not last
long. On Wolsey's fall, Katherine's wardship was granted to
Anne Boleyn's grandmother, and not long afterwards the girl was
married to Anne's uncle, Lord William Howard.[46] Anne and her
protégés now had everything, and Russell, who seems only to
have wanted the happiness of his wife and stepdaughters, had
nothing. A long feud with Cheney ensued, and it is no surprise,
either, to find Sir John less than enthusiastic for Anne Boleyn.[47]

Anne, therefore, was beginning to collect allies among existing
members of the king's immediate entourage, and it may be that
she also had some influence on admission to the privy chamber.[48]

[41] Ibid., iv.4584; for the vulnerability of Wolsey, see also ibid., iv.4556.
[42] RO, SP1/49, f. 175 [*LP*, iv.4584].
[43] *Ambassades de du Bellay*, 188 at p. 543 [*LP*, iv.5210].
[44] Ibid., iv.5624; *House of Commons*, i.634–7.
[45] *LP*, v.pp.311–12, 315.
[46] Ibid., iv.6072(21), 6187(12); v.318(21).
[47] Ibid., vi.462.
[48] For the following, see ibid., iv.3213(18), 3869(29), 3964, 4005, 4081, 4335.

This can hardly have been so as early as June 1527, when a post as gentleman of the privy chamber was given to Richard Page, who was later to be one of her loyal supporters and barely to escape with his life in 1536. In January 1528 Nicholas Carewe was recruited; a long-term boon companion of the king, he would be one of Anne's bitterest enemies. On the other hand, Wallop was appointed at the same time, and we have seen how he turned to Anne over Katherine Broughton. Thomas Heneage, whom Wolsey had insinuated into the department some weeks after Carewe and Wallop, was clearly *persona grata* with Anne, and this was probably a factor in his selection. Then there is the case of Francis Bryan whom the king 'took into his privy chamber' on 25 June. Bryan – brother-in-law first to Carewe (and like him a victim both of the 1519 expulsions and the Eltham redundancies) and then to the controller of the household, Henry Guildford – had every credential for court office already, and Anne was away from court when he was appointed. Yet one must note that Bryan was a replacement for Anne's brother-in-law William Carey, who had died of the sweat, and that he was soon on the way to France to escort (and accelerate) the impatiently awaited Campeggio.[49] That this was not an uncongenial task is clear from his letters when, later in the year, he was sent to get further concessions from the pope. The letters show him to be a strong supporter of Anne, confidently presuming on his family relationship with her.[50] Bryan may not have needed Anne's help to become a gentleman of the privy chamber again, but there is at least good reason to suspect that Henry knew he would please Anne by appointing the sort of man who would later write to him:

> I pray God my fortune may be so good to come with the tidings. Sir, I would have written to my mistress that shall be, but I will not write unto her, till I may write that shall please her most in this world. I pray God to send your grace and her long life and merry, or else me a short end.[51]

There is no such intimate evidence to tell us about Anne Boleyn's early relations with other powerful groups and indi-

[49] *St. Pap.*, i.302; *LP*, iv.4656.
[50] Francis's mother and Anne's mother were half-sisters: E. W. Ives, *The Common Lawyers in Pre-Reformation England* (Cambridge, 1984), p. 377.
[51] *St. Pap.*, vii.145. NB also the appointment of George Boleyn as esquire of the body on 26 Sept. 1528: *LP*, iv.4779.

viduals at court, such as the king's sister Mary, and her husband
Charles Brandon, duke of Suffolk. There is, however, some sign
of a link with her uncle, now duke of Norfolk. He had, after all,
wanted to exploit Anne in 1520–1 to extricate himself from his
job in Ireland, and it would have been obvious for a man like
Thomas Howard to see what he could gain from the king's
interest in her.[52] He was already finding it less easy to accept
Wolsey's frustrating dominance than had his father, the old
duke, who had died in 1524. The attacks on Wolsey by the poet
John Skelton were very much Howard-inspired, and in 1525,
when royal taxation had provoked unrest in Suffolk, Howard
and Brandon had made joint, if half-hearted attempts to plant
doubts about the cardinal in the king's mind.[53] Anne Boleyn
might, as Cavendish suggests, appear a lever ready to hand.

The Life and Death of Cardinal Wolsey is, however, only partially
correct in suggesting that it was the summer of 1527 and the
need to send an embassy to France which opened Wolsey up to
attack, and that Anne was in the lead:

> You have heard heretofore how divers of the great estates and
> lords of the council lay in wait with my lady Anne to espy a
> convenient time and occasion to take the cardinal in a brake
> [thicket = trap]. [They] thought it then that now is the time
> come that we have expected, supposing it best to cause him to
> take upon him the king's commission and to travel beyond the sea
> in this matter . . . Their intents and purpose was only but to get
> him out of the realm that they might have convenient leisure and
> opportunity to adventure their long desired enterprise. And by
> the aid of their chief mistress (my lady Anne) to deprave him so
> unto the king in his absence that he should be rather in his high
> displeasure than in his accustomed favour, or at least to be in less
> estimation with his majesty.[54]

In fact, if we are to believe the new imperial ambassador who
arrived in March, there was already then much ill feeling against
the French alliance that Wolsey was pushing, and in May he was
able to name Norfolk as one of those principally involved.[55]
Nevertheless, the cardinal's absence was significant. Anne did
agree to marry Henry, and Wolsey had hardly been gone a

---

[52] See above, pp. 43–5.
[53] *LP*, iv.1319, 1329.
[54] Cavendish, *Wolsey*, pp. 43–4.
[55] *Cal. S. P. Span., 1527–29*, pp. 109, 190–3.

month before he learned that the king was quite unexpectedly hosting an enormous house-party at Beaulieu in Essex, with both dukes, Exeter, several other peers (including Rochford) and their wives – all the aristocratic heavy mob which the cardinal feared most.[56] Even worse, he found the king listening to them. Henry's regular supper companions were Norfolk, Suffolk, Exeter and Rochford; and Dr William Knight, whom Wolsey was expecting to hold the fort for him, reported: 'This is to advertise your good grace that my lords of Norfolk, Suffolk, and Rochford, and Mr. Treasurer [Fitzwilliam] be privy unto the other letter that I do send unto your grace at this time, with these, after the open reading whereof the king' – and Wolsey must have breathed a sigh of relief at this point – 'delivered unto me your letter, concerning the secrets.'[57] There were, then, still some secrets between the two!

The minister nevertheless felt he had to begin a counter-bombardment of flattery. The grossness of this demonstrates how scared he was – 'there was never lover more desirous of the sight of his lady than I am of your most noble and royal person'![58] And when Wolsey returned to court on 30 September he had a worse shock. The long-standing custom had been to warn the king that he had arrived, and to ask for a private appointment in the privy chamber to report on his mission. When the cardinal's man arrived it was to find, as the imperial ambassador reported, that 'the king had with him in his chamber a certain lady called Anna de Bolaine who appears to have little good will towards the cardinal, and before the king could respond to the message she said, "where else should he come, except where the king is?"'[59] Henry indulgently agreed, and Wolsey found himself playing gooseberry to a courting couple and trying to talk diplomacy at the same time. He also realized how wrong he had been. He had gone to France dismissing Anne as a flirtation, and confident that a divorce would free Henry to marry a French princess; he now knew things were serious, for him perhaps, deadly serious.

[56] *LP*, iv.3318.
[57] *St. Pap.*, i.261 [*LP*, iv.3360].
[58] Ibid., i.278–9; cf. ibid., i.267.
[59] *Cal. S. P. Span., 1527–29*, p. 432.

7

Anne Boleyn and the
Fall of Wolsey

~~~≈≈~~~

FROM THE events of July–September 1527 to Wolsey's fall in
1529, it is tempting to draw a straight line, and a short one.
The battle had been arrayed. Wolsey against Anne and her
allies, with the cardinal between the Scylla of Anne Boleyn as
queen, and the Charybdis of a king furious at being baulked of
his divorce. That was how Cavendish saw it in retrospect, and
others had thought the same at the time. The imperial ambassador, Inigo de Mendoza, reported in October 1527, in language
much as Cavendish would use later, that Norfolk, Rochford and
their friends had made a league against the cardinal and had
been trying to ruin him in his absence.[1] He was equally clear
what a threat Anne would be to Wolsey's power if she became
Henry's wife in place of the present queen, 'who can do him little
harm'. He traced her hostility to two reasons: Wolsey's assumption that the next queen would be French, and an earlier move
by him which had deprived her father of 'a high official post'.
This latter may refer to the pressure put on Boleyn in 1519 over
the post of controller of the household, but it more probably
hints at her resentment that Boleyn had, in effect, had to pay
for his peerage by giving up the treasurership without an
equivalent post in compensation.[2] Mendoza was sure that Wolsey
was doing his best to sabotage the divorce and was proposing to
call a conference of experts in the hope that they would convince
the king that the law was against him.

Mendoza, however, was only speculating, and he reported

[1] *Cal. S. P. Span.*, *1527–29*, pp. 432–3.
[2] This seems much more probable than that Anne bore a grudge over Henry
Percy.

also an alternative opinion held by a number of courtiers. This was that if Wolsey became convinced of Henry's determination to marry Anne, he would execute a volte-face and support her rather than lose royal favour. This was the more perceptive analysis. After all, had not Wolsey risen to power, as Cavendish would later explain, by observing the principle that 'to satisfy the king's mind . . . was the very vein and right course to bring him to high promotion'?[3] Opposition to the cardinal in the spring and summer of 1527 thus turned out to be only another brief probing of his position in royal favour, of the sort that tested him from time to time throughout his period in power, and certainly did not commit Anne against him. There was much to be said for her (and Henry) deciding, as they did, to stick with a man who knew his way about the international scene as well as Wolsey, and who exuded the confidence that, so long as they trusted him, all would be well. Wolsey had quickly re-established his psychological dominance on his return from France in a number of grand set pieces, culminating in the splendid ceremony of 1 November 1527 in which a French delegation invested Henry as knight of the Order of S. Michel, and as news filtered back to England of the failure of the king's go-it-alone attempt to get papal support behind Wolsey's back, the cardinal seemed even more the man to turn to.[4]

Anne Boleyn certainly thought so. Like her father before her, she decided that there was a greater percentage in becoming a client of the cardinal than in continuing to oppose him. Despite her increased role in affairs, all through the first half of 1528 her efforts were to stand well with the man who would give her what she wanted. The brunt of this fell on Thomas Heneage, newly arrived in the privy chamber from Wolsey's own household.[5] At dinner on Tuesday 3 March Anne complained to him that the cardinal was neglecting her, and at supper when Heneage was sent down to Anne from Henry, with a special dish for her meal, she prevailed on him to join her at table – an act of the greatest condescension which Heneage well knew was not primarily intended for him. As the meal progressed, Anne's overtures to the cardinal became even plainer. How pleasant it would be, she mused, to have some carp or shrimps during Lent, from Wolsey's

---

[3] Cavendish, *Wolsey*, p. 12.
[4] Ibid., pp. 64–7; Hall, *Chronicle*, pp. 733–4; see above, pp. 103, 108.
[5] Ellis, *Letters*, 3 ii.131 [*LP*, iv.4005].

famous fishponds. Heneage offered a wry masculine apology when passing on the request: 'I beseech your grace, pardon me that I am so bold to write unto your grace hereof, it is the conceit and mind of a woman.' The minister, however, had not put one of his best men to 'mind' Anne for nothing, and a fortnight later Heneage was writing again to thank Wolsey for his 'kind and favourable writing unto her' – whether this accompanied a parcel of fish is not stated – and to pass on her 'humble' request for Cheney to be forgiven.[6] In June Heneage reported on the news of Anne's health after some ailment: 'Mistress Anne is very well amended, and commendeth her humbly unto your grace, and thinketh it long till she speak with you.'[7]

Wolsey marked Anne's recovery from the much more serious sweating sickness by 'a kind letter' and a 'rich and goodly present', which she acknowledged directly along with her indebtedness to Wolsey for his help:

> of the which I have hitherto had so great plenty, that all the days of my life I am most bound of all creatures, next the king's grace, to love and serve your grace: of the which I beseech you never to doubt that ever I shall vary from this thought as long as any breath is in my body. And as touching your grace's trouble with the sweat [in his household], I thank our Lord that them that I desired and prayed for are scaped, and that is the king and you.

The letter ends with a promise of what she will do for Wolsey when, as she puts it, 'this matter' is at 'a good end', a promise she repeated in another letter soon afterwards.[8] Most striking of all is a joint letter from Anne and Henry when an end to the epidemic allowed them to be together at the start of August.[9] She began it with good wishes to the cardinal and an expression of her debt to him 'never like to be recompensed on my part', and a mention of her anxious waiting for Campeggio. Then Henry followed: 'The writer of this letter would not cease till she had caused me likewise to set my hand; desiring you, though it be

---

[6] *LP*, iv.4081; see above, p. 126.

[7] *St. Pap.*, i.289 [*LP*, iv.4335]. The movements of Henry and Anne necessarily date this letter before the sweat.

[8] BL, Cott. MS Otho C x.f. 220. The MS is mutilated; for a full text see Burnet, *History*, i.104 [*LP*, iv.4480]; *LP*, iv.App. 197.

[9] BL, Cott. MS Vit. B xii.f.4. The MS is mutilated; for a full text see Burnet, *History*, i.103–4 [*LP*, iv.4360].

short, to take it in good part.' He was also more open about the
purpose of all this. The two of them had got into a state because
no news had reached England about Campeggio arriving in
France. Very probably 'your loving sovereign and friend, Henry
K' and 'your humble servant Anne Boleyn' got the reassurance
they wanted by return of post; Wolsey had an excellent professional manner.[10]

Not everyone has read the correspondence of 1528 in this way.
Those convinced by Cavendish that Anne had a settled hostility
to Wolsey from the time of the Percy episode have accused her of
obvious insincerity. Others have seen evidence of volatile moods.
It is true, too, that Wolsey was busy trying to stand well with
Anne. We may note that although Heneage had made the
appropriate excuses for the cardinal that Tuesday in March
1528, and although the privy chamber had been exceedingly
short-staffed and he was exhausted after a day attending the
king, he had felt Anne important enough, fish or no fish, to settle
down at eleven o'clock at night to warn Wolsey. The French
ambassador, writing in August 1528, was full of gloom about
Wolsey's prospects and reported that he was planning to retire,
knowing that his influence would not survive the marriage to
Anne.[11] A month later the imperial ambassador also reported
the cardinal's difficulties and his incentive to delay – the more
difficult the divorce could be made, the more Henry would need
him, and the longer it could be strung out, the longer it would be
before Anne could destroy his influence.[12] Cavendish remembered
how Wolsey 'ordered himself to please as well the king as her,
dissimulating the matter that lay hid in his breast, and prepared
great banquets and solemn feasts to entertain them both at his
own house'.[13] All this and more does suggest a stand-off in
insincerity. Yet Cavendish was writing with hindsight, and
diplomats are expected to be suspicious. It is worth noting that
by November the imperial ambassador was qualifying his assessment by passing on the alternative rumour that Wolsey had
done a deal with Anne and her father, as well as his own

[10] The reference to Campeggio establishes the date as after Anne had
returned to court following the sweat: *LP*, iv.4538, 4649. It was known on 28
June that Campeggio had not set off [ibid., 4430], by which time Anne and
Henry were separated.
[11] *Ambassades de du Bellay*, 132 at pp. 363–4 [*LP*, iv.4649].
[12] *Cal. S. P. Span., 1527–29*, p. 790.
[13] Cavendish, *Wolsey*, p. 36.

conclusion that Wolsey would, in the end, go the way the king wanted – exactly what he had said a year earlier.[14]

There was, indeed, no reason for Anne and Henry not to trust Wolsey, for 1528 did bring progress: first the commission brought back by Fox in May, and then the progressive news of Campeggio's preparations and eventual departure for England. What frayed their nerves was the time it all took. Wolsey's nerves, though, were frayed by something different: not as ambassadors thought, fear for his own future once a divorce was achieved – he was sanguine enough to believe that he could cope with that, however much he affected a desire to retire! His fear was that he would not be able to secure a divorce on the terms Henry demanded. It was perfectly clear that Henry's vision about the meaning of Leviticus 20 would get nowhere. Campeggio arrived fully and firmly convinced that the king was wrong in law, and Wolsey could share this realization with no one.[15] As early as July 1527 he had been accused by the king of being lukewarm to the divorce because he suggested an alternative (and altogether stronger) line of approach; in June 1528 the king lost his temper when Wolsey again tried to explain the problem.[16] All this forced the minister to concentrate on two outside chances, either to try to bring about a French hegemony in Italy which would then make the pope the prisoner of an ally of England, or to deafen him with pleas to grant the divorce somehow while lamenting about what would happen if he did not. So long as that policy seemed to produce results, as it appeared to do in 1528, so long Wolsey seemed to justify the trust Henry and Anne had in him. The question was, how long would the impossibility of success by that route remain a secret?

It would be satisfying to be able to point to a single event, a precise occasion that broke the illusion of progress behind which Wolsey sheltered for so many months, but the realization was slow to dawn, especially on Henry. Campeggio wrote a very revealing report on 9 January 1529 showing that despite what he had tried to explain, the king had supreme confidence that 'his merits and the urgency he uses therein' could not fail; assurance

[14] *Cal. S. P. Span., 1527–29*, p. 847.

[15] Except, perhaps, du Bellay: *Ambassades de du Bellay*, 162 at pp. 454–5 [*LP*, iv.4915], and 163 at p. 463 [*LP*, iv.4942].

[16] *St. Pap.*, i.194–5 [*LP*, iv.3217]; *Ambassades de du Bellay*, 132 at p. 363 [*LP*, iv.4649].

of divine revelation is not always an advantage.[17] Wolsey, by
contrast, was brutally pragmatic: 'I speak freely with his lordship to know his mind, and he generally ends by shrugging his
shoulders and has nothing else to say but that the only remedy is
to satisfy the king's wish in some way or other, and let it stand
for what it is worth.'

It was, perhaps, Anne who got to the truth first, possibly at
the time when she insisted on being brought back to court, where
Henry was soon, in the words of Campeggio, 'kissing her and
treating her in public as though she were his wife'.[18] She had
been frustrated by the legate's slow journey; she had been
suspicious at being kept out of Campeggio's way and ignored by
him; she had been expecting rapid progress once he did arrive on
8 October, and a month later all that had been achieved was the
ruin of Henry's self-confidence. Already on 1 November, Wolsey
had warned the pope that 'many people were again and again
insinuating to the king' the necessity of adopting policies which
would inevitably threaten the authority of Rome; and at the end
of the month the king did send Anne's cousin, Francis Bryan,
with Peter Vannes, his Latin secretary, to Clement VII with
instructions personally approved by Henry to force the Holy
Father into submission, if necessary with the threat that otherwise England would withdraw its allegiance to the see of
Rome.[19] About the same time there was the first sign of another
policy that would also be very definitely associated with the
Boleyns – the preparation of a monster petition to the pope from
the English political elite, urging him to grant the divorce in the
national interest.[20]

It may, of course, be premature to see in all this the signs of a
serious rupture between Anne Boleyn and Wolsey in November
1528, but if so it is premature by only a month or so. It was
about the third week in January that Anne had her second brush
with the cardinal over Cheney, and when the French ambassador
reported her victory in this, he also noted that Norfolk and his
faction (*'le duc de Nortfoch et sa bande'*) were already 'talking big'.[21]
A few days later Mendoza had picked up the news. Anne had
decided that Wolsey was trying to frustrate, not assist, the

[17] Brewer, *Henry VIII*, ii.486.
[18] Ibid., ii.486.
[19] *St. Pap.*, vii.106 [*LP*, iv.4897]; *LP*, iv.4977, p. 2159.
[20] *Cal. S. P. Span., 1527–29*, p. 861.
[21] *Ambassades de du Bellay*, 188 at p. 543 [*LP*, iv.5210].

divorce, and had formed an alliance with Rochford and with both Norfolk and Suffolk.[22] The naming of Suffolk for the first time as one of the group attacking Wolsey is significant, and so too the mention of Anne as an equal party, indeed, an initiator in the move – in the brief 1527 skirmish, Mendoza had treated her as an adjunct of her father. The confidence of the group increased as letter followed letter from Rome. Sending Bryan, a man committed to Anne and Henry, and renowned for his plain talking to the king as much as to lesser mortals, had placed in Rome a source of information quite independent of Wolsey.[23] And it was not only Henry who now received the unvarnished truth; Bryan wrote direct to Anne, although when the news was particularly grim he asked her to consult the king!

> I dare not write unto my cousin Anne the truth of this matter, because I do not know your grace's pleasure, whether I shall do or no; wherefore, if she be angry with me, I must humbly desire your grace to make mine excuse. I have referred to her in her letter all the news to your grace, so your grace may use her in this as you shall think best.[24]

From the start the news was bleak. Bryan had arrived on 14 January, but because of the pope's ill-health he had not even presented his credentials before Gardiner arrived a month later to strengthen the team, and it was another month before they achieved their first substantive session with Clement.[25] Their reports were full of despair. On 20 March Henry read to Tuke, the treasurer of the chamber, the letters which had just arrived from Rome, and Tuke warned Wolsey:

> Mr. Bryan's letter, for as many clauses as the king showed me, which was here and there, as his grace read it, was totally of desperation, affirming plainly that he could not believe the pope would do anything for his grace, with these words added: 'It might well be in his paternoster, but it was nothing in his creed' [i.e. the pope might well pray that Henry would have his problem solved, but he would not commit himself to doing anything about it].[26]

[22] *Cal. S. P. Span.*, *1527-29*, pp. 885-6.
[23] For Bryan's role see *St. Pap.*, vii.166 [*LP*, iv.5481] and above, p. 128.
[24] Ibid., vii.170 [*LP*, iv.5519]; cf. ibid., vii. 167 [*LP*, iv.5481].
[25] Ibid., vii.149 [*LP*, iv.5213]; *LP*, iv.5294, 5315, 5344, 5348.
[26] *St. Pap.*, i.330 [*LP*, iv.5393].

Bryan also communicated from time to time with 'my masters
and fellows of your grace's chamber', and although he was no
doubt discreet, his failure to announce the great breakthrough
could be interpreted by everyone, partisan of Anne or not.[27]
Very soon, too, we find that one of the most brilliant of the king's
advisers, Stephen Gardiner, had swung to Anne's support. A
protégé of Wolsey and noted in August 1527 as a supporter of
Katherine, the future bishop of Winchester had decided, with
that acute political 'nose' which would only desert him on a
couple of occasions in his life, that Anne was going to win.[28] He
wrote in March assuring her of his devotion, and she replied in
phrases typical of the patron to the client: 'I pray God to send
you well to speed . . . so that you would put me to the study, how
to reward your high service. I do trust in God you shall not
repent it.' Anne took the chance, at the same time, to tie up the
rest of the embassy by sending cramp-rings for Gardiner and the
two other envoys (Bryan excepted): 'And have me kindly
recommended to them both, as she that, you may assure them,
will be glad to do them any pleasure which shall be in my
power.'[29]

The one person whom Anne found difficult to motivate
against the cardinal was, ironically, the king himself. Whether
we explain this by, in the event, a well justified scepticism about
Norfolk's ability to succeed if Wolsey failed, or by the habit of
dependence engendered over fifteen years, or by the minister's
unrivalled ability and his proven record of success, Henry was
anxious to cling to his right-hand man. There was certainly a
rumour in January that he was beginning to distrust Wolsey's
promises, and he did keep Norfolk, Suffolk and Rochford more in
the picture.[30] Yet throughout the spring of 1529, Henry and
Wolsey made common cause in an effort to force concessions
from the pope. King and minister were united in the illusion that
the pope was genuinely anxious to help and that he only needed
encouragement. On 6 April they wrote in parallel to the English
envoys to reject the 'desperation' in the reports from Rome, to

---

[27] Ibid., vii.143 [*LP*, iv.5152].
[28] *Cal. S. P. Span.*, *1527–29*, p. 327.
[29] Burnet, *History*, v.444 [*LP*, iv.5422]. Cramp-rings (allegedly so-called
because they were a prophylactic against cramp) were a frequent gift in this
period.
[30] *Cal. S. P. Span.*, *1527–29*, p. 877.

imply lack of zeal and to urge greater efforts, although when Bryan's even gloomier next letter could not resist a suitably expressed 'I told you so', it was Wolsey who had to make apologies on behalf of the king.[31] Every piece of correspondence from Rome, every word, was scrutinized for evidence of papal good intentions.[32] Clement would yield.

All was based on nothing. In January the resident English ambassador at Rome had sent an envoy to explain that the pope would budge no further, and Campeggio had tried again and again to convince both Henry and Wolsey that the pope could not bend the law in their favour, that he was adamant.[33] Clement would not quash the dispensation for Katherine's second marriage. The very idea that the English should expect this offended him deeply, as did their relentless pressure – what Bryan had described as 'first by fair means and afterward by foul'.[34] When eventually letters from Rome did carry conviction, Henry and Wolsey attributed failure entirely to imperial blocking; and they turned on Campeggio, or rather, since they still needed him, on his senior staff, with a joint display of criticism which was only partly engineered by Wolsey to put the blame for his own over-confidence on the pope's deceit.[35] Already, however they had decided on a new tack: to go for a rapid decision on the suit in England. 'The king's highness,' wrote Wolsey, 'is minded for the time to dissemble the matter, and taking as much as may be had and attained there to the benefit of his cause, to proceed in the decision of the same here, by virtue of the commission already granted unto me and my lord legate Campeggio.'[36]

How proud Henry VIII was of his ability to 'dissemble'! Securing a favourable judgement in England would outflank the

---

[31] Burnet, *History*, iv.115–17 [*LP*, iv.5427]; iv.79–92 [*LP*, iv.5428]; *St. Pap.*, vii.169–70 [*LP*, iv.5519]; Burnet, *History*, iv.93 [*LP*, iv.5523]. This last can be dated *c*.9 May and was sent on 13 May: *LP*, iv.5535, 5576.

[32] Ibid., iv.5572 at p. 2461; Burnet, *History*, iv.112–13 [*LP*, iv.5576].

[33] *LP*, iv.5302 [for the date see ibid., iv.5037, 5073], 5535 at p. 2450, 5572 at p. 2461.

[34] Ibid., iv.5447, 5477; *St. Pap.*, vii.169 [*LP*, iv.5519].

[35] The crucial letters were dated 21 Apr., received early May: *St. Pap.*, vii.166–9 [*LP*, iv.5481]; *LP*, iv.5476. For the scene with Campeggio's secretary: ibid., iv.5572 at pp. 2463–4. But Wolsey told Campeggio that the decision to press the pope was Henry's, in spite of his telling him the facts: ibid., iv.5584 at p. 2470.

[36] Burnet, *History*, iv.94 [*LP*, iv.5523]; cf. ibid., iv.108–13 [*LP*, iv.5576]; *LP*, iv.5535 at p. 2450.

emperor's pressure and give the pope just the excuse he was supposedly looking for to help Henry. Confidence was maintained even when news arrived that imperial envoys were pressing Clement to revoke the case to Rome. Henry and Wolsey were sure the pope would never do that, any more than Francis I, who up to that time had stood solidly with them against Charles V, would at the international conference then being planned for Cambrai, make peace with England left out. Suddenly Campeggio found himself rushed into action. A decision was wanted, now![37]

The opening of the legatine court at Blackfriars on 31 May 1529 was, therefore, the latest in a succession of manoeuvres that king and cardinal were confident would give them what they wanted and vindicate Henry's faith in his minister. Few other people were as sure. Campeggio knew he was under papal orders to avoid a decision at all costs.[38] Anne and her allies went on with their preparations against the cardinal, confident that only the miracle of a legatine decision could now save him. The letters from her supporters in Italy kept up an insidious denigration of Wolsey. Ostensibly Campeggio was the target, but there is little doubt who Bryan had in mind when he wrote: 'Whosoever made your grace believe that he [Clement] will do for you in this cause hath not, as I think, done your grace the best service.'[39] On his way to Italy in December, Bryan had already passed on to Henry a warning from Francis I that he had quislings among his advisers.[40] In May, when Sir John Russell was ordered to France as Wolsey's representative and to stiffen the war effort there, he was recalled when actually in process of embarking his horses at Sandwich. Anne Boleyn had reminded the king of Bryan's warning, and had Suffolk despatched to France instead, with secret orders to probe the matter.[41] He did this in a transparent attempt to implicate Wolsey, and although Francis had actually

---

[37] Du Bellay, *Correspondance*, i.14 at pp. 44–8 [*LP*, iv.5702], 15 at pp. 48–51 [*LP*, iv.5701]; *LP*, iv.5681 at pp. 2510–11, 5703, 5710, 5713, 5733.

[38] Ibid., iv.5604.

[39] *St. Pap.*, vii.167 [*LP*, 5481]; cf. *LP*, iv.5518; *St. Pap.*, vii.170 [*LP*, iv.5519].

[40] Bryan's interview with Francis I must have been on the way out, since Suffolk left England while Bryan was still at Rome: *LP*, iv.5585, 5606.

[41] Du Bellay, *Correspondance*, i.4 at p. 14 [*LP*, iv.5541]; *St. Pap.*, vii.182–4 [*LP*, iv.5635]. Anne's response is made clear by du Bellay, *Correspondance*, i.17 at p. 58 [*LP*, iv.5742 is inaccurate]. Suffolk had arrived by 18 May: *LP*, iv.5562.

meant Campeggio and spoke well of the minister's loyalty, he did under pressure add the innuendo (or so Suffolk reported) that Wolsey had 'marvellous intelligence with the pope, and in Rome and also with Cardinal Campeggio. Wherefore, seeing that he hath such intelligence with them which have not minded to advance your matter, he [Francis] thinketh it shall be the more need for your grace to have better regard to your said affair.'[42] There was a second motive, too, behind the sending of Suffolk: to have a partisan of Anne Boleyn to represent England at the peace conference which was beginning to assemble in Flanders, to put him in a position 'to do "a cardinal of York at Amiens"'.[43] Wolsey had intended to go himself, if the king had been in favour, but he had to content himself with hamstringing Suffolk's instructions and precipitating his early return.

When Brandon got back in the first week of July, he found that Anne's faction was ready for the showdown.[44] His wife's humanist schoolmaster John Palsgrave, who also had links with the duke of Richmond and his mentor the duke of Norfolk, had been called up to prepare a propaganda pamphlet mocking Wolsey's period in office as a time of pride, waste, autocratic repression and ineffective tinkering.[45] Lord Darcy, one of the principal supports of the previous reign who considered that he had been very badly treated by the cardinal, had provided the political planning – the immediate arrest of Wolsey and his agents, the impounding of their papers and a thorough investigation of his administration: precisely the sort of coup that had destroyed Empson and Dudley in 1509.[46] The points to be scrutinized were listed in detail, the texts drafted of proclamations inviting complaints, all with the obvious end of securing a parliamentary act of attainder. The only refinement Suffolk needed to add when he got back to England was to have his own men keeping watch on the posts going across the Channel. All that seemed to be lacking was the occasion for Anne to 'prove' to Henry that the suspicions about Wolsey that had been fed to him were justified.

---

[42] *St. Pap.*, vii.183 [*LP*, iv.5635].

[43] Du Bellay, *Correspondance*, i.17 at p. 58. The reference is to the notorious ostentation shown (and success gained) by Wolsey at the conference with Francis I at Amiens in 1527.

[44] *LP*, iv.5723, 5741, 5771.

[45] Ibid., iv.5750. For this highly individual character see ibid., ii.295, 3486, 3659, 3831, pp. 1459, 1460; iii.3680, 3681; iv.39, 955, 4560, 5459, 5806–9.

[46] Ibid., iv.5749; cf. Guy, *Public Career of More*, pp. 106–7, 206–7.

Deprived of royal favour, the cardinal would then be 'naked to his enemies'.[47]

That occasion appeared to be the fiasco at Blackfriars. Anne herself was close enough to Henry during the hearings there to deliver the *coup de grâce*, so close, indeed, that du Bellay, the French ambassador, confidently expected to hear that she was pregnant.[48] Katherine of Aragon had no doubt that a failure of the legatine hearing would provide the opportunity to break the bond between king and cardinal, and Edward Hall certainly states that it was the failure there which convinced Henry of Wolsey's double dealing.[49] This allowed the attack prepared by Anne and the rest to go in, and Hall tells of a 'book' detailing the charges against the minister and signed by thirty-four of the council, which was presented to Henry before he left for his summer progress, that is, between 31 July and 4 August; and it is the case that an integral part of the scheme was put in hand on 9 August, with the issue of writs to summon parliament.[50] But then nothing more happened; the attack stalled, or, rather, Wolsey had blocked it. The day the Blackfriars court had closed, he had moved to conciliate Rochford and the king with what each appreciated most, money.

The previous February the cardinal had exchanged the bishopric of Durham (which he held in addition to the arch-bishopric of York) for the richest English see, Winchester. This had left the revenues of Durham at the king's disposal, and in the last week of July he had granted them to Anne's father. Wolsey thereupon threw in the four months' income due to him for the period October 1528 to February 1529, saying that he had always regarded that as belonging to the king and offering to expedite payment to Rochford.[51] Wolsey's indispensability rapidly re-asserted itself, not only in the management of the divorce where he

[47] Wolsey's own phrase.

[48] Du Bellay, *Correspondance*, 11 at p. 40 [*LP*, iv.5679].

[49] *Cal. S. P. Span.*, *1529–30*, p. 133; Hall, *Chronicle*, p. 758; cf. du Bellay, *Correspondance*, 7 at p. 19 [*LP*, iv.5582]. Gardiner also warned the envoys at Rome of the danger to Wolsey, though this could have been a diplomatic tactic: *LP*, iv.5715.

[50] Hall, *Chronicle*, pp. 758–9. The 'book' could have been the final version of Darcy's charges. Henry intended to leave Greenwich on 2 Aug., and had left by 4 Aug.: *LP*, iv.5965, 5825. The decision to issue the writs for a parliament was clearly made before the close roll entry date of 9 Aug.: ibid., iv.5837.

[51] Ibid., iv.5816. The fact that the grant to Rochford is called a (signed) bill shows that it was very recent.

was still the key man in relations with Rome, but also in diplomacy, and all the evidence suggests that the summer vacation of 1529 began and promised to continue in the normal way, with the king and minister separated until Michaelmas and communicating by letter. It is true that Henry called off an intended visit to Wolsey's country home at The More near Rickmansworth during which the cardinal would have stayed ten miles away at his abbey of St Albans, but this was for fear of the sweat – a motive which, given his terror the previous year, one may well credit – and he went instead to Wolsey's other house, Tittenhanger, which had kept him safe in the 1528 epidemic and was even nearer St Albans.[52] When drafting his plans Darcy had noted that, if Wolsey were pushed to answer the complaints against him, 'he clearly doubts not, as he and his affirms, but that he hath the guile and understanding to discharge him of all this light flea-biting or flies-stinging, and yet so to handle all matters that he shall reign still in more authority than ever he did, and all to quake and repent that hath meddled against him.'[53] It began to look as if he was right.

There was, however, when Henry and Wolsey separated for the summer progress of 1529, one change from the year before. Anne Boleyn was now the cardinal's enemy. There would be no more of the courteous communications and elegant gifts of 1528. Instead, as Wolsey well knew, Anne would have the field to herself and her supporters, who were dedicated to bringing him down and who now had a ready welcome at court – Norfolk, Suffolk, and particularly Rochford, whose duties as chaperon made him almost 'counsellor in residence'. Increasingly, the letters from the royal household show that Henry was listening to other advice; Wolsey was no longer able to monopolize him. As the end of August approached, the cardinal was having to wait for council decisions and was even reduced to asking for instructions.[54] Yet progresses did end, and Wolsey could know that if he sat tight, the autumn would come and with it the chance to work his magic with the king once again; he could still prove himself too strong for them.

But then, with a month or six weeks still to go, the cardinal began to make mistakes, mistakes which handed his enemies the

---

[52] Ellis, *Letters*, 3 i.345 [*LP*, iv.5825]; cf. *LP*, iv.4428.
[53] Ibid., iv.5749 at p. 2549.
[54] *St. Pap.*, i.337 [*LP*, iv.5864]; *LP*, iv.5865.

issue that they had been looking for in order not merely to curb his authority but to destroy him completely. His own errors did what the carefully planned coup in July had failed to do, and, incredibly, these were in the two areas of his greatest competence – his understanding of the king and his handling of diplomacy. Cardinal Wolsey was not deprived of royal favour following the abortive divorce hearing at Blackfriars, or even after the aristocratic attack on his position which followed that fiasco. He lost Henry's confidence from late August onwards by miscalculating the king's mood and by mishandling the Treaty of Cambrai, in which Francis I totally deceived him and caused him, in turn, to mislead his master.

Exploring the diplomatic maze of 1529 would take us too far from Anne Boleyn herself, but a brief account will reveal how it enabled her and her faction to bring him down. Wolsey had for months recognized the probability of peace between Francis I and Charles V, and as early as March 1529 had begun to behave again as the doyen of European summit diplomacy, his favourite role, and one which opened up the possibility that Anglo-French co-operation might force the emperor to abandon Katherine of Aragon as part of the price for peace.[55] Wolsey and Henry were agreed on this approach, but the decision in early May to go for a legatine trial in England posed the question of priorities, and the cardinal found to his horror that the king believed that Blackfriars took precedence over international trouble-shooting.[56] Wolsey knew the odds against a decision there and that the only hope was to keep up diplomatic and military pressure to persuade the pope to oblige Henry, but he had to acquiesce.

The consequence was, first, that Russell had to be sent to France instead of Wolsey, only to be recalled, as we have seen, at the insistence of Anne, in favour of Suffolk. Then when Wolsey had managed to neutralize that embassy and, in the process, engineer the despatch to Paris of another enemy, Francis Bryan, he found to his horror that his requests to have the peace conference delayed until after the Blackfriars verdict were being ignored by the French, thanks in part (though he was not aware of this) to the obstructive tactics of the French ambassador in

---

[55] *Cal. S. P. Span.*, *1527–29*, p. 927.
[56] *LP*, iv.5700, 5710, 5712; du Bellay, *Correspondance*, 17 at p. 58 [*LP*, iv.5742].

London, du Bellay, whom he imagined was his firm ally.[57] Even
then with the negotiations at Cambrai beginning on 5 July,
Henry still refused to let Wolsey go, sending instead Bishop
Tunstall and Thomas More, and the cardinal had to waste his
time at Blackfriars while 175 miles away Europe's future was
being settled between France and the Empire, with the English
envoys (once they had arrived) kept in ignorance and on the
sidelines.[58] Something of Wolsey's frustration became evident in
an attempt he made in July to embarrass Suffolk (and Anne).
The duke's probing of Francis I on the cardinal's loyalty had
been under a strict pledge of secrecy, but Francis told du Bellay
and the ambassador let something of this slip to Wolsey, who
promptly complained to Henry that Suffolk had maligned him to
the French king.[59] The king, unable to admit publicly his own
complicity, had to side with the minister until a fortunate (or
perhaps wise) indisposition kept Suffolk away from court and,
with the simultaneous absence of du Bellay, made it difficult for
Wolsey to make more of the affair.

The Treaty of Cambrai was signed on 3 August 1529, but this
did not mean the end of Wolsey's nightmare. He had been forced
to stand by powerless as the French had duped him.[60] Henry
now faced the situation that he had most feared: a pope who was
the emperor's man; the ending of the pressure that had kept
Charles out of Italy; and the revocation of the divorce suit to a
hostile Rome. How could Wolsey now rescue his king and his
own credit? The answer seemed to be to exploit the detailed
implementation of the Cambrai accords. The French needed the
English, for without the rescheduling of French and imperial
debts to England (an integral part of the Cambrai settlement),
Francis I stood no chance of raising the money to redeem his two
sons, who were hostages in the emperor's hands. In spite of a
boast to Campeggio in June that England would come to terms
with Charles V irrespective of France, the cardinal recognized
that there was a danger that if the French and the imperialists
ratified the Treaty of Cambrai bilaterally, Henry might be left to
face Katherine's nephew unsupported.[61] Nevertheless he believed

---

[57] See above, pp. 140–1. Du Bellay, *Correspondance*, 17 at pp. 58–60 [*LP*, iv.5742].
[58] Ibid., 16 at pp. 52–3 [*LP*, iv.5741]; *LP*, iv.5733.
[59] Du Bellay, *Correspondance*, 22 at pp. 64–5 [*LP*, iv.5862]. See above, pp. 140–1.
[60] Ibid., 17 at p. 58 [*LP*, iv.5742].
[61] *LP*, iv.5713, 5893.

that France could be pushed to give England more support, and
in particular to do more for the king's divorce – and, no doubt,
for Wolsey.[62]

Wolsey's notion of keeping the French under pressure enjoyed
considerable support during August because of the suspicious
behaviour of the ambassador, who pressed to have the treaty
implemented by Henry but failed again and again to provide
him a full text of it.[63] Wolsey did his best to indicate where such
information as London had, revealed provisions less advan-
tageous than he himself had negotiated at Amiens two years
before, and after du Bellay saw the king on 29 August, Henry
expressed grave doubts about the French demands.[64] When, the
next day, he examined advice from Wolsey which raised considerable suspicion about his supposed allies, he was 'much
kindled and waxed warm and thought himself not well handled
by them'.[65]

The king had however, received Wolsey's letter late in the day
after coming in from hunting; he ordered an overnight check of
Wolsey's detailed criticisms, against the text of the Treaty of
Madrid (to which the Cambrai accords frequently alluded), and
the agreement the cardinal had himself made with Francis I at
Amiens in 1527.[66] Rochford and Gardiner were in attendance,
and, fatal to Wolsey, the task was given to them. The outcome
was that the next day Henry changed his mind and his policy;
full concessions would be made to France, and Wolsey was told
that he was allowing resentment at the Cambrai débâcle to cloud
his judgement.[67] The true reason was that any coolness towards
France could be represented as risking the chance of a quick
divorce. If he was to get free from Katherine, Henry needed
Francis, and that took priority above everything. Du Bellay was
thus able to report on 1 September that he and his brother had
fully satisfied most English doubts, that Norfolk, Suffolk and
Rochford were in high favour, and that Wolsey was now clearly
on the way out.[68] And he was right, for the cardinal made

[62] Ibid., iv.5801, 5891.
[63] Ibid., iv.5881; du Bellay, *Correspondance*, 24 at pp. 70–1, 26 at pp. 73–4
[*LP*, iv.5911, 5912].
[64] *LP*, iv.5882, 5883.
[65] *St. Pap.*, i.340, 342 [*LP*, iv.5885, 5894].
[66] Ibid., i.342 [*LP*, iv.5890].
[67] Ibid., i.342–3 [*LP*, iv.5894]. Gardiner quoted the tag: 'we can more easily
regret the past than put it right.'
[68] Du Bellay, *Correspondance*, 24 at pp. 70, 72 [*LP*, iv.5911].

matters worse by challenging Gardiner on the change in direction and making his resentment plain.[69] His erstwhile protégé replied, vindicating his own good faith and reading back to the cardinal his own recipe for success with Henry: 'If your grace had been here and seen how the king's highness took it [you] would rather have studied how by some benign interpretation to have made the best of that which is past remedy than to have persisted in the blaming of not observation of covenants on the French part.'[70] Wolsey excused himself to Gardiner by return, but the slide was on.[71]

Only one thing could have saved Wolsey, and that was access to Henry in person, but while he was trying to work through the unreliable Gardiner, Norfolk, Suffolk and Rochford as the courtiers in favour and on the spot simply took over the execution of policy, while Anne conducted an open campaign of character assassination.[72] All Wolsey's anxiety to go to Cambrai in June and July was now represented as an attempt to delay the Boleyn marriage. He was also accused of having been for years in the pocket of Francis I's mother and mentor, Louise of Savoy; even Suffolk's ignominious retreat when only fifty miles from capturing Paris in 1523 was now attributed to Wolsey withholding the necessary cash at her behest![73] Sometime in the second week of September Wolsey took the plunge and asked directly for an interview with Henry in order to impart information too sensitive for a letter, normally an infallible way to touch the suspicious Henry. But although the appointment was arranged, he was told to indicate in writing the subject he wished to raise.[74] Henry was not going to trust blindly again – or was it Anne and her allies determined not to be caught out?

Whether or not Wolsey did see Henry as a result of this letter is not clear. There are two versions of events. One is most fully worked out in Cavendish, but has contemporary support from the newly arrived Chapuys.[75] According to this Wolsey was

[69] This is clear from the following.
[70] RO, SP1/55 f. 120 [*LP*, iv.5918].
[71] *LP*, iv.5883, 5923.
[72] *Cal. S. P. Span., 1529–30*, p. 195.
[73] Du Bellay, *Correspondance*, 43 at pp. 109–10 [*LP*, iv.6019].
[74] *St. Pap.*, i.344 [*LP*, iv.5936]. The date of the proposed interview has been lost through damage to the MS.
[75] Cavendish, *Wolsey*, pp. 92–7; *Cal. S. P. Span., 1529–30*, pp. 214, 235, 257; cf. Hall, *Chronicle*, p. 759.

refused access to court until Campeggio insisted that he should accompany him when he came to take his leave of the king, but even then the two legates were told to come without pomp and ceremony. The date chosen was Sunday 19 September and the place, the king's hunting lodge at Grafton near what is now Milton Keynes, a house so small that half the court had to sleep at Richard Empson's old house at Easton Neston three miles away.[76] Concerned that the cardinal's magic might still work on the king, Suffolk arranged for only Campeggio to be given lodgings at Grafton. Norris, the groom of the stool, lent Wolsey his room to change in, and the cardinal's supporters flocked in to welcome and warn him of the latest situation. Then the two legates were called to the presence chamber, packed with every courtier who could find a place, with polite greetings, sincere and insincere, all the way. Henry then entered, and the old magic did begin to work again. Raising the kneeling Wolsey, the king took him to one of the great window embrasures, made him put his hat on and engaged in a long and earnest conversation. The climax came when Henry produced against Wolsey one of his own letters, saying 'how can that be? Is this not your own hand?', only to be given a full and, as far as the observers could tell, entirely satisfactory explanation.

Dinner then followed with Anne and her supporters more than worried. Norfolk dined with Wolsey and tried to make him angry. Anne herself, entertaining Henry to dinner in her own chamber, tried to make *him* angry:

> 'Sir', quoth she, 'Is it not a marvellous thing to consider what debt and danger the cardinal hath brought you in, with all your subjects?' 'How so, sweetheart?' quoth the king. 'Forsooth, Sir', quoth she, 'There is not a man within all your realm worth £5 but he hath indebted you unto him by his means' (meaning by a loan that the king had but late of his subjects). 'Well, well', quoth the king, 'As for that there is in him no blame, for I know that matter better than you or any other'.

Even this did not discourage Anne, or so the attendants who reported the conversation retailed:

[76] *Cal. S. P. Span.*, *1529–30*, p. 222.

'Nay, Sir', quoth she, 'Besides all that what things hath he wrought within this realm to your great slander and dishonour. There is never a nobleman within this realm that if he had done but half so much as he hath done but he were well worthy to lose his head. If my lord of Norfolk, my lord of Suffolk, my lord my father, or any other noble person within your realms had done much less than he but they should have lost their heads [bef]ore this'. 'Why then I perceive', quoth the king, 'Ye are not the cardinal's friend'. 'Forsooth, Sir then', quoth she, 'I have no cause nor any other man that loveth your grace. No more have your grace if ye consider well his doings'.

Despite this barrage, Henry went back to the presence chamber and had another long, private conversation with Wolsey, followed by an even more secret *tête à tête* with him in the privy chamber until bedtime, when the king told him to return early next day to continue their discussion. So Wolsey set out for Easton, and there he was joined by Gardiner, either to find out what he could for Anne, or else mend his relationship with his old master. When, however, Wolsey got to Grafton the next morning, he found the plan changed. Anne was going riding with Henry to a new park three miles away, and had quickly arranged a picnic dinner to ensure that the cardinals would be gone before the king returned.

It is a good story. It is psychologically right; it illustrates to perfection the importance of access to the monarch – and the ability to deny access; it ought to be true. Unfortunately it does not square with the report of Thomas Alward who, like Cavendish, accompanied Wolsey to Grafton.[77] Alward had certainly heard the rumour that his master's days of power were numbered, but he himself said he had seen nothing out of the ordinary in the regular exchange of letters and messages between the cardinal and the court that vacation, and he seems to suggest that Wolsey attended court as much as would be expected. In particular Alward noticed nothing unusual in his master's reception at Grafton, either by the king or by the courtiers, and nothing strange in lodgings at Easton for, he says, both Wolsey and Campeggio. His letter confirms Wolsey's lengthy sessions with

[77] Ellis, *Letters*, 1 i.307–10 [*LP*, iv.5953]. The reading 'Grene[wich]' by Ellis and *LP* is incorrect.

Henry on the Sunday, but gives no support to the story of a change of plan for Monday. According to him, Wolsey sat in council with Henry all morning, and the king did not go hunting until after dinner; even then Wolsey did not leave until after dark. As for Suffolk, Rochford, Brian Tuke and Gardiner, Alward had heard stories but had noted 'as much observance and humility to my lord's grace as I ever saw them do', although he did add, 'What they bear in their hearts I know not.' Clearly not the most sensitive of men, and one, also, wanting to believe that things were as usual, but unlike Cavendish he was writing five days, not almost thirty years, after the event. Regretfully we must discard the brilliantly opportunistic ride and picnic, and assume that if Henry did go out riding with Anne that day it was after he had completed business with the two legates.

On this reading, Grafton was not the victory tradition has given to Anne, but as a successful recovery by Wolsey it was short-lived. The day before, du Bellay had noted that the cardinal was counting on the support at court of certain people 'made by him' – undoubtedly Gardiner, and possibly Heneage and Tuke too – who had already turned their coats.[78] They would defer to his face and observe the proprieties, but they were unwilling to support him otherwise. Meanwhile at court Anne was ever closer to Henry. Now the king even needed her to start the hunt, almost like the goddess Diana![79]

Wolsey retained office and chaired council meetings in the normal way as late as 3 and 6 October, but on the first day of the law term, 9 October, he found himself deserted in his own court and charged in king's bench with praemunire, that is, the offence of introducing (in this case by accepting the office of papal legate) an illegal foreign authority into England.[80] A week or so later he was dismissed as chancellor, and on 22 October he pleaded guilty to the charge, surrendered all his property to Henry and threw himself on the king's mercy.[81] As du Bellay (who was still in touch with Wolsey) explained to Montmorency, the constable of France, he had been offered his chance with

---

[78] There is a curious letter of 29 Aug. in which Tuke provides an encomium for Gardiner: *St. Pap.*, i.339 [*LP*, iv.5885].

[79] *Cal. S. P. Span., 1529–30*, p. 234.

[80] Ibid., pp. 276–7; Cavendish, *Wolsey*, p. 97; *LP*, iv.6035; du Bellay, *Correspondance*, 37 at pp. 91–2 [*LP*, iv.5982].

[81] Either 17 or 18 Oct.: Guy, *Public Career of More*, p. 31 n.179; *LP*, iv.6017.

either king or parliament and had no doubt which threatened less even though Anne had removed all hope of a recovery at court by making Henry promise never to receive him; there would be no more Graftons.[82] How wise she was is clear from the evidence that Henry continued for many months to feel that Wolsey had value, and even to communicate with him in secret. Meanwhile the lovers went to inspect his Westminster house, York Place, gloated over the treasures he had lost and decided that there they would build the palace of their dreams.[83]

All the faction opposed to the cardinal rejoiced, and began to argue about the spoils. Chapuys, quite rightly, congratulated Norfolk as the man who would be the king's new chief counsellor.[84] Yet the fall of Wolsey was first and foremost Anne's success. Without her they would not have made it. Wolsey himself explained his decision not to fight the praemunire on the grounds that it was impossible to challenge her influence, 'a continual serpentine enemy about the king'.[85] Anne had made the difference; Anne now had the triumph. Du Bellay reported: 'The duke of Norfolk is made chief of the council and in his absence the duke of Suffolk, and above everyone Mademoiselle Anne.'[86] He made it clear, indeed, that Anne and her father were determined to be recognized as enjoying and deserving the king's highest favour. Even before Wolsey's fall Thomas Boleyn was seeking to impress his value on the French by deliberately frustrating the agreement du Bellay was trying to negotiate: 'at least he is the one who is keeping the dance going, expressly against the dukes and the cardinal of York whom I had so convinced that I thought I had gained my objective.'[87] What was needed was a letter from Louise of Savoy acknowledging Boleyn's new standing. With still no such letter of greeting to hand, du Bellay wrote again a week later. Anne Boleyn and her father were continuing their obstruction in order to demonstrate that they were as zealous in the king's affairs as Wolsey had been, and because they saw that Henry himself was already

---

[82] Du Bellay, *Correspondance*, 43, 44 at pp. 110–12 [*LP*, iv.6011, 6018].
[83] Ibid., 46 at p. 115 [*LP*, iv.6030]; *Cal. S. P. Span., 1529–30*, p. 303 [*LP*, iv.6026].
[84] Ibid., pp. 295–6 [*LP*, iv.6026].
[85] Cavendish, *Wolsey*, p. 137.
[86] Du Bellay, *Correspondance*, 44 at p. 113 [*LP*, iv.6019].
[87] Ibid., 38 at p. 94 [*LP*, iv.5983].

inclined against the ambassador's proposal. They were well aware, he noted, 'that one of the principal devices which the cardinal of York had to maintain his influence (given the nature of his master) was to heap praise on his opinions.'[88]

Du Bellay was now even more pointed about the relative importance of Anne and Thomas. During the discussions,

[Boleyn] allowed everything to be said, and then came and suggested the complete opposite, defending his position without budging, as though he wanted to show me that he was not pleased that anyone should have failed to pay court to the lady [Anne], and also to make me accept that what he had said before is true, that is, that all the rest have no influence except what it pleases the lady to allow them, and that is gospel truth. And because of this he wanted with words and deeds to beat down their opinions before my eyes.[89]

The ambassador's firm advice to Paris was to flatter Boleyn pretensions and in particular to lionize the family's *petit prince*, George, who was just going on his first diplomatic mission. The arrival at the French court of such a young man as ambassador would probably provide a few laughs, but the new realities of power had to be recognized.[90]

[88] Ibid., 41*bis*, at pp. 104–5.
[89] Ibid., 41*bis*, at p. 105.
[90] Ibid., 41*bis*, at p. 105; *LP*, iv.5996.

8

Stalemate, 1529–32

~⟞⟝~

WHAT PUZZLED Henry VIII's European contemporaries most was that he went about his divorce the hard way. Wanting Anne as a wife instead of a mistress was eccentric in the first place, but determination to bludgeon the pope into guaranteeing in advance not only the outcome he wanted but also his own distinctive interpretation of the law, was unprecedented. Pressure on the pope – yes, that was expected; but 'the urgency used' by Henry was a principal cause of his humiliation at Blackfriars.[1] Even then the king would not resign himself to the fact that he would have to wait for the pope to adjudicate, and swallow the ruling if he did not like it. The struggle began again. Henry had, it is true, good reason to distrust Clement VII, but there was more than that behind the enormous effort set in train to force the pope to admit that in allowing Henry to marry Katherine his predecessor Julius II had exceeded his powers.

Part of the explanation is that Henry was passionately and openly in love with Anne. In his second despatch to Charles V, written after only a week in England and without needing to go to court, Chapuys reported: 'The king's affection for La Bolaing increases daily. It is so great just now that it can hardly be greater; such is the intimacy and familiarity in which they live at present.'[2] Henry's favour to the Boleyns was publicly demonstrated seven weeks after Wolsey's dismissal, when on 8 December Rochford was not only raised to the coveted earldom of Ormonde but created earl of Wiltshire in addition, a title

[1] *LP*, v.App.26.
[2] *Cal. S. P. Span.*, p. 196.

previously associated with the Stafford family and the duke of Buckingham's brother. George Boleyn thereby became Viscount Rochford and, soon after his return from the embassy to Paris, a nobleman of the privy chamber.[3] At the same time as Wiltshire, two others of the anti-Wolsey faction were similarly promoted, becoming the earls of Sussex and Huntingdon respectively. The next day there was a grand celebration to which, if we are to believe Chapuys, the king's sister Mary and both the dowager duchess and the current duchess of Norfolk (the highest-ranking noblewomen in the land) were summoned to watch Anne taking the place of the queen at Henry's side.[4]

There were, too, the strains the couple had to face. Katherine of Aragon still lived at court, formally recognized as queen by the king no less than the rest of the royal household, a permanent reproach to Henry and an irritant to Anne.[5] On the whole it was Anne who coped best, allowing Katherine's mixture of martyr-dom and complaint to drive Henry into her company. Thus on St Andrew's Day, a week before the promotion of the earls, Katherine had turned on Henry after dining with him, taxing him with unkindness and private neglect.[6] Defending himself, he boasted that the opinions on his case which were being collected were so weighty that the decision must go in his favour at Rome, and if it did not he would 'denounce the pope as a heretic and marry whom he pleased'. Katherine poured scorn on his argu-ments and Henry walked out in a huff. Anne did not fail to take advantage of the opening:

> Did I not tell you that whenever you disputed with the queen she was sure to have the upper hand? I see that some fine morning you will succumb to her reasoning and that you will cast me off. I have been waiting long and might in the meanwhile have contracted some advantageous marriage, out of which I might have had issue, which is the greatest consolation in this world. But, alas! Farewell to my time and youth spent to no purpose at all.

Even though Henry hoped to pacify her by placing her at his side

---

[3] Returned from Paris mid-Feb., in post by 21 Dec. 1530: ibid., pp. 467, 854.

[4] Ibid., p. 366; cf. *St. Pap.*, vii.370 [*LP*, v.1025].

[5] Cf. the comments on the polite formality of Henry and Katherine: *Cal. S. P. Ven.*, *1527–33*, 584.

[6] Ibid., 224.

at the 9 December banquet, it seems that Anne was careful not to appear at the Christmas festivities at Greenwich which Henry celebrated with Katherine 'in great triumph'.[7] The tactic worked. On 31 December Henry sent Walter Walsh, groom of the privy chamber, to Anne with a gift of £110, while the imperial ambassador noted early in February 1530 that Henry was spending all his time at York Place with Anne, leaving Katherine alone at Richmond for their longest separation yet.[8]

The story of Anne Boleyn's outburst on St Andrew's Day is recorded in one of Eustace Chapuys' letters, and it is a problem for anyone studying Anne Boleyn that from the autumn of 1529 the sheer immediacy and commitment of the ambassador's reports begin to impose his view of events and personality. We would, however, be wrong to accept his picture of Henry as merely the besotted victim of a shrewd and calculating harpy whom Wolsey was to stigmatize as 'the midnight crow'.[9] Irrespective of his passion for Anne, the frustrations and obstruction which the king was subjected to were bringing to the surface far more significant feelings that belonged to the core of his own self-awareness, his personal identity. What was going on was revealing him to be less than the king God had made him. The drive to marry Anne was thus not only an attempt to satisfy his emotions and desires, it was a way to vindicate his kingship.

As early as 1515, the crisis in Church–state relations which is known in history as 'the Hunne affair' had seen Henry publicly intervene to back the judicial ruling that canons enacted by the pope which were not demonstrably based on divine law were only admissible in England by prior royal approval: 'By order and sufferance of God we are king of England and kings of England in time past have never had any superior but God only. . . . Consent to your desire more than our progenitors have done in time past we will not.'[10] Although the king then still recognized traditional Church liberties and the accepted exclusion of the crown from spiritual matters, he was already sensitive over what he defined as 'spiritual'.[11] With the long frustration of the

[7] Ibid., 241; Hall, *Chronicle*, p. 768.

[8] Nicolas, *Privy Purse*, p. 13; *Cal. S. P. Span., 1529–30*, p. 446.

[9] Cavendish, *Wolsey*, p. 137.

[10] Robert Keilway, *Reports d'Ascuns Cases* (1688), f. 185; J. A. Guy, 'Henry VIII and the *praemunire* manoeuvres of 1530–31', in *EHR*, 97 (1982), 497.

[11] Cf. E. W. Ives, 'Crime, sanctuary and royal authority under Henry VIII', in *On the Laws and Customs of England*, ed. M. S. Arnold et al. (Chapel Hill, Carolina, 1981), pp. 299–303.

divorce suit, part of Henry's mind became increasingly doubtful about the extent to which a pope could tell a king, a man appointed directly by God, what he could or could not do. He might campaign with a frantic intensity for papal approval of his divorce, but casual remarks and speculation in the course of private conversation showed that more and more the king was beginning to question the whole status of the pope's authority in his 'great matter'. The threats made to Clement VII that England would withdraw allegiance from Rome, or appeal over the pope's head to a general council of the Church, were far more serious than the huffing and puffing which his holiness and, it seems, Henry's own men took them to be. In a world in which all orthodox Western Christians accepted that Jesus Christ had, by a specific act on a known historical occasion, delegated power over the Church to St Peter the first bishop of Rome, the possibility that this power was not given in that way and handed on to sucessive popes was to most men inconceivable. Yet, increasingly, not to Henry VIII of England. Anne Boleyn, and his determination to marry her, corresponded to something deep in the king's psychology.

Eustace Chapuys and other Catholic writers at the time and since have, therefore, been wrong to suggest that it was the advent of Anne Boleyn which made Henry begin to think these radical thoughts. She certainly provided them with a ready and discreditable explanation for the change in a king who in 1521 wrote the apparently pro-papal *Assertio Septem Sacramentorum*, but who later became ready, even eager, to butcher anyone who persisted in upholding the thousand-year-old Christian conviction that the pope of Rome was head of the Church. Yet the intense preoccupation with what it meant to be a king antedates Henry's interest in Anne Boleyn by many years, and the changes which made the Reformation were less unprecedented novelties than extensions beyond traditional boundaries of convictions long held by the king. The result was revolution, but a revolution produced more by writing out the independence of the Church than by writing in royal authority. This is not to say that in 1529 Henry VIII had grasped the 1532 principle that he was 'Supreme Head of the Church of England' – there was still a long way to go before that. It is, however, correct to say that many of the raw ingredients for that concept were already present in the king's mind and personality, and that the heat of adversity was beginning to act as a catalyst.

To all this, the new regime which replaced Wolsey had nothing agreed to contribute. The object of the new men had been to topple Wolsey; they had not been concerned to offer Henry a new way out of his matrimonial dilemma. Perhaps there had been some feeling that a parliament might offer a way forward, but if so, nobody knew what that was, and in the intentions of Norfolk and the others the principal purpose of calling the session had been to destroy Wolsey.[12] That, indeed, had been the one cause which held them together and they grew terrified when it became clear at the beginning of December that the king would not permit a parliamentary bill of attainder, and showed every sign that he would bring the cardinal back into government.[13] Norfolk did his best to keep Henry and the former minister apart, but he had to yield to the king and to the cardinal's support at court, and permit him to be pardoned and restored to royal favour on 12 February, retaining the arch-bishopric of York and a pension of 1000 marks from the see of Winchester, plus over £6000 in chattels returned by the king, which made him at least as wealthy as the duke![14] By May the council was widely known to be discussing the need to bring him back to run things, and Wolsey was doing everything to recruit support. Norfolk began to alternate between vindictive fright and sycophantic self-preservation, as he faced the problem of what to do if Henry did bring Wolsey back into government. It was ominous that by the autumn the king was making trenchant comments on the incapacity of his new advisers.[15]

The one person who kept her nerve in all this was Anne. It was thanks only to her that Wolsey's 'hinderers and enemies' retained the initiative and were able always to count on having 'time with the king before his friends'.[16] Wolsey had recognized this from the start. He wrote to his agent Thomas Cromwell soon after his surrender: 'If the displeasure of my lady Anne be somewhat assuaged as I pray God the same may be, then it should [be devised] that by some convenient mean she be further laboured [for] this is the only help and remedy. All possible means [must be attempted for the] attaining of her favour'; and

---

[12] Du Bellay, *Correspondance*, 46 at p. 115 [*LP*,iv.6030].
[13] *Cal. S. P. Span.*, *1529–30*, p. 368; and above p. 157[12].
[14] Ibid., pp. 449–50, 469; *LP*, iv.6094, 6181–2, 6262, 6411, 6436, 6447.
[15] Ibid., iv.6579, 6688; *Cal. S. P. Span.*, *1529–30*, pp. 630, 819; cf. *Cal. S. P. Ven.*, *1527–33*, 637: 'Everyday I miss the cardinal of York.'
[16] *LP*, iv.6112.

when he fell ill in January 1530, he played on the king's genuine concern to extract a message of sympathy from Anne.[17] She was, however, only superficially won over and, according to Chapuys, was more interested in whether or not Wolsey was genuinely ill, or merely milking the king's good nature.[18] Her response to the news that Wolsey had been pardoned was to lash out at Norfolk for caving in so abjectly; she cold-shouldered the cardinal's supporters at court and a letter from him in May, even though brought by one of her own faction, was met only with politeness and the message that she 'will not promise to speak to the king for you'.[19] At the same time Anne was making it clear to the French, Wolsey's strongest supporters, that she could do more for their interests than he ever would.[20]

Perhaps this failure to regain Anne Boleyn's favour explains why Wolsey in the latter part of 1530 changed direction and began to work for a *rapprochement* with Katherine, Charles V and Rome. The result was that by October preparation for a counter-coup was well advanced, and the signal was to be the arrival of a papal edict ordering Henry to leave Anne. Since the duke of Norfolk was for the moment away from court, Anne and her father had to move directly to forestall this disaster.[21] She whipped up the king's anger against such presumption on the part of Clement and treated Henry to a scene, or a series of scenes, which reduced him to tears. She brought out again her wasted youth and the reputation she had risked for Henry; she would leave him. In the end, Henry could only pacify her by agreeing to move against Wolsey. Even Anne, of course, could not have urged Henry to arrest Wolsey without offering some colourable excuse. What this was is not known in detail – the cardinal died on 29 November 1530 on the way to interrogation – but it was certainly a revelation of Wolsey's recent dealings with Rome and, perhaps, with Francis I and the emperor also. The most likely source is a deliberate leak to Anne or her father by a French ambassador concerned to prevent a swing back by England towards an imperial alliance.[22] Chapuys certainly

---

[17] *St. Pap.*, i.352 [*LP*, iv.6114]; Cavendish, *Wolsey*, p. 121.
[18] *Cal. S. P. Span.*, *1529–30*, p. 450.
[19] Ibid., p. 449; *LP*, iv.6076.
[20] Ibid., iv.6290; *Cal. S. P. Span.*, *1529–30*, pp. 436, 630, 711, 721.
[21] Ibid., p. 819. Walsh left to arrest Wolsey on 1 Nov. 1530. For Norfolk's absence and recall on 29 Oct.: ibid., p. 788.
[22] L. R. Gardiner, 'Further news of Cardinal Wolsey's end', in *BIHR*, 57.99–107; *LP*, iv.6720; *St. Pap.*, vii.211 [*LP*, iv.6733].

suspected that the surprisingly dismissive reaction of the French at the news of Wolsey's death indicated that they had earlier refused to go with him in abandoning support for a marriage with Anne 'on which alone depend the credit and favour the French now enjoy at this court'.[23]

Anne Boleyn's defeat of Wolsey's attempted come-back meant that those who had ridden to power behind her could sleep more peacefully. Yet not too peacefully; 'the king's great matter' continued to defeat them in November 1530, as it had done from the start.[24] Suffolk had wanted to pillage the Church and reduce the pretensions of the English clergy, which would have done nothing to advance Henry's matrimonial suit. Thomas More, the new chancellor, had been determined to block this anti-clericalism and to have nothing to do with the divorce, and although in private Norfolk felt much the same on both issues, he had been able to support More only in the attempt to hold the religious status quo. Not that the duke's calculated commitment to Henry's divorce had achieved anything, but this stemmed not from unwillingness but from lack of ideas – Thomas Howard would have helped his king to hell if Henry had wanted to go there.[25] Even the brilliant Stephen Gardiner, imprisoned by his high view of the clerical office, had had nothing to suggest.

The only support for Henry and the moving ferment of his ideas had come from Anne and the more committed of her backers. When the court had arrived at Waltham in early August 1529, in the aftermath of the Blackfriars hearing, Stephen Gardiner, the new secretary, and Edward Fox, the provost of King's College, Cambridge, shared lodgings together as they had earlier in the year on their Italian embassy.[26] They were billeted on a certain Mr Cressey, only to discover that the sons of the family were being tutored by an acquaintance from university days, Dr Thomas Cranmer of Jesus College. Academic gossip over supper turned to discussion of the king's predica-

---

[23] *Cal. S. P. Span., 1529–30*, pp. 805, 820; *Cal. S. P. Ven., 1527–30*, 642.

[24] For a detailed study of the period 1529–32: Guy, *Public Career of More*, although the following differs at a number of points.

[25] For Norfolk's desperation to move Charles V and Clement VII: *Cal. S. P. Span., 1529–30*, pp. 510–11. This may be connected with Wolsey's doctor being still in Norfolk's hands on 1 Mar. but at Ghent by 23 Mar. 1531, representing the duke to the imperial government: *LP*, v.120, 153, 283.

[26] The source followed here is Cranmer's secretary, Morrice [*Narratives of the Reformation*, pp. 240–2], not the reworking by Foxe, *Acts and Monuments*, viii.7–8, with the king's supposed remark that Cranmer had 'the sow by the right ear'.

ment, and Cranmer, trained in theology where Gardiner had
been trained in law, made the perceptive comment that proceedings at canon law would get Henry nowhere; the problem was
theological and theologians would give him the answer, 'Whose
sentence may be soon known and brought so to pass with little
industry and charges ... And then his highness in conscience
quieted may determine with himself that which shall seem good
before God, and let these tumultuary processes give place unto a
certain truth.'[27] A couple of days after, Fox (also a theologian)
told the king of Cranmer's opinion, which struck an immediate
chord in the royal mind; was not his case precisely that canon
law said one thing and divine revelation the other? Let this
perceptive scholar be sent for. Not that the king waited until his
summer progress was over and Cranmer could be interviewed.
Within days the French ambassador was being badgered by
Wolsey and Henry to find an excuse to return to France and
consult the theologians there, a task he did not relish.[28]

Cranmer was eventually interviewed by the king at Greenwich
in October 1529. There Henry recruited him to write a thesis on
the divorce question which could be used when consulting
university faculties of theology – such was the programme that
his initial suggestion had now grown into – and who was backing
this suggestion was made clear when Henry passed Cranmer
over to Rochford to be cared for at Durham House while he got on
with the writing.[29] Successfully completed, that task led to a
further appointment as royal agent collecting the views of the
Italian universities, and Cranmer left England in January 1530
in the entourage once more of Anne Boleyn's father, who was
being sent to argue Henry's case yet again, this time to Charles V
and Clement VII at the long conference they were having at
Bologna.[30] A new and highly important member had been added
to the Boleyn team.

The arrival on the scene of Thomas Cranmer showed Henry a
way to bypass the papal Curia and establish before all the world

[27] *Narratives of the Reformation*, p. 242.
[28] Du Bellay, *Correspondance*, 22 at p. 65 [*LP*, iv.5862].
[29] The difficulties re this meeting [Ridley, *Cranmer*, pp. 24–8] are overcome
by dating it soon after Henry's return to Greenwich following the summer
progress, i.e. the earliest practical moment. Cf. Scarisbrick, *Henry VIII*, p. 255.
[30] Ridley, *Cranmer*, pp. 29–31.

that his personal divine revelation was in very truth the age-old law of God. Already, however, Anne Boleyn herself had introduced the king to precisely that coherent political expression of his feelings about royal authority that he had been groping after. This was *The Obedience of the Christian Man and How Christian Rulers Ought to Govern*, published in October 1528 by the exiled William Tyndale, whose English translation of the New Testament, with its Lutheran prologues, had been pouring illegally across the Channel since 1526. Tyndale's book brought to England the revolutionary ideas circulating in Germany about the true place and role of the ruler in God's scheme of things, and is an uncompromising declaration that kings govern by divine right. The ruler is anwerable to God alone; the obedience of the subject to the ruler is an obedience required by God. There is no distinction in position between the clergy and the laity, Church affairs and temporal affairs: all is under the sole control of the monarch. For the Church to rule the princes of Europe – as it did – was not only 'a shame above all shames and a notorious thing', but an inversion of the divine order: 'One king, one law is God's ordinance in every realm.'[31] Tyndale did not say what a monarch was to do to recover the rights usurped by the Church: as with many thinkers, it was enough to say with Ko Ko, 'When your majesty says, "Let a thing be done," it's as good as done – practically, it *is* done – because your majesty's will is law.' Yet if *The Obedience of the Christian Man* did not tell Henry VIII how to realize his innermost convictions, it did articulate them for the first time. He did not surrender at once. After all, Tyndale was tarred with the brush of heresy; and the whole ordering of things, as well as the assumptions of almost everyone around the king, reinforced tradition. Nevertheless, he had been shown the radical alternative and was mightily attracted by what he saw.

The grounds for believing that it was Anne Boleyn who brought the radical option to Henry's attention are good. The source is Anne Zouche to whom Anne lent the book, but this time we have her story not later than 1579 – and at only one remove – through John Lowthe the Elizabethan archdeacon of Nottingham, who spent part of his career in the Zouche house-

[31] William Tyndale, *Works*, ed. H. Walter, Parker Society (1848–50), i.206–7, 240.

hold.[32] The story also has its own intrinsic verification, for if we were being offered a piece of Protestant hagiography it is far more likely that Anne would be credited with lending out Tyndale's *New Testament*, of which she also had a copy, rather than a political text which was soon overtaken by events. How Anne Boleyn came by the book was not reported by Mrs Zouche. The outside limits of dating are October/November 1528 when the text could have reached England and August 1529 when the court went on progress, but the most likely time was the spring, when the drive against subversive literature, required by the story, was taking place.[33] Anne had clearly by that stage had the book for long enough to be willing to lend it, and it is reasonable to assume that she had obtained it soon after publication and about the time that she abandoned hope of Wolsey and the legatine hearing. This suggests, indeed, the answer to an obvious problem – what did Anne and her supporters have in mind when they began to urge Henry to act unilaterally? Was it anything more than the somewhat irresponsible French advice to marry at once and hope the pope would accept the *fait accompli*?[34] That policy would have left Henry with no accepted second marriage, the hoped-for son a bastard in the eyes of most of Europe and many of his subjects, and England open to the dreaded papal interdict, something which Clement VII would, in fact, specifically threaten when in March 1530 he forbade any remarriage before Henry's divorce was granted; memories were still preserved of the havoc which that sanction had brought to the England of King John.[35] Yet, guided by Tyndale, Anne now had a positive alternative, a programme throwing off the judicial and administrative tyranny of Rome, restoring the proper God-given status and power to the prince, who would then reform the Church over which he ruled and bring it back to true biblical purity.

The fact that Anne lent her copy of Tyndale to her waiting-woman may be an indication that she was actively spreading this promising antipapal iconoclasm.[36] In the version of the story

---

[32] *Narratives of the Reformation*, pp. 52–7; George Wyatt, in *Wolsey*, ed. Singer, pp. 438–41.

[33] For the campaign see *LP*, iv.5416.

[34] *Cal. S. P. Span., 1529–30*, p. 708.

[35] *LP*, iv.6256; repeated Jan. 1531: ibid., v.27.

[36] George Wyatt, in *Wolsey*, ed. Singer, pp. 438–41.

Wyatt tells, she certainly intended to show it to Henry, having marked the passages he would be especially interested in. In the event, while Anne Zouche had the book it was taken from her by her future husband George, 'among other love-tricks'. George was much taken with so shocking a text and refused to return it, despite Anne's entreaties, who feared both for her mistress's property and the danger the book represented. Inevitably he was caught reading it by the dean of the Chapel Royal, whom Wolsey had instructed to carry out the purge on heretical books at court. The confiscated item was passed to Wolsey, but whether he would have used Tyndale's heretical reputation to smear Anne Boleyn we cannot know. Anne had been informed of the confiscation and had gone immediately to Henry, vowing 'it shall be the dearest book that ever dean or cardinal took away.' Henry listened, and sight of his ring caused the clerics to return the book to Anne, but she did not leave it there. Henry, she suggested, would find the work worth reading, especially the passages she had marked. She was right. He declared, 'This book is for me and all kings to read.' Not, it is true, for ordinary folk; it had too much about it of the heresies Henry disliked, and it remained on the list of banned works.[37] Yet to kings, and most pointedly to the king of England in 1529, *The Obedience of the Christian Man* did have much to say, and Henry set about trying to recruit William Tyndale as a propaganda writer![38]

The Boleyns were thus feeding the king with ideas.[39] They also began to move on the vital matter of policy; nurturing the feelings Henry had about what the situation ought to be was useless, unless at the same time he was given some idea how to

[37] *Tudor Royal Proclamations*, i.129.

[38] He failed, and *The Practice of Prelates* (Antwerp, 1529) showed that Tyndale opposed the divorce: R. Marius, *Thomas More* (1985), pp. 387–9.

[39] Foxe, *Acts and Monuments*, iv.656–8 claims that Anne introduced Henry to *The Supplication of Beggars* by a critic-in-exile of Wolsey, Simon Fish. Allegedly a copy was sent to Anne and she, after discussion with her brother, gave it to Henry, who was once again pleased and put in hand a pardon for Fish and his recall to England. Foxe also prints another version of events which he claims originated with a royal footman who drew the king's attention to the book and to two merchants who read the tract to Henry then and there. The king's comment was, 'if a man should pull down an old stone wall and begin at the lower part, the upper part thereof might chance to fall upon his head.' Probabilities strongly favour the latter version, for the names of the footman and the merchants can be substantiated in other sources [*LP*, iv.2839(24), 4595, App.78; v. p. 305]. The Boleyn story can be explained as a confusion with the Tyndale episode which Foxe does not record.

get there. The first tactic was the one that the Boleyn faction had mooted towards the end of 1528, a monster petition from the elite of England to the pope, begging for the divorce in the national interest. The original text was apparently too blunt in its threats against the pope to win sufficient acceptance at an initial meeting called in June 1530, but the modified text which was in the end sent to Rome was still full of menace, warning Clement that, although refusing Henry the divorce would make the condition of his subjects 'more miserable, . . . it will not be wholly desperate, since it is possible to find relief some other way.'[40] The advice to ignore the pope, which Wolsey had, months before, warned was being poured into the royal ear, had now helped to shape a formal communication to the Holy See. This revision was carefully not put to a second full meeting, but touted round the country from individual to individual at a brisk canter. The man in charge was William Brereton, groom of the privy chamber, the first association with Anne's cause of a man who was to die as her alleged 'lover' in 1536.[41] Assisting him was Thomas Wriothesley, a Gardiner man but one who may have owed his training at Cambridge to support from Thomas Boleyn.[42] All the adult peers available signed the petition, with a handful of exceptions who were apparently too far off the route of Brereton's team and too unimportant to make a detour worth while. Twenty-two abbots also signed but only six bishops – the remaining fourteen in England and three in Wales were not asked. All the senior officers of the royal household, clerical and lay, signed as well.

Few of those promoting this petition could have had much hope that it would have an impact at Rome, but it had the great domestic advantage of whipping grumblers into line and isolating Katherine's more determined supporters. At the June meeting, however, the king also took the opportunity to test reaction to the more positive approach suggested by Cranmer.[43] Could not the king, armed with the opinion of the theologians of the Western Church, marry at once without obtaining papal approval? The suggestion was greeted with stunned silence, until 'one of the king's chief favourites' fell on his knees to warn Henry

[40] Herbert, *Henry VIII*, pp. 446–51.
[41] Ives, in *Trans. Hist. Soc. Lancs. & Ches.*, 123. 7–8.
[42] *House of Commons*, iii.664.
[43] *Cal. S. P. Span., 1529–30*, p. 599.

of the danger that this would provoke popular unrest and to beg him at least wait until the cold and wet of winter would help to discourage the troublemakers. Who this favourite was we do not know. Of the signatories, the one best fitting both the description and the opinions expressed was the marquis of Exeter, but irrespective of his identity, he had faced Henry with the further unpleasant reality that radical policies once formulated might be politically impossible to implement.

Some weeks after the suggestion at the June meeting, a new and potentially even more radical initiative emerged from the Boleyn camp. Thomas Cranmer was again deeply involved, along with other experts, but the leading role was taken by Edward Fox, who now dedicated himself wholly to securing Henry VIII's divorce. We may also note that in December 1529 he was granted a benefice in the bishopric of Durham, whose revenue was, pro tem., assigned to support the Boleyns, and it is hard to doubt that he was by then close to Anne.[44] What Fox and his team produced was not a finished thesis but a data bank of scriptural, patristic and historical arguments which justified Henry taking into his own hands the solution of his matrimonial problem. The collection, known as the *Collectanea satis copiosa*, was sufficiently advanced to be shown to the king in the late summer of 1530, and he greeted it not so much as a drowning man greets a straw but as he might a rescue party from outer space![45]

Two lines of argument from first principles were made possible by the material Fox and the others collected. The first was that each province in the early Church had its own jurisdiction, independent of the rest and of the pope's nominal leadership; the proper body to settle Henry's divorce suit was, therefore, the English Church, and the English Church alone. The second line of argument was more radical, cutting out the pope entirely, and proving that a king was, by God's institution the sole possessor of all authority over Church and state in his realm – exactly that divine right over the whole of English life that Henry hankered after. This, of course, was just what Tyndale and Anne Boleyn had told him did belong to him, but there was a vital difference.

[44] *LP*, iv.6088.
[45] G. D. Nicholson, 'The nature & function of historical argument in the Henrician Reformation', Cambridge Ph.D. thesis (1977).

All they had been able to suggest was the arbitrary nationalization of the Church by royal will; what Fox offered Henry was the demonstration that he was already head of the Church – all that was required was to behave as such. It was the Church which was the intruder, usurping power which did not belong to it. Tyndale had called on Henry to invade previously sacrosanct territory against all accepted law and public opinion; Fox had made this superfluous. Henry was already in possession, an emperor answerable to God only for the conduct of every aspect of life in his realm, a conservative standing for the innate rights of himself 'and all kings'. He had only to exercise his power.

By June 1530 it was obvious to observers that Anne Boleyn and her supporters believed themselves to be on the brink of a major advance, and when the *Collectanea* reached the king, the impact on the tone and content of royal pronouncements both in Rome and in England was immediate.[46] Henry went further in October, as a new parliamentary session approached, and put to a gathering of clerics and lawyers a plan to empower the archbishop of Canterbury by statute to decide the divorce suit, notwithstanding the papal prohibition. When told that parliament could not act in this way, he reacted angrily, postponing parliament until the New Year and belabouring the papal nuncio with both *Collectanea* arguments: that the pope was ignoring English provincial privilege and that all but his power to determine doctrine was 'usurpation and tyranny'.[47] Anne Boleyn and her father kept up the momentum of these radical ideas, with antipapal tirades so violent as to shock the unshockable Chapuys and drive him from the court uttering warnings that together they would alienate England from the Holy See.[48] Wiltshire pressed the same line in council, as Henry told the ambassador, and the king himself was similarly violent, especially on one occasion when Chapuys noticed Anne Boleyn listening at a nearby open window.[49] When Charles V's man seized the chance to get in some home truths of his own, Henry quickly took the conversation out of earshot and the danger of an outburst from Anne. Propaganda was put to the press, and Wiltshire oversaw an English translation of the opinions of the

[46] *Cal. S. P. Span., 1529–30*, p. 601.
[47] Ibid., pp. 758–9.
[48] Ibid., p. 790.
[49] Ibid., pp. 797–8, 803.

European universities, possibly for Cranmer's treatise, the *Determinations . . . that it is so unlawful for a man to marry his brother's wife* (1531), which also picked up a number of points from the *Collectanea*.[50] Nor was diplomatic activity ignored, and Anne in particular went out of her way to entertain the French envoys over Christmas, while Henry gave the senior of them rooms in Bridewell Palace itself.[51]

The climax came when parliament, and the Church's equivalent, the convocation of the Province of Canterbury, assembled in the second and third weeks of January 1531.[52] Since the previous summer the king had been planning to extort a substantial sum from the English clergy towards his serious financial difficulties, and had begun a number of exemplary prosecutions of likely opponents for their involvement in Wolsey's offences. Convocation took the hint and quickly offered £100,000, in return for a pardon which was initially drafted to cover complicity with Wolsey. The Boleyn faction had not, however, relaxed its pressure. Chapuys reported Anne on New Year's Day as being full of confidence and brave as a lion, declaring 'that she wished all Spaniards were at the bottom of the sea . . . that she cared not for the queen or any of her family, and that she would rather see her hanged than have to confess that she was her queen and mistress.'[53] Katherine and a number of the courtiers were sure that Henry was going to act unilaterally, while even Norfolk, who privately found the implications of the *Collectanea* too extreme for his taste, was found expounding the new orthodoxy to a bemused Eustace Chapuys.[54]

The outcome of all this was that royal policy became ever more radical by the day. The original plan, that in return for a substantial sum in clerical taxation a royal pardon would cover complicity in Wolsey's offences, was amended by the council, and became a pardon for the illegal exercise of the Church's

[50] Ibid., pp. 818, 821, 847. The *Collectanea* was also the basis for much in the legislation of 1532–3 and in various other tracts, including the king's own *Glass of Truth* (1532).

[51] *Cal. S. P. Span.*, *1529–30*, p. 862.

[52] J. J. Scarisbrick, 'The pardon of the clergy', in *Cambridge Historical Journal*, 12 (1956), modified by Guy, in *EHR*, 97.481–503. The convocation for the province of York was much smaller and normally met later, since its bishops were required at parliament.

[53] *Cal. S. P. Span.*, *1531–33*, p. 3 [*LP*, v.24].

[54] Ibid., pp. 16, 22–3, 26 [*LP*, v.40, 45].

spiritual authority; coupled with it was a description of Henry as 'protector and highest head' of the Church and clergy.[55] When the convocation drew back at the new definition of its supposed offence and asked that the liberties of the Church granted by Magna Carta should be formally ratified, the king became more specific and demanded on 7 February that it immediately recognize him 'sole protector and supreme head of the English church and clergy'. Anne Boleyn's reaction was to make 'such demonstrations of joy as if she had actually gained Paradise'.[56] The king at last was moving in the direction she wanted.

Some days of haggling followed the claim to the supreme headship, and all doubt about who was advising the king is dispelled by the prominent part played here by George, Lord Rochford, Anne Boleyn's brother. Henry's agents were prepared to accept modifications on other concessions he had demanded, and to add the words 'so far as the law of Christ allows', if that made the title easier for the Church to swallow. Henry himself at first favoured the headship without qualification, and it was at this point that he sent in Rochford with a number of tracts to persuade convocation of the scriptural case for the supremacy. The clergy showed that they were well aware who was feeding the king by attempting, without success, to open a direct line of communication to Henry and to ignore Rochford. Eventually Henry realized, or it was explained to him, that he would lose nothing by the qualified formula. The Church might believe that the phrase neutralized the new title, and an impressive list of subsequent protests at home and to Rome would make clear that this was how the clergy did take it. But because Henry knew that the headship of the Church was precisely what the law of Christ

[55] J. A. Guy has resolved some of the difficulties in Hall's account [*Chronicle*, pp. 774–5] by demonstrating [pp. 492–3] that there were two bills for the pardon of the clergy, the first for involvement in Wolsey's offences and the second, 10 March, for exercising an illegal spiritual jurisdiction. However, the reason in the first bill (stated by Hall to have been introduced at the start of the session [pp. 774–5] but logically post 24 Jan., when the clergy resolved to make a grant) conflicts with a pre-7 Feb. council draft mentioning church jurisdiction [Guy, in *EHR*, 97, pp. 488–91]. This can be resolved by suggesting that the council draft was (*pace* Guy, p. 491) an assertion of royal status in spirituals, which was later made more explicit in the demands of 7 Feb. On this reading, disagreement in council antedated the draft and the shift from Wolsey's offences to an illegal spiritual jurisdiction, and the move from the term 'protector and highest head' to 'sole protector and supreme head of the English church and clergy' mark the increasing dominance of Boleyn influence.

[56] *Cal. S. P. Span., 1531–33*, p. 63 [*LP*, v.105].

did provide, the added phrase strengthened his title and became a way of rebutting the contention that he was trenching on the mystical headship of Christ over the Church militant and triumphant.[57] The fact that he knew perfectly well that the clergy would take the concession in a different way was a characteristic piece of Henrician sharp practice.[58] In a similarly dishonest way Henry would deny to the papal nuncio that he had usurped the pope's authority by creating *'ceste nouvelle papalité,'* but Chapuys could see that it almost made the king 'pope in England' and that in the king's eyes the supposed limitation was nothing of the kind. He noted too how Anne and her father had been the chief promoters of the measure, and Wiltshire told Katherine's champion, Bishop Fisher, to his face 'that when God departed from this world he left behind him no successor or vicar on earth'.[59]

The Pardon of the Clergy in the opening months of 1531 was a second triumph for Anne Boleyn and her supporters – first Wolsey, now the pope. It was not, however, a conclusive victory. There was no immediate divorce between Katherine and Henry, and eighteen months would elapse before his marriage to Anne. Instead of applying the logic of the radical success, a great deal of time and effort was devoted to blocking any hearing of the divorce suit at Rome and to securing papal approval for a trial elsewhere – policies which should never have bothered a king fully determined to trust in his God-given *imperium*. Such a king should, instead, have been pushing forward with a hearing at home before the authorities of the Church of which he was now head – but that was not the case in England in 1531.

A number of reasons help to explain this strange reversal in the story of Henry VIII and Anne Boleyn. One undoubted factor was the situation in Europe. Francis I was anxious, in the face of the all-conquering Charles V, to retain the friendship of the pope as well as of Henry, and in 1531 he began a series of diplomatic moves to bring England and Rome together, which raised the

---

[57] Henry used this implication to reject the qualification 'in temporal matters'.

[58] *Cal. S. P. Ven.*, *1527–33*, 656 must suggest that the ambiguity was deliberate, for the crowns rejected the extra-qualification 'as far as canon law allows'. Cf. Henry's tendentious reply to Bishop Tunstall.

[59] *Cal. S. P. Span.*, *1531–33*, pp. 63, 71, 75 [*LP*, v.105, 112].

possibility that Henry might, after all, secure the generally recognized papal divorce he had struggled for so long.[60] More important, perhaps, had been the firm resistance which the Church had offered to the claim for headship, and in particular the blunt refusal of Archbishop Warham to act in defiance of long-established papal authority. Early in the 1531 session of convocation he had been subjected to a private interview with Henry, and he had not budged.[61] The Church might have accepted, more or less, Henry's own definition of his position, but the king as yet had no way to compel it to do what he wanted. And beyond the hierarchy there was, as Chapuys liked to point out, the menace of a conservative-minded political elite and the nation at large.[62]

It was this in particular that gave Henry great and increasing pause. The faction which came to power in 1529 had united only on the negative, 'Wolsey must go'; Anne Boleyn and her pretensions had for many been no more than a convenient tool. The realization that she was the true inheritor of that ultimate royal favour which had been Wolsey's strength came, therefore, as an unpleasant surprise. Even worse was the realization of the radicalism being advanced by the Boleyn faction and the imminent possibility that Anne would replace Katherine as queen. For those of Wolsey's opponents who had always been loyal to the queen and to tradition, men like More or the earl of Shrewsbury, the result was merely to confirm the rightness of their position and the size of the stakes for which they were playing. For others it was a case of changing or taking sides for the first time, so that through 1530 and 1531 there was a steady growth in the weight of opinion at court and in the council, which was hostile to Henry's plan to marry Anne Boleyn. One of the earliest of those presumed to be an ally who declared, albeit privately, in favour of Katherine was the king's favourite of the tiltyard, Nicholas Carewe. Although a cousin of Anne, by background strongly Francophil and as late as June 1531 one of the few who accompanied Henry on his more intimate courting expeditions, Sir Nicholas made it clear when serving as Henry's ambassador at the imperial court in 1529 whose side he was really on, and on his return he immediately opened up com-

---

[60] Ibid., p. 152 [*LP*, v.238]; cf. Knecht, *Francis I*, pp. 223–6.
[61] *Cal. S. P. Span.*, *1531–33*, p. 26 [*LP*, v.45].
[62] Ibid., *1529–30*, p. 511.

munication with Katherine and with Chapuys.[63] Another defector
was the duke of Suffolk. Uncomfortably aware that the coup
against Wolsey had left him in the cold, and with a wife who had
seen her precedence as the king's sister and dowager queen of
France rudely set aside in favour of Anne Boleyn, Suffolk made
no secret of his hostility.[64] Indeed, if we are to believe a rumour
which reached Chapuys in May 1530, he actively set out to drive
a wedge between Henry and Anne.

Chapuys' story was that Suffolk had tried to convince Henry
that Anne was a woman with a past, and as a consequence the
duke had been banned from appearing at court.[65] He had named
as her former lover a courtier who in fact had been rusticated
some time before, precisely on suspicion of too great an interest
in Anne, so that on Suffolk's revival of the scandal she had asked
Henry to send the man away again. The king had done so, but
had soon interceded with Anne for the courtier and brought him
back into favour. Though Chapuys certainly believed the tale, he
did admit that it was only a rumour and could give no other
details, but commentators have generally accepted that the
person in question was Thomas Wyatt. It is a plausible identification, for Suffolk certainly nurtured an 'immortal hate' against
Sir Thomas, and would be responsible for his arrest in 1536 as
one of Anne's faction.[66] There is, however, no evidence that
Wyatt was sent down from court during Anne's lifetime, though
that was to happen to him later; nor, as we have seen, is there
much reason to believe that Anne was seriously involved with
him. A possible resolution is suggested by taking the somewhat
different reference which Chapuys made to the same person in
1533 (again unnamed), as one 'whom she [Anne] loves very
much and whom the king had formerly chased from court for
jealousy of her', and coupling with it the curious episode of
Wyatt's going to Italy early in January 1527.[67] According to the
latter story, Sir John Russell was travelling by boat down the
Thames on the first stage of his journey as Henry's envoy to the
pope, when he encountered Wyatt. Hearing of his mission,
Thomas announced then and there, 'I, if you please, will ask

---

[63] Ibid., pp. 279, 470, 514, 536, 587, 692; *1531-33*, p. 198 [*LP*, v.308].
[64] Ibid., *1529-30*, p. 421; see above, p. 154.
[65] Ibid., p. 535.
[66] Muir, *Life and Letters of Wyatt*, p. 201.
[67] Friedmann, *Anne Boleyn*, i.190 n.1; George Wyatt, *Papers*, p. 27.

leave, get money and go with you' – and promptly did just that. Since it was about this time that Wyatt realized that he was competing with a king who was seriously in pursuit of Anne, he might well have seized the chance of (and Henry given permission for) a visit to Italy in order to extricate himself tactfully. Add a strong seasoning of malice and a routine absence of Wyatt from court at the time that Suffolk spoke to Henry in 1530, and you have the story Chapuys tells.[68]

The rustication of Suffolk (if it was that and not just the duke making himself scarce) did not teach him the wisdom of supporting Anne in future. In August or September when the French, with the support of Wiltshire and Norfolk, pressed the council to go ahead with the marriage and trust that the pope would regularize it *post facto*, it was Suffolk who led the rest of the councillors to reject the scheme emphatically.[69] In the spring of 1531 he openly espoused a pro-imperial policy in the council, while in the summer he told Henry that the king was the third person Katherine would obey; when Henry asked who the first two were, expecting the reply, 'the pope' and 'the emperor', the duke answered that God was the first and her conscience the second.[70] Some days after this well placed barb, Suffolk discussed the divorce with Fitzwilliam, the treasurer of the household, and agreed that the time had come to co-operate together 'to unseat the king from his folly': the signal would be the papal decision in Katherine's favour – and the sooner the better.[71] It is small wonder that Anne exploited Suffolk's colourful private life to hit back with the allegation that he had an incestuous relationship with his son's fiancée, and the accusation was the sweeter since the girl was the daughter of one of Katherine of Aragon's Spanish attendants![72]

Another surprising defector from the ranks of Anne's supporters was her aunt, the duchess of Norfolk – surprising that is, unless the background and circumstances of Elizabeth Howard are recalled. A daughter of the attainted duke of Buckingham and with many years of service as a lady-in-waiting at court, the

[68] For the possible source of Suffolk's information see below, pp. 377–8.
[69] *Cal. S. P. Span.*, *1529–30*, pp. 708–9. The reference to 'Norfolk' [p. 709] should read 'Suffolk': Friedmann, *Anne Boleyn*, i.120 n.2.
[70] *Cal. S. P. Span.*, *1531–33*, p. 177 [*LP*, v.216].
[71] See above, p. 172[70].
[72] Ibid., p. 214 [*LP*, v.340].

duchess had had no cause to love Wolsey but plenty to revere Katherine. She also had what was a most powerful motive for returning to this earlier allegiance – a desire to strike at her husband the duke, who for three or four years had been quite blatantly keeping a mistress.[73] Dislike of Anne also played a part. Elizabeth Howard had earlier clashed with Katherine over her claim that she took precedence over the dowager duchess of Norfolk, the duke's stepmother, so to see Anne exalted over both of them could have been no pleasure.[74] She also resented Boleyn interference in the marriages of her children, and especially Anne's insistence that her daughter should marry the duke of Richmond. Sharp words between them on this subject were soon followed by Elizabeth Howard sending Katherine a secret message hidden in an orange, and thereafter a series of reports about *la partie adverse* (some highly informative).[75] By Christmas 1530 the duchess's Stafford blood could not resist some acid comments on the family tree of the upstart Boleyns – and not for the first time, either – and her strident support for Katherine led to her being banned from court in the following spring.[76]

Chapuys is, of course, the only source for all this, and one must continue to test the characterization of Anne that he offers, but it is hard to imagine her assertive personality not becoming waspish under the strain of her situation.[77] As Christmas 1530 approached, she proclaimed her defiance of the world by having the livery coats of her servants embroidered with a version of the arrogant motto she had learned from Margaret of Austria: '*Ainsi sera, groigne qui groigne*' – 'Let them grumble, that is how it is going to be!'[78] Anne seems even to have inspired a carol by her gesture – equally defiant, though more subtle:

---

[73] Ibid., p. 814 [*LP*, v.1164]; for the duchess see Wood, *Letters*, ii.360–72; *LP*, vi.474, 475.

[74] *Cal. S. P. Span., 1529–30*, p. 368.

[75] Ibid., pp. 762, 819 [*Correspondence of Charles V and his ambassadors*, ed. W. Bradford (1850), p. 323]; ibid., *1531–33*, pp. 44, 154 [*LP*, v.216, 238]. The ambiguity of the first reference is settled by Wood, *Letters*, ii.363, 368; it was the marriage with the son of the earl of Derby which the duchess preferred. Chapuys' gossip on the Howard marriages is contradictory, e.g. *Cal. S. P. Span., 1529–30*, 279, 360, in part because of his wish to detach Norfolk from Anne by suggesting the marriage of Surrey to Mary.

[76] Friedmann, *Anne Boleyn*, i.128 n.1; *Cal. S. P. Span., 1531–33*, p. 154 [*LP*, v.238].

[77] September 1530 found Anne trying to force courtiers to abandon Katherine: ibid., *1529–30*, p. 422.

[78] Ibid., pp. 710, 852; literally: 'thus it will be, grudge who grudges.'

Grudge on who list, this is my lot:
Nothing to want if it were not.

My years be young, even as ye see;
All things thereto doth well agree;
In faith, in face, in each degree,
Nothing doth want, as seemeth me,
  If it were not.

Some men doth say that friends be scarce,
But I have found, as in this case,
A friend which giveth to no man place
But makes me happiest that ever was,
  If it were not.

A heart I have, besides all this,
That hath my heart, and I have his.
If he doth will, it is my bliss,
And when we meet no lack there is,
  If it were not.

If he can find that can me please,
A-thinks he does his own heart's ease,
And likewise I could well appease
The chiefest cause of his mis-ease,
  If it were not.

A master eke God hath me sent
To whom my will is wholly lent
To serve and love for that intent
That both we might be well content,
  If it were not.

And here an end: it doth suffice
To speak few words among the wise;
Yet take this note before your eyes:
My mirth should double once or twice,
  If it were not.[79]

The piece is anonymous, but even if not by Anne it is certainly expressive of her position. Indeed a bold hypothesis would seize on the personal allusions and suggest Anne as the performer of the song. 'If it were not' – the marriage of Katherine is now a

---

[79] R. L. Greene, 'A carol of Anne Boleyn by Wyatt', in *Review of English Studies*, n.s.25 (1974), pp. 437–9. It is not by Wyatt: Harrier, *Canon*, p. 54. Line 11 might well be a pre-echo of Anne's later motto: 'The Most Happy'.

publicly derided obstacle to Anne's happiness, and to Henry's.

The blatant tone of Anne's motto and the carol probably explains why the device was dropped after only a few weeks. Chapuys snidely suggested that it was because Anne had been told of the original imperialist version, *Groigne qui groigne et vive Bourgoigne*, but he had forgotten – perhaps did not know of – her time in Mechelen and Brussels years before.[80] More probably it was because a blatant perversion of a motto belonging to the highly respected imperial family was hardly the way to encourage English men and women to accept her in place of a Habsburg queen they had known for twenty years. Anne's attitude could certainly be counterproductive – witness the shock when soon after the affair of the motto she publicly declared that she wished all Spaniards at the bottom of the sea, clearly including Katherine in her ill wishes.[81] One unfortunate in the privy chamber caught the full force of her wrath when she discovered him one day taking fabric to Katherine to make into shirts for Henry, and this despite his excuse (which the king confirmed) that he was doing so on instructions.[82] One may sympathize with Anne, but it was not the fault of the hapless courtier that Henry saw no significance in expecting the wife he was claiming to have rejected to continue caring for his clothes! Anne was too fond of threatening to have members of the royal household dismissed, and several went the way of the duchess of Norfolk.[83]

On occasion, even Anne's father got the rough edge of her tongue for his timidity – the new earl now had, after all, a lot to lose – while the duke of Norfolk found his position increasingly

[80] Friedmann, *Anne Boleyn*, i.128 n.3.

[81] *Cal. S. P. Span.*, *1531–33*, p. 3 [*LP*, v.24]. Cf. Henry's reported response to the vandalizing of Katherine's barge: ibid., p. 693 [*LP*, vi.556]. See above, p. 167.

[82] Ibid., *1529–30*, p. 600. Some of Anne's anger might be accounted for if she also was making shirts for Henry: Nicolas, *Privy Purse*, p. 97.

[83] *Cal. S. P. Span.*, *1529–30*, p. 600; ibid., *1531–33*, pp. 214, 239 [*LP*, v.340, 416]. Chapuys regularly refers to 'the young marquis', which from 10 Oct. 1530 should mean Henry Grey, marquis of Dorset (b.1517) and not Henry Courtenay, marquis of Exeter (b.c.1498), although the references only make sense if the latter is meant. Chapuys began the practice in the last months of Grey's father's life, hence 'young marquis' = Exeter [ibid., *1529–30*, pp. 430, 600]; hence, also, the wife dismissed from court was Katherine's former attendant, Gertrude Courtenay, née Blount, not Frances Grey, the daughter of Charles Brandon and Mary Tudor. Cf. Friedmann, *Anne Boleyn*, i.146 n.3.

unenviable.[84] He was out of sympathy with the radical Boleyn line which he found himself more and more called upon to present, and (as his wife gleefully passed on to Katherine) had been heard to mutter that Anne would be the ruin of the Howards.[85] Norfolk's ally, Stephen Gardiner, on the other hand, was careful to give her no opening to test her growing suspicion of him, and she met her match in Henry Guildford, controller of the household.[86] Although he had signed the loyalty petition to the pope in June 1530, he had spoken out in council in favour of Katherine and, after accompanying an abortive delegation in May 1531 to persuade the queen to 'be sensible', had been heard to wish that all the lawyers and theologians arguing for the king could be put in a cart and shipped to Rome, there to be exposed for the charlatans they were. Anne was furious and warned Guildford that as soon as she was queen she would have him out of office. Sir Henry retorted that in that case he would save her the trouble, and marched off to the king to resign then and there. Henry tried to smooth his old friend down with excuses about 'woman's talk', and Guildford did eventually take back the white stave of office, but he still showed his displeasure by retiring to his home in Kent to cool off.

The courtly opposition to Henry VIII's divorce proposals also began to argue back in defence of tradition. A large proportion of the clergy had protested against the title 'supreme head', and Bishop Fisher and others had written effective pieces in defence of Katherine.[87] In the spring of 1531, however, court preachers began to speak openly against Henry's claims, while the manipulators of the Canterbury mystic Elizabeth Barton, 'the Nun of Kent', were busy dispensing her anti-Boleyn 'prophecies' to Katherine and her circle of supporters.[88] Reginald Pole, the king's cousin and a man with a fair prospect of ending up as cardinal-archbishop of Canterbury, abandoned his lukewarm assistance to the divorce suit and wrote a critique of the king's

[84] *Cal. S. P. Span.*, *1531–33*, p. 699 [*LP*, vi.556]. The evidence, however, is retrospective. For Norfolk on Boleyn, see ibid., *1529–30*, pp. 442–3.

[85] *LP*, v.216; *Cal. S. P. Span.*, *1531–33*, pp. 152–3 [*LP*, v.238]. For Anne's open rejection of Katherine as queen, see ibid., p. 3 [*LP*, v.24; Friedmann, *Anne Boleyn*, i.129 n.1].

[86] *Cal. S. P. Span.*, *1531–33*, pp. 175–7 [*LP*, v.287].

[87] Scarisbrick, *Henry VIII*, pp. 276–8; Mattingly, *Catherine of Aragon*, p. 232; Guy, *Public Career of More*, pp. 175–6.

[88] *LP*, v.216; vi.1464–6, 1468, 1470.

position so effective as to make Cranmer afraid that it would get into general circulation.[89] Particularly powerful were the pragmatic political arguments he advanced: the dangers of a disputed succession which would revive the disasters of Lancaster and York, and the economic damage which England would suffer if Charles V blocked the two vital trade routes to Flanders and Spain.[90] The points were shrewdly made and struck home. Increasingly it began to look as though if Henry insisted on taking a new wife, he might lose, or at least risk, his very crown.

Anne Boleyn must have felt very often at this time that apart from the fluctuating support of the king, her only firm allies were her brother, Thomas Cranmer and Edward Fox, and none of these had political weight or belonged to the council. She had influence, as can be seen in ambassadorial appointments or in the readiness of Anthony Browne of the privy chamber to surrender to her father and brother the crown office which he held in Rayleigh, Essex; but no leading politician was ready to commit himself openly to the implications of the radical victory over the Church.[91] Anne had helped Henry to conceptualize his instinctive feelings about kingship; the researchers she patronized had shown him that he had rights over the Church, and she had stood behind the king as he had made his claim. Yet what would ensure, if not the support of the people who mattered, at least their acquiescence? Or were Katherine's supporters right in believing that unilateral action was impossible? Francis Bryan no longer wrote hopefully to Anne or indeed mentioned her in the despatches he sent to Henry from his diplomatic post at the French court.[92] The renewed diplomatic initiative had even robbed her of Edward Fox, her ablest adviser, whom Chapuys called 'a sophisticated negotiator and a firebrand on the divorce issue'. He was away from May until the end of the year when he and Bryan came back together.[93]

One success alone gave Anne hope as 1531 reached towards midsummer and beyond. Henry left Katherine. The curious *maison à trois* inaugurated at the end of 1528 had become more

---

[89] W. Schenk, *Reginald Pole* (1950), pp. 28–9.

[90] *Cal. S. P. Span.*, *1531–33*, p. 322 [*LP*, v.563].

[91] Ibid., *1529–30*, p. 586; *1531–33*, pp. 239–40 [*LP*, v.416]; *LP*, v.364(28).

[92] But Bryan and Fox did pray for Henry to receive 'your heart's desire': Pocock, *Records*, ii.140 [*LP*, v.427].

[93] *Cal. S. P. Span.*, *1531–33*, p. 152 [*LP*, v.238]; *LP*, v.1025. He did make a brief return visit in Sept.: ibid., v.401, 427.

and more a matter of comment, and most European observers drew the simple conclusion that Anne was the king's mistress. If, as seems to have been so, this was not the case, it was not because they had maintained a decorous separation: quite the contrary. Anne's mother might usually be somewhere about, but the couple were always together and Henry's privy purse expenses show how tied up with each other their lives were.[94] Anne would lay out money if Henry had no ready cash; far more often it was Henry who paid – for Anne's clothes, for her gambling debts, for furring her gowns, for gold arras to hang in her chamber. When spring approached in 1530 he had set her up for travelling with him, with three saddles and a large quantity of tack, splendidly decorated in black and gold, and a set of harnesses for the mules which carried her litter.[95] It was perhaps in celebration of this present that Henry made an exhibition of himself on a journey from Windsor, by taking Anne up on his horse to ride pillion – and two observers who were ill advised enough to comment found themselves in trouble.[96] Anne was also active in field sports, Henry's great passion. The same month in which she received her harness, she was supplied with a full set of equipment for archery – bows, broad-head arrows, bracer, shooting glove – with a further four bows to follow.[97] On one autumn hunt, one of her greyhounds got out of control, along with one belonging to Urian Brereton of the privy chamber (William's brother), and the two of them savaged a wretched cow.[98]

This is not to say – and here is the key to the relationship between Henry and Anne – that all was pastoral bliss, nymphs and shepherds, hearts and flowers. As a self-made woman, Anne saw no percentage in bloodless simpering. Her attraction was that of challenge; she had not won the king by being submissive. When a poison-pen drawing came into her hands showing a male figure labelled 'H', and two female figures 'K' and 'A', and 'A' had no head, she called her maid Anne Gainsford: 'Come hither Nan, see here a book of prophecy; this he saith is the king, this the queen, and this is myself with my head off.' The maid said sensibly, 'If I

[94] Nicolas, *Privy Purse, passim*; *LP*, v.App.10.
[95] RO, E101/420/1 [*LP*, iv.App.256].
[96] *Cal. S. P. Span.*, *1529–30*, p. 536.
[97] Nicolas, *Privy Purse*, pp. 47, 50.
[98] Ibid., p. 74.

thought it true, though he were an emperor, I would not myself marry him with that condition.' To which Anne replied: 'Yes, Nan, I think the book a bauble, yet for the hope I have that the realm may be happy by my issue, I am resolved to have him whatsoever might become of me.' The patriotic desire for pregnancy has the ring of an Elizabethan accretion, but not the resolution.[99] It meant that Henry found himself facing a person prepared to stand up to him. When in the summer of 1530 he dared to remind Anne how much she owed him and how many enemies she had made him, her reply was reported as: 'That matters not, for it is foretold in ancient prophecies that at this time a queen shall be burnt. [Were they, by chance, discussing the poison-pen drawing?] But even if I were to suffer a thousand deaths, my love for you will not abate one jot.'[100]

Henry, we must suppose, generally found this exciting – after all, he became more and more committed to Anne. But he could grizzle and he could grumble. At the start of 1531 Paris and Rome were laughing at the story that Henry, having quarrelled with Anne, had been reduced to begging her relations 'with tears in his eyes' to mediate between them.[101] In April when the two fell out over Princess Mary, Henry complained to Norfolk about her arrogant words and the domineering attitude Anne took towards him, saying plaintively that she was not like Katherine, who had never in her life spoken harshly to him.[102] From Katherine's point of view it might have been better if she had. Observers noted that once Henry had made it up with Anne, as 'happens generally in such cases, their love will be greater than before.'[103]

Through all this, Katherine had kept her hollow status, presided at court and, remarkably, continued the custom she and Henry had followed all their married life of communicating if not in person at least by messages every three days. Henry sometimes made half-hearted gestures towards a greater separation. After a

---

[99] George Wyatt, in *Wolsey*, ed. Singer, pp. 429–30.

[100] *Cal. S. P. Span.*, *1529–30*, p. 634.

[101] Ibid., *1531–33*, p. 35 [*LP*, v.64]. The probable cause of the quarrel was Anne's ill-treatment of a courtier: ibid., p. 33 [*LP*, v.61].

[102] *LP*, v.216.

[103] *Cal. S. P. Span.*, *1531–33*, p. 33 [*LP*, v.61].

formal state dinner on 3 May, Holyrood Day, had turned out very well, Katherine ventured the next morning to suggest that Mary should pay them both a visit.[104] Henry, however, once more mindful of Anne, replied brutally that Katherine could go and visit her if she wanted to, and stay there too, whereupon the queen replied that neither for her daughter nor anyone in the world would she dream of leaving him; her proper place was at his side.[105] Anne Boleyn's one refuge was Wolsey's former palace of York Place, soon to be known as Whitehall. It had no separate 'queen's side' for Katherine and her suite to occupy, but Anne and her mother could lodge in the chamber under the cardinal's library, and her father and brother also had their own rooms elsewhere.[106] It was, thus, very much to her taste when Henry began the extensions at York Place in the spring of 1531, necessitating frequent visits to supervise the building which went on round the clock.[107] The only disappointment was that as the decorations went up in the window glass and on the striking new gate later to be misnamed 'the Holbein Gate', there were none of Anne's leopard badges or the monogram 'HA'.

There were, however, none of Katherine of Aragon's pomegranates either, and with Anne and Henry having a common project and a shared refuge in York Place, the queen's situation deteriorated. At the end of May the king was threatened with the supreme insult of having to appear before the pope at Rome; there could be no more delay, Clement informed him. After intense discussion it was decided to make one last appeal to Katherine, and she was visited at Greenwich on the evening of the 31st by the most powerful delegation possible – some thirty nobles, courtiers and clerics.[108] For the sake of the country, they told her, she must save Henry from this indignity and consent to having the case settled in England. But Katherine was as impervious to their cross questions as to their speeches, and they went away empty-handed. A few days later Henry began an almost continuous series of hunting trips, circulating restlessly

[104] Alternatively on the feast of SS Philip and James: *LP*, v.p. 325.
[105] *Cal. S. P. Span., 1531-33*, p. 153 [*LP*, v.238], but preferring Friedmann's reading: *Anne Boleyn*, i.148 n.3.
[106] *Cal. S. P. Span., 1531-33*, p. 154 [*LP*, v.238]; RO, E36/252 ff. 419-20 [*LP*, v.p. 448].
[107] Colvin, *King's Works*, iv.306-12; Hall, *Chronicle*, p. 774; see below, p. 298.
[108] Ibid., p. 781.

between Hampton Court and Windsor and local hunting boxes, where he and Anne were accompanied only by Nicholas Carewe and two other attendants.[109] Katherine moved with the court to Windsor. Then on Friday 14 July, after Henry had dealt with an important despatch to Bryan and Fox, without warning he left for Woodstock and his summer progress, leaving Katherine only the instruction to stay where she was.[110] It was almost five weeks past their twenty-second wedding anniversary, and this treatment hurt her as nothing had before.[111] Her next regular message to Henry, authenticated by the countersign they had used for so long, made this hurt obvious, and the king exploded in anger. Katherine, he returned, had brought on him the indignity of a personal citation to Rome, him, the king of England; she had turned down the delegation he had sent of the wisest and most noble of his counsellors; he wanted no more messages. Katherine answered nevertheless, but her self-righteous tone, however justified, might have been calculated to make matters worse. Henry sulked for four days and then sent a bitter and formal reply advising her to attend to her own business.[112]

Predictably, Eustace Chapuys attributed even this letter to the malevolence of Anne Boleyn, and we may imagine that Anne had time and again urged Henry to pluck up his courage, leave Katherine and join her. Yet this was not quite what he had done; rather, he had egotistically chosen to suit himself. There was little to reassure Anne in this. The separation from Katherine left her in command at court, with an enormous advantage over the queen in the battle to control the king's mind; it was a position to exploit. But it did not mean that Henry had taken a final decision. He had whipped himself into a sense of grievance against a woman who had rubbed raw his kingly pride, and what he had done in irritation he could undo as easily; as late as November 1531, Henry and Katherine were attending state occasions together, though apparently they did not meet.[113]

---

[109] *Cal. S. P. Span.*, *1531–33*, p. 198 [*LP*, v.308].
[110] *LP*, v.337; Hall, *Chronicle*, p. 781.
[111] *Cal. S. P. Span.*, *1531–33*, p. 291.
[112] Ibid., pp. 222–4 [*LP*, v.361].
[113] John Stowe, *Survey of London*, ed. C. L. Kingsford (Oxford, 1908), ii.36. 'King Henry and Queen Katherine dined' at the feast for the new serjeants-at-law at Ely House 'but in two chambers, and the foreign ambassadors in a third chamber'.

Anne's own marriage was no nearer – indeed, as the months went by the obstacles must have seemed ever more formidable. The Venetian Mario Savorgnano, visiting England soon after the separation, had no doubt where the odds lay:

> There is now living with him a young woman of noble birth, though many say of bad character, whose will is law to him, and he is expected to marry her, should the divorce take place, which it is supposed will not be effected, as the peers of the realm, both spiritual and temporal, and the people are opposed to it.[114]

Katherine, he noted, though the king's pressure had somewhat reduced visits to her court, still had a household of two hundred and thirty maids of honour.

[114] *Cal. S. P. Ven., 1527–33*, 682.

9

The Turning-point, 1532–33

CHRISTMAS 1531 was the most miserable anyone at the court of Henry VIII could remember. The king made a great show, but 'there was no mirth because the queen and the ladies were absent.'[1] Anne Boleyn herself was in no position to replace Katherine. She might occupy the consort's lodgings at Greenwich and have a flock of attendants, but the increasing polarization of opinion had made her position more and more isolated.[2] She continued to extend her influence within the court and outside, and her word began to command attention as far away as Calais.[3] Yet the continuation of that influence was wholly precarious; this, indeed, may explain why she was – so it was said – anxious to see Princess Mary lodged as many miles away as was possible.[4] At Rome the divorce suit was going from bad to worse; in December Henry had been reduced to attempting to bribe enough cardinals to achieve a six-month hold-up.[5] That in turn was a reflection of the situation in the king's council, where the majority continued to resist the radical alternative, but had nothing to suggest instead other than further appeals to Katherine's good nature![6]

The events of New Year's Day 1532 certainly made clear who held the moral initiative.[7] Tradition dictated that on that day the

---

[1] Hall, *Chronicle*, p. 784.
[2] *Cal. S. P. Span.*, *1531–33*, p. 354 [*LP*, v.696].
[3] *LP*, Add.746.
[4] *Cal. S. P. Span.*, *1531–33*, p. 278 [*LP*, v.512].
[5] Pocock, *Records*, ii.144–5.
[6] *Cal. S. P. Span.*, *1531–33*, pp. 263–4 [*LP*, v.478].
[7] For the following see *Cal. S. P. Span.*, *1531–33*, pp. 353–4 [*LP*, v.696].

members of the royal family and the court exchanged gifts. Anne duly gave Henry an exotic set of richly decorated Pyrenean boar spears and, in contrast to New Year 1531, Henry does not seem to have had to pay for his present in advance. His gift to her was a matching set of hangings for her room and bed, in cloth of gold, cloth of silver and richly embroidered crimson satin.[8] As for Katherine, the king had decided for the first time not to give presents to her or to her ladies, and had, rather meanly, ordered the courtiers to follow suit.[9] He had not, however, forbidden Katherine, who realized that the custom gave her a splendid opportunity to circumvent the continuing prohibition on her sending messages to Henry. Nothing had been said about gifts! Carefully choosing a gold cup of a highly distinctive design and of obvious expense, the queen sent it to be presented to her husband. The unfortunate gentleman of the privy chamber on duty to receive gifts could not refuse it, but he found himself the target for predictable royal fury when he came to present the cup. Two hours or so later Henry realized what he had done and sent to get the cup back, frantic that it might already have been returned to Katherine. In that case it could have been re-presented later in the day during one of the court functions, when Henry would have found it almost impossible not to accept and thereby recognize publicly his relationship with Katherine! Fortunately the privy chamber still had the cup, and orders were given to return it only in the evening, when it would be too late for Katherine to try that ploy. It was not a happy Christmas for either Henry or Anne.

Behind the scenes, however, and probably unrecognized by Anne or many of the others involved, movements had already been set in train which would break the political impasse and transform stalemate into victory. The first sign was a break-through on the vital question, 'By what means could a lay monarch assert his God-given authority over the Church?' The way this could be answered was triumphantly demonstrated in 1531 in 'new additions' appended by the septuagenarian lawyer,

[8] Ibid., p. 354: *'certain dards faytz a la biscayne'*. 'Une darde' was a short spear with a two-edged, leaf-shaped blade, which, given the source (or perhaps the fashion) of the weapons, suggests 'boar spear'. For the 1531 gift see Nicolas, *Privy Purse*, p. 101.
[9] Chapuys says that the prohibition included Mary, but she did receive a gift: *LP*, v.p. 327.

Christopher St German, to a work already in print, *A Dialogue betwixt a Doctor of Divinity and a Student in the Laws of England, of the Grounds of the said Laws and of Conscience* – better known to later generations as *Doctor and Student.*[10] In the general text St German had shown by arguing from specific cases that only the sacramental functions of the Church were really outside the concern of human, that is secular, law. In practice, however, the Church was possessed by ancient prescription of a great deal more than this, and in the 'new additions' St German faced head-on the key question in the royal supremacy: what was 'the power of the parliament concerning the spiritualty and the spiritual jurisdiction'?[11] Traditionalists such as Thomas More believed that no local legislature could prevail against the universally recognized liberties of the Church. St German showed otherwise. A statute binds all men because all have assented to it, the Lords directly and the Commons through their representatives. It can, therefore, properly regulate all the actions of the Church which belong to the temporal sphere, prescription or no. In effect whenever the Church wanted to do more than exhort, it needed statutory authority. 'The king in parliament' is 'the high sovereign over the people which hath not only charge on the bodies but also on the souls of his subjects'.[12]

It would be a piece of felicitous plotting for Christopher St German to arrive on the scene as a protégé of Anne Boleyn. Alas, history is not so neat. There is, however, direct evidence that he was in touch with Henry VIII himself and working as a parliamentary draftsman on many of the proposals in the 'new additions' to *Doctor and Student.*[13] In other words, however St German had come to royal attention, he was not just another theorist, albeit the one who had at last found the magic way forward. He was, rather, actively in process of drafting the legislation which would give statutory effect to the supreme headship with, as the ultimate prize, the achieving of the king's divorce by parliamentary authority.

[10] St German, *Doctor and Student*, pp. 315–40. See J. A. Guy, 'The Tudor commonwealth', in *Historical Journal* 23 (1980), 684–7; *Public Career of More*, pp. 151–6; 'Thomas More and Christopher St German', in *Moreana*, 21 (1984), 5–25; *Christopher St German on Chancery and Statute* (Selden Society, 1985), pp. 19–55.
[11] St German, *Doctor and Student*, p. 315.
[12] Ibid., p. 327.
[13] Guy, in *Moreana*, 21.8; *Public Career of More*, pp. 151–2, 156.

The second development that promised hope to Anne Boleyn in 1531 was the arrival not of a book, but of a man: Thomas Cromwell. Since Cromwell would bring Anne to the English throne at last – and himself, in the process, to high favour with the king – and since he would, within three years of that, destroy her as he manoeuvred to become supreme in government, a good dramatist would have scripted a memorable first encounter. Yet this would be false, and not merely because life is not art or, more prosaically, because the first evidence we have is of Anne sending him a verbal message in March 1529, but because Cromwell would have seemed nothing remarkable at any first meeting.[14] A man of about forty-five, for fourteen years a business agent and solicitor for Thomas Wolsey, he had saved himself from the wreck of the cardinal's enterprises by neat manoeuvring which had left him in charge of salvage operations on behalf of the king! He also worked for the duke of Norfolk, particularly on parliamentary matters, but by the opening of 1531 Cromwell had risen to the position of sworn royal counsellor. Opinions about him were fiercely discrepant while he was alive, and historians today are no more in agreement. For some a fixer, a hit-man firing bullets others made to bring down men better than himself. Alternatively the bureaucrat, the agent, the archetypal staff officer. Or, yet again, the perceptive statesman, the original mind which reallocated the atomic weights in the periodic table of English politics.

What, then, did the arrival of Thomas Cromwell in 1530–1 mean for Anne Boleyn? The difficulty in answering this question is, of course, the difficulty of separating the man then from the man we know later. It is all too easy to see the ferment in royal ideas and policies in 1532 and afterwards, and to argue that he was the new yeast. What we do need to ask, is what our assessment would be if Cromwell had died in 1532. The working papers he left show him already active in a myriad of matters, but there is no reason to believe that if the papers processed by other busy counsellors had survived we would not have material of much the same character. Certainly by Wolsey's standards, his archive suggests an executive and not yet a policy-maker. And we have no need of a policy-maker. Tyndale's unitary sovereign state,

[14] *LP*, iv.5366.

Fox's supreme headship, St German's king-in-parliament – here already is the philosophy, the proclamation and the mechanism of the Henrician Reformation. Not that Cromwell had nothing to contribute. He was quickly associated with the new thinking; the offer to convocation in February 1531 of the Trojan Horse formula 'as far as the law of Christ allows' was probably his, and he was perhaps already playing in his mind with the implications of 'empire'.[15] Yet in ideas Cromwell was a latecomer, and to load him with too much responsibility for the innovative thinking behind the Reformation is to distract from his real originality in the Boleyn camp. At last Anne was backed by a first-rate politician.

Henry VIII had initially planned to recall parliament for October 1531, but the lack of clear policies among the counsellors put back the meeting twice, eventually until 15 January 1532.[16] Hard though it is to follow the arguments of these preliminary weeks, it is clear that several options were being canvassed. Anne spoke defiantly of achieving the divorce irrespective of Charles V, and her alliance with the French (who themselves exuded confidence in a rapid divorce) was demonstrated to all at a banquet in late October, when she sat at the head of the table between Henry and the senior French envoy, Jean du Bellay, while his colleague sat with Norfolk and her parents and, less comfortably, Gardiner and Fitzwilliam.[17] Her faction succeeded in having Cranmer's version of the *Collectanea* published in November, and Cromwell and his ally Thomas Audley, speaker of the Commons and from November a king's serjeant-at-law (senior legal adviser to the crown), produced drafts for legislation to enable the divorce to be granted by the English Church and papal counter-measures to be ignored.

On the other hand, Cromwell and Audley were also busy drafting, under instructions, bills which envisaged a quite different scenario – the continuation of the struggle for a divorce at Rome; one draft would have made it treason to bring into

[15] Lehmberg, *Reformation Parliament*, p. 114.
[16] For the following see Guy, *Public Career of More*, pp. 180–201; Lehmberg, *Reformation Parliament*, pp. 131–53; M. Kelly, 'The submission of the clergy', in *Transactions of the Royal Historical Society*, 5th series, 13 (1965), pp. 97–119; G. R. Elton, 'Thomas More and the opposition to Henry VIII', in *Studies in Tudor and Stuart Politics and Government* (Cambridge, 1974), i.155–72, although the interpretation below differs at certain points.
[17] *Cal. S. P. Span., 1531–33*, pp. 272, 295 [*LP*, v.488, 546].

England any sentence by Clement against Henry, while another
would have curbed the activities of English clerics abroad,
possibly to tie the tongue of Reginald Pole before his departure
to Avignon and Padua was permitted in January 1532. That
Henry or Norfolk or both were behind this planning seems
probable, but we do not know for certain. A third scheme in
preparation was an attempt to hit the pope financially by cutting
off annates from England (payments made by new appointees to
major benefices). This may have begun as a radical plan
based on the *Collectanea*, and it certainly included clauses to
ensure that the English Church would function irrespective of
any papal censures, but it was drafted to use language about the
pope which it is mild to describe as sycophantic.[18] Norfolk
certainly presented the annates bill only as a device to put more
pressure on Clement VII, and never seriously believed that it
threatened the link with Rome.[19] Even so it ran into vigorous
opposition in both houses of parliament, which was only quelled
by the personal intervention of the king, and that more than
once, and even then only after a late concession suspending the
operation of the act unless confirmed in whole or part by royal
letters patent.

The act threatening to restrain annates was passed, but the
manner of its passage did not augur well for parliament's
willingness to adopt the full gospel of St German. In any case,
opposition at court and in the council was becoming outspoken.[20]
Early in the New Year Anne's uncle – desperate to find the least
traumatic way to make progress – tried with the assistance of her
father to persuade Archbishop Warham to defy the pope.
Having failed at that, Norfolk called a meeting of his supporters,
and putting as strongly as he could the lesser *Collectanea* argument about English privilege (topped off with the St German-
like argument that matrimonial causes belonged to the temporal
sphere and so to the crown), he asked for their commitment in
defence of these royal rights. The faction broke, then and there,

[18] 23 Henry VIII, c.20: 'our said sovereign lord the king, and all his natural
subjects as well spiritual as temporal be as obedient, devout, Catholic and
humble children of God and Holy Church as any people be within any realm
christened.'
[19] *Cal. S. P. Span.*, *1531–33*, p. 417 [*LP*, v.898]; cf. *St. Pap.*, vii.349 [*LP*, v.868,
831].
[20] *Cal. S. P. Span.*, *1531–33*, p. 384 [*LP*, v.805].

under the weight of his challenge. Thomas Lord Darcy, who had been with Norfolk all the way since the attack on Wolsey, spoke bluntly and for the majority. His life and his property was at the king's disposal, but matrimonial cases belonged without question to the Church courts. And, he added ominously, king and council knew perfectly well what to do without trying to put a cat betwixt other people's legs and dragging in outsiders.[21] If the king heeded the advice and the implied warning, there was no future for Anne.

After this episode, Cromwell could have had little hope that the legislation necessary to secure Henry's divorce was politically possible. The odds, however, are that he had never had much hope of this at all and had been going through the motions, while the exertions of Henry and Norfolk on the annates bill proved to them that they were up against an impenetrable wall of opposition. Cromwell, instead, had realized that there was only one way forward. This was to 'bounce' the king into a whole-hearted acceptance of the radical gospel – all doubts, all caution, all the warning voices swept aside by the rush of events and the force of the king's emotion. The occasion was to hand – the meeting of the next session of parliament – for the issue was bound to be raised there of the way the Church handled people accused of heresy. It is a fashion of some historians in the later twentieth century to discount hostility to the Church in pre-Reformation England by pointing to evident signs that it was popular and played a valued part in the life of the individual and the community. Yet to say this is to misunderstand anticlericalism. Orthodox belief and support for the existing Church as an institution were not incompatible with severe criticism of the way in which the clergy abused its privileged position; take, for example, the Catch 22 system in heresy trials.[22] Cromwell was well aware how many of the elite present in parliament had these doubts. Already in 1529, in the first session of parliament, a sizeable number of voices had been able to carry some reform of clerical abuses, particularly abuses of the Church courts. Since then, however, and largely by More's own enthusiastic use of the chancellor's office to encour-

---

[21] *'sans vouloer mestre le chat entre les jambes d'autres'.*
[22] Innocent people accused of heresy, who refused to abjure errors they did not hold, were burned.

age persecution, heresy had become the issue – with five men burned, the first for more than fifteen years. In one notorious case, that of Thomas Bilney, there was real doubt whether the victim was in any way a heretic; and although More had not been directly involved, as soon as it had become clear that the matter would be aired in parliament he had set to work on a massive cover-up.[23]

All this Cromwell could see. He had memories of the 1529 agitation, probably some of the anticlerical material prepared at that time, and he may even have noted that Bilney (and other alleged heretics) had attempted to appeal from the verdict of the Church courts to Henry himself as 'supreme head', and had been ignored. Here was the point where the Church was vulnerable to challenge.

Complaints in the Commons about the prosecution of heresy became louder – fuelled, no doubt, by signs in convocation that the Church was determined to increase the pressure against unorthodox opinions but, we can assume, also discreetly encouraged by Cromwell himself. Then at an opportune moment we find the House debating a petition against the Church courts drafted by Cromwell and his assistants, the so-called 'Supplication against the Ordinaries' (ecclesiastical judges), and this was submitted to the king on 18 March. Henry seems not to have recognized the special significance in the Supplication, and neither did convocation when it received the text for comment on 12 April, but the document was in reality a brilliantly conceived booby trap. It invited the king as 'the only sovereign lord, protector and defender' of both clergy and laity to legislate in parliament to 'establish not only those things which to your jurisdiction and prerogative royal justly appertaineth, but also reconcile and bring into perpetual unity your said subjects, spiritual and temporal.'[24] The overtones clearly echo St German and the *Collectanea*, and when the Church was called on for its view it was at once put on the spot. It had either to abandon its traditional independence or tell Henry to his face what had been said so far only privately or unofficially – that the title 'supreme head' meant nothing.

It was here that chance took a hand. Convocation gave to

---

[23] Guy, *Public Career of More*, pp. 164–74.
[24] Ogle, *Lollards' Tower* (1949), p. 330.

Stephen Gardiner the job of preparing an immediate response to the first and most dangerous clause of the Supplication, which queried the independent jurisdiction of the Church. An obvious choice – brilliant, the king's secretary, the odds-on favourite to succeed Warham at Canterbury – Gardiner had two fatal disabilities. First, he was an uncompromising advocate of a clerical privilege that had raised the son of a Suffolk cloth-maker to the richest bishopric in England, and, in Henry's own words, to be the king's 'right hand'. In the second place, Gardiner had been out of England for ten weeks and had returned only in time to see how difficult the crown had found it to get the annates bill through, even in a modified form.[25] The conservatives had fought. Warham had had a violent altercation with Henry across the House of Lords; More had organized an almost subversive opposition in the council and in the Commons; on Easter Sunday, William Peto, head of the Observants (the order of friars peculiarly in favour at court) and a noted partisan of Katherine, had preached a sermon telling Henry to his face that he would end up like the Old Testament tyrant Ahab (though he left unspoken the implication that Anne Boleyn was Jezebel). Then, when the following Sunday a royal chaplain was put up to reply, he was barracked by another of the friars and, for good measure, hauled before convocation for breaching ecclesiastical discipline – a convocation which already had its claws into Hugh Latimer, one of Henry's favourite clergy and later a chaplain to Anne Boleyn.[26] And when parliament reassembled after the Easter recess and Henry asked the Commons to vote him money, he was told by Katherine's sympathizers there that to take her back was the best way to guarantee national security. Given that the anti-Boleyn faction, clergy as well as laity, was everywhere standing up to be counted, it would have required a man of much less assurance than the bishop of Winchester not to feel that now he had returned, a counter-attack must be successful. His earlier support of Anne Boleyn was a thing of the past; the independence of the Church was too great a price to pay for the king's happiness.

So Gardiner's reply to the Supplication of 18 March was an unequivocal assertion of the ancient privilege of the Church: 'We

[25] Muller, *Gardiner*, pp. 45–6.
[26] BL, Sloane MS 2495, ff. 15v–16; *Cal. S. P. Span., 1531–33*, pp. 427–8 [*LP*, v.941].

your most humble subjects may not submit the execution of our charges and duty, certainly prescribed by God, to your highness's assent.'[27] Henry reacted as Cromwell knew he would once his God-given position was impugned. If churchmen believed this, the supreme headship was a title empty of meaning and their concession in 1531 had been a dishonest attempt to deceive their sovereign. Gardiner's reply reached the king about 27 April, and Henry reacted with stunning force. He unmanned Gardiner by his fury, and called up Thomas Audley to invite the Commons to renew agitation against the Church; then on 10 May he sent Edward Fox to convocation to demand the unequivocal surrender of the Church's independence. When the clergy showed signs of fight, Henry stepped up pressure in parliament and Cromwell produced a bill to strip the Church of its powers. Thomas More, realizing that the crisis had come, threw his weight openly against the king, most probably by mobilizing again the conservative lobby in the Lords which had emasculated the annates bill, and he too received the full blast of Henry's wrath.

With Gardiner and More both in disgrace the Church offered a compromise, but the king promptly prorogued parliament, so blocking the ability of the bishops, abbots and lay peers of a conservative turn of mind to support from the Lords the sort of rearguard action that had won the day in 1531. Instead, convocation was ordered on 15 May to itself adjourn that same day – having first, of course, given the king what he wanted – and to make the point clear a party of leading courtiers and counsellors made a quite unprecedented descent on the upper house of convocation (the bishops and abbots). Significantly this was made up of Norfolk, Anne's uncle, Wiltshire and Rochford, her father and brother, Oxford, father-in-law to Norfolk's son and on close terms with Cromwell, Sandes, the lord chamberlain and an archetypal sycophant, and Katherine's ally the marquis of Exeter, in yet another exhibition (or test) of his loyalty to Henry rather than to principle.[28] Their ultimatum given, they took the Church's answer back to the king, only to return later in the day with Henry's final terms. Warham knew he was beaten. Resistance would only invite a massive series of praemunire

---

[27] Ogle, *Lollards' Tower*, p. 340.
[28] *LP*, v.479, 679.

prosecutions, then action by statute in the next session of parliament, and it would infuriate the king; better to save what could be saved. Sending the hot-headed lower house of convocation back home, he gathered varying degrees of support from six other bishops and perhaps a further half-dozen abbots, and surrendered to the king's demands. The following day, when the king's anger had sufficiently cooled, Norfolk was able to arrange a relatively harmonious surrender, by Sir Thomas More, of the great seal.

There is no contemporary evidence of Anne Boleyn's reception of the news of the Submission of the Clergy, but it revolutionized her position. Thomas Audley replaced More at the chancery, though initially with the title 'keeper of the great seal', and Thomas Cromwell became undeniably the key man in government. Within the royal household where in May 1532 death had conveniently removed Anne's old critic, Henry Guildford, his place as controller was taken by another of Cromwell's allies, William Paulet.[29] With her brother already one of the two noblemen of the privy chamber and her father, lord privy seal, Anne Boleyn now had supporters in many of the vital positions in government and court. As always, of course, her uncle the duke of Norfolk had survived, despite growing disquiet at Anne's independence of mind and hatred of the religious radicalism with which she was associated, and despite the defeat of the alternative policy he had been advocating of even more pressure on Rome. But whatever his doubts and however substantial the lead that Cromwell now had over him in royal favour, the duke, with his willingness to 'suffer anything for the sake of ruling', had predictably finished up on the winning side and remained, if somewhat shaken, still a piece on the political board for Cromwell and Anne to reckon with.[30]

Amongst those who had overtly resisted the radicalism of Anne Boleyn and her supporters, the rush was on to make amends as quickly as possible – and none moved more rapidly than Stephen Gardiner.[31] In 1530 he had marked his successful beginning as the king's secretary by buying out Sir Richard

[29] Ibid., v.1069.
[30] Ibid., v.1059.
[31] Cf. John London, 'wherever I find occasion to oblige the king or any pertaining to my lady marquess [Anne], I do my duty as Mr. Barlow and Mr. Taylor her servants can testify': ibid., v.1366; cf. 1034, 1632.

Weston's interest in the royal estate at Hanworth in Middlesex. Henry VIII and his father before him had created a fine country property there, with a moated manor house connected by bridges to the gardens (which were noted for their strawberries), an aviary, ponds, an orchard and a park beyond – and very convenient for Hampton Court and the River Thames. All this the bishop now surrendered to Anne in an effort to retrieve his monumental error over the Supplication.[32] Henry moved in workmen, fitted out the house with specially made furniture and instructed his Italian experts to provide the latest fashion in Renaissance ornament (see plate 42).[33] Not that the king was wholly mollified. Gardiner was never entirely comfortable as secretary thereafter, and his formal replacement by Cromwell in the spring of 1534 was only a recognition of the realities. Even his brilliant exposition of the royal supremacy in his 1535 best-seller, *De Vera Obedientia*, never quite persuaded Henry to trust him as he once had.

We may also detect signs that realists were recognizing where the future lay. Honor the wife of Arthur Plantagenet, Viscount Lisle, made strenuous efforts in the summer of 1532 to secure Anne's attention, sending first a present of peewits and then a bow, a gift which fell somewhat flat when it proved too heavy for Anne to draw. What Lady Lisle wanted was some concessions for a trading venture she was starting with her own ship, the *Sunday of Porchester*, and although Anne informed her that the time for such a request to the king was not right 'for certain causes' – no doubt the unhappy state of the royal coffers following the failure of parliament to vote adequate taxes in May – she did promise 'to do you good in some other way'.[34]

Court gossip also blamed Anne for the shocking spectacle of a young priest being drawn and hanged without first being degraded from his orders, and this for a coining offence which was naive rather than treasonable. When her own father had

---

[32] BL, Harl. MS 303, ff. 13–15v [cf. *LP*, iv.6542(23); v.1139(32), 1207(7)].
[33] Colvin, *King's Works*, iv.147–9; W. H. Tapp, *Anne Boleyn and Elizabeth at the Royal Manor of Hanworth* (1953).
[34] *Lisle Letters*, i.xxxii [*LP*, ix.402]. M. St. Clare Byrne pointed out that the *LP* date is wrong, and proposed May/June 1530 to Summer 1532. The letter, however, clearly comes at the start of a summer progress and must refer to a royal visit to Waltham on a Monday in July/Aug., i.e. 8 Aug. 1532. The other possible date is 9 Aug. 1529, which seems too early [*LP*, iv.5825; v.pp. 314, 320–1, no. 1152 and above, p. 142].

asked her to intercede for the prisoner, she was supposed to have replied that there were too many priests in the country already.[35]

It was clear too that the relationship between Henry and Anne had moved on to a different level: marriage was now a real and immediate possibility. The granting and furnishing of Hanworth was one sign; another was the very considerable increase in Henry's spending on Anne. In both 1530 and 1531 he had paid out from his privy purse about £220 on or for Anne. In 1532 the figure jumped to £330, although that did include nearly £50 lost to her in ten days playing 'Pope Julius', an early version of Commerce. Much of the extra went on clothes, and while it is anachronistic to talk of a 'trousseau', Anne was certainly being fitted out for the role of queen. Two garments are described in particular detail. One was an open-sleeved cloak of black satin, lined throughout in the same material and with three and three quarter yards of matching velvet at the collar and hem. The other was a black satin nightgown (dressing-gown), lined with black taffeta and edged with velvet. And lest we forget how striking this must have been with Anne's dark hair, there was an equally calculated gown in green damask.[36]

Given the dramatic moves in the early months of 1532 and the new relationship between Henry and Anne, it is easy to see the rest of the year as a run-up to their wedding. It is, however, wiser to see first the way in which events seem to follow a natural line of development, but then to observe the doubts and difficulties which that interpretation leaves unresolved. Certainly from May 1532, marriage was in the air. The king talked openly of marrying again.[37] Building workers were impressed in every part of the land to assist in the renovation of the royal lodgings in the Tower of London, which played an important role in the ritual of coronations.[38] Cromwell was soon busy drafting legislation to protect the king's new powers from opponents at home and abroad. Archbishop Warham – a longed-for bonus, this – died after forty years of service to the crown and two in defence of the Church, and the Boleyns were able to secure the immediate selection of Cranmer to succeed him, a remarkable demon-

---

[35] *Cal. S. P. Span.*, *1531–33*, p. 481 [*LP*, v.1165].
[36] Nicolas, *Privy Purse*, pp. 274–7; 222–3.
[37] *Cal. S. P. Span.*, *1531–33*, p. 489 [*LP*, v.1202].
[38] *LP*, v.1307.

stration of influence, since it was usual to leave a bishopric vacant for a year in order to milk the income for the crown.[39] And the imperial ambassador became aware that something else was afoot that summer. The English were, in great secrecy, feeling their way towards a meeting between Henry VIII and Francis I.[40]

The plan was for Henry to spend some time on French soil at Boulogne, and for Francis to visit Calais in return, but filling in the detail proved difficult. Henry and Anne wanted as public a triumph as possible, in order to give her the European recognition she needed, and they angled for the attendance of Marguerite d'Angoulême and an impressive array of French noble women (Francis's second wife, Eleanor, was a niece of Katherine of Aragon and, of course, quite out of the question).[41] At first this was agreed, but later Marguerite withdrew, pleading ill-health – a polite way, it was said, of showing her disapproval of Henry's intended marriage.[42] More likely, she was responding to second thoughts on the part of Francis, who was anxious to avoid anything that could hinder the alliance he was hoping to make with the pope: his second son, Henry, would marry Catherine de' Medici at Marseilles in October 1533. The French did suggest the duchesse de Vendôme in place of the king's sister, but she was too closely associated with the livelier side of Francis I's court to please Henry, who was intent on the utmost propriety. In the end it was agreed that no ladies would be officially present on either side, but as Anne would go to Calais with Henry, Francis would meet her when he arrived there.

The proposal was kept secret for as long as possible, between Henry, Anne, the French ambassador and a very few others. As in 1520, the possibility of a summit meeting with the French was guaranteed to rouse English hostility. In the event, much of the

[39] Ridley, *Cranmer*, pp. 50–3.
[40] *Cal. S. P. Span.*, *1531–33*, pp. 464, 488 [*LP*, v.1109, 1202]. For the conference, see P. A. Hamy, *Entrevue de François Premier avec Henry VIIIᵉ à Boulogne* (Paris, 1898); *Cal. S. P. Ven.*, *1527–33*, 822–4; *LP*, v.1485; *The Maner of the Tryumphe at Caleys and Bulleyn*, Wynkyn de Worde (1532), ed. A. F. Pollard, in *Tudor Tracts* (1903).
[41] Hamy, *Entrevue*, pp. ix–xii [*LP*, v.1187]. Hamy, following *LP*, attributes this item to du Bellay. Friedmann, *Anne Boleyn*, i.165 corrects to de la Pommeraye; du Bellay was in France: du Bellay, *Correspondance*, i.p. 280. *Cal. S. P. Span.*, *1531–33*, p. 494 [*LP*, v.1256].
[42] Ibid., p. 528 [*LP*, v.1377]; Hamy, *Entrevue*, p. 143; *LP*, vi.134; P. Jourda, *Marguerite d'Angoulême* (Paris, 1930), p. 172; see above, pp. 40–2.

credit for agreeing and putting into operation this less grandiose final scheme belonged to Anne herself. Giles de la Pommeraye, the French ambassador, was invited on the royal progress that summer, and at each of the houses visited, Henry made time to point out the new building he had had done and what his future plans were.[43] The king took the ambassador hunting all day, the two of them together, and went out of his way to show him English methods. Often de la Pommeraye was asked to escort Anne, sharing a butt as they shot the deer with crossbows or going with her to watch coursing, and she presented him with a huntsman's coat and hat, a horn and a greyhound. When the arrangements for the Calais meeting were complete, Anne had de la Pommeraye as a guest at the dinner she gave for Henry at Hanworth.[44] The ambassador claimed in his despatches that Anne was doing all this at the behest of the king to honour Francis I, but he admitted privately to Chapuys that her services to France were more than could ever be repaid.[45]

This is not to say that Henry did not join in with enthusiasm. He was determined to make a good show, and, silencing the grumblers, he called up almost all of the English aristocracy which was healthy and could be spared from duties in England.[46] An agreement was made to limit display by both sides, especially the wearing of cloth of gold or silver, but even so, Henry's own expenditure on the spot may have exceeded £6,000, and the limitation on attire did not, of course, apply either to the king or to Anne.[47] Henry also seems to have seized the opportunity to reset much of the royal jewellery, setting aside many of the best stones for her, as in the case of four bracelets which yielded Anne no fewer than eighteen tabled rubies.[48] On top of this, Henry stripped Katherine of her jewels. The indirect message, that he wished her to give them to him – the customary way in which the king expressed requests that could not be refused – elicited the response that ever since the New Year she had been forbidden to give Henry anything, and the rare barbed comment that it

[43] Hamy, *Entrevue*, pp. ix–xii [*LP*, v.1187].
[44] See above, p. 60; *Cal. S. P. Span., 1531–33*, p. 525 [*LP*, v.1377]; *Cal. S. P. Ven., 1527–33*, 808.
[45] Hamy, *Entrevue*, pp. xi–xii [*LP*, v.1187]; *Cal. S. P. Span., 1531–33*, p. 511 [*LP*, v.1316].
[46] Ibid., p. 511 [*LP*, v.1316]; Hamy, *Entrevue*, p.l.
[47] *LP*, v.1373, 1600.
[48] Ibid., v.1237; BL, Roy. MS 7 C.xvi, f. 41v [*LP*, v.1376].

would be a sin to allow her jewels to adorn 'the scandal of Christendom'. This thrust forced a typically self-righteous reply from the king, and the vulgarity of a direct order to send the jewels.[49]

Jewels were not, however, all that Anne needed to be fitted for the European stage. When Francis I had last seen her she had been a lady-in-waiting to his wife. If she was to meet him now as England's intended queen, she needed status. This she was given at an impressive ceremony in Windsor Castle on the morning of Sunday 1 September.[50] There, her hair about her shoulders and her ermine-trimmed crimson velvet hardly visible under the jewels, Anne was conducted into the king's presence by Garter King at Arms, with the countesses of Rutland and Derby, and her cousin Mary Howard, the duke of Richmond's prospective wife, carrying the crimson velvet mantle and gold coronet of a marquis. Henry was flanked by the dukes of Norfolk and Suffolk and surrounded by the court, with the officers at arms in their tabards and de la Pommeraye as a guest of honour. Anne kneeled to the king, while Stephen Gardiner read out a patent conferring on her in her own right and on her offspring the title, marquis of Pembroke.[51] Henry then placed on her the mantle and the coronet and handed her the patent of nobility, plus another granting lands worth £1,000 a year. Anne thanked him and withdrew to her chamber, after which Henry proceeded to St George's Chapel and a solemn high mass sung by Gardiner. Here the king and de la Pommeraye (on behalf of Francis) swore to the terms of a treaty between England and France; Edward Fox preached a sermon extolling the intention of Henry and Francis to co-operate against the Turkish infidel, and announced publicly the plan for the two to meet at Calais. The service ended with a magnificent Te Deum, with trumpets and orchestration,

---

[49] *Cal. S. P. Span.*, *1531–33*, p. 525 [*LP*, v.1377].

[50] Ibid., p. 508 [*LP*, v.1292]; *Cal. S. P. Ven.*, *1527–33*, 802; *LP*, v.1274(3), (4). Hall, *Chronicle*, p. 790. The partisan nature of the ceremony was emphasized by the countess of Rutland being a daughter of Sir William Paston, a Norfolk neighbour of the Boleyns, and the countess of Derby being the stepsister of Anne's mother. The duke of Norfolk's estranged wife was intended to be present, but probably refused: *LP*, v.1239.

[51] Anne was described as both 'marquis' and 'marchioness' of Pembroke. The point in the former title was that she held a newly created peerage in her own right, not (as was the case otherwise) by virtue of marriage. But for convenience I have used 'lady marquis' or the female form.

after which everyone returned to the castle for a great banquet.

For several weeks afterwards the embassies of Europe buzzed with rumour and counter-rumour about the prospective meeting – would it take place after all? Speculation was ended on Friday 11 October when before dawn Anne took ship with Henry at Dover, on *The Swallow,* and found herself at 10.00 am, and after almost twenty years, landing once more at Calais. But this time she was at the side of her intended husband and being greeted by the thunder of a royal salute, the attentions of the mayor and lord deputy of Calais and a parade of the garrison. Not that her own party was very prominent. Her twenty or thirty ladies must have been almost lost among the two thousand or so nobles, knights and lesser men escorting Henry, and despite his best efforts they were only from the Boleyn faction, or else were time-servers.[52] Many of the more important Englishwomen were missing – most noticeably his sister Mary.

Anne had ten days in Calais with Henry, living like a queen, escorted by him everywhere and lodging with him at the Exchequer, the only interruption being the surprise arrival of a delegation of welcoming notables from Francis I on the 15th.[53] Then on the 21st the king left to meet 'his beloved brother' and to spend four days at the French court at Boulogne for what has been described as a 'stag party' – 'the great cheer that was there, no man can express it.' Then it was England's turn, and Henry arrived back at Calais with Francis on Friday 25 October.

We hear nothing of Anne Boleyn during Francis's magnificent reception in Calais – all told, 3,000 guns were fired in his honour – and his lodgings at Staple Hall on Calais' main square were some distance from the Exchequer. One of his first actions on arrival was to send the provost of Paris to her with the present of a diamond worth £3,500, but still she made no appearance. Evidently Anne had a sense of theatre, and she was reserving her entry as the climax of the great banquet Henry was to give on the Sunday night. The room for this was magnificently prepared, with hangings of cloth of tissue and cloth of silver, ornamented with gold wreaths encrusted with precious stones and pearls, and a display of seven shelves of gold plate – not a single piece of

---

[52] *Cal. S. P. Ven., 1527–33,* 802 gives thirty, 822 gives twenty; a French report, *LP,* v.1485, gives ten or twelve only.
[53] *Cal. S. P. Ven., 1527–33,* 824.

silver or silver gilt – and all of it lit by twenty candelabra of silver and silver gilt carrying one hundred wax candles.

It was after the dinner and its one hundred and seventy different dishes prepared alternately French style and English style that Anne made her entry, leading a masque of six ladies 'gorgeously apparelled'.[54] There was her sister Mary Carey, her aunt Dorothy, countess of Derby, one of her supporters at Windsor, another aunt, Elizabeth Lady Fitzwalter, her sister-in-law, Lady Rochford, her client (or dependant) Lady Lisle and lastly Lady Wallop, wife of the ambassador to France and at least a former client.[55] They wore costumes 'of strange fashion' – loose, gold-laced overdresses of cloth of gold, with sashes of crimson satin ornamented with a wavy pattern in cloth of silver. All were masked, and they were escorted by four maids of honour in crimson satin and tabards of cypress lawn. Each chose a Frenchman to dance with: the countess of Derby led out Marguerite d'Angoulême's husband the king of Navarre, and the other ladies their partners, but Francis himself was, of course, claimed by Anne. After a couple of dances, Henry could no longer restrain his childlike excitement and removed the masks 'so that there the ladies' beauties were showed'. Dancing then went on for another hour, but Francis and Anne spent much of this in private conversation before Henry escorted his guests back to Staple Hall.

The last full day of the Calais visit, 28 October, soon passed in holding a chapter of the Order of the Garter and a wrestling match which saw Henry's specially imported Cornish wrestlers restore the national honour lost at the Field of Cloth of Gold, though the king very wisely did not again take on Francis in person.[56] Thus the atmosphere of amity persisted to the end, Tuesday 29 October, when Henry accompanied the French king to say farewell at the border-crossing into France. That done, there was a rush to get back to England, but the brilliant weather which had so far graced proceedings now broke in a furious north-westerly gale which, coupled with a spring tide, drove the lucky ones back to Calais and the unlucky on to the inundated shores of Flanders.[57] Someone, however, must have

---

[54] Thus *The Maner of the Tryumphe*; cf. Hall, *Chronicle*, p. 793.
[55] See above, pp. 126–7; *Cal. S. P. Span., 1531–33*, p. 466 [*LP*, v.1109].
[56] *LP*, v.1093, 1168.
[57] Hall, *Chronicle*, p. 794.

got over, to set in motion the propaganda that Henry saw as one major object of the meeting with Francis. Wynkyn de Worde had his pamphlet, *The manner of the triumph at Calais and Boulogne,* on the streets of London within the week. Its one reference to Anne Boleyn may, indeed, be a government-inspired piece of disinformation. Her name heads the list of those who danced on the Sunday night, the second is that of 'my lady Mary', followed by the countess of Derby and Lady Fitzwalter. In no way did Mary Carey take precedence over a countess (or her aunts), nor would she immediately spring to mind as 'my lady Mary'. There must be a real suspicion that readers were intended to assume that Henry's daughter Mary had been at Calais and had countenanced the precedence given to Anne Boleyn.[58]

Henry and Anne had intended to stay at Calais until the 8th and so they missed the dangers and the shipwrecks, but the storm which only began to slacken on Monday 4 November must have kept them confined to the Exchequer. Not that that was much of a hardship. It was a large house with extensions including a tennis court, with a gallery to walk in, a king's garden and a queen's garden and, if Anne occupied the accommodation designated for her on a planned later visit, she had a suite of seven main rooms (including a chamber overlooking the garden), and her bedroom backed onto Henry's own, with interconnecting doors.[59] All the while the wind remained foul for the Channel crossing, and when the intended departure day arrived it rose to a new violence which cleared pedestrians from the Calais streets. The return of fine weather on Sunday 10 November encouraged Henry to have his bed and baggage sent aboard, but then a Channel fog put an end to any immediate departure. They got away eventually at midnight on Tuesday 12 November, and reached Dover early on Thursday morning after a painfully slow crossing lasting twenty-nine hours. The counsellors at Westminster breathed a sigh of profound relief at the news of the king's safe return, and rapidly organized a Te Deum at St Paul's Cathedral. Henry, however, took his time; he had only reached Eltham by the 24th.[60] And the explanation we know. Somewhere, sometime, perhaps as the wind tore through

[58] The 'lady Mary' cannot be Henry's sister, who is always called 'queen of France'.

[59] Colvin, *King's Works*, iii.349–51.

[60] *Cal. S. P. Span.*, *1531–33*, pp. 556–7 [*LP*, v.1579].

the Calais streets, or in a manor house in Kent, Anne at last slept with Henry.[61]

With Anne Boleyn and Henry VIII now living together, albeit discreetly, the time of doubt and irresolution was finally over – or so it would seem. To many historians the decision to cohabit was made possible by the Anglo-French treaty of the previous summer, and whatever was finally agreed at Calais. The first promised Henry a large force of French ships and troops, should Charles V attempt an invasion. As for Calais (about which Henry and Francis later disagreed), the English king seems to have been convinced that the French would make a further attempt to bring Clement to heel – the proposed match with Catherine de' Medici was an obvious bargaining counter – but that if the pope did not yield, they would then join England in appealing over his head to a general council of the Church. Armed with this guarantee, Henry (it is suggested) had at last felt secure enough to consummate his relationship with Anne – and she, for her part, must have been convinced at last that it was safe for her to respond. By the end of December 1532 she could suspect that she was pregnant, and about 25 January the two were married.[62] The wedding was kept secret, although Henry realized that he could not expect to keep the news from Rome much after Easter (13 April). Montmorency, the *grand maître* of the French royal household, was still writing to Anne as *Madame la Marquise* in March, not knowing that her brother was then on the way to make Francis the first to know that she was now both wife and expectant mother.[63] Chapuys did report in February that Henry had been formally betrothed, but he was still at the end of March only able to report that there were

---

[61] This is the probability; Anne was pregnant by the beginning or at least the middle of December; see below, p. 212.

[62] Cranmer, *Letters*, p. 246. Hall, *Chronicle*, p. 794 gives St. Erkenwald's Day, 14 Nov. 1532. This was adopted by later Protestants anxious to protect Elizabeth's reputation. Hall, however, had no such motive, and his date does coincide with the probable start of cohabitation (which must have been known in court circles). He may, therefore, preserve the genuine date when, by sexual intercourse, Henry and Anne turned their vows into a canonically valid marriage – always assuming that there was no valid marriage with Katherine. The marriage ceremony *c.*25 Jan. 1533 (on which Friedmann's arguments, *Anne Boleyn*, ii.338–9 are conclusive) would thus be the formal regularizing of the relationship before a priest.

[63] *LP*, vi.230, 242.

strong rumours that the marriage would take place after Easter
and it was Carlo Capello from Venice who was the earliest
ambassador to report (12 April) that Henry had already been
married for several months.[64]

The news was hardly much quicker to circulate in England,
and the slowness of observers to tumble to what was going on
again shows how strong the assumption was that Henry simply
could not remarry without the pope's consent. However, for eyes
which avoided this conditioning, the signs had been clear. In the
second week of December Henry had gone with Anne to view the
new building in the Tower and, most exceptionally, he had
shown her the royal treasure in the treasure room. When the
French ambassador arrived with an important message, Anne
apparently persuaded Henry to open the room again and show
the ambassador also, something which Henry had specifically
avoided doing when he had taken the envoy over the Tower
some days previously. Once Henry began to reveal financial
secrets the relationship had gone deep indeed.[65]

On 24 January it became common knowledge that Anne's
protégé, Cranmer, was to be the next archbishop of Canterbury;
he had got back to England earlier in the month, having been
collected by special messenger sent by Henry to hasten his
return.[66] On the 26th Thomas Audley was promoted to the title
of chancellor, and a few days later Chapuys reported what seems
to have been a meeting to discuss the penultimate draft of the
Act of Appeals which Cromwell had been preparing, to put on
the statute book a statement of the royal supremacy and to break
the judicial links between England and Rome.[67] Meanwhile
Henry and Anne were beginning to talk even more freely about
getting married, and applicants for places in her household were
told that they would not have long to wait.[68] Her father the earl
of Wiltshire told the earl of Rutland on 7 February that the king
was determined to marry Anne at once, and sounded him out on
his reaction to the forthcoming appeals bill. When Rutland
(even though a Boleyn supporter) said that parliament had no

[64] *Cal. S. P. Span.*, *1531–33*, pp. 609, 625 [*LP*, vi.180, 296]; *Cal. S. P. Ven.*,
1527–33, 870.
[65] *Cal. S. P. Span.*, *1531–33*, pp. 566–7 [*LP*, v.1633].
[66] *Cal. S. P. Ven.*, *1527–33*, 846; Ridley, *Cranmer*, pp. 52–3.
[67] Lehmberg, *Reformation Parliament*, pp. 161, 168.
[68] *Cal. S. P. Span.*, *1531–33*, pp. 598–600, 602 [*LP*, vi.142, 160].

competence in spiritual matters, Boleyn flew into a rage and browbeat him into agreeing to vote for the king; other peers were probably handled similarly.[69]

Anne's pregnancy was generally known of within the court before the news of her marriage, if only from proud hints dropped by the new queen herself.[70] Chapuys reported that on 15 February she had said quite openly to the duke of Norfolk that if she was not pregnant by Easter she would undertake a pilgrimage to pray to the Virgin Mary. A week later she said to one of her favourites, probably Wyatt, and again in the hearing of many courtiers, that she had developed a craving for apples, which the king said was a sign that she was pregnant but which she had denied – clearly in jest, as she went back into her room laughing loudly. On St Mathias' Day, 24 February, Anne held a sumptuous banquet for the king in her own rooms which were hung for the occasion with the best tapestries, and the tables were set with a mass of gold plate. Henry was in fine form. He spent the whole meal bantering and flirting with Anne and her ladies and ignoring the duke of Suffolk, the chancellor and his other guests, although he was heard to ask the dowager duchess of Norfolk, Anne's stepgrandmother, whether she did not think that 'madame la marquise' had made a good marriage and had a great dowry, for all the furnishings and all the plate belonged to her.[71]

By the second week of March Henry was confident enough to put up preachers at court who proclaimed the immorality of his marriage with Katherine and (by implication) 'the virtues and secret merits' of Anne, while on the 14th Cromwell introduced the appeals bill in the Commons and on the 26th convocation was asked to pronounce on the validity of a dispensation to marry a brother's widow.[72] By then the papal bulls allowing Cranmer to be consecrated under the traditional forms had arrived, and on 30 March the ceremony took place, a few days before the appeals bill cleared both Houses of Parliament and convocation gave its decision in Henry's favour. There was now nothing to stop Anne's public recognition.[73] By the end of March

[69] Ibid., p. 602 [*LP*, vi.160]. Chapuys seems to have believed that what was being proposed was a bill to approve the marriage to Anne.

[70] Friedmann, *Anne Boleyn*, i.189 n.2, 190 n.1.

[71] *Cal. S. P. Span.*, *1531–33*, p. 617 [*LP*, vi.212].

[72] Ibid., p. 618 [*LP*, vi.235]; Lehmberg, *Reformation Parliament*, pp. 174–8.

her household had at last been formed.[74] On the Wednesday of
Holy Week Katherine was told that she had to reduce her title
and lifestyle to that of dowager princess of Wales; already Bishop
Fisher, the lone voice speaking up for her, had been silenced by
detention.[75] And the following Saturday, the eve of Easter Day
1533, Anne went to mass as queen, at last. Glittering with
jewellery, wearing a pleated gown of cloth of gold, her train
borne by her cousin the future duchess of Richmond and with
sixty maids of honour in attendance, Queen Anne was prayed for
by name and given full regal honours.[76]

Told in this way, the story of the months before Easter 1533 does
appear to be one of ever increasing tempo leading towards the
inevitable climax of the long years of courtship. The Submission
of the Clergy was the decisive breakthrough; mass on Easter eve,
the victory parade. Yet despite the coherence and the pace of the
story, despite its romantic conviction, there are disturbing pieces
of evidence which do not fit in, suggesting that the courtship of
Henry VIII and Anne Boleyn remained difficult to the end and
that the outcome even after May 1532 was by no means certain.
In the first place, there was the eight-month delay after the
Church had been reduced to submission; Archbishop Warham
could not be pressured into defying the pope, and the decision,
on his death, that Cranmer was the man who could be relied on
to grasp that nettle, necessarily meant more delay. Secondly,
even though French protection against Charles V had been
forthcoming since the summer, and even though the drafting of
legislation on the relation between England and the papacy was
well advanced, Henry decided at the end of September to
postpone parliament until the New Year.[77] Then there are signs

[73] The annulment of Katherine's marriage postdated the public recognition
of Anne, and was achieved at an archiepiscopal court at Dunstable, 10–23
May. It was followed on 28 May by a hearing which confirmed the legality of
the union already effected between Anne and Henry.
[74] *Cal. S. P. Span.*, *1531–33*, p. 625 [*LP*, vi.296].
[75] Ibid., p. 629 [*LP*, vi.324].
[76] Ibid., p. 643 [*LP*, vi.351]; *Cal. S. P. Ven.*, *1527–33*, 870.
[77] Parliament was prorogued by a commission dated 4 Nov., on the excuse
of the king's absence in Calais. The decision, however, had been taken before a
letter from Audley to Cromwell, which was written prior to the last Wednesday
before the king left Greenwich, i.e. 2 Oct. The alleged reason would have
justified a brief prorogation (the Calais meeting was over by 29 Oct.), but not
until Feb. 1533 [*LP*, v.1406, 1514–15].

that loss of nerve and dislike of the king's policies were not entirely quelled by the Submission. The duke of Norfolk claimed that he, and particularly Anne's father had blocked a wedding in May 1532; he even told Chapuys that Wiltshire had *contrefit le frenetique* ('pretended insanity') on that occasion and that both had earned black looks from Anne as a result.[78] Be that as it may (and Chapuys had detected no hint of this performance at the time), it does seem possible that Norfolk may have been more than a little involved on the conservative side over the Submission. He certainly made a curious trip to Dover in March 1532 which allowed him to meet Stephen Gardiner on his return from France and to escort him back to London.[79] In June the duke quarrelled with the French ambassador, and Anne had to move in to save the Calais meeting.[80] As late as the end of May 1533, Chapuys was still reporting tension between Anne, and Norfolk and Wiltshire, and he passed on the story that when the latter saw his pregnant daughter enlarging her gowns and had remarked that she should not try to hide the baby but thank God for the condition she was in, he had been publicly crushed by Anne's reply that she was in a better state than he had wished her to be![81]

Outright opposition persisted as well, and from a very difficult quarter: Henry's sister Mary and her husband Charles Brandon, duke of Suffolk. During the Easter break between the two parliamentary sessions in 1532, Mary made a number of opprobrious remarks about her brother's choice of Anne, and these set off an affray in the Sanctuary at Westminster which, quite in the style of Capulet and Montague, had left one of the Brandons' principal gentlemen dead and the court in an uproar. The duke had to promise to control his men, the killers were then in June allowed to purchase a pardon, and the duke and duchess apparently made themselves scarce in their house in Oxford-

---

[78] *Cal. S. P. Span.*, *1531–33*, p. 699 [*LP*, vi.556].
[79] Ibid., p. 405 [*LP*, v.850].
[80] Ibid., pp. 476–7 [*LP*, v.1131].
[81] Ibid., p. 699 [*LP*, vi.556]. Chapuys' report 'that . . . the Lady taking a piece of material, as is the custom with pregnant women here to add to gowns which are too tight, her father said to her that she should take it out and thank God to find herself in such a condition' is often interpreted as criticism of Anne by Wiltshire. The advice not to disguise the pregnancy only makes sense if interpreted as above. The alternative reading in Friedmann, *Anne Boleyn*, i.158 n.1, amounts to much the same.

1 *Anne Boleyn*, by an anonymous painter.

2 (above) *Anne Boleyn*, by an anonymous painter.

3 (left) *Anne Boleyn*, attributed to John Hoskins.

4 (above) *Unknown Lady*, by Hans
Holbein the younger, inscribed *Anna
Bullen decollata fuit Londini 19 May 1536*.

5 (right) *Unknown Lady*, by Hans
Holbein the younger, inscribed *Anna
Bollein Queen*.

6 (facing page, above left) Queen
Elizabeth's ring.

7 (facing page, above, middle) *Anne Boleyn?*,
attributed to Lucas Hornebolte.

8 (facing page, above right) *Princess Mary*,
attributed to Lucas Hornebolte.

9 (facing page, middle) *Katherine of Aragon*,
attributed to Lucas Hornebolte.

10 (facing page, below) A portrait medal of
Anne Boleyn, inscribed *A.R. The Moost Happi
Anno 1534*.

11 (above) *Henry VIII*, attributed to Lucas
Hornebolte.

12 (right) *Jane Seymour*, attributed to Lucas
Hornebolte.

13 (below, right) *Henry Fitzroy, duke of
Richmond*, attributed to Lucas Hornebolte.

15 (above) *Margaret of Austria*, by Bernard van Orley.

14 (facing page) *Elizabeth I as Princess*, by an anonymous painter.

16 (above) *Charles V*, attributed to Lucas Hornebolte.

17 (left) *Claude of France*, by Jean Clouet.

18 (below) *Francis I*, by Godefroy le Batave.

19 (top) Mechelen, the palace of Margaret of Austria: the southern range from the courtyard.

20 (bottom) Blois, the palace of Claude of France: the 'façade of the loggias', under construction during Anne Boleyn's residence with Queen Claude.

21 (top) *The Privy Stairs of Whitehall Palace*, by Antony van Wyngaerde. In the foreground the privy stairs lead from the river. At the back of the courtyard beyond is the innerface of the Court Gate. From the Holbein Gate to the left a gallery leads to the box overlooking the tiltyard and to the octagonal building, the Cockpit, beyond. St James' Palace is in the background, to the right.

22 (bottom) A letter from Henry VIII to Anne Boleyn, September 1528: 'the reasonable request off your last lettre with the pleasure also that I take to know them trw, causyth me to send yow now thes news. The legate whyche we most desyre aryvyd att Parys on Sonday or Munday last past, so that I trust by the next Munday to here off hys aryvall att Cales, and then I trust within a wyle after to enyoy that whyche I have so long longyd for, to God's pleasur and owre bothe comfortes. No more to yow at thys present, myne owne darlyng, for lake off tyme, but that I wolde you were in myne armes or I in yours, for I thynk it long syns I kyst yow. Writtyn affter the kyllyng off an hart at xj off the kloke, myndyng with God's grace tomorow mytely tymely to kyll a nother. By the hand off hym whyche I trust shortly shallbe yours. Henry R.'

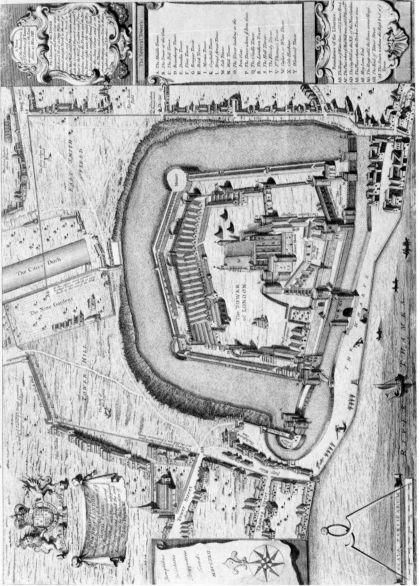

23 The Tower of London, 1597. The royal apartments are to the south-east of the White Tower; note the scaffold on Tower Hill; the scaffold on Tower Green was erected twenty yards due south of the chapel of St Peter ad Vincula, in the north-west of the Inmost Ward.

24 (above) *The Mount Parnassus*, Hans Holbein the younger's design for the tableau at Gracechurch Street for Anne Boleyn's coronation procession.

25 (left) *Henry VIII dining in the Privy Chamber* (after Holbein?).

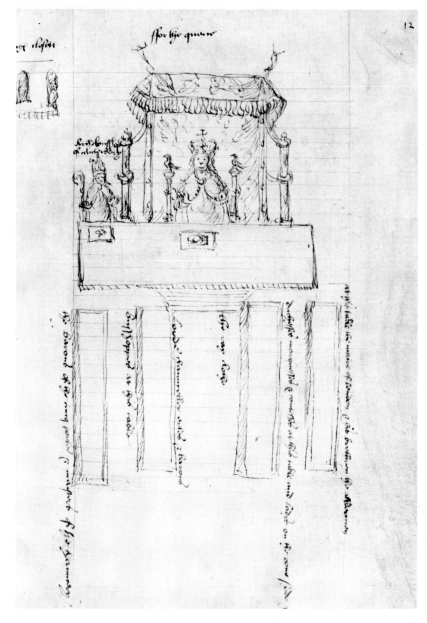

26 The seating plan for Anne Boleyn's coronation feast in Westminster Hall. Top
left – 'kinges closett'; top centre – 'ffor the quene'; next to Anne –
'Archebusshop of Canterbury'. The legends by the tables read, from the right:
'at this table the maire of london & his brethren the alldermen': 'duchesses
marquesses & contesses at this table and ladys on the oone syde &c'; 'the ray
clothe'; 'lorde chauncelleer erles & barons'; 'busshoppes at this table'; 'the
barons of the cincq portes & maisters of the chauncery'.

27 (above) *The Annunciation*, in an illuminated book of hours (King's MS 9). Anne's signature has been cut from below the couplet she wrote to Henry:

> Be daly prove you shalle me fynde,
> to be to you bothe lovyng and kynde.

28 (facing page) Coffer of the organ screen, with the cipher 'HA' and the falcon badge, in King's College Chapel, Cambridge.

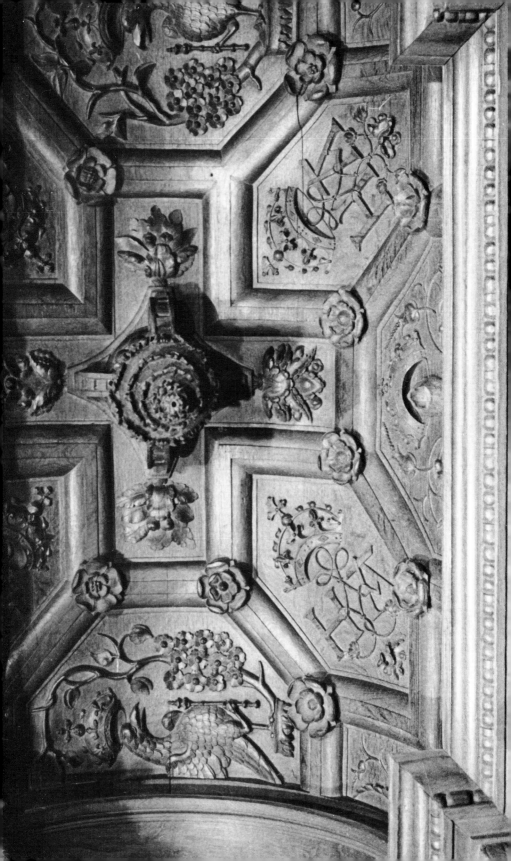

29 (top) Anne Boleyn's book of hours (printed in Paris).

30 (bottom) Anne Boleyn's psalter.

31 A page from 'Motets and Chansons', a music book in the Royal College of Music (MS 1070): the lower design shows a falcon pecking at a pomegranate.

32 Anne Boleyn's New Testament, translated by William Tyndale (Antwerp, 1534).

33 The back cover of volume 2 of Anne Boleyn's copy of *La Saincte Bible en Francoys*, translated by Lefèvre d'Etaples (Antwerp, 1534).

34 The front cover of Anne Boleyn's copy of 'The Ecclesiaste': the arms are of Henry VIII impaling those of Anne Boleyn; the badges are (clockwise from top left): lion, dragon, falcon, greyhound.

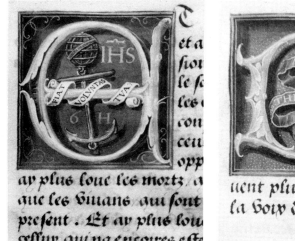

Illuminated letters from 'The Ecclesiaste': 35 a falcon badge; 36 a symbolic design; 37 a motto.

38 *Design for a Standing Cup*, by Hans Holbein the younger. Anne's falcon badge is visible between the left and centre satyrs.

39 The Boleyn cup (1535), now in Cirencester parish church.

40 A carving of Anne Boleyn's shield of arms at the Beauchamp Tower, Tower of London. The adjacent carvings were made by prisoners later in the sixteenth century.

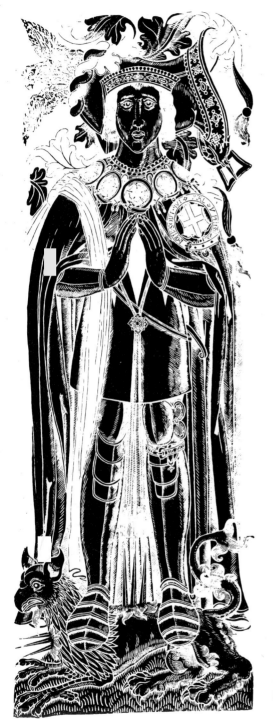

41 (left) A brass of Thomas Boleyn, at Hever Church.

42 (below) A terracotta plaque of the Goddess Minerva, by Giovanni da Maiano, formerly at Anne's house at Hanworth and now at Hanworth Park.

43 (top left) *Thomas Wyatt*, and 44 (top right) *James Butler, earl of Ormonde*, both by Hans Holbein the younger.

45 (bottom left) *Thomas Howard, duke of Norfolk*, by Hans Holbein the younger.

46 (bottom right) *Thomas Wolsey*, by Jacques le Boucq.

47 *Thomas Cromwell*, by Hans Holbein the younger.

48 *Mary Tudor, Queen of France, and Charles Brandon, duke of Suffolk,* by an anonymous painter.

Fitz Williams Earl of Southampton.

Russell B Privy Seale.

with one E.

Borbonius Poeta.-

49 (top left) *William Fitzwilliam*, and 50 (top right) *John Russell*, both by Hans Holbein the younger.

51 (bottom left) *Nicholas Bourbon*, by Hans Holbein the younger.

52 (bottom right) *Jean de Dinteville* (School of Clouet).

53 *William Warham*, by Hans Holbein the younger.

54 *Thomas Cranmer*, by Gerlach Flicke.

Tho: Moor Ld Chancelour

55 (top) *Thomas More*, and 56 (bottom) *Nicholas Carewe*, both by Hans Holbein the younger.

shire. The matter, however, did not end there. A group of Suffolk's servants swore to take revenge, and Cromwell promptly told the king.[82] We may note that it was a week after this that Henry paid an apparently unscheduled visit to his sister and brother-in-law, very probably to insist that they accept Anne. According to Chapuys, Henry had to repeat the lesson a month later, before Charles Brandon would at least do his duty at Boulogne, although he was again deliberately absent at Shrovetide 1533 when Anne presided at a great feast in honour of the French ambassadors.[83] His wife, Mary – the only person in England in a position to do so – seems never to have accepted her brother Henry's will. Her absence from Calais was widely interpreted as a direct snub to Anne Boleyn.

Some of Anne's enemies were able also in the summer of 1532 to threaten her with a ghost from the past, the earl of Northumberland. We have seen how marriage to Mary Talbot quickly became a disaster, and by 1530 the earl had effectively separated from his wife. When, in the course of yet one more marital altercation, Mary charged her husband with neglecting her, he replied that they were not married, because he had previously been legally contracted to Anne Boleyn. Seeing a way out of her own troubles, the countess reported the matter to her father who was a staunch supporter of Queen Katherine. He, however, chose not to send the news to Anne's more obvious opponents, but to the duke of Norfolk; Thomas Howard, in his turn, took a cautious line and showed the letter to Anne. Each peer was clearly aware of the danger of alienating both the favourite and the king if the matter did not stand up to examination. Anne's characteristic response was to take the letter to Henry himself and insist that it be investigated. So during July 1532 Northumberland was interrogated on oath by the two archbishops and then, in the presence of the duke of Norfolk and the king's canon lawyers, he swore on the Blessed Sacrament that there had been no precontract with Anne.[84]

---

[82] *Cal. S. P. Ven., 1527–33,* 761; 25 Henry VIII, c.32; *LP,* v.1139(11), 1183, 657. This last should be dated post 8 June 1532, the date of the election of the abbot of Northampton: ibid., v.1139(23).

[83] *Cal. S. P. Ven., 1527–33,* 792, 802; *Cal. S. P. Span., 1531–33,* pp. 509, 512, 613 [*LP,* v.1292, 1316; vi.212].

[84] Vienna, Haus-, Hof- und Staatsarchiv, England Korrespondenz Karton 5, Konvolut 1532, ff. 81–2; Friedmann, *Anne Boleyn,* i.159–61; *LP,* x.864.

Another sign that progress from the defeat of the Church to pregnancy and marriage was less than straightforward is the probability that Henry had at one time considered marrying Anne at Calais, even perhaps in the presence of Francis I. Gossip in England warned that this was the plan; both the imperial and the Venetian ambassadors reported to the same effect; Charles V, although horrified, also expected that the marriage would go through.[85] Observers of the conference itself believed the story right to the last, and one even suggested that Sunday 27 October was the appointed day and that the officiating priest would be the former French ambassador to England, Jean du Bellay, now bishop of Paris, a favourite with Anne.[86] When no marriage took place, this was put down to fear of the emperor or, more likely, advice from Francis.[87] In fact Anne had announced in late September that 'now, if the king wished to marry she would not consent', as her desire was to be married at Westminster, but her remark nevertheless indicated that the idea of a wedding at Calais had been under consideration.[88] Indeed, if we are to trust reports, in August she was dropping palpable hints in her correspondence that she would marry there.[89] Other indications, however suggest that there was another plan: to marry before the journey to France. As well as the informed guesses of the ambassadors, an incident which pointed to this option having been considered was the bitter reception Anne gave to Sir Gregory Casale, Henry's Vatican agent, when he arrived at Calais. She rounded on him, accusing him of managing the divorce incompetently, and was all the more angry, we are told, because she had hoped to be married in mid-September.[90] Quite clearly the marriage plans of Henry VIII and Anne Boleyn were anything but settled.

Perhaps the most significant evidence of continuing uncertainty about the future of their relationship is the text of Henry's grant to Anne of title to the marquessate of Pembroke, for this

[85] Ibid., v.1524, 1679; *Cal. S. P. Span., 1531–33*, p. 986 [*LP*, v.1256]; *Cal. S. P. Ven., 1527–33*, 803, 811, 816.

[86] Ibid., 824; the Milanese envoy in France even called Anne 'the king's beloved wife': *Cal. S. P. Milan*, ed. A. B. Hinds (1912), 900.

[87] *LP*, v.1538; *Cal. S. P. Ven., 1527–33*, 822; ibid., *1534–54*, 1035.

[88] *Cal. S. P. Span., 1531–33*, p. 527 [*LP*, v.1377].

[89] Ibid., p. 495 [*LP*, v.1256].

[90] *LP*, v.1538.

provided that her title would descend to her son, whether or not he was born in lawful marriage.[91] To achieve this unusual provision, all that was needed was the omission from the patent of two words – lawfully begotten – and it is doubtful whether this was noticed by those who heard the document proclaimed in Latin at Anne's investiture. It is, of course, a possibility that the almost unprecedented creation of a woman as a peer in her own right posed problems in drafting, but omission of such a standard form by accident seems unlikely. If, then, the wording was deliberate, what was its significance? Friedmann argued (and others have read the grant in the same way) that with Warham's death removing the last major obstacle to their marriage, Anne began to live with Henry, but that the grant of the title and the wealth to support it was an insurance against any last-minute disaster for herself and any children she might have by the king.[92] It is, however, strange that Anne should, on this argument, stand out for marriage for six years and then gamble on a divorce still in the future; no doubt she could have got as good terms for at least several months. Why wait? Equally, it is strange that Henry, desperate for a legitimate heir, should at this late stage have chosen to contemplate the possibility of a bastard child. Perhaps we should turn Friedmann's argument on its head and see Henry insuring himself by the patent against the continuing doubt that despite all his efforts, when at last he and Anne had married, it might not be possible to vindicate the legality of the relationship. The patent is, thus, not an announcement by Anne to the world that she is going to sleep with Henry, nor an admission, at last, that she did have a lower price than she had been asking. It is yet more evidence that Henry is still not certain that he is going to succeed.

We may add, finally, the clear indications that Henry, whatever Cromwell's legislative drafts told him, had still not been completely liberated from a psychological dependence on the papacy. Negotiations with Rome continued – in part, no doubt, in order to delay Clement VII's judgement in favour of Katherine, but also to ensure that the new archbishop was canonically appointed in the traditional way.[93] What is more, signs began to

[91] BL, Harl. MS 303 f. 1; cf. *LP*, v.1370(1).
[92] Friedmann, *Anne Boleyn*, i.162–3.
[93] *LP*, v.1493; *Cal. S. P. Span., 1531–33*, pp. 585, 599 [*LP*, vi.89, 142].

appear of a compromise with Rome. It is hard to say who took the initiative here or how serious it all was. Apparently a softer tone from Henry after the Calais meeting, plus a tactful suppression by his Vatican agents of earlier more aggressive instructions, had coincided with increased willingness at Rome to find a way out of the impasse. By the date of his marriage to Anne, Henry was boasting that Clement was beginning to yield, and only a day or two after, news was received from Francis I that his cardinals had reached the pope and were making good progress.[94] The papal nuncio was soon heavily involved in secret negotiations with the king and his council, much to the concern of Chapuys who feared the pope would desert Katherine.[95] Of course this, as well as the strict secrecy surrounding the marriage, may have been primarily intended to pull the wool over Clement's eyes, but it was at least partly for home consumption, an attempt to create the impression that at last the pope had given Henry what he wanted. So on 8 February the papal nuncio was invited to attend the king to the House of Lords, where he was placed at the right of the throne. Since the French ambassador was put at the left, the object of the tableau was clearly to suggest that Henry enjoyed full support from both Francis I and Clement VII.[96]

All this makes a good deal more plausible the recusant tradition that Henry tricked the priest who conducted his marriage to Anne by claiming that he had papal approval. Sander reports the story, apparently from Harpsfield, and it occurs in an anonymous attack on Henry that is independent of but related to the Harpsfield text.[97] According to this tradition the wedding took place in the upper chamber over the Holbein Gate of Whitehall, before dawn and with very few witnesses. When the celebrant asked if the king had the pope's permission, he was given a somewhat ambiguous assurance that this had been received. Not happy with this, he asked again and suggested that the document should be read out; the king, with a smile, effectively challenged him to call him a liar and declared that the licence was among his private papers, but that 'if I

[94] Ibid., 585–7 [*LP*, vi.89]; *LP*, vi.91.
[95] *Cal. S. P. Span., 1531–33*, 592–8 [*LP*, vi.142].
[96] Ibid., 594 [*LP*, vi.142].
[97] Sander, *Schism*, pp. 93–4; Harpsfield, *Pretended Divorce*, pp. 234–5; BL, Sloane MS 2495, ff. 13–14.

should, now that it waxeth towards day, fetch it, and be seen so
early abroad, there would rise a rumour and talk thereof other
than were convenient. Go forth in God's name and do that which
appertaineth to you.'[98]

Some details in the story are independently vouched for – for
instance the tiny number of witnesses and the extreme secrecy.[99]
Others are very plausible, such as the attendance of Henry
Norris and Thomas Heneage of the privy chamber, the two men
one would expect to be in the king's confidence. Anne's attendant
was supposedly Lady Berkeley, and this again is credible. Anne
Savage, as she then was, had been a gentlewoman at court for
some years and was a dependant of William Brereton, groom of
the privy chamber; one account states that a groom was also
present, and if so this was most probably William. On the other
hand, not all the details of the story are reliable.[100] The celebrant
was remembered in recusant circles as Rowland Lee, later
bishop of Lichfield, but evidence from Chapuys – though
admittedly from 1535 – identifies the priest as George Brown,
the prior of the Augustinian Friars of London and later archbishop of Dublin. But that aside, the story also has a ring of truth
about it.[101] Though the recusants were intent on suggesting that
Henry uttered a blatant lie, the words credited to him are typical
of the king's penchant for qualified honesty: ' "I trust you have
the pope's licence . . ." "What else", quoth the king.' Or again,
'Think you me a man of so small and slender foresight and
consideration of my affairs that unless all things were safe and
sure I would enterprise this matter? I have truly a licence . . .
which if it were seen, should discharge us all.' The king, of
course, still had the papal licence to marry Anne, which was
conditional upon a declaration that his marriage with Katherine
was void, but it did not specify who would make that declaration
of nullity.[102] Assume that Henry was certain either that the pope
would, after all, oblige or that Cranmer would, and the assertion
becomes at least a half-truth. Little can be certain about that
pre-dawn gathering over the Whitehall gate; but the probability

[98] Harpsfield, *Pretended Divorce*, p. 235.
[99] *Cal. S. P. Span., 1531–33*, p. 608 [*LP*, vi.180].
[100] *LP*, v.p. 327; vi.p. 14; Brereton, *Letters and Accounts*, pp. 243, 248.
[101] *LP*, viii.121.
[102] Pocock, *Records*, i.25.

is that even then Henry felt he had to imply papal consent to his marriage.[103]

If we put together all this evidence of uncertainty, even after the dramatic collapse of convocation in May 1532, that victory begins to look somewhat less decisive. What appears to be the steady movement thereafter towards marriage with Anne and a breach with Rome was achieved only by continuing struggle. It is here that we have to make a fundamental choice in interpretation over the decision to consummate the relationship between Henry and Anne. Was it Anne's decision, now that the prize was in sight? Henry's, now that he could be certain of victory? Each view has had its advocates. Or was it a deliberate device by Anne to force Henry to act? She knew that there was now no obstacle to her marriage except the king's indecision. She could also be sure that Henry would be certain that any child she might conceive would be a son, and would never permit it to be born illegitimate. Throughout their relationship it had been Anne who had stiffened Henry's resolve; perhaps even at the last she had to precipitate the necessary crisis.

That this last is the true reading is strongly suggested by the circumstances of Elizabeth's birth on 7 September 1533. If Anne's pregnancy lasted the full term she must have conceived in December 1532; hence the conclusion that she might have begun to guess her condition by the end of the month. Yet Anne had not entered the maternity rooms specially prepared for her until ten days before Elizabeth arrived, whereas protocol and custom dictated that she should do so a month or six weeks before the expected birth.[104] To explain this we have to conclude that Elizabeth was born at least a fortnight early. That, in turn, would indicate that it was probably only at the end of the third week in January that Anne began to suspect that she had conceived. And if this deduction is correct, then other events of that month fall into place: the appointment of Cranmer, the promotion of Audley, the flurry of parliamentary drafting and,

---

[103] Elizabeth believed in a papal bull covering her mother's marriage and set Matthew Parker to search for it. He at first reported no success, but later found 'matter of that bull' and sent William Cecil 'some quires': Parker, *Correspondence*, pp. 414, 420. Even Cranmer did not know the exact date of the marriage: 'about St. Paul's Day'.

[104] See below, p. 229.

most of all, the hurried wedding on the 25th. The news of her pregnancy was the ultimatum that Anne used to force Henry into action at last. The hugger-mugger of that pre-dawn ceremony in the Whitehall gatehouse and the king's attempts still to keep it quiet are a measure of the psychological block in Henry which Anne had forced him to overcome.

Some observers of the behaviour of Henry and Anne, and many more commentators at second hand, would have found this discussion quite unnecessary. All over Europe the assumption was that Henry had married his mistress. There was even gossip that they had already had a child, or children.[105] Yet the grounds for believing that Anne remained a virgin until the last months of 1532 are strong. Sander might claim that she was promiscuous at a very early age, but the equally Catholic George Cavendish who had known her was, we have seen, unequivocal:

> The noblest prince that reigned on the ground
> I had to my husband, he took me to his wife;
> At home with my father a maiden he found me.[106]

There is no evidence that she bore any children before 1533, neither in the comments of informed observers nor – and this is more significant – in any administrative or financial records. No process was ever made at Rome on the ground of her immorality, and Katherine's case suffered by its eagerness to assume the worst without proof; actual evidence of adultery would have decisively weakened Henry's claim to be acting on conscientious grounds – it was never forthcoming.[107] Anne's determination to be a wife and not a mistress meant that self-interest lay in morality. Henry's need for a legitimate heir made for the same – and the argument is the stronger if we should see the king doubtful about the success of his divorce almost to the last. Neither could afford the risks of incautious passion. That the relationship had a physical element – at least on Henry's side – is well attested, and how this could be expressed yet controlled over six years may intrigue the curiosity and challenge the belief

[105] *Original Letters*, ii.552–3.
[106] Cavendish, *Metrical Visions*, p. 41; cf. also BL, Sloane MS 2495 f. 2v.
[107] *LP*, vi.438.

of a generation brought up to different norms of behaviour. We may also wonder how strong was that physical element. But controlled it was; when full sexual relations began, they were initiated by calculation – and the calculation was very probably Anne's.

10

A Coronation and a Christening

⟨⟨ornament⟩⟩

L ONDON WAS all a-bustle as the Easter season of 1533 came to an end. Anne Boleyn, now the king's 'most dear and well-beloved wife', was to be crowned on Whit Sunday, 1 June, and orders had arrived for the full panoply of a royal coronation.[1] The city had to 'make preparation aswell to fetch her grace from Greenwich to the Tower by water, as to see the city ordered and garnished with pageants in places accustomed, for the honour of her grace when she should be conveyed from the Tower to Westminster', and there was barely a month in which to get ready for what was to be the first major exhibition of civic pageantry since 1522 – indeed, only the second of its kind in the whole reign.[2]

Now scores of participants were mobilized – nobles and others who claimed the right to serve in particular capacities, those selected to be knighted in honour of the occasion and those who were to take part in the processions.[3] Lady Cobham found herself allocated the role of attendant horsewoman and required to find white palfreys for herself and her own ladies, and although her own robes and the long cloth of gold (or perhaps red velvet) trapper for her horse were provided, she was expected to equip her attendants herself, 'as unto your honour and that solemnity apperteineth'.[4] And the lesser folk were busy on the construction, the decoration, the railing, and the gritting of the

---

[1] *Cal. S. P. Ven., 1527–33*, 878.
[2] Hall, *Chronicle*, p. 798.
[3] E.g. *LP*, vi.396.
[4] Ellis, *Letters*, 1 ii.32–3.

streets to give footing to the horses – all the preparations, large and small, inseparable from the great occasion.

The pageantry of a coronation spread over four days.[5] On the first, the monarch would be escorted by river to the Tower; the next was devoted to court rituals, and on the afternoon of the third took place the road procession from the Tower, through the city to Westminster; the final day saw the actual coronation and the great banquet in Westminster Hall. There were some half-dozen 'places accustomed' for pageants on the route through the city, and all were decorated on the occasion of Anne's coronation, plus three more, making the show as big as that for Charles V in 1522 and larger than Katherine of Aragon's in 1501. The water pageant, too, was outstanding.

It was about one o'clock on Thursday 29 May that the fifty great barges of the London livery companies set out, with numerous smaller vessels, from the rendezvous at Billingsgate. They were even more elaborately dressed than for the lord mayor's procession, with flags and bunting overall, hung with gold foil which glistened in the sun and with little bells that tinkled; the vessels were packed with musicians of every kind, and carrying more cannon than seems safe on such a crowded waterway. The fleet was led by a light wherry in which had been constructed a mechanical dragon that could be made to move and belch out flames, and with it were other models of monsters and huge wildmen, who threw blazing fireworks and uttered hideous cries. A very safe distance behind came the mayor's barge, with the aldermen in scarlet and the common councillors. To the starboard of the mayor's craft came the famous 'bachelors' barge, provided by the Haberdashers, the company of the then mayor. This was hung with cloth of gold and silk, with great banners (one fore, one aft), blazoned with the arms of Henry and Anne, and the port gunwale was covered with thirty-six shields showing the two coats of arms impaled. The port escort of the mayor's barge was another wherry, this time carrying an outsize

---

[5] The following is based on *The noble tryumphant coronacyon of Quene Anne*, Wynkyn de Worde (1533), ed. A. F. Pollard, in *Tudor Tracts* (1903); Hall, *Chronicle*, pp. 798–805; Dublin, Trinity College MS 518, ff. 30–2; BL, Harl. MS 41 [*LP*, vi.561, 601]; RO, PRO31/8 ff. 50v–54 [*LP*, vi.585]; Spelman, *Reports*, i.68–70 [*LP*, vi.583]; Wriothesley, *Chronicle*, i.18–22; *Cal. S. P. Ven.*, *1527–33*, 912; *Ordinances for the Household*, pp. 123–211; *LP*, vi.396, 562–3, 584, 701; Cranmer, *Letters*, pp. 245–46; cf. Anglo, *Spectacle*, pp. 246–61.

representation of Anne's principal badge, a white falcon crowned, perching on red and white roses which grew out of a golden tree stump, with the green hill on which the tree stood surrounded by 'virgins singing and playing sweetly'.

Rowing against the tide, it took the procession two hours to reach Greenwich, reverse its order and come to anchor off the palace steps. In mid-afternoon Anne entered her own 'sumptuously' decorated barge, along with the principal ladies of the court. A second barge carried the rest of her women, then came the king's barge full of his guard 'in their best array', with the royal trumpets and minstrels, followed by the barges of the courtiers – totalling, with the livery company vessels, some 120 large craft and 200 small. Observers rhapsodized about:

> the banners and pennants of arms of their crafts, the which were beaten of fine gold, illustring [reflecting] so goodly against the sun, and also the standards, streamers of the cognisances and devices, ventalling with [waving in] the wind, also the trumpets blowing, shawms and minstrels playing, the which were a right sumptuous and a triumphant sight to see and to hear all the way as they past upon the water, to hear the said marvellous sweet harmony of the said instruments, the which sounds to be a thing of another world.[6]

Now rowing with the tide, the flotilla was making better than seven knots. All sea-going vessels had been ordered out of the fairway, but they joined in with gun salutes as Anne passed, almost as though officially lining the route. When the main anchorage of the Pool of London was reached, the salvoes became so many, drowning the continuous ripple of the cannonfire among the barges, that observers lost count. But the best was yet to come. As the procession rounded the bend of the river at Wapping and came in sight of the Tower, the gunners there received the order they had been waiting for and 'loosed their ordinance', four pieces at a time! While the rest of the fleet 'hovered' – backed water – off Tower Wharf, to one final crescendo of noise the barges carrying Anne and the lord mayor pulled in to the landing steps. They were greeted first by a party of the Tower officers and the heralds; then Anne and the London notables proceeded through the crowd to a second reception

[6] *LP*, vi.563.

party, the officers of the royal households, next to be greeted by
the great officers of state; then finally through the postern gate
into the fortress and to the king himself who, that day, as
throughout the coronation festivities, had been compelled by
ancient tradition to observe in secret. Henry embraced his wife,
who turned to thank the citizens 'with many goodly words', and
so too the king. In an age when magnificence was one of the
qualities that gave a monarch authority, London had done him
proud.

Henry, too, had achieved something more than magnificence
by mobilizing city and court to do honour to his new wife. What
the feeling of observers and participants was we do not know, but
even if we discount as wishful thinking many of the assertions
that, whenever they appeared in public, Katherine of Aragon
and her daughter Mary were greeted with enthusiasm, there still
must have been many in both the court and the city who had
mixed feelings about this new marriage. But just as it was
intended to do, this magnificent river pageant had drawn
thousands of excited spectators, and what they had seen was the
city oligarchy and the elite of the realm uniting to honour the
king's second wife. As one herald put it, 'all the lords that might
come, but especially temporal peers of all the realm in their
barges', while another seems to imply that before the queen and
her entourage embarked there had been some formal reception
of Anne 'as queen of England by all the lords of England'.[7] Who
could blame the populace for concluding that those who knew,
agreed with what Henry had done? And who could expect critics
such as the duke of Suffolk not to look at the banks as they
passed by and decide that Henry had popular support for his
actions? The pageant had been engineered as a piece of cor-
porate idolatry. All had apostacized before the king's command;
all had bowed the knee to the new goddess. And even for those
with harder heads and less imagination, there was an equally
significant lesson. Henry had had his way; the king's will was
irresistible.

The first public part of the ceremony over, the royal couple
spent the next forty-eight hours in the seclusion of the Tower,
enjoying the reconstructed apartments which had been readied
for the occasion at Cromwell's personal direction. Virtually

---

[7] Dublin, Trinity College MS 518, f. 30v; Wriothesley, *Chronicle*, i.18.

nothing of them remains, but they were in the south-east corner, in the innermost ward, between the White Tower and the main curtain wall. As well as lesser rooms, Anne had available a rebuilt great chamber and a rebuilt dining-room, while a new bridge across the moat gave access from her private garden into the city. The plans for a private gallery for the queen had been dropped, but there was the restored great gallery to do double duty. And within the privacy of the Tower, the court rituals of the coronation continued to proclaim the lessons of the day, particularly this time to the nobility and gentry. Eighteen Knights of the Bath were created, in ceremonies which lasted from dinner on Friday to Saturday morning, and involved a special overnight vigil in chambers fitted up for each candidate in the White Tower. These included up-and-coming courtiers such as Francis Weston, the king's former page, and William Windsor, the son of Lord Windsor, keeper of the great wardrobe, but many were connected with Anne Boleyn or her Howard relations. Henry Parker, George Boleyn's brother-in-law; the earl of Derby, whose wife was Anne's aunt; Thomas Arundel, who had recently married Anne's cousin; Henry Saville of Thornhill in Yorkshire, who was already identified as the man to block the pretensions of her open enemy, Thomas Lord Darcy; possibly Lord Berkeley, whose wife had been Anne's bridesmaid back in January – all these and others were object lessons in the new way to honour: support for the new queen.[8] Then on the Saturday Henry dubbed nearly fifty knights bachelor.[9] Since the honour was in some ways a burden that could only be avoided by paying a fine, some men were probably there under compulsion, but we can again pick out the names of protégés of such Boleyn supporters as Cromwell, Henry Norris, William Brereton and the earl of Derby. There could be little doubt who it was 'the king delighteth to honour'.[10]

The weather on Saturday 31 May 1533 was perfect for the procession to Westminster. By about midday the mayor had made one last check on the arrangements, riding back to the Tower from the spot allocated to the aldermen near the Cross in Cheapside, past the craft guilds and the merchants lined up

[8] For Arundel and Saville, see *House of Commons*, i.337; iii.280.

[9] Wynkyn de Worde in *The noble tryumphant coronacyon* gives 46 names; *LP*, vi.563 gives a figure of 63.

[10] Also in securing exemptions; cf. ibid., vi.746.

behind railings on one side of the street, and on the other, the general populace, held back by a line of constables. In addition to the special pageants, the houses of Cheapside had been hung with cloth of gold, velvet and tissue, while Cornhill and Grace-church Street were decorated in scarlet and crimson, with arras, tapestry and carpets on display (see plate 24). There had been some difficulty in getting the procession organized, and instead of starting from the Tower at two o'clock it did not leave until five, but now, as it began to make its way through the crowds, the message of the river procession was again reflected bright and clear.

Anne herself chose to dress in the French fashion, and the procession was headed by twelve servants of the new French ambassador, Jean de Dinteville, Francis I's *maître d'hôtel*. They wore blue velvet with yellow and blue sleeves, and had white plumes in their hats, while their horses had trappers of blue sarcenet, powdered with white crosses. (In December, Francis would reimburse the ambassador for his outlay with a gift of 500 gold *écus* (£100).[11])

Then came the gentlemen of the royal households, marching two by two, each man by tradition the eyes and ears of the king he served. They were followed by the nine judges riding in their scarlet gowns and hoods and wearing their collars of SS; each one had been summoned individually, so that the law would be seen to warrant the coronation. They had been unable to get into the Tower in time to form up, and had had to slip into place as the procession passed Tower Hill. Next came the new Knights of the Bath, followed by the full weight of government and social status – the royal council, the ecclesiastical magnates and the peers of the realm. Individuals could then be seen, making their act of support: the chancellor; both the archbishops; the am-bassador of France emphasizing again his monarch's personal backing; the ambassador of Venice, implying European recog-nition; the lord mayor; the deputy earl marshal and beside him the lord constable of England, Charles Brandon, the king's brother-in-law, keeping his thoughts to himself but showing all outward acquiescence. As the two or three hundred filed slowly past the waiting crowds, this massive demonstration of solidarity with the king and his new marriage could not have failed to make its point.[12]

[11] *Actes de François I⁽ʳ⁾*, ii.590, no. 6639.
[12] The procession was half a mile long: *LP*, vi.661.

At last, behind the courtiers and magnates, came the queen in her litter. She was dressed in filmy white, with a coronet of gold. The litter was of white satin, with 'white cloth of gold' inside and out, and its two palfreys were clothed to the ground in white damask. In ravishing contrast was the queen's dark hair, flowing loose, down to her waist. Over her, the barons of the Cinque Ports held a canopy of cloth of gold. Then came her own palfrey, also trapped in white. Twelve ladies in crimson velvet rode behind, then two carriages decked in red cloth of gold. Next, seven more riders, two more carriages – one white, one red – and thirty gentlewomen on horseback, this time in black velvet. These were followed by the king's guard in two files, one on each side of the street, 'in their rich coats' 'of goldsmiths' work', and lastly all the servants in the livery of their masters or mistresses. It was, said the published report, a 'most noble company'. Anne might not be universally popular, but she was magnificent.

Knowledgeable observers would, admittedly, have noticed significant absences. Neither the king's sister Mary nor her daughter Frances was there, nor was the premier English duchess, the duchess of Norfolk. The first carriage had, therefore, to be occupied by the dowager duchess, Anne's stepgrandmother, with (and reports vary) either her mother or the dowager marchioness of Dorset. But Mary was near to death and her daughter hardly out of childhood, while the absence of the duchess could be easily discounted, given her notorious quarrel with her husband. The earl of Shrewsbury, another doubter, was also missing, but he had taken care to claim his traditional coronation role and to send his son to represent him. The wisdom of showing at least acquiescence was illustrated by the fate of Thomas More, who did deliberately refuse to attend. Sent £20 to buy a suitable gown for the occasion by Tunstall, Gardiner and John Clerk, bishop of Bath and Wells, in the hope that he might be able to recover at least some royal favour, More took the money but declined to join his former conservative allies in a procession which, he was quite explicit, must undermine their integrity. As far as we know he never saw Tunstall again, and within a year of this declaration of intransigence More was in the Tower.[13]

---

[13] R. Marius, *Thomas More* (1985), pp. 438–40.

It is, however, hard to assess wider reaction to the coronation procession. Hostile accounts delighted in knocking everything they could. The report that reached Brussels, the one containing the story that Anne concealed a goitre behind her high collar, says quite uncompromisingly that the crowds did not cheer or even take their hats off when Anne passed.[14] When challenged on this, the mayor said that he could not command the hearts of the people, and it was left to Anne's fool to retort that they were keeping their caps on to cover their scurvy heads. The 'HA' monogram of the king and his new queen was maliciously read as 'Ha, Ha!', and the French presence was greeted with the cry, 'Whoreson knave, French dog'. A similar recollection is preserved in the *Cronica del Rey Enrico*, which has Anne replying to a question from Henry about the decorations in London, 'Sir, I liked the city well enough, but I saw a great many caps on heads, and heard but few tongues.'[15] On the other hand we must remember that the *Cronica* is a compote of truth, half-truth, rumour and nonsense, while the overstatement in the Brussels account invites suspicion. It is extremely unlikely that so disciplined an assembly as the livery companies, and their journeymen and apprentices, denied the minimum courtesies. The most objective eyewitness, the Venetian ambassador, stresses 'the very great pomp' and the enormous crowds, and remarked on 'the utmost order and tranquillity' of the occasion.[16] 'Dumb insolence' is, however, hard to estimate, and as no comment is made on any positive show of enthusiasm, perhaps the safest conclusion is that the Londoners crowding the streets that day were more curious than either welcoming or hostile. And in any case, in contemporary thinking what mattered more than crowd reaction was what we might call the psychological impact of the procession and the careful observance of all the right ritual. As Edward Baynton, Anne's worldly-wise chamberlain, wrote to George Boleyn on 9 June, the coronation had been performed 'honourably' and 'as ever was, if all old and ancient men say true'.[17]

This was undoubtedly true of the actual coronation at Westminster Abbey on Whit Sunday, despite the fact that Anne was

---

[14] RO, PRO31/8 f. 51 [*LP*, vi.585].
[15] *Cronica del Rey Enrico*, pp. 17–18 [*Chronicle*, ed. Hume, p. 14].
[16] *Cal. S. P. Ven.*, *1527–33*, 912.
[17] *LP*, vi.613.

almost six months pregnant. The advantages of a crown for his new wife must have been considerable for Henry to accept the risk of such an ordeal. The great procession began to assemble in Westminster Hall from seven in the morning but it was just before nine that Anne herself entered. They then set out along a railed route carpeted with cloth of blue ray all along the seven hundred yards between the dais of the hall and the high altar of the abbey.[18] For this occasion, the court and the peers in their parliament robes were joined by the lord mayor, aldermen and judges, each in scarlet; the monks of Westminster and the staff of the Chapel Royal, all in their best copes; four bishops, two archbishops and twelve mitred abbots in full pontificals; and the abbot of Westminster with his complete regalia. Anne was resplendent in coronation robes of purple velvet, furred with ermine, with the gold coronet on her head which she had worn the day before, though it is not clear that she followed tradition by walking barefoot. Over her was carried the gold canopy of the Cinque Ports, and she was preceded by the sceptre of gold, the rod of ivory topped with the dove and the crown of St Edward carried by the lord great chamberlain, the earl of Oxford. Anne was supported, again as tradition dictated, by the bishops of London and Winchester; the dowager duchess of Norfolk carried the train – a very long one – and she was followed by a host of ladies and gentlewomen dressed in scarlet, with appropriate distinctions of rank.

Special stands had been erected in the abbey, and in particular one from which the king could watch proceedings incognito from behind a lattice-work screen. In the choir stood St Edward's Chair, draped in cloth of gold, on a tapestry-covered dais two steps high, which was itself set on a raised platform carpeted in red. Here Anne rested for a moment before resuming her endurance test. As tradition dictated, the coronation was set in the context of a solemn high mass, sung, apparently, by the abbot of Westminster. It was, however, Cranmer who prayed over Anne as she prostrated herself before the altar. Then he anointed her, before she returned to St Edward's Chair, where he crowned her and delivered the sceptre and the rod of ivory. After the Te Deum, St Edward's crown was exchanged for a lighter one and the service continued for Anne to take the

[18] Colvin, *King's Works*, iv.290–1.

sacrament and to make the customary offering at the shrine of the saint. Then a break for some brief refreshment, and the procession back, past the clock tower in New Palace Yard and its five cisterns running with wine, and into Westminster Hall beneath the splendidly redecorated north front. If More had seen taking part in the procession on the Saturday as an assault on his integrity, how much more the actual coronation. The elite of the land had taken Anne as queen in the sight of God, and under the most solemn and hallowed sanctions of Holy Church. Shakespeare would declare a generation later:

> Not all the water in the rough rude sea
> Can wash the balm from an anointed king.

This mystique of monarchy now belonged to Anne Boleyn. Only death could take it away.

Even with the procession over, Anne had several hours more to face, and on her return she withdrew to her room while the guests were settled in the hall for the coronation banquet.[19] The judges had been turned out days before, their courts dismantled, the windows reglazed, the seating and statuary gilded, and the hall hung with arras for the occasion. Two long tables had been laid on the right and two on the left side of the hall, where the diners sat in order of precedence (see plate 26). At the upper and more honourable end, at the table nearest the south wall, sat the barons of the Cinque Ports and the masters in chancery; at the middle one sat the peers on one side and the bishops on the other, and below them the judges and the royal council. On the opposite side of the great blue carpet, and only on the north side of the table so that they could each be served formally and directly from the centre aisle – as befitted a day of triumph for women – sat the duchesses and great ladies and the gentlewomen. The remaining table, against the north wall, held the mayor and aldermen of London and the senior freemen.

Then, when all was set, Anne herself entered. She sat at the long marble table across the hall, on the king's great marble chair mounted on the dais twelve steps up, under a cloth of estate. Only the archbishop of Canterbury shared the table with her, and he was a good way to her right. Nothing and nobody

---

[19] For the length of the ceremony see Cranmer, *Letters*, p. 245 and *LP*, vi.601.

must be allowed to blur the focus of the occasion. Beside the queen stood the dowager countess of Oxford and the countess of Worcester, who held a cloth up to conceal her from time to time, whenever Anne wished 'to spit or do otherwise', and two gentlewomen sat at her feet, under the table, to do her bidding. To ease her during the lengthy proceedings, a comfortable inner chair had been purpose-made to fit inside the marble one! Henry, meanwhile, occupied a specially built box above where the court of king's bench normally sat, from which he would watch events in privacy, along with the ambassadors of France and Venice.

Given the enormous numbers of important folk on duty that day, it seems hardly credible that eight hundred people remained to sit down. One list of attendants names almost one hundred gentlemen and higher ranks, as well as scores of lesser mortals. Only the eight nobles appointed to serve the queen were allowed on the holy ground surrounding her, but there were about 120 more support staff for the top table alone. Overall responsibility lay with the duke of Suffolk as high steward, a function that he discharged in a doublet and jacket dripping with pearls, and from the saddle of a horse magnificently trapped in crimson velvet. Also on horseback, and all in crimson, was Lord William Howard, with his horse's purple velvet trapper embroidered with the Howard white lion and slashed to show the white satin lining. He was deputizing throughout the coronation as earl marshal – the duke of Norfolk had been sent with Anne's brother on an embassy to France – and was in charge of serving the banquet. The two of them now escorted in the first course, twenty-eight dishes for the queen and the archbishop, which were carried by the new Knights of the Bath. Twenty-four dishes followed for the second course and thirty for the third – each heralded with as much noise as the king's trumpets and minstrels could make – and even though the lower tables had less, according to a carefully graded scale, the lord mayor and his companions were very satisfied with their two courses of thirty-two. The king had exacted tribute from far and wide, and the lavishness and magnificence of the food (provided from specially enlarged kitchens) was set off by a profusion of 'subtleties', those curious devices so beloved of the Burgundian tradition of royal feasting.[20] The wax ships were singled out for particular praise.

[20] Ibid., vi.554; Hall, *Chronicle*, p. 804.

It was 'the most honorable feast that hath been seen'. And even when the banquet was over, there were still the closing ceremonies to get through before the queen was able to retire. It was nearly six o'clock. She had been 'on parade', almost continuously, for nine hours.

How much all this cost we do not know, still less the expense for the whole four days. The Milanese ambassador guessed that it cost the City an incredible £46,000 (200,000 ducats) and the king half that amount, but whatever the figure, it was clearly immense. Equally clearly, Henry found it all worthwhile.[21] Chapuys' description of the events as 'cold, meagre and uncomfortable' is sour grapes; the 'concubine' had been accorded the fullest possible inauguration as queen.[22] No doubt the elaboration, the attention to detail, the evident 'overkill', does indicate a measure of insecurity, and we must remember that all the participants knew that the king was watching, just as he had watched the court's original acceptance of Anne the previous Easter. Nevertheless, in the same way that the popular and the religious liturgies had been performed, so had the banquet. It had been a test, a sacrament of loyalty. The great of the land had dined to honour Anne Boleyn, their queen; they had drunk to their sovereign's new consort; whatever their inner doubts, they had identified with her. In More's simile, they had been 'deflowered' – raped. The seductiveness of the old magic is seen in the reactions of those hard-headed judges for whom Westminster Hall was the normal workaday environment. When summoned to the coronation, they had felt it necessary to meet to discuss how to respond. There is even, in Justice Spelman's account, a hint of minimal acquiescence, of the tradition of avoiding as far as possible taking political sides. But by Sunday they were scrambling for places on the stands in the abbey and flattered by the honourable positions accorded them at the feast. Spelman noted with pride that, as they kneeled to Anne as she left the hall, she smiled and said, 'I thank you all for the honour ye have done to me this day.' And even though we may suspect that this was a general thankyou to the company, the judges clearly thought it was just for them.

The coronation banquet marked the end of the official cere-

[21] *Cal. S. P. Milan*, 911; cf. Colvin, *King's Works*, iv.290.
[22] *Cal. S. P. Span.*, *1531–33*, p. 704 [*LP*, vi.653].

monies, but custom dictated that a court celebration should follow. Monday 2 June, therefore, was devoted to jousting, balls and a 'goodly banquet in the queen's chamber', though it is only the first that we know much about. The original plan had been to have the jousters, challengers and answerers, ride in the coronation procession with all the elaborate costumes and devices that had been prepared for the tilting, but when Lord William Howard, who was to lead the challengers, had been obliged to deputize for his brother as earl marshal elsewhere in the procession, the idea was dropped.[23] These 'great jousts' were perhaps the first to be held in the new tiltyard that had been built opposite the gate of the new palace of Whitehall, and as usual there were plenty of guests as well as the general public.

The entertainment, however, was not a success. The eight jousters in each of the two teams ran six courses apiece but there were not, as the published account pretended, 'broken many spears valiantly'.[24] Very many of the horses veered away from the central barrier, or tilt, so that the riders found it difficult to secure flush hits on their opponents. In other circumstances one might suspect deliberate lack of enthusiasm, since Anne's enemy, Nicholas Carewe, was leading the answerers, but one can hardly imagine that he would publicly invite the suspicion of the king or risk his own standing in jousting circles. Whatever his private emotions, he knew very well that refusing to accept Anne would destroy his career. A more mundane but likely explanation for the poor sport would seem to be some unexpected problem presented by the new arena. Carewe, along with everyone else, except for More and a few stiff-backed men like him, was busy doing his best to impress the royal couple with his enthusiasm to honour them. That was certainly the atmosphere remembered by a somewhat effusive French tradition:

> The initiatives of the gentlemen and lords were notable as the English sought, unceasingly, to honour their new princess. Not, I believe, because they wanted to, but in order to comply with the wishes of their king. The lords and ladies set to dances, sports of various kinds, hunting expeditions, and pleasures without parallel. Numerous tournaments were held in her honour – each man

---

[23] *LP*, vi.561.
[24] Hall, *Chronicle*, p. 805. Wynkyn de Worde, *The noble tryumphant coronacyon*, and Wriothesley, *Chronicle*, i.22 say that 18 took part.

put his lance under his thigh or fought to the death [!] with the
sword – and everything a success. And as well as magnificent and
joyful celebrations, everyone strove to be as attentive and solicitous
as possible to serve their new mistress.[25]

The psychological dominance that had been established over the
court was very real.

The end of the celebrations did not, however, mark any end to
the high spirits at court. Anne's chamberlain, writing to her
brother in France, reported that 'pastime in the queen's chamber was never more. If any of you that be now departed have any
ladies that they thought favoured you, and somewhat would
mourn at parting of their servants, I can no whit perceive the
same by their dancing and pastime they do use here.'[26] The
death of the king's sister Mary on 24 June seems to have made
little difference. Any mourning was brief. What mattered was
the delivery at Greenwich on the 28th of Anne's wedding gift
from Francis I, a magnificent litter with three mules specially
purchased from the dauphin, and originally presented to her
brother in Paris. She immediately took it on a three mile trial.[27]

Henry did find time to issue a proclamation warning of the
penalties of according royal honours to anyone but Anne.[28] The
authority for this was the Act of Appeals, though it is doubtful
how many of the members of parliament or peers who passed the
bill had expected it to be used to outlaw a lifetime of respect to
Katherine and Mary, a habit which even the duke of Norfolk
found it embarrassingly hard to break.[29] Neither mother nor
daughter had been willing to accept relegation to the status of
'princess dowager' and 'Lady Mary', while their household
servants backed them in every way they could – with shows of
dumb stupidity or feminine tantrums to the limits of caution
and beyond. There was, after all, remarkably little that Henry
could do when Katherine put her people into new liveries
embroidered, as for the last twenty-four years, with 'H' and 'K' –
remarkably little, that is, unless Chapuys' wilder fantasies about
poison and treason trials were turned into fact.[30] Efforts to

[25] De Carles, in Ascoli, *L'Opinion*, lines 111–27.
[26] RO, SP1/76 f. 195 [*LP*, vi.613].
[27] *Actes de François Ier*, ii.393, no. 5721, ii.416 no. 5829; *Cal. S. P. Ven.*, *1527–33*,
893; *Cal. S. P. Span.*, *1531–33*, pp. 721, 724 [*LP*, vi.720].
[28] *Tudor Royal Proclamations*, i.209.
[29] *Cal. S. P. Span.*, *1531–33*, p. 794 [*LP*, vi.1125]; *St. Pap.*, i.408 [*LP*, vi.1252].
[30] *Cal. S. P. Ven.*, *1527–33*, 923.

deprive Mary of plate and jewels now thought excessive were defeated by the disappearance of the inventory, while Katherine, who was willing to surrender like a dutiful wife everything Henry had ever given her, refused point-blank to let Anne have the splendid christening robe she herself had brought from Spain:[31] 'God forbid that I should ever be so badly advised as to give help, assistance, or favour, directly or indirectly in a case so horrible as this.' And for once Henry had to acquiesce.

More and more, indeed, attention began to focus on Anne's fast-approaching confinement. For some time after the coronation, reports of her health continued to be good, but there is reason to believe that the advanced stages of the pregnancy were, in fact, difficult. Henry, it was later said, had been at his wits' end, even hoping for a miscarriage if it would save Anne's life.[32] Certainly, he declined to go on the usual summer progress because of his wife's condition, and the couple retired to Windsor where he could hunt in the forests thereabouts, while she waited until it was time for her 'to take her chamber'.[33] This was a curious custom, part religious, part medical, part feminine mystery, by which a queen entered a sort of purdah from a month or six weeks before her expected confinement until she was 'churched', or purified, some six weeks after delivery.[34] 'Chamber' must be understood in the usual court sense of a suite of rooms, duplicating the normal privy chamber suite but specially prepared, with an oratory (prayer was often the only obstetric help available), 'the rich font of Canterbury' (in case a weak baby needed instant baptism), and heavy, draught-proof hangings. Outside, her presence chamber was divided by a curtain, beyond which the queen stayed for the whole time; a special 'bed of state' was built there for her to preside on, instead of the usual chair. The male officers of her household were never openly allowed further than the outer, or great, chamber, where they had to kick their heels in attendance while their duties were taken over by the ladies of the court. Details of the arrangements were handed on from one royal confinement to the next, so that in late July Katherine of Aragon's former chamberlain had sent

[31] *LP*, vi.1009; *Cal. S. P. Span.*, *1531–33*, p. 756 [*LP*, vi.918].
[32] De Carles, in Ascoli, *L'Opinion*, lines 148–64.
[33] Hall, *Chronicle*, p. 805; *LP*, vi.895.
[34] *Ordinances for the Household*, pp. 125–6; Dublin, Trinity College, MS 518 ff. 117–19.

the necessary papers to Cromwell to be passed to the new incumbent, and in early August the carpenters and joiners moved into Greenwich, where the confinement was to take place.[35]

On Thursday the 21st Anne and Henry together left Windsor for Whitehall. After spending the weekend there they went on to Greenwich, where Anne took formal leave of the masculine world on the Tuesday following.[36] With his wife in her chamber, Henry took his mind off his anxieties by planning a splendid joust to mark what he hoped would be the safe delivery of a son to be called Henry or Edward, but he was not left in suspense for long. His daughter was born at 3 pm on Sunday 7 September.[37]

The sex of the baby was some disappointment to Anne and Henry. The pundits (all but one) had been predicting a son, and Chapuys made the most of this. There is, however, no evidence of the crushing psychological blow that some have supposed. After all the alarms, Anne had had an easy labour; the child was perfect and took after her father.[38] Henry's predominant emotion was relief. The jousts, of course were abandoned; as with the arrival of Mary in 1516, public celebrations for the birth of a princess were low-key, but a herald immediately proclaimed this first of Henry's 'legitimate' children, while the Chapel Royal sang the Te Deum.[39] Letters announcing the news were sent out far and wide, a second and public Te Deum was sung at St Paul's, and preparations were at once put in hand for a magnificent christening on Wednesday 10 September, to be followed by bonfires and free wine in London.[40] Edward Hall waxed eloquent over the ceremony: the procession from the Great Hall at Greenwich, along a carpet of green rushes and between hangings of arras, to the Church of the Observant Friars; the lavish arrangements in the church, and the splendour of those taking part. Elizabeth was brought back from the

---

[35] *LP*, vi.890; J. W. Kirby, 'Building work at Placentia, 1532–33', in *Transactions of the Greenwich and Lewisham Antiquarian Society*, 5 (1954–61), 22–50.

[36] *LP*, vi.948, 1004 [*Lisle Letters*, i.35].

[37] *Cal. S. P. Span.*, *1531–33*, p. 788 [*LP*, vi.1069]; *LP*, vi.1070; Hall, *Chronicle*, p. 805.

[38] De Carles, in Ascoli, *L'Opinion*, lines 168–76.

[39] *LP*, vi.1166; Hall, *Chronicle*, p. 805.

[40] *LP*, vi.1089; Wriothesley, *Chronicle*, i.22–3, which contradicts Chapuys: *Cal. S. P. Span.*, *1531–33*, p. 795 [*LP*, vi.1125]. For the christening, see also Hall, *Chronicle*, pp. 805–6; *LP*, vi.1111.

ceremony that autumn afternoon, escorted by over five hundred lighted torches. Henry had ensured, as the French noted (their ambassador was a guest of honour), that again 'the whole occasion was so perfect that nothing was lacking.'[41]

The occasion was also used to humiliate Anne's critics yet again. The friary itself had been the centre for the most vehement and public opposition to the divorce. The name Elizabeth was given to her rather than the name of one of the godmothers, deliberately to identify her with the royal dynasty, especially Henry VIII's mother. The marquis of Exeter was called on to carry 'the taper of virgin wax'; the duke of Suffolk escorted the child; John Lord Hussey, 'Lady Mary's' chamberlain, helped to carry the canopy. Most striking of all, Katherine's friend the marchioness of Exeter was one of the godmothers, and it was common knowledge that 'she really wanted to have nothing to do with this', but took part 'so as not to displease the king'; the need for her to give an impressive christening present as well – three engraved silver-gilt bowls with covers – can only have rubbed salt into the wound.[42] Humiliation for the conservatives was accentuated by the triumphant role played by the Boleyns and the Howards and their allies. Among the twenty-one participants listed by Hall, there was Anne's father and brother and eight Howard connections, Thomas Cranmer (as godfather), one person who was linked to William Brereton and another to Thomas Cromwell.[43] We also know that Cromwell himself was amongst the observers; he had been largely responsible for the success of the coronation and it seems probable that he organized the christening as well.[44] Those who had backed the Boleyn marriage might well triumph. Anne and Henry had won.

Or had they? Hindsight suggests that there is another and more disturbing conclusion that should have been drawn from this

---

[41] De Carles, in Ascoli, *L'Opinion*, lines 181–2.

[42] Ibid., lines 183–5. The godmothers were Agnes, dowager duchess of Norfolk, Margaret, dowager marchioness of Dorset, and the godfather, Cranmer; the marchioness of Exeter was godmother at the confirmation which followed immediately on the baptism, but her name was Gertrude, not Elizabeth ['Ysabeau'], as de Carles assumed from the name given the child.

[43] Henry, earl of Worcester; John Dudley.

[44] *LP*, vi.1111(4).

impressive end to a climactic twelve months – twelve months that had made Anne, still only the younger daughter of a newly elevated earl, first marchioness of Pembroke, then the king's wife, next the queen crowned and finally mother of the heir to the throne. The birth of Elizabeth, which had cemented the relationship between the parents, had undeniably weakened Anne's position in the eyes of the world. Before the marriage she had seemed to embody the hope of a son for England; in pregnancy she could be presented as the promise that that hope would be fulfilled. But with a daughter in the cradle, Anne had still to establish her claim to the throne. The birth of Elizabeth undid much of what the coronation had set out to achieve; Anne Boleyn remained a pretender. If she had had a son in September 1533, her position would have been beyond challenge. All but the most intransigent of Katherine's friends would have seen the wisdom and advantage of accepting the new heir and his mother; the Boleyn marriage would have become the accepted reality in political life, and court faction would have realigned accordingly. Even Charles v would have recognized that the restoration of Katherine and Mary was a lost cause. Even Mary herself would have been hard put to resist the prior claims of a boy. As it was, the birth of a daughter ensured that Anne would continue under pressure from both enemies at court and hostility abroad. It also kept Mary's claim alive; even if she were of doubtful legitimacy, so was Elizabeth, and age and the imperial connection made her much the stronger candidate as heir presumptive. Thus instead of faction being stabilized by the marriage, the coronation and the birth of a prince, the arrival of Elizabeth revived and perpetuated instability. Security would only come if Anne could have a son.

III

A Royal Marriage

I I

Anne and Henry

❦

THERE IS among the relics of Mary Tudor a book of prayers where the page devoted to intercessions for women with child is said to be stained with tears.[1] In the later twentieth century the problem of childlessness attracts considerable attention in the Western world, but no pressure on the would-be mother today can match the peculiar strain on a sixteenth-century queen. Her essential function was to bear sons; otherwise she was a failure. Princesses of the blood were brought up to see this as their destiny. Anne Boleyn had won her way by education, personality and courage, but now she had to accept that success as an individual was unimportant against biological success or failure. It is partly for this reason that the years 1534 and 1535 are comparatively light on information about her. She was no longer, of course, the immediate issue in politics, but the silence also reflects the fact that there was now only one thing expected of her. Her stepdaughter Mary fiercely resented Anne and rejoiced at her discomfiture, but she too would come to know the private physiological hell of the childless Tudor wife. Anne had described children as 'the greatest consolation in the world', but the Spanish ambassador had the right of it when he wrote of Mary years later that 'the queen's lying-in is the foundation of everything.'[2]

To have a son, one son – that was all that was necessary. Surely that was not too difficult in an age of large families; surely that could not be difficult with a husband like Henry, who at the

---

[1] C. Morris, *The Tudors* (1955), p. 151.
[2] Quoted Prescott, *Mary Tudor*, p. 307.

time (and since) was recognized as a 'fleshly' man, fond of women, and a sexual predator?[3] All that might seem necessary was a healthy wife, and sons would arrive; Anne had only to lie back and do her duty for England. And when healthy sons did not arrive – as they had not arrived to Katherine before her – it was obvious where to place the blame. Yet this is wide of the mark. The popular idea that our ancestors reproduced themselves with the efficiency of Third World populations today is a fallacy. Even among the nobility, where birth rates and child survival rates were higher than among the general population, large families were by no means the rule, and there were many instances of childlessness or of couples that only produced daughters. Guaranteeing a male heir was no more possible than it ever has been. Nor was Henry as the popular image would have him. As well as the difficulties and hazards of conception and pregnancy in an age when medical knowledge and practice were more of a danger than a help, Anne had to contend with a husband who was anything but a good prospect for paternity.

The evidence that Henry VIII had sexual problems is, first of all, circumstantial. Between 1509 and 1547 he is known, or can be presumed, to have had sexual relations over some months or years with eight women – that is, his six wives and his two known mistresses, Elizabeth Blount and Mary Boleyn. Only four of the eight conceived, and we may note that the last time was in 1536 when Henry was only forty-five. As well as the poor record of conceptions, Henry's partners had a poor record of maternal success. Only four pregnancies produced a healthy infant, one each for Katherine of Aragon, Elizabeth Blount, Anne Boleyn and Jane Seymour. There were other pregnancies that ended in miscarriage, stillbirth or death in the first days of infancy. Anne herself had two miscarriages – that is, in two of her three known pregnancies. Katherine her predecessor had an even poorer record – five failures in six, and over a much longer period.[4]

---

[3] George Wyatt, *Papers*, p. 141; for a concurrent Catholic view, BL, Sloane MS 2495 f. 2: 'King Henry gave his mind to three notorious vices, lechery, covetousness and cruelty, but the two latter issued and sprang out of the former.'

[4] J. Dewhurst, 'The alleged miscarriages of Catherine of Aragon and Anne Boleyn', in *Medical History* 28 (1984), 49–56, has significantly revised the number of Katherine's supposed pregnancies, although I disagree with his

This case history raises the possibility that it was Henry and not his wives who was responsible for silence in the nurseries of the Tudor royal palaces. At a distance of 450 years, deficiencies in fertility or genetic defects can be nothing more than suspicions, and the one thing which seems clear is that venereal disease was not to blame (as is sometimes suggested). The king did not suffer from syphilis. His medical history and the record of the treatments he received are quite unlike those of Francis I, for instance, who was heavily infected with the pox, and it has been convincingly argued that the leg ulcer which periodically darkened Henry's life from 1528 and is often assumed to be venereal, was actually caused by osteomyelitis resulting from falls in the tiltyard.[5] We have, of course, to take into account the medical condition of the women concerned. There is the evidence about the difficulty of Anne's first pregnancy, and the five years' delay between her agreement to marry Henry and the commencement of sexual relations in 1532, when she was over thirty, must have lessened her chances of successfully having children. But all eight women could not have been bad risks. There is nothing in the history of Katherine of Aragon's sisters to suggest a tendency to impaired childbearing; Mary Boleyn became pregnant as soon as she left Henry for her husband, William Carey; the same was true of Katherine Parr when she married Thomas Seymour after the king's death in 1547.

Whether or not Henry suffered from any congenital impairment, there is direct evidence to support the suggestion that he was, or became, partially impotent. In 1540 his divorce from Anne of Cleves was secured on the ground of the king's sexual incapacity. Henry's own deposition admitted his lack 'of the will and power to consummate the same', though he slept regularly with his fourth wife for several months.[6] But the blame was

---

reduction of Anne's pregnancies to two (1533 and 1535/6), omitting that in 1534 (see below, p. 239). The report of 24 June 1535 that Anne was visibly pregnant [*LP*, viii.919], redated 1533 or 1534 in *Lisle Letters*, i.10, belongs to 1533, as the court was at Hampton Court in 1534. The Milanese report in May 1535 that Anne was pregnant seems to refer to the events of the previous summer: *Cal. S. P. Milan*, 962.

[5] Scarisbrick, *Henry VIII*, p. 485. Alternatively, the ulcer could have been varicose. For Francis I see Knecht, *Francis I*, pp. 418–19.

[6] Burnet, *History*, iv.427, 430. The phrase in Henry's declaration that if Anne 'brought maidenhead with her' he never 'took any from her by true carnal copulation', seems to suggest that he had attempted intercourse. He

placed on his German bride's lack of attractiveness (and allegedly
suspect virginity), while concern for the obvious reflection on
Henry led his doctors to pass on to the court (with some details
decently veiled in Latin) the king's assurance that he 'thought
himself able to do the act with other but not with her'.[7] The same
problem had bedevilled the relationship with Anne Boleyn. At
his trial in May 1536, George Boleyn was asked whether Anne
had told his wife that the king was incapable of sexual intercourse, implying that he was unable to attain or sustain an
erection (*le Roy n'estoit habile en cas de soy copuler avec femme et qu'il
n'avoit ne vertu ne puissance*). Such a delicate question was handed
to Rochford in writing, and the story was that it was reading the
allegation out aloud which sealed his fate.[8] That is improbable,
but the asking of such an amazing question is proof enough that
doubts about the king's vigour did circulate.

We can, indeed, take the matter a little further.[9] No hint of
impotence had prevented Anne rapidly becoming pregnant in
December 1532, and she was pregnant again just over a year later,
three or four months after the birth of Elizabeth. But we have a
most revealing insight into the way Henry's mind worked in an
interview with Chapuys in April 1533.[10] When the ambassador
pointed out that a new wife to replace Katherine by no means
necessarily guaranteed children, Henry asked excitedly, 'Am I
not a man like other men? Am I not? Am I not?' The ambassador
had, he declared, no reason at all to deny this – he was not privy to
all the royal secrets (that is, that Anne was four months
pregnant). Quite obviously Henry associated virility and sexual
potency with having children. The birth of Elizabeth reassured
him, as did the second pregnancy, and Chapuys noted in
February 1534 that Henry was quite happy that he would have a

---

consulted his doctors several times about the inability to consummate, and Dr
Chamber 'counselled his majesty not to enforce himself, for eschewing such
inconveniences as by debility ensuing in that case were to be feared'. Chamber
reported that Henry could not, in Anne's company, 'be provoked or stirred to
that act': John Strype, *Ecclesiastical Memorials* (1822), I ii.460–1.
   [7] Thus Dr Butts, ibid., p. 461.
   [8] *Cal. S. P. Span.*, *1536–38*, p. 126 [*LP*, x.908], quoted from Friedmann, *Anne
Boleyn*, ii.280 n.1. Cf. Henry's phrase re Anne of Cleves: 'neither will nor
courage'.
   [9] But for more speculative psychological discussion see L. B. Smith, *Henry
VIII, the Mask of Royalty* (1971), pp. 64–6.
   [10] *Cal. S. P. Span.*, *1531–33*, p. 638 [*LP*, vi.351].

son this time.[11] By April the queen's condition was obvious, and Henry's confidence is seen in the highly elaborate silver cradle which was ordered from his goldsmith, Cornelius Hayes, with Tudor roses, precious stones, gold-embroidered bedding and cloth-of-gold baby clothes.[12] All was well as late as July, and then tragedy struck.[13] Anne miscarried.[14]

The secret of the disaster was so well kept that it was only on 23 September that Chapuys reported that the queen – or 'the lady', as he insisted on calling her – was not, after all, to have a child.[15] We have to remember that the ambassador had been out of touch with the court while it was on summer progress. Away from the public eye, with a smaller number of attendants than at other times and with both Anne and Henry desperate to conceal it, total discretion was achieved. But the damage had been done. The ominous reminder of Katherine's history brought all Henry's doubts flooding back. It is notorious that anxiety about virility can lead to a loss of sexual potency, and this is what seems to have happened with Henry. Perhaps, after all, he was not 'like other men'. The confidence and stimulation of the new marriage was shattered, and it would be more than a year before Henry could make Anne pregnant again.

[11] Ibid., *1534-35*, p. 67 [*LP*, vii.94]; *Lisle Letters*, ii.175 [*LP*, vii.556]. J. Dewhurst, in *Medical History* 28, rejects this pregnancy, and suggests pseudocyesis, the exhibition of pregnancy-like symptoms as a result of psychological stress. Anne, however, had no reason to be under stress at this date, having produced a healthy female child eight months earlier. If she had 'a goodly belly' in late April (and the informant is her receiver-general), she would then be 16-plus weeks pregnant, i.e. conceiving not later than the start of the year. Imperial sources at Rome had been informed by 23 Jan. 1534 that Anne was pregnant, allegedly by a letter from the newly arrived English ambassador in France. If this was Lord William Howard, the date of arrival must have been the beginning of December [*LP*, vi.1438], suggesting that Anne became pregnant in November 1533. This could just make good sense, but the chain of information is too long for complete confidence: ibid., vii.96.

[12] RO, SP1/88 f. 116 [*LP*, vii.1668]. Since Hayes' bill was for items delivered to 'Mr Secretary' (i.e. Cromwell) it must have been prepared post April 1534. It is unlikely that the detailed bill for a cradle for Elizabeth would be delayed so long. Alternatively, it could have been ordered for the expected birth in 1536. It was not for the future Edward VI: Cromwell would then have been addressed as 'lord privy seal'.

[13] *St. Pap.*, vii.565 [*LP*, vii.958]; *Cal. S. P. Span.*, *1534-35*, p. 224 [*LP*, viii.1013].

[14] That it was a miscarriage and not a stillbirth or neonatal death is indicated by the queen not having 'taken her chamber'.

[15] *Cal. S. P. Span.*, *1534-35*, p. 264 [*LP*, vii.1193].

It is significant that it was after the miscarriage in the summer of 1534 that the first hints appear of a rift between Henry and Anne. Tradition regularly backdates these by a year, to the last weeks before Elizabeth was born. On 13 August 1533 Chapuys had reported that he saw signs of hope for Katherine in Henry's long absence from Anne.[16] Even more dramatic, the imperial ambassador at Rome passed on to Charles V the news that the king's loss of affection in the face of Anne Boleyn's arrogance had led him to switch his attentions to someone else.[17] On 3 September Chapuys had remarked on how lucky Anne was to have received her magnificent state bed (for her presence chamber) two months previously, since:

> Full of jealousy – and not without reason – she used words to the king which he did not like, and he told her that she must shut her eyes and endure, just like others who were worthier than she, and that she ought to know that he could humiliate her in only a moment longer that it had taken to exalt her!

After this, Henry refused to speak to her for two or three days.[18]

The case looks ominous. Yet under scrutiny the story evaporates. The report from Rome of the alleged mistress is an error in dating by a modern editor: it belongs to the late autumn of 1534.[19] Several letters from different sources quite independently reported that in July and August 1533 the royal couple were in good health and enjoying life; Henry was in tearing high spirits at the thought of the new baby.[20] As for Chapuys' tales in August, he was in London, so how could he know that Henry was neglecting Anne at Windsor? Furthermore, the ambassador himself tells us that when Henry specially summoned him to meet the king and his council, the meeting was away from the court, at Guildford, and was disguised as a hunting trip precisely to avoid causing Anne anxiety.[21] In any case, a second letter from Chapuys admitted that he had got things wrong.[22] His September report of Henry's bitter remarks to Anne is also

---

[16] Ibid., *1531–33*, p. 760 [*LP*, vi.995].
[17] *LP*, vi.1054.
[18] *Cal. S. P. Span.*, *1531–33*, p. 788 [*LP*, vi.1069]; Friedmann, *Anne Boleyn*, i.213 n.1.
[19] Cf. *LP*, vi.1054 with *Cal. S. P. Span.*, *1534–35*, pp. 292–3.
[22] *LP*, vi.879, 891, 948, 963, 1004.
[21] *Cal. S. P. Span.*, *1531–33*, p. 755 [*LP*, vi.918].
[22] Ibid., p. 777 [*LP*, vi.1018].

suspect. By that time Anne had 'taken her chamber', so all the ambassador could have had to work on was gossip about what had allegedly been overheard by an attendant during one of the king's private visits. For a husband who, a few weeks before, had been concerned to protect his wife from anxiety, the speech as recorded seems inconsistent, to say the least. Perhaps in the discomfort of her late pregnancy Anne did make a scene, perhaps Henry's own worry caused him to bite back – such an episode would be neither surprising nor significant. Or perhaps the whole was exaggerated by the wishful thinking of Katherine's ally, the marchioness of Exeter, who was probably the ambassador's informant.[23] Whatever occurred or did not occur, we need to note that Chapuys himself dismissed it as 'a lovers' quarrel'. So should we.

The rumours reaching the Low Countries via the Hanse merchants painted quite a different picture – not of a besotted king coming to his senses but of one who was more besotted than ever, constantly at his wife's side and letting court discipline go to the dogs![24] And that may be much nearer the truth. In late October 1533 Anne's maids of honour were repeating Henry's brazen remark that he loved the queen so much that he would beg alms from door to door rather than give her up. The two are still described as 'merry'. Henry kept Anne, as always, in selective touch with diplomatic affairs, visited Elizabeth after the baby was given her own special establishment in December 1533, and gave the general impression of remaining firmly under his wife's thumb. As the session of parliament due in January 1534 approached, Anne helped her husband to whip opinion into line and Henry warned the marquis of Exeter that the least signs of disloyalty would cost him (and any one else) his head.[25]

Like almost all the specific stories of friction between Henry VIII and Anne Boleyn, the story that trouble arose between them in the autumn of 1534 after the failure of Anne's second pregnancy began with Chapuys.[26] It was his report that the

---

[23] Ibid., p. 800 [*LP*, vi.1125].

[24] *LP*, vi.1065.

[25] For the above see ibid., vi.1293, 1510, 1528; vii.83, 126, 556, 682, 888; *Cal. S. P. Ven.*, *1527–33*, 924; *Cal. S. P. Span.*, *1531–33*, p. 842 [*LP*, vi.1392].

[26] The imperial envoy at Rome reported rumours about bad feeling between Anne and Henry, which were circulating in France on 20 Sept., but withdrew them on 3 Oct., having received Chapuys' letter dated 27 Aug.: *Cal. S. P. Span.*, *1534–35*, pp. 260, 268–9 [*LP*, vii.1174, 1228].

imperial ambassador at Rome was echoing, and the first notice
of the affair is in the despatches sent to Brussels in late
September. What Chapuys reported was that with the ending of
his hope for a child, Henry had 'renewed and increased the love
that he had had previously towards another very beautiful maid
of honour [*demoiselle de court*]'. Anne had responded by wanting to
dismiss the girl, but Henry had been most upset and had
informed her that 'she had good reason to be content with what
he had done for her, which he would not do again, if he were
starting afresh, that she should remember where she had come
from, and many other things'.[27] A fortnight later Chapuys had
more to tell. George Boleyn's wife had been forbidden the court
because she had plotted with Anne to pick a quarrel with
Henry's new lady so that she would have to withdraw.[28] Anne's
influence was wilting daily, and the rival was sending encouraging messages to Mary that her trials were nearly over. Many of
the courtiers were encouraging Henry's new interest, with the
intention of separating him from Anne. The affair was still going
on in December when the king was again annoyed at Anne's
complaints, but by the end of February it was finished. In her
place was Anne's own cousin, Margaret Shelton, the daughter of
the governess in charge of Elizabeth and Mary.

What should be made of all this? The conventional interpretation is that the marriage of Henry VIII and Anne Boleyn was
breaking or had broken up. Descriptions of Anne after her fall
are projected back to present Henry as a king whose life was
made 'hell' by a 'barren, old and ill-natured baggage'. 'Im-
portunity' (nagging) and 'cursedness' had destroyed every vestige
of the king's great passion. Henry the great lover was looking
elsewhere.[29] Yet the facts do not justify such a picture. We have
to remember the tainted sources of so much of Chapuys'
information – it was Anne's enemy Carewe who passed on the
story of the king's annoyance at her complaints in December
1534.[30] The ambassador could also be led astray, as he himself
recognized. His pleasure on New Year's Day 1535 that even such

[27] Ibid., p. 264 [*LP*, vii.1193].
[28] Ibid., p. 280 [*LP*, vii.1257]. For the rest of the paragraph see ibid.,
pp. 293, 294–5 & 299–301, 344 [*LP*, vii.1279, 1297, 1554]; *LP*, viii.263 at
p. 104.
[29] *Cal. S. P. Span., 1536–38*, p. 127 [*LP*, x.908]; *LP*, x.1047.
[30] *Cal. S. P. Span., 1534–35*, p. 344 [*LP*, vii.1554].

a Boleyn partisan as the earl of Northumberland was turning against the regime had changed to doubt within the month.[31] His earliest mention of the alleged romance carried the warning not to attach too much importance to it, since Henry was so fickle and Anne knew how to manage him. Even in the last weeks of her life when she faced the threat of Jane Seymour, Chapuys would still be sceptical.

There are, too, reasons why we should be sceptical. Who was this new flame? Some have supposed that the favourite was Jane Seymour, but there is nothing to support this, and when Jane does appear on the scene there is no reference to any earlier affair with Henry. How are we to understand the arrival of Margaret Shelton? This has been variously interpreted as a deliberate piece of procuring by Anne in order to supplant her anonymous rival, or by Norfolk to supplant Anne, from whom he was now estranged. And why does Margaret Shelton suddenly drop out of the limelight? Another problem is the role of Lady Rochford, who is otherwise known as Anne's enemy. As to the reference that the king was renewing a previous relationship, that too becomes mysterious with the redating of the supposed 1533 Rome despatch, unless this is what was alluded to in Chapuys' remark that Anne's jealousy in 1533 was 'not without reason'.

A far more likely explanation for the evidence than the 'irretrievable breakdown of marriage' is, in fact, suggested by Chapuys' own description. The relationship between Henry and his new lady was first of all a limited one; it would be significant, he said, only if it lasted and if it became warmer than it had been. And what that limitation was is indicated by the description of the girl as 'the damsel whom the king has been accustomed to serve'. 'Accustomed to serve' – this is the language of chivalry. What Henry had done was to offer his knightly service to a new 'mistress' for the game of courtly love. As in the case of Anne Boleyn herself, this could sometimes lead to a genuine relationship, but Chapuys is clear that in this case it did not do so, nor when the king's interest turned to Madge Shelton. Indeed it is easy to see why an amour which remained superficial should attract a man anxious to appear a terror with the women, but deeply uncertain of his capacities.

It is nevertheless obvious why Anne should object to Henry's

---

[31] Ibid., p. 354 [*LP*, viii.1]; *LP*, viii.121.

gallantry. She had for six years been Henry's 'sovereign lady'; she had been the adored mistress. How could she accept the new situation and see Henry become the 'servant' of another woman? And she must have suspected as we do, that Henry would not have relegated her to conventional treatment as queen if she had had a son. It was not, however, a mere matter of pride or hurt feelings, or of failure to adjust to her new position. Henry might well get annoyed at such over-sensitiveness: he was behaving as the rules said a king should behave, so why could not she? But a royal consort occupied a place at the head of the court and of society which was hers by incontestable right. There had never been any rivalry between Katherine and the ladies whose praises Henry had sung over the years, who had danced with him, who had played the game of flirtation with him; she was the queen. Anne, however, knew that her right to that title was contested. She could not take for granted the protection of recognized status; she still had to compete for and win the king's favour. She was in the contradictory position of being expected to behave as a queen, but having to continue to challenge as a mistress.

The place that Anne occupied was flawed in another way. She was now a wife and mother. Convention – and Henry was nothing if not conventional – dictated that she should now take a subservient role, neither disputing with nor presuming to criticize her husband. Once the honeymoon period was over, the husband was expected to find his concerns in the masculine world; he was certainly not expected to live in his wife's pocket. One of the worst things that Flemish rumour could say about Henry was that he did just this and let the court go to the devil. Anne, however, as we have seen, was that Tudor rarity, the self-made woman. She was where she was by virtue of her own abilities. It was asking a great deal of her after so many years, and years which had brought her the most amazing success, to change her lifestyle so drastically.

There was one thing more. However complicated the motivation, however we gloss the phrase, Henry and Anne had been in love. In an outburst against the new regime, a Colchester monk had declared with contempt that when the two had been at Calais in 1532, Anne had followed Henry round like a dog.[32] Certainly they quarrelled, and not simply on Chapuys' evidence.

[32] *LP*, vii.454.

The Venetian ambassador reported in June 1535 that Henry had had more than enough of his new queen.[33] The alleged remark of 1534 that he could reduce Anne as rapidly as he had raised her only makes sense if Henry was blazingly angry at the time, for at the very same moment he had Cromwell hard at work drafting the statute which would vest the succession to the crown in the children of the Boleyn marriage! If he said it, he certainly did not mean it. As Chapuys had said of the friction between Henry and Anne over the new 'mistress', these were lovers' quarrels and not much notice should be taken of them. If some were provoked by the king's shallow gallantries to other ladies, at other times the queen could laugh about such flirtations. Anne nearly caused an international incident at a banquet on 1 December 1533 by bursting into laughter when she was talking to the French ambassador. Offended, he had asked, 'How now, Madam! Are you amusing yourself at my expense or what?' Trying to mollify him, Anne explained that Henry had gone to bring another guest for her to entertain, and an important one, but on the way he had met a lady and the errand had gone completely out of his head.[34]

In the relationship between Henry and his second wife, storm followed sunshine, sunshine followed storm. A fortnight after the Venetian report that Henry was satiated with her, the returning French ambassador told Paris that she was very much in charge.[35] In an ultimate sense, the problems of Henry and Anne arose from the fact that there was emotion in the relationship. The conventions of the day, of courtly love, of sovereign and consort, of husband and wife, were simply not capable of accommodating the fierce passions which united Anne Boleyn and Henry Tudor.

The tensions within the marriage were undoubtedly made worse by external problems. The most immediate was Katherine's daughter, Mary. Seventeen at the time of the second marriage, she was adamant in her refusal to recognize Anne and her child, despite her father's determination that she should do so. Though

[33] *Cal. S. P. Ven., 1534–54*, 54.
[34] *Cal. S. P. Span., 1534–35*, p. 338 [*LP*, vii.1507]; ibid., p. 376 [*LP*, viii.48]; Friedmann, *Anne Boleyn*, ii.45 no.1.
[35] *LP*, viii.909.

Katherine helped to inspire Mary, his ex-wife could be largely ignored by Henry. Relegation to a modest establishment away from court was a proper fate for a princess dowager, and Katherine was not one who would, so he believed, ever plot against him. Mary, on the other hand, was undeniably part of the royal family. Intelligent, gifted, not unattractive and of a winning disposition, popularity made her adherence more important and her opposition more dangerous. Disloyalty to Henry did not seem like disloyalty when it was thought to be support for the rightful heir, and increasingly Mary became the focus for all dislike of Anne and everything she appeared to represent.

Henry saw Mary's behaviour as a straightforward case of disobedience and, despite his obvious affection for her, put increasing pressure on his daughter to conform.[36] She lost her royal style and her household; she was forced as 'a bastard' to join the household of the 'legitimate' Elizabeth and give her precedence at all times, under the oversight of Elizabeth's governess, Anne Shelton, who was Anne's aunt. Mary was kept away from her mother, isolated from her former friends and servants, and deliberately slighted and ignored by Henry. The result was a head-on clash with a Tudor obstinacy as great as his own, but at the cost of permanent damage to Mary. The story is not pleasant to modern reading, although what was questioned at the time – and not only by her committed supporters – was not so much the treatment for her disobedience as the unfairness of it. According to Chapuys, when Norfolk and Rochford rebuked Anne Shelton for being too lenient with Mary – the family must not fail the king – Anne's aunt replied that even if Mary was the bastard daughter of a poor gentleman she would deserve respect and kindness because of the girl she was.[37] Henry disagreed. He was determined to break his daughter's will. It was Anne Boleyn, however, who got the blame. To believe this made it much easier for Charles V to keep up some civil relationship with Henry, much easier for Mary (and Katherine) to resist pressure. Her father could not really know; he was not to blame; it was the harpy who had her claws in him. When Anne

---

[36] Prescott, *Mary Tudor*, pp. 45–57.
[37] *Cal. S. P. Span.*, *1534–35*, p. 57 [*LP*, vii.214].

was dead Mary discovered the truth, and the abasement which Henry exacted then was to scar her for life.

This is not to say that Anne was guiltless. Chapuys' letters are full of her railing against Mary and of her lurid threats to curb 'her proud Spanish blood'.[38] But much though the ambassador warned of poison and worse, Anne was ranting, not thinking. There is an obvious ring of truth in his story that, assuming she would be regent if, as expected, Henry went to Calais to meet Francis I again, Anne swore to seize that chance to put Mary to death. When her brother pointed out, very simply, that this would anger the king, she retorted that she did not care, even if she was burned for doing it.[39] So Anne's language was violent and threatening, but this sprang not from malevolence but from self-defence. For Henry, Mary was a disobedient child. For Anne, she was much more. Her obstinacy was an insult, a denial of Anne's own identity and integrity. If Katherine's marriage was valid, then she, Anne, was a whore. And there was an added twist. In canon law – and this fact was widely appreciated at court – a child born to a couple who believed that they were properly husband and wife remained legitimate even if it was subsequently found that the marriage was invalid.[40] Mary, if anyone, had been conceived 'in good faith', as the lawyers put it, and by refusing to recognize the priority of Elizabeth she was in effect asserting her own claim to be the heir to the throne. For Anne, therefore, the negative policy of disciplining Mary and excluding her from court was a defeat; every day that she withheld the positive endorsement of Anne's title made the queen's weakness more obvious. Active conformity alone would do. Anne knew that the stakes could not be higher: 'She is my death, and I am hers.'[41]

Mary was certainly frustrating to deal with, and this is another explanation for Anne's outbursts and her support for harsh treatment. All the same, on three distinct occasions Anne put out feelers for a better relationship. In February or March 1534, when on a visit to Elizabeth, she offered to welcome Mary if she would accept her as queen, and to reconcile her with her

[38] Ibid., p. 72 [*LP*, vii.296].
[39] Ibid., p. 198 [*LP*, vii.871].
[40] The bona fide argument was being canvassed in 1533 – see Cromwell's note of April: *LP*, vi.386 ii.
[41] *Cal. S. P. Span., 1534–35*, p. 573 [*LP*, ix.873].

father.[42] Mary's response was that she knew no queen but her mother, but that if the king's mistress would intercede with her father she would be grateful. Even after this offensiveness Anne tried again, before leaving the house in high dudgeon, vowing to repress such impudence. It was perhaps a few months later, when the two half-sisters were at Eltham, that Anne and Mary found themselves in the palace chapel together.[43] An attendant, either out of kindness or in order to see the fun, or as part of a deliberate plot to set Anne up, told her that Mary had acknowledged her before leaving. The queen immediately sent a message to the princess apologizing for not noticing, saying that 'she desires that this may be an entrance of friendly correspondence, which your grace shall find completely to be embraced on her part.' Mary's reply could not have been ruder. From the publicity of her dinner table she declared that the queen could not possibly have sent the message; she was 'so far from this place'. The messenger should have said 'the Lady Anne Boleyn, for I can acknowledge no other queen but my mother, nor esteem them my friends who are not hers.' Her curtsey, she explained piously, had been made to the altar, 'to her maker and mine'. The story has a good pedigree, but it is a late one, and we may doubt whether even Mary dared to be this offensive. But even allowing considerable discount, Anne would still have been justified in being offended.

It is not surprising to find after this that Anne left Mary to reflect for eighteen months before trying again, but with Katherine on her death-bed and Anne certain that she was pregnant again, Lady Shelton was instructed to press once more the queen's desire to be kind.[44] This was followed, after the old queen had died, by a message that if Mary would obey the king she would find Anne a second mother, and be asked for minimal courtesies only. When Mary replied discouragingly that she would obey her father as far as honour and conscience allowed, Anne tried to frighten and warn her at the same time. She wrote a letter to Anne Shelton, which was left 'by accident' in Mary's oratory where she read it, as clearly she was expected to do. Efforts to persuade Mary were, Anne wrote, to cease; they had been an

[42] Ibid., p. 72 [*LP*, vii.296].
[43] Ibid., p. 224 [*LP*, vii. 1013]; Clifford, *Dormer*, pp. 81–2.
[44] *Cal. S. P. Span., 1536–38*, p. 12 [*LP*, x.141]; ibid., p. 44 [*LP*, x.307].

attempt to save her from her own folly, not because Anne needed
her acquiescence. One may think that only partly true, but there
is no doubt of the chilling realism of Anne's warning of what
would happen to Mary if, as she expected, the child she was
carrying was a son: 'I have daily experience that the king's
wisdom is such as not to esteem her repentence of her rudeness
and unnatural obstinacy when she has no choice.' This was only
literal truth, as anyone knew who was familiar with Henry's
behaviour towards those who had offended him but sought
mercy too late.[45] Mary took a copy of the letter for Chapuys,
restored the original to its place and ignored the warning.

Mary's failure to accept Anne was one problem, but it was
linked to another: an increasing opposition to the queen among
the nation at large and among the elite. There is no doubt that a
good deal of Anne's unpopularity was on account of Mary and
the repudiation of Katherine. The sentiment was frequently
found among women, for obvious reasons.[46] Margaret Chanseler
from Bradfield St Clare in Suffolk demonstrated a particularly
personal line in invective when she said that Anne was a 'goggle-
eyed whore ... God save Queen Katherine.'[47] Feelings were
usually more circumspect among the elite, but no less real. Anne
could not but notice the readiness of the courtiers who accompanied her to see Elizabeth, to slink off at the same time to pay
their respects to Mary.[48]

Much of the hostility to Anne, however, was also associated
with a dislike of royal policies of recent years: in the first place
taxation, but even more, interference with the Church. During
the attack on the Church, the abbot of Whitby declared com-
prehensively that 'the king's grace was ruled by one common
stewed [professional] whore, Anne Bullan, who made all the
spirituality to be beggared and the temporalty also.'[49] The less
educated could be just as direct, in their own way. On Monday 4
May 1534, one Henry Kylbie was attending to his master's horse
in the stables of the White Horse in Cambridge. Perhaps the

---

[45] Cf. the king's remarks in Nov. 1535: *Cal. S. P. Span.*, *1534–35*, p. 572 [*LP*, ix.862].
[46] *LP*, vii.840.
[47] Ibid., viii.196.
[48] E.g. *Cal. S. P. Span.*, *1534–35*, p. 299 [*LP*, vii.1297].
[49] *LP*, v.907.

horse was lame; we do not know. At any rate, Kylbie had arrived with his Mr Pachett the Saturday before on the way from London to Leicester, and he was heartily sick of waiting. The ostler of the inn strolled over and the two got into conversation. Did he know, the ostler asked, that there was no longer a pope, only a bishop of Rome? As a man who may well have stabled the horses of the Cambridge Reformers when they met in the inn for their evenings of convivial but risky debate, the ostler evidently was well up in religious gossip. Not so Henry Kylbie. There was a pope, he insisted, and anyone who said contrary was 'a strong heretic'. When the ostler, playing his ace, said that 'the king's grace held of his part', Henry lost his common sense and his temper. Both ostler and king were heretics, and 'this business had never been if the king had not married Anne Bullen.' Angry words became blows, and ended with Henry breaking the ostler's head.[50]

Those at court in the forefront of the battle for the papal headship did their best to exploit such plebeian sentiments. When two of the Observant Friars on the run from Greenwich were asked whether Elizabeth had been christened in cold water or in hot they replied, 'hot water, but it was not hot enough.'[51] When the Blessed Richard Reynolds, 'the most learned monk in England', went to the scaffold with the Carthusian martyrs in May 1535, he took with him John Hale, a Cambridge fellow and vicar of Isleworth in Middlesex who was part of a cell which Reynolds had been feeding with gossip about the morals of the Boleyn family and the falseness of Henry's claim to be supreme head.[52] It was Hale that confessed that he had had pointed out to him as the king's son, Mary Boleyn's son by William Carey. The group also dabbled in the cryptic prophecies that circulated widely in moments of crisis – that a queen (Anne) would be burned, that Henry was the cursed Mouldwarp prophesied by Merlin, and so forth.

We know of all these cases, and more, because of the tireless efforts of Thomas Cromwell to monitor every possible source of discontent. He also put together an armoury of statutory weapons for use if necessary.[53] The Succession Act required every person

---

[50] Ibid., vii.754.
[51] Ibid., vii.939.
[52] Ibid., viii.565, 567.
[53] On this see G. R. Elton, *Policy and Police* (Cambridge, 1972).

to take an oath to support the Boleyn marriage, and a massive attempt was made to swear all adult males in the country.[54] The act also made it a treasonable offence to write or act against the marriage with Anne, with lesser penalties for gossip or for refusing to take the oath specified, while the clergy and Church institutions were also forced, in a variety of ways, to abjure the power of the pope. Another act, passed later in the year, extended the definition of treason to cover anything spoken, written or done which deprived the king of his title or seriously defamed him.[55] And as the acts came into force the popular voice was clear – the blame rested on Anne. George Cavendish would write later:

> I was the author why laws were made
> For speaking against me, to endanger the innocent;
> And with great oaths I found out the trade [method]
> To burden men's conscience: thus I did invent
> My seed to advance; it was my full intent
> Lineally to succeed in this Imperial crown:
> But how soon hath God brought my purpose down![56]

Anne was assumed to be encouraging her husband's brutality, particularly the deaths of the Carthusians, Fisher and More.[57] 'The people, horrified to see such unprecedented and brutal atrocities muttered in whispers about these events and often blamed Queen Anne.'[58] Since, according to the report which circulated on the continent within weeks of his death, Sir Thomas himself had said at his trial that the real reason for condemning him was his refusal to assent to the Boleyn marriage, it was all too plausible to present Anne as a latter-day Salome demanding the head of a new saint.[59]

How much Anne, or Henry for that matter, knew of the more serious opposition within the political establishment, it is impossible to say. Henry was aware of the possibility of it. He said of Katherine: 'The lady Katherine is a proud, stubborn woman of very high courage. If she took it into her head to take her

---

[54] 25 Henry VIII, c.22.
[55] 26 Henry VIII, c.13.
[56] Cavendish, *Metrical Visions*, p. 42.
[57] Harpsfield, *More*, p. 264; see above, p. 60.
[58] De Carles, in Ascoli, *L'Opinion*, lines 209–13.
[59] Harpsfield, *More*, p. 264.

daughter's part, she could quite easily take the field, muster a great array, and wage against me a war as fierce as any her mother Isabella ever waged in Spain.'[60] Yet the evidence of any actual conspiracy was hidden deep in the correspondence of Chapuys, and only began to leak after the failure of the rebellion which did break out in the north in 1536, the Pilgrimage of Grace. If we are to believe the ambassador, there was a majority of the magnates – in importance, if not in numbers – who were critical of the way matters were going, and many who were talking of actual revolt against Henry. But as with most magnate conspiracy, it was only talk. Apart from the initial psychological effort needed to break free from the chain of loyalty to the king, the odds against a successful concerted rising were high, and dissatisfaction with affairs had to compete with the very real desire not to come into the open before success was assured. Much of the conversation and messages reaching Chapuys were, indeed, attempts to avoid that decision by having Charles v take the first step.[61]

The duke of Norfolk's increasing dissatisfaction was of a different kind. Anne and her supporters were leaving him behind. He had been prepared for her to be a Boleyn when taking risks, but he fully expected her to be a Howard when enjoying success. The queen, however, had a good memory. Despite the fact that his mistress was one of her ladies-in-waiting, the duke found himself in much less favour than he felt was his due. Perhaps Anne felt that she had paid her debts to the Howards by persuading Henry to marry his illegitimate son, the duke of Richmond, to her cousin Mary without the large payment the king would normally have expected for disposing of so valuable a match.[62] Norfolk, however, was soon complaining that the sweets were going elsewhere.[63] Perhaps even more than by Anne, Thomas Howard was put out by Cromwell, who was now in effective and obvious charge. The secretary's usefulness and record of success was, in fact, taking him out of the Boleyn clientage and making him an independent political figure in his own right, but he maintained his links with the queen and to

---

[60] *Cal. S. P. Span.*, *1534–35*, p. 430 [*LP*, viii.429], trans. Mattingly, *Catherine of Aragon*, p. 291.

[61] E.g. *Cal. S. P. Span.*, *1534–35*, pp. 608–11 [*LP*, vii.1206].

[62] Nov. 1533: *LP*, vi.1460; Wood, *Letters*, ii.362–3.

[63] *LP*, viii.263 at p. 104.

outward appearances was still her man – perhaps Anne herself did not recognize the change.[64] Yet Norfolk, though sometimes goaded into grumbling in public, remained loyal to Henry and acquiescent towards the Boleyn marriage. And this was not only because his only known principle was self-advantage ensured by spaniel-like sycophancy to the king, or because there was still some advantage in having a niece on the throne. The point was that Anne had only a daughter and a miscarriage to her credit; for Norfolk to have the king's only living son as a son-in-law was too good a hand to throw away. And it was one which Anne and her brother were increasingly suspicious of.[65]

The problems facing Anne – the lack of a son, the intransigence of Mary, increasing unpopularity – were compounded by the international situation. As always, the controlling reality was the hostility between Francis I and Charles V. It was one of the periods of 'cold' rather than 'hot' war, with the antagonists each regarding Henry and his quarrel with the pope as one extra circumstance to be exploited or contained, as appropriate. Henry's principal reliance continued to be on his 'good brother Francis', but he was never confident that England's interests were wholly safe there. Thus in a relationship which has rightly been described as 'ambiguous', Henry and Francis each tried to exploit their alliance in a thoroughly selfish fashion.[66] The result was a great deal of suspicion, one of the other, and with Anne personifying to the English the French connection, the opprobrium fell on her.

Anne had been fully involved in the attempt to postpone the proposed meeting between Henry and Francis proposed in the summer of 1534, and the expected arrival of a French embassy in the following November was prepared for with care and enthusiasm.[67] The Admiral of France was, however, bringing an imperial suggestion for a settlement between Charles and Francis which involved the marriage of Mary to the dauphin. This shocked Anne because it implied that her patron, Francis,

[64] *Cal. S. P. Span.*, *1534-35*, p. 217 [*LP*, ix.681].
[65] Ibid., p. 484 [*LP*, viii.826]; *LP*, viii.985.
[66] Knecht, *Francis I*, pp. 234-5.
[67] See above, pp. 41-2; for the following see *Cal. S. P. Span.*, *1534-35*, pp. 327-9, 330-3, 335-8, 339-40, 345, 376 [*LP*, vii.1437, 1482, 1507, 1554; viii.48]; *St. Pap.*, vii.584-7 [*LP*, vii.1483].

considered that Mary had a better claim to the English throne than her own daughter, and matters were made even worse when the French were lukewarm at Henry's counter-proposal for a marriage between Elizabeth and Francis's third son. The result was a perceptible coolness on the side of both the French envoy and the queen. Anne nevertheless did her best to improve matters towards the end of the mission, and we hear of her entertaining the admiral at the final great banquet, while Henry sought out Gontier, the ambassador's secretary and a man of considerable influence, to come to talk with his wife. It was a different story when she saw Gontier again, on his return with the answer to the proposal about Elizabeth.[68] It had taken him almost two months, and she upbraided him for the delay, which had aroused all Henry's suspicions. If the French did not allay them at once, her own position would become impossible, for she felt herself more precarious than even before she was married; she could say no more, with everyone watching, including Henry, and she could not write to him or see him again. She then withdrew, and Henry went off dancing.

We have to remember that in sixteenth-century diplomacy – if not in diplomacy generally – what is said often had an ulterior motive, and in February 1535 the intention of the English was certainly to frighten the French.[69] However, on this occasion Anne's concern convinced Gontier: 'I assure you, my lord, by what I can make out, she is not at her ease.'[70] And there is no doubt that she had good cause to fear the loss of French support, as their hard bargaining caused Henry to press Francis for more and more public commitment to his cause.[71] Nor were matters improved by a banquet given by the resident French ambassador, where many of Anne's critics were present to hear gruesome tales of the persecution of unorthodox religious opinions then in full swing in Paris.[72] Eventually a meeting of representatives was arranged for Calais in May 1535. Cromwell was at first to go himself, but he fell ill, and the Boleyn interest was represented instead by Rochford – characteristically, Chapuys supposed that

[68] *LP*, viii.174, at p. 61.

[69] Ibid., viii.189, 263.

[70] Ibid., viii.174 at p. 61; Friedmann, *Anne Boleyn*, ii.51.

[71] *LP*, viii.336–8; *St. Pap.*, vii.584–90, 592–9, 602–3, 608–15 [*LP*, viii.339–41, 557, 793].

[72] *LP*, viii.174.

Cromwell was evading the responsibility for any failure.[73] And fail the negotiations did, despite a rapid return to England by Rochford in search of further instructions.[74] When he arrived, it was significant that he first had a long discussion with his sister before reporting to the king himself; and it was noted that Anne's conversation had suddenly become bitterly anti-French. Nor did she stop at talk. Within a fortnight she had put on a notable entertainment at Hanworth with a guest list both large and select, but she pointedly omitted the French resident, who was duly and satisfactorily incensed.[75] Soon after, Bishop Fisher and Thomas More were executed, and Francis I's reaction to the news, laced with comments about Anne's morals, lowered the temperature of Anglo-French relations still further.[76] Anne might be 'wholly French', but by the summer of 1535 this threatened to become yet another liability, and a serious one.

[73] *Cal. S. P. Span.*, *1534–35*, p. 452 [*LP*, viii.666].
[74] Ibid., p. 476 [*LP*, viii.826].
[75] Ibid., p. 493 [*LP*, viii.876].
[76] *LP*, viii.985; ix.157; Burnet, *History*, vi.116.

Anne the Queen:
Influence, Power and Majesty

~~~~~~~~~~~~

I T IS a reflection on the essential maleness of history, of those
who made most of it and those who have written most of it,
that we have no study of the position of the queen consort in
England. Of the supporting role of the king's wife in public
affairs, yes; of success or failure as a mother, yes; but very little
about the queen in her own right, and this despite the fact that in
the royal household 'the king's side' was always matched by a
smaller but parallel 'queen's side'. Much of the material for such
a study has, indeed, been lost or is almost inextricably mixed up
with the king's archive.

Anne Boleyn is no exception to this, but if anything the brevity
of her reign accentuates the problem. The 1534 parliament
confirmed to her as part of her jointure the lands and revenues
she had been granted in 1532, especially those received as
marchioness of Pembroke, plus two more grants made on 21/22
March 1533.[1] The property listed in these latter patents had, up
till then, been held by Katherine of Aragon as part of her
jointure, and parliament now gave retrospective sanction to this
diversion of property from 'the princess dowager'. A good deal of
the income came in fee farms charged on particular properties,
but a proportion arose from estates which Anne was given to
administer and exploit.[2] The statute which vested this extra
property in the new queen also cancelled all existing offices and
leases except where these were straight economic contracts, in
which case titleholders were given until the autumn to establish

---

[1] 25 Henry VIII c.25; BL, Harl. MS 303, ff. 16, 23v, 24 [*LP*, vii.419(25)].
[2] *LP*, vi.1189.

that they were exempt from this resumption. The measure (which had the immediate effect of negating all the favours granted by Katherine) raised a number of eyebrows, but we would be wrong to see it primarily as a political move.[3] Even someone as obviously committed to Katherine as Sir Edward Neville of the privy chamber was confirmed by Anne in the tenancy he had had from her predecessor.[4]

The resumption seems, in fact, to have had a primarily economic intention – to squeeze more money from the tenants – and a number of papers have survived from what was obviously a serious attempt at tighter management. There was a detailed settlement of accounts to March 1533 with Katherine's receiver, and a careful note of outstanding liabilities. A complete list of annuitants was prepared as well.[5] That Anne herself was directly involved in what was going on is clear from a memorandum evidently drawn up for a discussion with her.[6] It brought the queen up to date with the activities of her council, which directed and supervised the commissioners actually involved in the resettlement of the tenancies, and it listed major policy issues which required her decision. Thus she was asked what should be done with former tenants of Katherine who were offering good terms for the renewal of her titles, what the policy should be towards applicants for replacement leases who missed the Michaelmas deadline, and what the position was of those who had offered an increased rent instead of a lump sum cash down. All this makes it very much more likely that Anne herself had been similarly involved in the ripple of activity which had followed the grant to her of the lands to support her new dignity as marchioness of Pembroke in September 1532.[7] A commission of her men had taken immediate possession of the properties and set to work on a detailed survey of the estates, which was completed by the following March.

Only one account has so far been identified which gives a general outline of Anne's expenditure, though it does not go into

---

[3] *Lisle Letters*, ii.147 [*LP*, vii.349]; cf. the appearance of even-handedness in the act for Katherine as princess dowager: 25 Henry VIII c.28.
[4] *LP*, iii.2239; viii.962(1).
[5] Ibid., vi.1189; vii.352.
[6] Ibid., vi.1188. This is wrongly dated in *LP*; it follows the legislation that received the royal assent on 20 Mar. 1534.
[7] Ibid., v.1274(3). A few of Anne's leases do survive in RO, E328.

detail.[8] It shows that George Taylor, Anne's receiver-general, had a total liability in 1534–5 of £6,381 8*s.* 9¾*d.* Of this, £4,423 3*s.* 1¾*d.* came from her English estates, and £633 13*s.* 10*d.* from Wales, giving £5,056 16*s.* 11¾*d.* from lands, overall. Taylor received the remainder, £1,324 11*s.* 10*d.*, from the queen's 'coffers', clearly to fund expenditure at seasons when the flow of rents proved inadequate for day-to-day expenses. This shows that already, after only two and a half years of marriage, Anne's reserves were at least equivalent to 25 per cent of her annual income. In fact they were evidently more, for at the end of the 1534–5 account Taylor returned £2,508 13*s.* 1½*d.* to the coffers, a net surplus of £1,184, or over 20 per cent, on this one year. As this implies, Anne was not saddled with many bad debts or arrears as yet; Taylor had to carry forward a liability for a mere £32.

On the expenditure side, by far the largest specific sum, almost £1,000, went on wages and annuities, with nearly £200 on gifts and rewards – a useful reminder of the patronage at the queen's disposal, which meant for her, as well as for lesser lords, income as well as the exercise of favour. Thomas Cromwell was her high steward at £20 a year, but even he had to pay £99 15*s.* for the post.[9] Also in the category of patronage and good lordship must be put the 'rewards for New Year's gifts' which amounted to more than £250 in all, although once again there was some quid pro quo in the form of New Year's gifts received. It may be, however, that although the king gave plate and very often received plate at New Year, which could easily be sold, the fashion in the queen's household was different. The Manners family, for instance, continued to give Anne, as they had before her marriage, elaborately embroidered clothing – frontlets and sleeves – while Anne's first gifts to her ladies as queen were palfreys and saddles.[10] That decision seems to have been agreed with Henry himself – which raises the question of the extent to which the patronage exercised by Anne was independent. The gifts of the queen's ladies to Henry were certainly of the same personal sort. In 1534 Anne's mother gave him a velvet case

[8] RO, SC6 Hen. VIII, 6680 [*LP*, ix.477].

[9] *LP*, ix.478.

[10] Hist. Mss. Comm., *Rutland Mss.*, iv.272, 276–7; *LP*, vi.1194, 1382, 1589. No doubt the object was to enhance the appearance of Anne's attendants when on progress etc.

embroidered with the royal arms, containing six collars, three worked with gold and three with silver; her sister-in-law, Lady Rochford, presented a shirt with a collar of silver work.[11]

Perhaps it is no surprise to find close collaboration between king and queen on such a family matter as New Year's gifts. For many, indeed, interest in Anne existed precisely because of her closeness to Henry. In 1532 Richard Lyst, a Franciscan lay-brother at Greenwich, sent her news of the misdeeds of his superior, John Forrest, in the clear expectation that she would pass it on to Henry and Cromwell; while a petition to the king in 1535 describes her as having 'the name to be a mediatrix betwixt your grace and high justice'.[12] The earl of Oxford, frustrated by two years of nothing but kind words from Henry in reply to his claim to certain hereditary offices, was much encouraged when he turned to petition Anne.[13] The success she had in securing for her uncle, the duke of Norfolk, the grant of the wardship and marriage of the king's own son, the duke of Richmond, free, gratis and for nothing, demonstrates how effective the queen's influence could be.[14] Anne used that influence with circumspection, as her refusal to seek a customs exemption for Lady Lisle in 1532 demonstrates; but it was there.[15]

Anne Boleyn was nevertheless more than a seductive voice in the ear of her husband. As early as 1531 the duke of Milan was advised to treat her as a force in her own right, and to equip his ambassador with some novel and flashy Italian knick-knacks for her, worth 1,200 crowns or so.[16] With marriage bringing to an end many of the struggles in which Anne was a front-line combatant, it may be that her active participation in affairs did diminish; evidence of her involvement certainly does. Yet there are still glimpses. When Lord Leonard Grey returned to Ireland in the autumn of 1535 with considerable forces and substantial rewards from the king, Anne had been at the final briefing session, for she had given him herself the chain round her waist, worth 100 marks, and a purse of twenty golden sovereigns.[17]

[11] RO, E101/421/13.
[12] Ellis, *Letters*, 3 ii.249 [*LP*, v.1525]; *LP*, ix.52.
[13] Ibid., vii.594.
[14] See above, p. 252.
[15] See above, p. 194.
[16] *Cal. S. P. Milan*, 843.
[17] *Lisle Letters*, ii.468 [*LP*, ix.700].

More often to be found is evidence of her continued involvement in patronage. One of Lisle's correspondents assured him that 'I have moved a friend of mine about the queen concerning Master Howard's matter, and I mistrust not but that I shall obtain your desire in that behalf.'[18] On another occasion the dean and chapter of Exeter, expecting soon to have a farm to rent on the expiry of the lease, found themselves invited by Anne to grant a new sixty-year term to a nominee of hers at the existing rent; a letter from Anne was reckoned in 1531 to smooth matters at Calais for her uncle Lord Edmund Howard, the controller there; when she became aware of an excessive delay in one chancery suit, she thought nothing of writing directly to the chancellor requesting speedier action.[19] A dispute between rival claimants to a vacancy in the Calais garrison, in which Cromwell and everybody who mattered at court seem to have had one special interest or another, saw Anne, too, supporting one of the candidates. Then she changed her mind and issued letters in favour of George Gainsford, a relative of her receiver-general George Taylor, which were described 'as a stay' if 'the worst fall' – in effect, a veto.[20]

Anne was, of course, no isolated figure. She still had behind her the faction that had brought her to power, which was now intent on reaping the fruits of that power. Not enough is yet known of the articulation of the Boleyn faction, whose presence and policy can be principally demonstrated in religious matters, but its dominance in affairs generally is beyond doubt. The lord privy seal was Anne's father, the king's secretary was Thomas Cromwell; the lord chancellor was Thomas Audley, Cromwell's ally and Anne's – she lent him her house at Havering in 1535 to escape the plague in London – and the archbishop of Canterbury was Cranmer.[21] Of these posts, all but the privy seal had at the start of 1532 been in the hands of men loyal to Katherine of Aragon and her daughter Mary. In the privy chamber, Anne's brother was one of the two noblemen, and Henry Norris groom of the stool and the king's right-hand man, while lesser men like Brereton occupied a number of the other places there. Potential rivals were in eclipse.

---

[18] Ibid., ii.147 [*LP*, vii.349].
[19] Hist. Mss. Comm., *Fifth Report*, p. 296b; *LP*, Add.746; ibid., 569 (possibly for one of her servants).
[20] *Lisle Letters*, ii.152, 298, 299 [*LP*, vii.386, 1581, 1582].
[21] *LP*, ix.358, 450; cf. ibid., v.1430.

Stephen Gardiner was intent in these years on regaining royal favour and lay very low, and the first sign of forgiveness was his being sent to France as ambassador in the autumn of 1535.[22] The dukes of Norfolk and Suffolk continued to attend court from time to time, but Suffolk in particular counted for little. Not only had his wife, Mary Tudor, died in 1533, but by 1535 he was being stripped of his assets to pay outstanding debts to the crown.[23] Chapuys' letters show how often he had to deal with Cromwell now, instead of either Brandon or Howard. This is not to say that all supporters of Katherine and Mary were displaced. Several of the privy chamber were as high in royal favour as ever – Carewe, Neville, Browne and Russell – while even Exeter kept his place as a counter to Rochford. There can, however, be no doubt where the weight of royal favour lay. Chapuys told the emperor's adviser Granvelle in November 1535 that the secretary then stood above everybody except 'the Lady'.[24]

In all this, particular interest inevitably concentrates on this last, the relationship between Anne and Cromwell. Although he would eventually be shown to be a cuckoo in the Boleyn nest, there is nothing to suggest that until then Anne ever saw the secretary as other than her loyal dependant, and to all outward appearances he remained 'her man'. It was Cromwell who sent the warrant for the delivery to Anne of her letters patent creating her lady marquis of Pembroke, and who possibly drafted the writ requiring local officers to assist the survey of her Welsh properties; the file copy of the survey instructions remained with him, along with a copy of the commission and an estimate of the value of the properties inspected.[25] The success of the coronation was largely attributed to Cromwell. And this close relationship continued. Its tone is very clear in a letter Anne sent to the minister when his ally Christopher Hales, the attorney-general, began to meddle with a wardship which had been granted to her:

Master Secretary, I pray you despatch with speed this matter, for mine honour lies much on it, and what should the king's attorney do with Pointz's obligation, since I have the child by the king's

[22] Muller, *Gardiner*, pp. 51–66.
[23] *LP*, viii.1101, 1130; ix.21.
[24] Ibid., ix.862.
[25] Ibid., v.1450; vi.299 (cf. vii.p. 353); RO, E163/10/19 and 20.

grace's gift, but only to trouble him hereafter, which by no means
I will suffer, and thus fare you well as I would ye did. Your loving
mistress, Anne the Queen.[26]

She was also known to be an effective influence on Cromwell.
When a drive against river obstructions late in 1535 threatened
the weir which Lady Lisle's family owned at Umberleigh in
Devon, direct applications to Cromwell and the king were found
useless, but it was thought worth considering an alternative
application via the queen.[27] When the lord deputy of Ireland
died on the last day of 1535, his widow Anne Skeffington
petitioned Cromwell to secure payment of his overdue fees, plus
free passage from Ireland where the new lord deputy, Leonard
Grey again, was trying to hang on to as many as possible of the
assets of his predecessor. Yet at the same time Lady Skeffington
wrote directly to Anne, imploring her to secure the king's
backing for her petition to the minister.[28] We may see something
of the same sort in the efforts of Elizabeth Staynings to secure
access to the queen.[29] Her husband, Walter, was in prison for
debt, but despite the king's instructions to Cromwell to sort the
matter out, as well as the reminders of Norris and other men of
standing, the minister always pleaded pressure of other work.
This has been interpreted as Cromwell frustrating the intervention of the privy chamber, but it reads more like an attempt
to use administrative delay to assist Staynings' creditors, or in
order to exact the price for Cromwell's own services too.[30] Mrs
Staynings, knowing that she would soon have to leave London to
have the child she was carrying, wrote to her aunt, the Viscountess
Lisle, then in Calais: 'Good madam, if there be any lady of your
acquaintance in the court that you think that is familiar or great
with the queen, that it please you to write unto her that I may
resort unto her sometime, for I feel me that trouble is not yet at
an end.'[31]

There is some evidence to suggest that Anne was particularly

[26] *LP*, viii.1057; cf. v.1398. Letters between Anne and Cromwell are rare; she
normally communicated by messenger.
[27] *Lisle Letters*, iv.841 [*LP*, ix.892].
[28] *St. Pap.*, ii.302 [*LP*, x.185]; *LP*, x.186.
[29] *Lisle Letters*, i.xxxviii, xxxviiia; ii.202, 202a [*LP*, vii.511–12, 734, 844]; *LP*,
vii.409–14, 845.
[30] *Lisle Letters*, ii. pp. 169–71.
[31] Ibid., ii.202 [*LP*, vii.734].

receptive to female petitioners. We have already seen instances concerning Lady Skeffington and Elizabeth Staynings. When the latter's husband was desperately looking for protection in April 1533, his immediate thought was that his wife's aunt was in attendance on Anne, who had just been proclaimed queen: 'I judge in my mind the queen will be good and gracious lady unto me upon your special request, to see me have the laws executed indifferently between me and my adversaries that keeps me in prison.'[32] Over the winter of 1535–6 Katherine Howard, Anne's aunt, was trying to secure a separation from her second husband Henry, Lord Daubeney. She told Cromwell that the only assistance she was receiving was from the queen herself, and this despite the strenuous efforts which were being made to destroy her standing with Anne.[33] The help may have been very practical indeed; Lord Daubeney, who was certainly pleading financial hardship at one stage, reached an amicable agreement with his wife after Anne's father had made available £400.

To the influence that Anne exercised over Henry and in her own right, must be added what can be called her official status. In common with other members of the royal family, her council performed semi-political functions in the lands assigned to her. One such was revealed in a mix-up of instructions about settling a local dispute in Worcestershire, where her attorney-general was issuing contrary orders to those her council had already issued, so that her officers on the spot were being 'dishonested'.[34] Her elevation to the throne also had repercussions within her family, of which she seems to have become the effective head. When the son of Sir William Courteney of Powderham died, the father was approached to assist in a match between his widowed daughter-in-law and Cromwell's nephew, Richard Cromwell.[35] Courteney, however, replied that the girl was a near relative of the queen and he would not move unless Cromwell could send him a request from the king that he should promote the match, to guarantee him against 'her grace's displeasure'. This puts into a somewhat different light the rustication from court of Anne's

[32] Ibid., i.xxxviii [*LP*, vii.512].
[33] Ibid., iv.841a [*LP*, x.416]; *LP*, ix.577.
[34] Ibid., Add.991.
[35] Ibid., vi.837.

sister Mary. She had secretly married in 1534 'young Stafford', one of the hangers-on at court, the second son of minor Midlands gentry, and the marriage had only been discovered when it became obvious she was pregnant. The reason for Anne's rigorous attitude was not pique or pride. It was that Mary had failed to recognize her position, both by making what was an obvious *mésalliance* for a queen's sister, and by failing to accept the directing role which the Boleyn family now owed to Anne.[36]

At a less intimate level, Anne could also exercise influence through her household. There were the jobs it could offer. Stephen Vaughan, a merchant adventurer and an old friend of Cromwell, tried very hard to get his wife accepted as the new queen's silkwoman, even to the extent of her submitting un-solicited – and in the event unnoticed – samples of her work.[37] Nor was this the only instance of competition for places in the queen's household, although few were as direct as David ap Powell, who applied to Cromwell for a post either as yeoman purveyor to the queen or yeoman of her carriage, because he had not the capital to trade any longer.[38] Anne's service was evi-dently lucrative – her uncle Edmund Howard saw it as much more profitable than his position as controller at Calais – and although, given only three years, relatively few of her men qualified for a bonus in the form of a royal grant of some kind, that would have become an increasing possibility.[39] A number of questionable characters even made a living by claiming to belong to the queen's staff. A priest called James Billingford alias Kettilbye had 'a good thing going in the Midlands in 1534–5, where he conducted visitations of a number of abbeys, styling himself variously as Anne's chaplain, her (or her father's) kinsman, her scholar, the nephew of the duke of Norfolk and servant to Thomas Cromwell – just the sort of person whom it would be wise to 'sweeten'; after all, Lady Lisle thought it an investment to send the queen's genuine servants venison.[40]

Anne Boleyn's royal household is known to have been headed by Lord Burgh, an insignificant peer whose first achievement for Anne was to vandalize Katherine of Aragon's barge for her use

---

[36] *Cal. S. P. Span.*, *1534–35*, p. 344 [*LP*, vii.1554]; *LP*, vii.1655.
[37] Ibid., vi.559, 917.
[38] Ibid., vii.1623.
[39] *Lisle Letters*, ii.428 [*LP*, viii.1103]; *LP*, vii.922(9), 1352(8); viii.1007.
[40] Ibid., vii.600, 641, App.22; viii.81(2), 94; *Lisle Letters*, i.xxxiii [*LP*, vi.126].

and his last to assist in her trial, and whose performance in the Lincolnshire Rising of 1536 was loyal but lacklustre.[41] Anne's chancellor was her uncle, James Boleyn, with whom she shared some sympathies, but her aunt by marriage was not among her favourite attendants.[42] The same could be said of the wife of her master of the horse, William Coffin.[43] He was a professional household administrator, actively concerned with the staffing of his department, and later to serve Jane Seymour in the same capacity. Lord Burgh's deputy was Sir Edward Baynton. He also, as we shall see, shared some of Anne's religious opinions, but he was primarily a career courtier, serving as vice-chamberlain to all Henry VIII's later wives.[44] John Uvedale (or Udall) her secretary had even longer in royal service, beginning as an exchequer clerk under Henry VII and ending as treasurer for the northern garrisons under Edward VI. He also combined what was obviously a part-time post under Anne with that of secretary to the duke of Richmond.[45] George Taylor the receiver-general we have already met. He had been in Anne's service for several years before the coronation and may have begun as a lawyer, but although his was a post of importance carrying a fee of £50 a year, he has correctly, if unkindly, been described as 'part of the background'.[46]

These senior men of the household, according to later stories, were forced to keep a wary eye on their mistress, who would intervene herself if things went awry. William Latimer, one of her chaplains, recalled that as soon as she had set up her household she called her 'council and other officers' to a formal meeting, where she lectured them on their duties. Her first requirements, he remembered (which, given Latimer's sense that religion should have priority, we may take as confirming the genuineness of his story), were honour, equity and justice, and value for money: 'such mediocrity [balance] that neither sparely pinching, nor prodigally consuming, may restrain you from the

[41] *Cal. S. P. Span.*, *1531–33*, p. 693 [*LP*, vi.556]; *LP*, xi.533, 590, 1155(5).

[42] *House of Commons*, i.456; 'I think it much unkindness in the king to put such about me as I never loved . . . I would have had [those] of mine own privy chamber which I favour most': *Wolsey*, ed. Singer, pp. 454, 457.

[43] *House of Commons*, i.666–7.

[44] Ibid., i.400–3. See below, pp. 304, 311, 314, 327.

[45] Ibid., iii.508–9.

[46] *Lisle Letters*, i.p. 519; *LP*, x.1009.

golden mean of frugal expending.' Virtue, however, was not to be neglected, especially among the lower members of the court, who were to attend chapel daily, behave with propriety, and keep away from 'infamous places' and 'evil, lewd and ungodly disposed brothels'. Persistent offenders were to be sacked and barred the court for life, 'to their utter shame'.[47] Nor was Anne's direction merely verbal. We know of an actual case where she intervened to get the bill of her cheese and butter supplier paid.[48]

Remarkably, we have for the whole period of Anne Boleyn's marriage a continuous record of the relationship of one couple with this court, Arthur Viscount Lisle and his wife Honor, and of their attempt to build up and exploit a relationship with the queen in every possible way. To the good fortune of the historian, Lord Lisle's posting to Calais as lord deputy necessarily meant not only that many things which in England might have been left to word of mouth had to be put down on paper, but that there was a positive demand for a steady flow of news and gossip to keep starved exiles in the swim. Lady Lisle's commitment to Anne had been demonstrated in 1532 when she accompanied her to Calais, and it is highly likely that her last engagement before leaving England had been to take part in the queen's coronation procession.[49] Once in Calais, Honor Lisle became meticulous in ensuring that she was recommended whenever possible to the queen and to the ladies of the court – out of sight was certainly not going to be out of mind if she could help it. A series of luxuries and elegant presents crossed the channel at suitable intervals, such as a dozen and a half dotterels (a special treat, and taken live to Dover so as to arrive fresh) accompanied with a linnet in a cage.[50] Lady Lisle's favourite dog had to go the same way to obtain one favour, with Francis Bryan getting some of the kudos for being the intermediary.[51] Anne became very fond of the animal, as Margery Horsman explained to Lady Lisle almost a year later: 'The queen's grace setteth much store by a pretty dog, and her grace delighted so much in little Purkoy that after he was dead of a fall there durst nobody tell her grace of it, till it pleased the king's highness to tell her

[47] Oxford, Bodl. MS C. Don. 42, ff. 22–4.
[48] *LP*, vii.415.
[49] *Lisle Letters*, ii.p.464.
[50] *Lisle Letters*, ii.182, 193, 207, 212a [*LP*, vii.613, 654, 795, 824].
[51] Ibid., ii.109, 114 [*LP*, vii.25, 92].

grace of it.'[52] Evidently the suggestion was that Purquoy should be replaced – with a dog, not a bitch, Mrs Horsman insisted – but subsequent advice was that the queen did not want another.[53] The proposal some months later of a monkey was firmly turned down. Anne could not abide the sight of them.[54]

The Lisle correspondence preserves an informative vignette of the business of New Year's gifts, seen from the point of view of the Lisle agent, John Hussey:

> On New Year's even, by the advice of Mr Taylor the queen's receiver, I delivered your gift unto her grace by the hands of Mr Receiver. And I then being in place where her grace's New Year gifts were appointing, her grace came in, and asked me how your ladyship did, and how you liked Calais. To which I answered that your ladyship did like it well, and that you humbly recommended you unto her grace, praying God to send her grace many good New Years.[55]

From all points of view a perfect occasion – a gift and its accompanying sentiments graciously received, and the interest of the recipient in the giver caught, if only for a moment. And Anne confirmed the renewed bond by a gift to Honor Lisle of a pair of gold beads, with tassels, weighing three ounces, and that value even greater since they were 'of her grace's own wearing'.[56]

It was soon after this that Lady Lisle decided that she must secure from the queen a livery kirtle to demonstrate that, though on detached duty with her husband, she was properly part of Anne's household.[57] A present of cloth, specially chosen and then submitted for approval beforehand to Taylor the receiver-general, reminded Anne of Lady Lisle, and the promise was graciously given. It was, however, a year before the kirtle was actually supplied, partly because the queen had to select a suitable one, but more because Taylor saw delay as a means to further with the Lisles the interests of his relative George

---

[52] Ibid., ii.299a [*LP*, ix.991].
[53] Ibid., iv.826 [*LP*, viii.119].
[54] Ibid., ii.421 [*LP*, viii.1084]; Katherine liked them, a memory of Spain.
[55] Ibid., ii.302 [*LP*, viii.15].
[56] Ibid., ii.307 [*LP*, viii.46].
[57] For the following see ibid., iv.828, 829, 830a, 830, 833; ii.380; iv.835, 836; ii.492a, 497, 502a, 506; iii.658a, 658, iv.842; iii.668 [*LP*, viii.232, 353, 371, 378, 545, 664, 939, 1028, 1084; ix.898, 951, 1004, 1033; viii.110; x.499, 559, 573, 608].

Gainsford. Lady Lisle was always careful to keep in with the queen's attendants with periodic messages and tokens, but in this case Taylor forbade any inducement to the wardrobe staff to expedite the gift, so that Hussey found himself 'driven off' five times in six days. Even when Hussey, it seems, slipped the staff a bolt of cambric behind the receiver's back, everything had to wait for Taylor's elegant note of apology – he had, he said, been away – and still it would be two months before the livery was actually handed over on 18 March to another of the Lisle servants, Thomas Warley:

> This day in the morning I had a token of Mistress Margery that the kirtle should be delivered to me in the queen's grace wardrobe, where upon sight of the said token I received the said kirtle, which is of cloth of gold paned . . . After I had received the kirtle I returned to the queen's chamber to give thanks to Mistress Margery, and to know if she would anything to your ladyship, which as then was returned into the privy chamber, so that since, I could not speak to her. But, God willing, I intend to be at the court tomorrow . . . And if it may please your ladyship to send a letter to Mistress Margery and another to Mr George Taylor, giving them thanks for their pains, as your ladyship knows better what is to be done than my simpleness can advise you . . . Also that it may please your ladyship to remember them of the queen's wardrobe, as shall be your pleasure.[58]

'Royal patronage' was definitely not a simple business of asking and receiving. It is sad that after such endeavours to secure so magnificent a garment, Lady Lisle could only have worn it for a matter of weeks; after May Day 1536, there was no value in the livery of a dishonoured queen.

All this has taken us a long way from that single financial account for the year 1534–5, following the trail of the categories 'Wages and Annuities', 'Gifts and Rewards' and 'New Year's Gifts'. Honor Lisle's livery kirtle, in fact, must have figured under another heading, 'Wardrobe of the Robes', with its very low expenditure – £69 in round figures; the 'Wardrobe of the Beds' was even lower, again in round figures, £44. The stables, by contrast, cost nearly £600, although the figure of £22 6s. 6d. for

[58] Ibid., iii.658 [*LP*, x.499].

the queen's barge can only have covered repairs, with the running costs lost in the general wages bill. There was, too, a huge rag-bag category, 'divers necessary emptions' – no less than £1,525 9s. 9¼d. The low figure for the Robes and the Beds suggests that either 1534–5 was a freak year or, much more probably, that bills in these departments were paid after very considerable delay. At the time of Anne's death, the Robes owed over £500 and the Beds £166, unlike the stables which owed only £157 – clearly only one quarter in arrears.[59] The list of suppliers to whom Anne owed money in May 1536 casts a revealing light on the often forgotten economic significance of a royal court, with its contingent of suppliers (mercers, drapers and clothier) and the army of craftsmen – tailors, embroiderers, fustian-maker, silkwomen, pinner, coffer-maker, gold-wire drawer, skinner, furrier, painter, farrier and a dozen more besides. One of the detailed bills behind this account has also survived.[60] It was presented by William Lok, the mercer most employed by the queen and a leading Londoner, who would be called on to assist in clearing the Tower of foreigners on the occasion of her execution![61] The bill covered the three months from late January to late April 1536, and shows Anne spending £40 a month, mainly on clothes for herself and Elizabeth. On top of this, the haberdashery bill for approximately the same period was £68 4s. 1½d., and there may have been supplements from the king also, if he continued the sort of gifts he was making in 1535 – over twenty yards of green satin and more than thirteen yards of green cloth of gold.[62]

These bills take us very much into the domestic life of a Tudor queen. Sewing, embroidery, making clothes – here were all the expected activities of the great lady and her maidens. Silks – black, white, orange, tawny, red, green, bought by the ounce and

---

[59] RO, SP1/104 ff. 1v–16 [*LP*, x.914].

[60] 'W. Loke, Account of materials furnished for the use of Anne Boleyn and Princess Elizabeth, 1535–6', in *Miscellanea of the Philobiblion Society*, vii (1862). The Lok bill covers the period 20 Jan. to 27 Apr. 1536, but the total, £124 15s 2d, disagrees with the equivalent figure in the list of debts, £123 10s 6d: RO, SP1/104 f. 1v. The end of the bill, however, is missing, and it is possible that there was a minor deduction which accounts for the difference; the bill does contain mistakes.

[61] Lok was also a keen reformer: see below, p. 317.

[62] RO, SP1/103 ff. 322–7 [*LP*, x.913]; J. Caley, 'Extract from a MS in the Augmentation Office', in *Archaeologia*, ix (1789), 248 [*LP*, viii.937].

half ounce; ribbon – red, tawny, black, purple, carnation; needle ribbon to roll the queen's hair; fringes, tassels, Venice gold with chain work for a nightgown. According to George Wyatt, Hampton Court in his day was sumptuous with 'the rich and exquisite works for the greater part wrought by her own hand and needle, and also of her ladies'.[63] Clothing Elizabeth as befitted a princess was another major occupation, with a gown of orange velvet, kirtles of russet velvet, of yellow satin, of white damask, of green satin, embroidered purple satin sleeves, a black muffler, white ribbon, Venice ribbon, a russet damask bed-spread, a taffeta cap covered with a caul of gold. Anne, apparently, was especially fussy about her daughter's caps: one made of purple satin required at least three journeys to Greenwich to get right.

The accounts also give glimpses of that deliberate ostentation which royalty was expected to show. In these last months before her execution, there were payments for chair decorations in crimson silk, in green silk, and in Venice gold with crimson fringes; for a red sarcenet 'great bed' with a matching sparver, or canopy, lined with blue buckram; for crimson and orange curtains; for a 'little bed' of green satin; for decoration of a pair of clavichords – perhaps the ones that Anne's 'lover' Mark Smeton was to play on? There was even a purchase of thirty-two and three quarter yards of green buckram to line the presses or cupboards in the queen's apartments. For the hunt or the progress, a set of elaborate decorations for Anne's own saddle cost almost £4 10s., four tassels of gold, silver and black silk a further 53s 4d. The gift of a saddle and harness decorations for Lady Margaret Douglas, the king's niece, cost £4 13s. 7½d.

Most striking of all is the size and elaboration of the queen's wardrobe. Between January and April 1536 she purchased, at the minimum, gowns in tawny velvet with black lambs' fur, velvet without fur, damask, and satin furred with miniver; a russet gown in caffa (heavy silk), two in black velvet, one in black damask, one in white satin and a second with crimson sleeves; a gown in purple cloth of gold lined with silver, and new carnation satin from Bruges to insert into the sleeves of a gown of tissue. Thirteen kirtles included white satin and white damask, black velvet embroidered and crimson satin 'printed', with

[63] George Wyatt, in *Wolsey*, ed. Singer, pp. 442–3.

matching sleeves. There were eight nightgowns, two embroidered and another in russet trimmed with miniver; and three cloaks – of black Bruges satin, of embroidered tawny satin and of black cloth lined with black sarcenet – while Arnold the shoemaker had eight lots of black velvet to make shoes and slippers. We may well believe the story told by Nicholas Sander that 'every day she made some change in the fashion of her garments.'[64] Had Anne lived, her wardrobe might well have rivalled the two thousand costumes which tradition assigns to that most fashion-conscious of monarchs, her daughter Elizabeth.

And what of that daughter? Although we can almost riffle at will through Anne Boleyn's finery, when we come to a question like that we can find practically nothing. Of course, in the expected fashion of a great lady, she did not have daily care of her child. Indeed, early in December 1533, at the age of three months, Elizabeth was sent to be fostered at Hertford, and thereafter Anne only saw her occasionally.[65] Nonetheless the queen was, as we have seen, very much involved with seeing that her daughter was turned out in the style to which her status entitled her.[66] She visited her, both alone and with Henry, and she was clearly in regular touch with Margaret, Lady Bryan (the mother of Sir Francis), who had actual charge of the child.[67] Yet as the mother of a princess, Anne could only have a partial say in the major decisions about her child; the king or the council had the last word.[68] When instructions were given to have Elizabeth weaned, at the age of twenty-five months, they were given 'by his grace, with the assent of the queen's grace'.[69] Anne, it is true, did send a private letter to Lady Bryan, no doubt full of maternal instructions and she may have felt a special affinity with the woman looking after Elizabeth for she was her mother's half-sister.[70] But that was accidental; Lady Bryan had not been chosen for that relationship, but because she had previously

---

[64] Sander, *Schism*, p. 25.
[65] *St. Pap.*, i.415 [*LP*, vi.1486].
[66] See above, pp. 269–70.
[67] See above, pp. 247–8; *LP*, vii.509.
[68] The decision to send Elizabeth to Hertford in December 1533 went through the council.
[69] *St. Pap.*, i.426 [*LP*, ix.568]. The initiative seems to have been taken by Lady Bryan and communicated to Henry via Cromwell.
[70] See above, p. 128.

watched over the infancy of the Princess Mary.[71] The choice was
clearly Henry's.

There are only a few vignettes of Anne with Elizabeth, or with
Elizabeth and Henry. One, two days before her arrest, shows
Anne attempting to appeal to Henry through the child and hints
at powerful emotions of which we know no more.[72] Already by
then Anne had begun to think about the future of Elizabeth.
Only a day or two earlier, she had had a conversation on the
subject with her chaplain, Matthew Parker. To his dying day he
believed that Anne had in some way commended Elizabeth to
his spiritual care, though whether this was more than a significance which he read into the discussion because it turned out to
be the last he ever had with Anne, we cannot know.[73] But even if
she was only sharing with him her hopes for Elizabeth's education, the fact that she chose to talk to a man of the kind we
shall find Parker to be is a significant pointer to the intellectual
and religious upbringing she wanted for the child.[74] It was the
upbringing she had had, but managed not with the facilities her
father had provided as a rising courtier, but as for a princess. In
the event others would train Elizabeth, but she would turn out to
be very much her mother's daughter.

[71] *Literary Remains of King Edward the Sixth*, ed. J.G. Nichols (1857),
pp. xxxii–xxxiii.
[72] See below, p. 364. For another, see below, p. 342.
[73] Parker, *Correspondence*, pp. 59, 400.
[74] See below, p. 312.

13

Anne Boleyn: Art, Image
and Taste

～～≫⊱≪～～

THE WAYS in which temperament and personality as well as
physique descend – or fail to descend – from generation to
generation is a never ending cause of discussion. With Anne
Boleyn and her daughter Elizabeth we can be sure of the facial
resemblance, less sure that the daughter's taste for things
scholarly or for music was inherited and not, instead, the
product of careful education and the atmosphere at the Tudor
court. The parallels, however, are there. It is clear that in dress
sense and wardrobe Anne Boleyn anticipated Elizabeth I's acute
awareness of the politics of ostentation. Each had more than a
love of mere finery – a recognition, rather, that in order to play
the part it is necessary to dress the part. The mother also
anticipated the daughter in another way: the exploitation of the
cult of monarchy which was to reach its height in England in the
reign of 'Gloriana'. The Bible, chivalry, art – above all, and most
original in 1533, the language of humanism – all were mobilized
to present Anne as a divine ruler. It was not, of course,
an approach peculiar to England. There was an international
technique to image-building. Yet between Anne and Elizabeth
there was an uncanny similarity of attitude towards the projection of monarchy, and of themselves as chosen by God to rule.

The most extensive demonstration of Anne's position and role
as queen is in the elaborate pageants prepared for her coronation
procession through the city of London on 31 May 1533. We have
followed the event, but we have not yet looked closely at the
devices that set the scene – and very revealing they are. They
have been criticized as lacking imagination and technical novelty,
but time was largely to blame for the latter: machinery could not

be built at a moment's notice. In 1522 there had been ten weeks to arrange the reception of the emperor Charles v, while the welcome in 1501 for Katherine of Aragon had been the climax of two years' work, not the bare month available to prepare to greet her successor.[1] In any case, the displays organized in 1533, if not of intrinsic originality, are of special interest in the story of Anne Boleyn, for they were officially commissioned; they represented what she and Henry wanted. That this is the way it was done we can be sure because of the survival of a commission for a series of pageants in honour of her successor, Jane Seymour.[2] This lays down the themes and even the mottoes to be used for twelve main displays, but then leaves fourteen 'other subtleties to be at the pleasure of the maker'. Apart from the absence of instructions about materials and colours, the order is very similar to a contract of the period for a painting or piece of sculpture. There were two 'makers' of Anne's six principal pageants: Nicholas Udall (possibly a relative of her secretary) and his friend John Leland, the king's antiquary. Udall did 80 per cent of the work. He was a former Oxford student who in the past had got into trouble over the sale of prohibited books and who would go on to become head of Eton, possibly because of the success of his work for Anne on this occasion. Leland's lesser share was made up for by the experience he could contribute, for he had been taught by William Lily, who had written the Latin verse for Charles v's entry into London in 1522.[3]

The first of the Udall–Leland tableaux was positioned at the turn from Fenchurch Street into Gracechurch Street, where a triple arch was erected across the street, decorated in antique or Renaissance style, and supporting a representation of Mount Parnassus, in classical legend the abode of Apollo and the Muses, all closely modelled on Virgil. The god of music and

[1] Anglo, *Spectacle*, pp. 57, 186, 248–9, 258.
[2] BL, Add. MS 9835, f. 22 [*LP*, x.1016]; see below, p. 281.
[3] *Ballads from Manuscripts*, ed. F.J. Furnivall (Ballad Society, 1868–72), i.373–401, from BL, Roy. MS 18A lxiv, ff. 1–16. This purports to be a copy of verses posted up or spoken during the course of the pageants, but the first two at least (by Leland on the river pageant and Anne's litter) and Leland's final piece on the coronation are probably additions, perhaps to prepare a presentation text to Anne. Omitting the 65 lines in these sections (35 plus 15 plus 12, all in Latin), Leland contributed 138 lines of Latin, Udall, 310 lines of Latin, 221 of English. The source for the non-Udall/Leland material is Hall, *Chronicle*, pp. 800–2. Cf. Anglo, *Spectacle*, pp. 246–61.

poetry was himself enthroned in the centre, with his eagle perching above, while the nine goddesses of art and learning were grouped on either side around a white marble fountain which ran with Rhenish wine: Helicon, the sacred fountain of poetic inspiration. Latin verses by Leland and Udall drew Anne into the scene as one whom the gods had come expressly to honour, and each of the deities in turn praised Henry's new queen. According to Edward Hall, the Muses did not actually speak their lines but had them displayed in letters of gold, while the goddesses themselves played on a variety of musical instruments; whether Apollo was similarly treated is not clear. The advantage of this was not just that it spared Anne lengthy Latin speeches which she probably could not have understood, but that she could have the verses pointed out and translated without embarrassment. Furthermore, it was probably asking a good deal of London's musical and dramatic talent to assemble at short notice a large consort, each of whose members could also declaim Latin verse effectively.

Beauty, chastity, virtue, noble descent, these were the qualities that Anne's tableaux proclaimed, along with the assurance that she was now to give Henry the companionship and consolation he had lacked for too long – and children, above all children, and male children at that. There was no diffidence about drawing glad attention to Anne's pregnancy. It was her supreme achievement and her greatest merit. Anne Boleyn was flaunting in front of critics and public opinion generally her divine right to the king's bed and to the throne.

To support this paean of praise to Anne, and to cry her challenge to the world, Udall plundered the full repertoire of classical myth and allusion. Here were the roses of Paestum; the festival of Ceres; Cybele. Henry was Nestor, Anne one of the Sibyls; he was to love her as Titus Sempronius Gracchus the elder loved his wife Cornelia; Anne was purer than the rigid morality of the Sabines; her love for Henry was the love of Portia for Brutus.[4] As Sydney Anglo has pointed out, this classical metaphor is in marked contrast to previous processions. Here we find humanism in the service of monarchy, whereas in 1501 it had been the medieval pageant tradition which was dominant and (despite Lily) even in 1522. Anglo does consider the

---

[4] *Ballads*, pp. 381–8.

humanism 'superficial': 'a self-conscious Latinity and a thin veneer of commonplace literary allusions covering what is, for the most part, a dull, trite and lamentably repetitious pageant series'.[5] Perhaps, but the fact that the classicism only, and somewhat thinly, overlaid traditional forms and ideas – as when the Muse Thalia based her speech on Anne's heraldic badge, the falcon – is more a comment on Tudor humanism generally, and Thalia was, after all, the Muse of Comedy. The significant point for our purpose is that Anne Boleyn should have committed herself so firmly to the new humanist style.

The Gracechurch Street tableau is also important for another connection. The design can be attributed to Hans Holbein the younger who had returned to England for his second and lasting stay in 1532.[6] With the one exception that, as executed, only the Muse Calliope was seated, the drawing now in the Staatliche Museen in Berlin closely matches Hall's description of the arch and also fits Udall's verse (plate 24). Scholars normally account for Holbein's design by his connection with the Steelyard, the community of North German merchants which, Hall records, 'made' the pageant. But if we allow at least a semi-official status to Udall's work, it seems likely that 'made' should be read as no more than 'paid for', and that Holbein was involved as the artist called in by the merchants to execute a design to a detailed English specification. And with Holbein (whose previous English contacts had been with men such as More, Warham and Guildford) having now executed a court design for Anne, it may be no accident that within months of the coronation his patrons began to include members of the new court circle, most notably Anne's ally, Thomas Cromwell.[7]

Holbein's presentation of Parnassus gave rise to one of the hostile canards which so bedevil the story of Anne Boleyn. On 16 June Chapuys merely dismissed the coronation as 'a cold, meagre and uncomfortable thing', but a month later he had got hold of the story that the eagle hovering over Apollo had been deliberately placed there by the German merchants as a reference to the emperor, Charles V, whose symbol thereby towered over the arms of Henry VIII and Anne which, the drawing suggests, were on antique pillars, framing the nine Muses. Three

[5] Anglo, *Spectacle*, p. 248.
[6] Ibid., pp. 249–50.
[7] See below, pp. 286–7.

weeks later he repeats the tale, and others have repeated it ever since. It is first of all improbable that foreign merchants who depended on the favour of the English crown should plan so offensive a gesture. Second, it is clear that the eagle in Holbein's drawing is not the two-headed bird of the Habsburgs. Third, the iconography of the tableau demands that the eagle be the one associated with Apollo; to have incorporated the imperial bird associated with Zeus, and without any justification in the text, would have been illiteracy of the first order. We may note, too, that according to the classical story the eagle was blinded by Apollo's brilliance – hardly a compliment to Charles V! Indeed, if we are at all to credit Chapuys' story of Anne's annoyance, it was probably irritation at the ignorance of the *hoi polloi*.[8]

Less than two hundred yards past the Parnassus display was the second Udall–Leland pageant, a castle-like structure, open on one side and roofed with a cupola, standing against the Leaden Hall. Inside, the roof was painted to represent the heavenly bodies, and the floor was a green field out of which rose a hill surmounted by a tree stump. The pageant combined – or rather confused – two themes. The first was an identification of the hoped-for fecundity of Anne Boleyn with the maternal success of the legendary St Anne. The saint sat to one side of the hill, surrounded by two of her supposed daughters, the Virgin Mary and Mary Salome, and the latter's two sons, St James and St John. On the other side was her third daughter, also Mary, with her husband and four children, one of whom spelled out the message in 'rude simpleness':

> We the Citizens, by you in short space
> Hope such issue and descent to purchase.[9]

The second theme exploited Anne Boleyn's badge, the crowned falcon, and was the only mechanical device that there had been time to make. When the child had finished his verses, the machinery brought the tableau to life. First the tree stump thrust

---

[8] *Cal. S. P. Span., 1531–33*, pp. 704, 740, 754–5 [*LP*, vi.653, 805, 918]. Rowlands, *Holbein*, p. 88, argues that the bird was a falcon, but this seems iconographically extraneous. For the suggestion of an identification between Apollo and Henry VIII see D. Cressy, 'Spectacle and power', in *History Today*, 32 (1982), 18–19.

[9] *Ballads*, p. 389.

out a mass of red and white roses – the life of the united Yorkist–Lancastrian dynasty bursting forth again from the apparent barrenness of the Tudor stock. Then a cloud painted on the roof opened and a white falcon swooped to settle on the roses, while another child explained the symbolism, to be followed from the same cloud by an angel who placed an imperial crown on the falcon's head, to the comments of a third child:

> Honour and grace be to our Queen Anne,
> For whose cause an Angel Celestial
> Descendeth, the falcon (as white as [the] swan)
> To crown with a diadem imperial!
> In her honour rejoice we all,
> For it cometh from God, and not of man.
> Honour and grace be to our Queen Anne![10]

Udall prepared three Latin verses in addition – on the St Anne theme, on the falcon and the roses, and on the coronation of the bird (that is, Anne), while a Leland stanza summed up. Finally, the queen left to the strains of a ballad about the white falcon. One would be tempted to see something biographical in Udall's fifth verse:

> Of body small,
> Of power regal
> She is, and sharp of sight;
> Of courage hault,
> No manner fault
> Is in this falcon white.

It is certain, however, that the final verses spelled out Anne's message of the day to the citizens of London. The Muse Clio had already put it in the sophistication of Latin:

> Anna comes, the most famous woman in all the world;
> Anna comes, the shining incarnation of chastity.
> In snow-white litter, just like the goddesses,
> Anna the Queen is here, the preservation of your future.[11]

[10] Ibid., p. 389.
[11] Ibid., p. 382.

Now Udall proclaimed it in the mother-tongue:

> And where by wrong
> She hath flown long,
>   Uncertain where to [a]light;
> Herself repose
> Upon the Rose
>   Now may this falcon white.
>
> Whereon to rest
> And build her nest,
>   God grant her most of might!
> That England may
> Rejoice alway,
>   In this same falcon white.[12]

The play made, in this and some of the other pageants, with the white falcon raises the question of Anne's use of the device. The white falcon was the crest of the Butlers, earls of Ormonde, whose heir had been recognized in 1529 to be Thomas Boleyn; as such it appears on the magnificent brass to Sir Thomas in Hever church (plate 41). Although Leland's verses for the St Anne pageant state that the falcon appears because of this family connection, all the symbolism of the crown, sceptre, roses and the tree stump was new – although each had antecedents (as did the falcon) in previous royal heraldry.[13] Between 1529 when her father became an earl and 1532 when she herself was raised to the peerage, Anne had used a simplified shield of arms showing her mother's descent from Edward I and from the earls of Surrey, and also her father's earldom of Ormonde and his earlier barony of Rochford. If she wanted a badge, she took the latter's black lion rampant. When she became marquis of Pembroke a coronet was added and the monogram 'AP' adopted, but not, it seems, the falcon.[14] What then appears to have happened is that on her marriage, or in anticipation of its announcement, Anne had been granted heraldic augmentations associated with the crown, to enable her to give an existing family badge that new and personal twist which Udall and Leland were able to exploit.[15]

---

[12] Ibid., pp. 390–1.

[13] H. S. London, *Royal Beasts* (1956), pp. 59–61.

[14] BL, Harl. MS 6561, f. 2.

[15] Anne's shield of arms was changed from quarterly: 1 Ormonde; 2 Brotherton; 3 Rochford; 4 Warenne, to 1 Lancaster; 2 Angouleme; 3 Guienne; 4 quarterly Ormonde and Rochford; 5 Brotherton; 6 Warenne.

After the odd conjunction of St Anne and the mechanical falcon at the Leaden Hall, the next pageant reverted to a classical subject, an encounter at the Conduit in Cornhill between Anne and the Three Graces: a somewhat incongruous display because, although framed by a Latin prologue and epilogue, the deities announced themselves by English equivalents typical of the chivalric disguising – Heart Gladness, Stable Honour and Continual Success. That mixture was also prepared at the Great Conduit and the Standard in Cheapside, where static displays of heraldic devices and coats of arms were coupled with Latin speeches, but at the Little Conduit in Cheapside the dramatic presentation of the Judgement of Paris, though largely in English, was much more convincingly classical.[16] Mercury gave Paris the golden apple to present to one of the three goddesses, the wealthy Juno, the wise Pallas Athene and the beautiful Venus, who each try to outbid the others.[17] Paris, in line with the story, awarded the prize to Venus:

> Yet to be plain
> Here is the fourth lady now in our presence,
> Most worthy to have it, of due congruence,
> As peerless in riches, wit and beauty,
> Which are but sundry qualities in you three.

> But for her worthiness, this apple of gold
> Is too simple a reward, a thousandfold.[18]

A child then capped what Paris had said by announcing that there was another reward prepared for Anne, the crown imperial, and pointing to Anne as a demonstration of divine providence. The parting song to Anne concluded with the stanza:

> The golden ball
> Of price but small,
> Have Venus shall,
>   The fair goddess,
> Because it was
> Too low and bare
> For your good grace
> And worthiness.[19]

---

[16] Two Latin verses were probably displayed, not spoken.
[17] The Greek and the Roman pantheon are confused here.
[18] *Ballads*, p. 396.
[19] Ibid., p. 398.

The most remarkable demonstration of the interest in things classical was, unfortunately, not part of the work of Udall and Leland, and thus is known only by descriptions, and not by the text. This was the bringing together of two hundred children on specially built staging at the eastern end of St Paul's churchyard, many, no doubt, from the nearby St Paul's School. They declaimed a series of translations from the Latin poets, praising both Anne and Henry. It is also the one episode to which we know Anne's spontaneous reaction on the day. She highly commended the children's efforts and 'said "Amen" with a joyful smiling countenance'. Confirmation that Anne was not merely being polite here, but that she had been given in the coronation procession something distinctive to her and that she wanted, can be found by comparing her pageants with those designed for her successor, Jane Seymour, possibly for her abortive coronation. Of the twelve described in detail, one was a display of caged singing birds in a meadow, one a maiden with a unicorn by a fountain and a third the new queen's badge and motto, but all the rest used traditional religious themes – the Vision of St John, the Coronation of the Virgin, the Transfiguration and so on – with not a classical allusion in sight.[20]

Seen in a European context, the classicism that distinguished Anne Boleyn's entry in 1533 is very much what we might expect. During her time in France she may have seen stirrings of this newer style. In the entry of Mary Tudor into Paris in 1514, Bacchus faced Ceres (but inside a replica of the city's emblem, the ship), while a display of heraldry had the morality characters Justice, Truth and Unanimity in discussion with Minerva, Diana and Apollo; at Francis I's entry into Lyons in 1515, he was depicted as Hercules gathering fruit in the garden of the Hesperides, while at Rouen in 1517 there was a depiction of the battle between the Gods and the Titans.[21] But the overriding fashion during Anne's years in France was, as in England, for chivalric myth and moralizing. For anything equivalent to her procession we have to wait until the entry of Francis I's second queen, Eleanor, into the city of Rouen in 1532, when she was accompanied by the chariots of Mercury (drawn by serpents), Juno (drawn by peacocks) and Pallas Athene (drawn by the

[20] BL Add.MS 9835 f. 22 [*LP*, x.1016].
[21] J. Chartrou, *Les Entrées Solennelles et Triomphales à la Renaissance* (Paris, 1928), pp. 32–3, 52–3.

Muses and escorted by Apollo).[22] It is unlikely that we should
assume any imitation in Anne Boleyn's entry; more probably the
fashion for *l'antique* was progressing approximately in parallel on
both sides of the Channel.[23] Where Anne's procession did reflect
her French tastes was in respect of the French language: the first
tableau (not by Udall and Leland) was a welcome jointly in
English and in French by children dressed as merchants. Even
more flattered was her interest in music. Apart from the playing
of the Muses in Gracechurch Street, the ballad of the falcon and
the song at the Judgement of Paris, music was also arranged at
the Great Conduit, with an ensemble of voices and instruments
on top of the Standard, and a choir of men and boys on the roof
of St Martin's, Ludgate. The Conduit in Fleet Street was
covered by a tower to conceal a chorus of children and 'such
several solemn instruments that it seemed to be a heavenly
noise', and at Temple Bar (the limit of the city's jurisdiction) a
choir of men and boys stood ready to serenade Anne's departure.

The design of the coronation procession thus demonstrates
Anne's participation in the cult of majesty. It can, however,
tell us more still. When her daughter Elizabeth was presented to
the world as 'Gloriana', this was not merely a formula for
adulation – what today might be called 'media hyperbole'. It
was, rather (as painstaking research has shown), underpinned
by an elaborate and complex foundation of ideas, metaphor and
symbol.[24] In the 1533 coronation pageants for Anne, the seeds of
this later image-building are clearly to be seen. Here, as elsewhere, Elizabeth was the daughter of her mother – or as
assiduous a follower of European fashion. That she should
continue to use the falcon and roses as a badge is understandable; its message of life from the dead had now a double
poignancy.[25] Yet the linking of minds is very much closer than
that. A famous painting of Elizabeth by the monogrammist HE
(and dated 1569) takes as its theme The Judgement of Paris, and
depicts the queen confronting the three goddesses, just as Anne
had done in Cheapside thirty-three years earlier.[26] The classi-

[22] Ibid. pp. 82–3.
[23] Cf. Lowinsky, *Florilegium*, p. 226 n.42.
[24] Yates, *Astraea*.
[25] See the use of the falcon badge on the 'mourning sword' of the City of
Bristol (1594) and the fireplace (1583), now in the library of Windsor Castle.
Elizabeth also used it on her books: Neale, *Queen Elizabeth*, p. 9.
[26] H.M. Queen, Hampton Court.

cism is now better integrated with the compliment; Elizabeth has absorbed the role of Paris and instead of the apple going to Venus and the crown to Anne, the apple is now the orb of England and is retained by the queen against all divine competition. Nonetheless, the essential exploitation of the classical myth is the same. Another parallel is the identification of both mother and daughter with the nymph Astraea, the goddess of Spring who (myth had it) had withdrawn from the world with Saturn at the end of the Golden Age, but was now returned to usher in a new golden era of wealth, prosperity, religion and virtue. The lord mayor's pageant in 1591 would say:

> Lo, the Olympus' king, the thundering Jove,
> Raught hence this gracious nymph, Astraea fair:
> Now once again he sends her from above,
> Descended through the sweet transparent air;
> And here she sits in beauty fresh and sheen,
> Shadowing the person of a peerless queen.[27]

In the verses which Udall wrote in 1533 for the Muses to greet Anne with, her arrival is hymned as the return of the age of Saturn and the start of eternal spring. Again, the image is elaborated in the case of the daughter, but the identification in the case of the mother is quite unequivocal.[28]

Perhaps the most striking of Elizabeth's identities is that of the Virgin Mary, a persona which might seem to be beyond her mother, on grounds both of her pregnancy and of the limited advance of Reformation ideas by 1533.[29] We would be wrong. In 1533, of course, drawing a parallel between Anne Boleyn and St Anne was the most immediate way to invest the new queen's image with a sacred identity, but early sixteenth-century attitudes saw no embarrassment in subsuming the Virgin Mary in the personality of an earthly woman, whatever the name. Thus the Marian motet *O salve genetrix Virgo* may possibly have been written or adapted deliberately for use at Anne's coronation while other Marian pieces could be sung unchanged because of the implication that the promised son was to be born.[30] The link

---

[27] Yates, *Astraea*, pp. 59–69; the quotation is from p. 61.
[28] *Ballads*, p. 388.
[29] Yates, *Astraea*, pp. 76–80.
[30] Lowinsky, *Florilegium*, pp. 180–1; see below, pp. 295–6.

was made specifically in the pageant (not by Udall and Leland) planned for the gate into the precinct of St Paul's.[31] It consisted of an empty throne surrounded by the motto (in Latin), 'Queen Anne prosper, go forward and reign!' In the foreground below this royal throne were placed three splendidly dressed women, unidentified but possibly some of the Sibyls of antiquity who prophesied the advent of Christ. The ones at the left and the right held silver placards with suitable general-purpose texts from the Bible written in blue, but the central figure held a gold placard with the inscription (also in blue), *Veni amica coronaberis* ('Come, my love, thou shalt be crowned'), under which sat two angels holding an imperial crown. This was the direct appropriation of the Marian hymn, *Veni coronaberis*, and the popular religious theme of the Coronation of the Virgin.[32] Beneath the tableau was stretched a long scroll with the inscription (again in Latin), 'Queen Anne, when thou shalt bear a new son of the King's blood, there shall be a golden world unto thy people.' This again harks back to the virgin Astraea, but also has overtones of the new heaven and the new earth won by the son of the Virgin Mary and even, perhaps, of the Annunciation promise of a 'kingdom that knows no end'. And the religious symbiosis of Mary's son and Anne's (expected) son was reinforced by the three ladies having supplies of wafers to throw to the crowds, wafers which carried not religious images but the message of the long scroll in letters of gold.

One motif which was strangely not exploited in the coronation was the motto that Anne had adopted on her marriage to Henry: 'the most happy'. Like her earlier short-lived mottoes it was a statement of defiance – 'the most happy', that is, 'the most appropriate' – but it also played on other senses of this multiple word: 'the most fortunate' – chosen by the king; 'the most propitious' – carrying the king's child; and 'the most content' – a statement of personal emotion quite at odds with Jane Seymour's servile choice, 'bound to obey and serve'. Anne's motto was, however, used on the medal which was, according to tradition, struck to mark her coronation; but, since it is dated 1534, the medal more probably records its anniversary, unless it was prepared to be in readiness for mass circulation when the

[31] Hall, *Chronicle*, p. 802.
[32] It was also proposed for Jane Seymour's pageant.

longed-for heir would be born (as expected) in late summer that year.[33] The latter conjecture would certainly explain why only one copy is known. The revival of the portrait medal of classical times was one of the most characteristic of Renaissance attempts to recover antiquity, but it only arrived in Northern Europe about the start of Henry VIII's reign. Anne Boleyn's medal is, therefore, interesting as one of the earliest examples of the genre in England. We cannot, however, hail it as a wholly successful effort at a humanist portrait medal, for it derives more from the first German attempts which used heads taken from full- or three-quarter-face painted portraits, rather than the classical pure profile which was eventually achieved by Matsys in his 1519 medal of Erasmus, made at Antwerp. Still, even though the Anne Boleyn medal is yet another example of Renaissance ideas reaching England at second and third hand, it must confirm Anne's awareness of the new intellectual fashions which is revealed in the coronation idiom.[34]

In the absence of diaries and personal correspondence the themes and language espoused in the coronation ceremony and the concern with identity revealed by the portrait medal are perhaps as near as we can come to the mind of Anne Boleyn. We can, however, also explore the hagiographical route – the search for relics. There is, first, her plate and jewellery. There was certainly plenty of it. Some time after her death a wooden desk was inventoried, full of pieces, including one diamond ring with the 'HA' cipher, another with the cipher and the text (in Latin), 'O Lord make haste to help me', while a third had a broken part of her motto, 'Moste ....'; amongst a quantity of jewellery in boxes were others with 'HA' and a brooch with 'RA' – 'Regina Anna' – in diamonds.[35] However, none of the personal jewellery Anne owned has survived to be identified. Items remaining from the hundreds of pieces made and remade for the Tudor sovereigns are extremely rare – the taste of one generation is raw material to the next. Of Anne's plate, on the other hand, one English item does survive, a 314 mm high silver cup and cover made in 1535 (plate 39) and now among the treasures of Cirencester parish

[33] G. Hill, *Medals of the Renaissance*, revised J. G. Pollard (1978), p. 145.
[34] J. Pope-Hennessy, *The Portrait in the Renaissance* (New York, 1966), pp. 64–6, 89, 92–3.
[35] *LP*, xii.(2). 1315.

church. It is topped by the falcon on the tree stump, but its chief interest is the design, which picks up once again Anne's interest in Renaissance fashion. The origin of the cup lies in a pattern in circulation abroad which was published in a German pattern book a decade later, but the inspiration appears to be Italian, an attempt to achieve in silver the form of Venetian glass of the period.[36]

Beyond this cup there have been, up to now, only descriptions to whet our imagination. Much work for Anne was undertaken by Cornelius Hayes, the king's Flemish goldsmith, and it was he who, as we have seen, made the highly elaborate but unused silver cradle ordered in 1534.[37] Other craftsmen employed included another Fleming, Thomas Trapper, who for £90 supplied a bowl in fine gold, with a cover, weighing 40 troy ounces (0.91 kg), with Queen Anne's cipher on it.[38] More revealing of Anne's personal choice is the present she gave to Henry at New Year 1534. It is listed as:

> A goodly gilt bason, having a rail or board of gold in the midst of the brim, garnished with rubies and pearls, wherein standeth a fountain, also having a rail of gold about it garnished with diamonds, out whereof issueth water at the teats of three naked women standing about the foot of the same fountain.[39]

Very clearly this was anything but a piece of gothic craftsmanship.

In all this, much interest attaches to the extent of the relationship between Anne and Hans Holbein. As well as the coronation arch, it is known that he designed a pendant with a central stone and the initials 'H' and 'A' combined, as well as drawing that cipher on a shield, but a great deal of speculation has had to be based on that little.[40] Holbein did not have a hand in the 1534 cradle – that suggestion depends on reading the calendar not the original itemized bill – and we have seen that no

---

[36] *Connoisseur Period Guides*, ed. R. Edwards & L. G. G. Ramsey, *The Tudor Period* (1956), pp. 69–70; *Jewels and Plate of Queen Elizabeth I*, ed. A. J. Collins (1956), p. 197 no.6.
[37] See above, p. 239.
[38] J. Williams, *Accounts of the Monastic Treasures Confiscated at the Dissolution*, ed. W. B. Turnbull (Abbotsford Club, 1836), p. 97.
[39] RO, E101/421/13 [*LP*, vii.9].
[40] Ganz, *Die Handzeichnungen*, xxxix.2(e); xxxix.4(d); cf. xxxix.3(d) and (f), while xix.9 could be Anne's gryphon supporter.

drawing or painting of Anne by him has survived.[41] Holbein was employed by the crown on occasions during Anne's career, but his first known regular employment dates from 1538.[42] All the time, however, the evidence for a close link has lain unrecognized in a Holbein pattern for a standing cup and cover, now in Basle (plate 38).[43] This can confidently be identified as a piece designed to Anne's order or else for her, because engraved on the side of the cup is the crowned falcon on the roses. At last we have a major item to see, and something which was certainly hers; the famous British Museum design for Jane Seymour's cup was not the first that Holbein had made for an English queen. In the Basle drawing the falcon and the imperial crown which forms the knop on the cover of the cup are somewhat incongruous against the mannerist style of the rest of the piece: the stem is supported by three semi-nudes in classical style, while the cover rests on a rim held up by four satyrs, and a band round the bowl of the cup is decorated with four antique heads. With the connection with Anne now established, it becomes plausible to believe that it was Holbein who designed her 1534 present to Henry: a sketch by him of the goddess Ceres depicts a nude female figure very much as the list describes Anne's gift.[44] Yet even if that conjecture is false, we can now be confident that Holbein's patron after his return to England in 1532 was Anne Boleyn.

A case has also been made in recent years for crediting Anne Boleyn with the patronage of another artist, or, rather, family of artists, the Horneboltes from Ghent: Gerard the father, Margaret of Austria's court painter, and his children Lucas and Susanna, each of whom had followed in the family profession.[45] Anne, however, was certainly not involved in their decision to try their

[41] RO, SP1/88 f. 116 [*LP*, vii. 1668]; see above, pp. 53–4.
[42] Rowlands, *Holbein*, p. 91.
[43] Offentliche Kunstsammlung, Amerbach-Kabinett, Basle: English Sketchbook 89 [Ganz, *Die Handzeichnungen*, vi.7].
[44] Ganz, *Die Handzeichnungen*, xxiii.5.
[45] For the following see J. Murdoch, et al., *The English Portrait Miniature* (1981) pp. 29–33; R. Strong, *Artists of the Tudor Court* (Victoria & Albert Museum, 1983), pp. 34–44; also *The English Renaissance Miniature* (1984), pp. 30–44; H. Paget, 'Gerard and Lucas Hornebolt in England', in *Burlington Magazine*, 101 (1959), 396–402. Tree-ring dating, however, shows that the surviving portrait of William Carey must be a later copy, or even an enlargement of a miniature: J. Fletcher, 'A portrait of William Carey, and Lord Hunsdon's Long Gallery', in *Burlington Magazine*, 123 (1981), p. 304.

fortune on this side of the Channel, for Lucas was in England at the latest by September 1525. What is possible is that he had a letter of introduction to Thomas Boleyn – even, perhaps, from the archduchess herself – for one of Lucas's first commissions was a portrait of Boleyn's son-in-law, William Carey. It has also been suggested that the Horneboltes were discreetly absenting themselves from the Low Countries, where an outburst of religious persecution was under way. There may be truth in this, despite the fact that Gerard Hornebolte seems to have returned to Habsburg employment without difficulty after 1531, for Lutherans were certainly quite numerous in the artistic world there. Yet once again the date rules out any connection with Anne.

At a later period, however, just as Anne did favour the slightly suspect Holbein, so she may have employed a reformist refugee like Lucas Hornebolte. He was appointed king's painter for life and made a denizen in June 1534, and the grant implies some personal involvement of the king. It records that: 'For a long time I have been acquainted not only by reports from others but also from personal knowledge with the science and experience in the pictorial art of Lucas Hornebolte.' This coincides with a high point in Boleyn influence, and it is very tempting to make the connection. A Hornebolte employee was busy in 1533 on the windows at Windsor, while another, Richard Atzell, figures in the 1534 New Year's gifts as a German 'polisher of stones'; in fact he came from Trèves and was naturalized in March 1535, certainly with Cromwell's assistance. On the other hand, Lucas Hornebolte had come to England early enough to acquire contacts with the circles around Katherine in the last years of her unchallenged supremacy, and many of the pieces attributed to him link the artist not with Anne but with her enemies. He is credited with four miniatures of Katherine herself, one of Princess Mary, two of Brandon and one of Charles V, and possibly with a half-length panel painting of the countess of Salisbury, Mary's first governess and the mother of the Pole brothers. There is still research to do, but it cannot be said that the omens for a close link between the Horneboltes and Anne Boleyn are good.

One aspect of the work of the Hornebolte family which Anne must have known, even if she did not employ them, was manuscript illumination, where they were unsurpassed. In the thinking of the day, such objects were more akin to jewels than to books, and Anne had an obvious enthusiasm for them as well as decided tastes of her own. Only a small number have survived or can now be identified as having belonged to her but the proof that she was an enthusiast is the trouble that was taken to prepare for her a presentation copy of the exemplification of the royal patents that she had been granted between June 1532 and her jointure on 21/22 March 1533.[46] The first item is the patent creating her lady marquis of Pembroke, which begins with a massive letter 'H', 114 mm by 107 mm, illuminated in gold and blue and incorporating the crowned falcon on the roses. The whole impressive document may well be 'the jointure of Queen Anne' for which the chancery provided four skins of, vellum along with silk and gold, at a cost of eighteen shillings in the year 1533–4.[47]

Among illuminated manuscripts proper, pride of place must go to 'The Ecclesiaste', now in the collection of the duke of Northumberland at Alnwick (plate 34).[48] A text of the Book of Ecclesiastes (with commentary), it is in such good condition that Anne herself could have just put it down. The velvet binding now grey but once black, shows exactly what those frequent payments to Hayes the goldsmith for fine velvet bindings were for. All four corners, front and back, are guarded with brass, decorated with a roundel on which is engraved a royal badge – the crowned lion rampant regardant, the dragon, the crowned falcon on the 'roses, and the greyhound – and there are two decorated brass clasps. At the centre of the front cover is Anne Boleyn's shield of arms in enamel on a metal base, possibly silver, surmounted by a crown. The title page is almost an imitation of printing, but it does introduce the ground colours for the illuminations, pink and slate, a combination which Anne seems to have favoured elsewhere.[49] The work itself has a running title in a brighter blue which is also used to number the twelve chapters and to divide the treatment of each into '*texte*',

[46] BL, Harl. MS 303.
[47] *LP*, vii.1204.
[48] Alnwick, the duke of Northumberland, Percy MS 465.
[49] I owe the suggestion re printing to Miss Janet Backhouse. Subsequent investigation showed that the ornaments imitated occur on the Alençon edition, *c*.1530: see below, p. 317.

sections of the biblical text of varying length and in French, and '*annotation*', commentary in English.

Each section of *texte* and *annotation* has its initial letter 20 mm square and illuminated alternately in sky-blue lit by white and in dusky pink, each on a slate-blue ground speckled with gold. The initial letters of each chapter are, however, treated in a far more magnificent fashion. Four times the size – 40 mm square – they comprise a series of eight designs: the arms of Henry VIII impaling those of Anne, as on the cover enamel (chapter 1), the initials 'H' and 'A' (chapters 2, 7, 11), the crowned falcon on the roses (chapters 3, 10), an allegorical design (chapter 4), the motto 'the most happy' (chapters 5, 9), oak tree foliage (chapter 6), Anne's own shield, crowned (chapter 8), and a gold filigree pattern (chapter 12) (see plates 35–37).[50] The quality of workmanship is very high indeed. Even what appears to be just a flower-like letter 'J' in pink on a slate ground with 'H' and 'A' in gold, turns out on closer examination to be lined with green and picked out in white, with a lace over the slate and the whole in perspective and shadowed, as though the letter were raised off the page; in one decorated letter 'I', an area the size of a postage stamp contains a curving tendril of gold with eleven oak leaves, a cluster of some nine or so catkins in white and gold, and seven acorn cups, four full and three empty; the first illumination of all, the combined shield of Henry and Anne, is in no fewer than seven colours and tones.[51]

The most remarkable of all the larger illuminations is, without doubt, the 'E' of '*Et me suis*' at the start of chapter 4.[52] The letter is in pink, picked out in white and lined with green, with a white scroll round the horizontal element bearing the motto '*Fiat voluntas tua*' – 'Thy will be done.' Behind the letter is an anchor in blue with a gold stock, hanging from a celestial sphere, also in gold; beside the sphere is the abbreviation 'IHS' and below the scroll, '6 H' – all these in gold also. The technique is superb; the shadow cast by the anchor on the background is lovingly

[50] Alnwick, Percy MS 465, ff. 2; 12v, 61v, 130; 23, 117; 34; 44, 100v; 54; 88; 139.

[51] Ibid., ff. 61v, 54, 2. Udall's coronation verses [p. 385] referred to Anne's capacity to attract the oak. If the blossom could be separated from the oak tendril and interpreted as a lime, the allusion could be to Philemon and Baucis, almost the only classical example of marital fidelity omitted by Udall and Leland.

[52] Alnwick, Percy MS 465, f. 34.

indicated, and the effect of light and shade on the cagework of the sphere is meticulous, inside and out. The precise significance of this symbolism has yet to be elucidated. The motto and the monogram for 'Jesus' suggest some reflection of the text at a point which deals with the reality of oppression in human experience, but the rest is more esoteric. The celestial or armillary sphere appears in a number of Holbein's designs for medallions, though without its meaning becoming apparent, but at the end of the century the device was being interpreted as a symbol of constancy.[53] This would make good sense of the anchor, another symbol of firm commitment, and relate nicely to the motto which is taken from the words of total dependence on God uttered by Christ in the Garden of Gethsemane.

Apart from any religious interpretation, one would also expect a layer of meaning in the illumination that referred directly to Anne or Henry, or both of them; nine of the other large illuminations do so without question, and a tenth, the blossom and fruit of the oak, might easily do so too. Such a double meaning could readily be drawn for the chapter 4 illumination, from the sphere, anchor and motto announcing fidelity and obedience. The key, however, must lie in the interpretation of '6 H'. If instead of '6' this is the Greek letter sigma, σ, the equivalent of 'S' in English, we have a letter which was used in royal monograms to mean 'Sovereign'. In that case, the religious level of meaning is indicated by the monogram 'IHS' for Jesus above the central scroll, and the secular by 'σH' for 'Sovereign Henry', below it, with the remaining symbols taking on meanings appropriate to the respective levels. Thus much is increasingly conjecture, but what is not in doubt is that there is another connection here between Anne and her daughter. Elizabeth, too, used the armillary sphere as a device, and from early on in her reign. A portrait of Sir Henry Lee shows him wearing one as her champion, as did his successor, the earl of Cumberland. Paintings of Elizabeth herself with a celestial sphere include some of the most famous, such as the 'Ditchley' and the 'Rainbow'.[54]

---

[53] Ganz, *Die Handzeichnungen*, xxi.6(a),(f); xl.7(c); R. Strong, *The Cult of Elizabeth* (1977), p. 52. The Van Dyck of the 9th earl of Northumberland (National Trust, Petworth), however, includes a sphere which indicates 'wisdom'.

[54] Yates, *Astraea*, p. 65 n.1; R. Strong, *Portraits of Elizabeth* (Oxford, 1963),

The Alnwick 'Ecclesiastes' was made for Anne during her three years as queen, although the exact date has been disguised by a deliberate erasure of part of the colophon, leaving only M¹CCCCC.[55] In style it clearly belongs to the tradition of illumination which she had first experienced at the court of Margaret of Austria twenty years before, but it is almost certainly the product of Flemish-trained craftsmen working in England, and not an item ordered from a studio in the Low Countries. An interesting possibility, indeed, is raised by comparing the Alnwick volume with another of Anne Boleyn's manuscripts, 'The Pistellis and Gospelles for the LII Sondayes in the Yere', now in the British Library.[56] This was produced between the time of Anne's becoming marchioness of Pembroke and her recognition as queen, that is, over the winter of 1532–3. It is less elaborate than the later volume. The first item is a large representation of Anne's original arms, quartering the arms of Ormonde, Brotherton, Rochford and Warenne on a lozenge surmounted by a coronet, with four complex gold monograms. The contents is listed between architectural borders in gold, while another architectural border, which includes figures of St Peter and St Paul and medallions of the evangelists, surrounds a depiction of the Crucifixion, with Mary, St John and Mary Magdalen. Thereafter, however, there are only small illuminated letters, containing Anne's arms on a lozenge or the initials 'AP'. Nevertheless, and despite the manuscript's much poorer condition, there are obvious similarities with the Alnwick 'Ecclesiastes', in penmanship, in adopting the form of *texte* in French and *exhortation* in English, and the use of blue for editorial matter. The case is not yet proven, but there is a real possibility that here are two volumes from a single studio under Anne's patronage.

Along with this evident appreciation of things Flemish came Anne Boleyn's other love, the art of France. The earliest example of this, either imported for her or brought back when she returned to England in 1522, is the book of hours printed at Paris

---

p. 134 no. 1; 'Lee' – NPG, no. 374; 'Cumberland' – National Maritime Museum; 'Ditchley' – NPG, no. 2561; 'Rainbow' – Hatfield House.
    [55] Alnwick, Percy MS 465, f. 148.
    [56] BL, Harl. MS 6561.

and now at Hever Castle (plate 29).[57] It qualifies as illuminated only by courtesy, for it is an example of a publishing initiative which started at the end of the previous century to make such devotional books cheaper and more readily available, by supplying a printed text and woodcut illustrations which could then be coloured by hand. This copy was produced on vellum, making it a more up-market product than one on paper; the cuts have been coloured, the initials also, and the pages have been given gilt borders in an architectural style. The book carries an inscription which is believed to be genuine:

> Remember me when you do pray,
> That hope doth lead from day to day.
> Anne Boleyn

It stands in striking contrast to the manuscript in italic script, delicately heightened with colour, of a specially adapted text of Clément Marot's poem, *Le Pasteur Evangélique*, which Anne received after her marriage to Henry VIII.[58] Speculation has suggested that Francis I may have been the donor, but irrespective of that, the volume is from one of the top ateliers in France. What is not certain, however, is whether the splendid illumination of Anne's arms surrounded by a wreath of oak leaves and Tudor roses, with the falcon badge almost as a pendant, came with the book, or was added in England so as to face the first page.

Another French manuscript, a psalter, is even closer to Anne.[59] It dates from the period between her father's elevation to an earldom in December 1529 and Anne's own promotion in September 1532, and was also specially ordered for her from one of the studios in Paris or Rouen which supplied the court and elite society of France. Whoever did so must have had Anne's tastes very much in mind, and it has been hinted that such an order might have been placed by Jean du Bellay, who as Francis's ambassador in England did become very friendly with Anne. It seems more probable, however, that the commission

---

[57] Hever Castle, *Hours of the Blessed Virgin Mary* (G. Hardouyn, Paris, n.d.). The conjectural date for the book is *c.*1528. I owe this information to the kindness of Mr Richard Allen.
[58] BL, Royal MS 16E13.
[59] Sold by Sotheby's 7 Dec. 1982: *Western Manuscripts*, Lot 62.

came from Anne personally or from someone exceptionally close to her, most plausibly, perhaps, from the king himself.[60]

The reason for suspecting this personal commission is the intimacy of one of the symbols used in the psalter (see plate 30). No surprises are presented by the two full borders in the book, one in French gothic style and one of Renaissance candelabra. Nor are there any in the armorial achievement facing the first folio: any good French atelier could produce such a display of Anne's arms on a lozenge, held up by two somewhat muscular winged putti within an architectural frame, and repeat the lozenge in a number of the specially large initial letters which occur at various points. However, the full-page illumination opposite the Renaissance candelabra is unusual. It has an architectural frame, with wingless putti holding a lozenge on which are three items, two monograms in purple and the black lion of Rochford at the bottom. This lozenge is again used in a smaller form elsewhere. The upper of the two monograms is a letter 'A' which has a stroke through the apex and the normal horizontal stroke written as a 'V'. That this is more than a fancy piece of penmanship is clear from the occurrence of exactly the same form in the sections of the coving of the organ screen of King's College, Cambridge, which, as we shall see, celebrate the marriage of Henry and Anne (see plate 28). Indeed, this seems to be a combination of the letters 'A', 'T', 'M' and possibly 'V' (or 'U'). What all this might mean is not obvious, but given its appearance in a French manuscript and in English carving of some years later, we must assume that we have here an important symbol particular to Anne, if still a riddle to us.

The larger monogram, placed centrally on the lozenge, is also to be found elsewhere. It was used with the coroneted lozenge of Anne's arms at the start of 'The Pistellis and Gospelles' of 1532–3, and a variant of it occurs also on the coving of the King's College organ screen. It is thus reasonable to conclude that the device was also specific to Anne. As Tudor monograms go (and by comparison with the 'A'), this second combination is very simple. It is formed of the letters 'H', 'E', 'N'

---

[60] The attempt to use du Bellay's letter of 13 Apr. 1530 [ibid., pp. 72–3] to infer a link between the MS and the bishop, Anne and Henry, and the humanist Jacques Colin, seems ill advised. The reference *'Je me trouveray continuellement autour du Roy et de Madame'* is to Francis I and Louise of Savoy [*Correspondance*, i.65 at p. 142].

(this last backwards), 'R', 'E', 'X', 'S', and 'L'. 'HEN ricus REX' is an obvious reading, but there are the last two letters to account for also. 'Sovereign Lord', 'Sovereign Liege', seem the likely interpretations. Perhaps the refrain of the court song, 'My sovereign lord', is relevant here, with its queen (or mistress) using that title to praise 'the eighth Harry' and his tiltyard exploits in her honour. Given the foreign provenance of the psalter and yet the use of such personal symbols, it is reasonable to assume that the order for the book must have come from somebody very close to Anne indeed.[61]

The one manuscript which belongs neither with the Flemish nor with the French ones that Anne owned is the music book in the Royal College of Music in London (plate 31).[62] It is a less than top-class production, on paper rather than vellum, unfinished, frequently corrected, and with the forty folios which do carry completed illuminations offering a decidedly old-fashioned collection of fruit, foliage, grotesques and monsters. Three things link the book with Anne: first, as we have seen, the occurrence of her name ('Mistress A Bolleyne', followed by the motto 'nowe thus' and the curious musical notation); second, a representation of what may be a falcon attacking a pomegranate (Katherine of Aragon's badge); and third, the contents.[63] A majority of the works included are in praise of the Virgin Mary or prayers to female saints, which suggests that the text was intended for a woman. Edward E. Lowinsky, who has made the authoritative study of the text, also suggests that several of the items are particularly appropriate to Anne as queen, and especially striking are the two, both by the French court composer Mouton, which directly mention the name, Anne. The one does so by including within a *mélange* of psalm texts, the prayer of rejoicing from the first book of Samuel, uttered by Hannah (Anna) when her son was born; the other, a prayer for progeny, mentions Anna by name. Since Mouton died in 1522 it is obvious that the

[61] One would expect the monogram to refer more directly to Anne, and hence that 'S' and 'L' might make *'Servant'* or *'Serviteur Loyal'*, but the *rex* make it certain that the letters refer to the king. The above only glances at the topic of Anne's monograms and ciphers. BL, Harl. MS 6561 has a more complicated monogram at f. 1v which may include the name BOLEYN.

[62] London, Royal College of Music, MS 1070. For the following see Lowinsky, in *Florilegium*, pp. 161–235.

[63] See above, pp. 30–1, 37, 283. Lowinsky reproduces the inscription in *Florilegium* at fig. 13.

person he had in mind was not Anne Boleyn! It was, rather, Anne of Brittany. Indeed, in the prayer for children, the name of the latter's husband, Louis XII, is left unchanged. Yet, as the migration of the famous motet *Quis dabit osculis nostris* from the funeral of Anne of Brittany to that of Maximilian I shows, courts were not averse to pirating a good thing when they heard it, and a secondary application of the texts to Anne Boleyn would be perfectly in accord with the thinking of the time, especially since Anne's patroness, Claude of France, had been Anne of Brittany's daughter.[64]

Intriguing though this hypothesis is, it does present some difficulties as it stands. The use of the expression 'Mistress Anne' with her father's motto would seem to suggest an early rather than a late date. Lowinsky's suggestion that it refers to Anne's execution, with the three notes and the *longa* signifying 'the end', has to overcome the objection that even after her fall she is still normally called 'the queen'; the simple Christian name and surname belong to the period before her father's earldom in 1529. Also, the falcon is not depicted with crown and sceptre, nor, apparently, is it perching on roses, although 'you outshine the roses' – a hitherto unexplained expression in a pastiche motet, *O salve genitrix Virgo* (apparently unique to the book) – could be a reference to the badge or to the early thinking which produced the badge.[65] One wonders, too, about the point of the bird pecking at pomegranates, once Katherine had been relegated to the status of dowager princess of Wales. We may note, further, that the form of the 'A' for Anne is a variant, not the final form of the monogram in the psalter and at Cambridge. All this, together with the quality of the piece and its incompleteness – it was not presented but put straight into use in performance – may suggest a date for the book before 1529. The parental motto, 'now thus', would in that case be a boast about Anne: that her situation as plain Mistress Boleyn was only temporary – the three notes; and then it would be gone for good – the *longa*.

Lowinsky, however, associates the first (and otherwise unknown) motet in the book with the themes of Anne's coronation – and the mixture of humanism, classical allusion and Christian

[64] '*Quis dabit*', attributed to Ludwig Senfl on publication (1538), but actually by Constanzo Festa.
[65] The perching falcon appears on p. 29 and is reproduced in Lowinsky, in *Florilegium*, as fig. 9; the text of the motet appears ibid., p. 180.

symbol is very much that of 1533. There are also a number of possible connections in several other pieces. He suggests too that the mediocre quality of the manuscript rules out the idea of a gift from the French court or of a gift commissioned by any courtier of standing. Searching for a donor of lower rank but some wealth, with musical skill, court connections, a thorough acquaintance with Anne's tastes in music and a repertoire which was appropriate to her time abroad (and therefore somewhat old-fashioned by European standards in the mid 1530s), Lowinsky puts forward the name Mark Smeton, the musician with whom she was accused of adultery in 1536. He certainly satisfies all the requirements, and an attempt by him to produce an illuminated manuscript for Anne would tally with the evidence at the time of her fall that Smeton was attempting to ape the manners of his social superiors.[66] Although there was good precedent at court for a musician presenting a music book to his patron, that was in the context of the New Year's gifts; how a gift would have been regarded at an unconventional time – implying, as it might some more personal link – is not at all clear.

Whether or not we accept Smeton as the possible editor of the music book, or whether we follow the indications of an earlier date and explain the abandoning of the work as a consequence of Anne's increasing status, which made such a relatively crude piece no longer acceptable, is of interest, but not the main point. Anne Boleyn's interests in music are well known, but it now appears that they extended beyond her own performance to the musical life of the court, and perhaps as far as the encouragement of a choral style that she had come to know in her formative years abroad.

One dimension of Tudor court life where it is difficult to measure the influence Anne might have had, is that of building. Although the flood-tide of Henry VIII's building activities did not set in until 1535, Anne's coming into favour had coincided with the acquisition of two major sites, the unfinished Hampton Court – which Henry continued and elaborated – and York Place (later Whitehall), where the site of the episcopal palace, already made magnificent by Wolsey, was enlarged many times over, and the

[66] See below, pp. 368–9.

existing buildings swallowed up in what was to be the king's main residence in (or rather, on the edge of) the city of London. For Henry, even this was not enough, augmented though it was by continual large and small building projects in his eighteen or so other properties, such as the royal apartments in the Tower that were renovated for Anne's coronation. In 1531 the king decided to start yet another house, St James'! Thus, Anne Boleyn's married life with Henry was a constant removal from one builder's yard to another. Since we know that the king discussed with her even the design of his personal jewellery, it is hard to believe that he did not talk buildings – and not just, as we might suppose, in order to listen to his own voice; on one occasion Anne herself was certainly expecting some message from Thomas Alvard, the paymaster of the works at Whitehall.[67] One area where she certainly did have an impact was in the frantic rush from 1531 onwards to build the one palace where there was to be no room for Katherine. Impressment of labour, construction by artificial light, canvas screens to allow work to continue in all weathers – everything was done to finish in record time, and it was in the new gatehouse of Whitehall that Henry and Anne were married.[68]

The final and public rejection of Katherine in 1533 meant further hours of work in all the royal palaces, replacing heraldic glass and decorations which employed her arms and symbols, and at Greenwich the opportunity was taken at the same time to erect Anne's arms in place of Wolsey's on the great organ in the chapel.[69] In the gallery at Eltham where the baby Elizabeth played in bad weather, ten of her mother's badges were inserted in the glass at a shilling each, and with a great deal of new glass elsewhere in the palace, no doubt similarly decorated, Mary's celebrated rudeness to Anne in the chapel there does seem at least more understandable.[70] At Hampton Court the queen's suite was removed from the floor above to the same floor as the

---

[67] *LP*, v. 1299.

[68] Colvin, *King's Works*, iv.307; BL, Sloane MS 2495 ff. 13–13v refers to 'York House in the high chamber over the West Gate'. The three gates at Whitehall stood north (Holbein Gate), south (King's St Gate – not yet built) and east (Court Gate – date unknown) of the centre line of the palace. From the position of the royal apartments both the Holbein Gate and the Court Gate were 'west'; since the former is the further west of the two, that is possibly the site intended.

[69] Colvin, *King's Works*, iv.105.

[70] Ibid., iv.82; see above, p. 248.

king's apartments – perhaps Anne favoured intercommunicating doors, as at the Exchequer at Calais.[71] The royal beasts in the gardens there had to make room for a newcomer, a leopard – Anne's secondary badge, derived from the Brothertons – and a leopard was also set up on the hall roof. Fortunately for economy, her successor's device was the panther, so all that was necessary in 1536 was some anatomical modification![72] No such modification proved possible to the roof of the Great Hall, which to this day continues to display Anne's arms and the 'HA' monogram. Of the more accessible locations, only one escaped the removal of every trace of Anne's existence which was attempted at her fall; this was a doorway in the St James' gatehouse, where the cipher remains still.[73]

From time to time we get glimpses of Anne's own taste. At Greenwich, the ceilings in her presence chamber and bed-chamber were decorated with gilded bullions and buds on a lattice of white battens; the areas in front of the chimneys in the main rooms were protected by Seville tiles, and the other alcoves paved in yellow and green Flanders tiles costing a third of the price.[74] At Eltham in 1534, arrangements 'against the coming of the prince' (the child Anne was to lose in the summer) included an iron canopy over the cradle, special measures to exclude draughts, and the redecoration of the suite in yellow ochre.[75] Occasionally we even meet Anne herself. Three bird coops had to be built on the king's orders at Sir Henry Norris's house in Greenwich town in 1534, for 'the peacock and the pelican that were brought to the king out of the New Found Land'. Anne had complained to Henry bitterly that the birds must be got out of the garden because she 'could not take her rest in mornings for the noise of the same'. Anyone who has had to live in the vicinity of a peacock will sympathize – and feel somewhat sorry for Norris too![76]

Anne's taste for the antique continues to come through from all the sources. At Hampton Court her new lodgings were

[71] Ibid., iv.136; see above, p. 201.
[72] Ibid., iv.26.
[73] Ibid., iv.241.
[74] Ibid., iv.104–5. Since the work was done after Henry had separated from Katherine, we can assume Anne's interest.
[75] Ibid., iv.82.
[76] Ibid., iv.105; 'Building work', in *Transactions of the Greenwich and Lewisham Antiquarian Society*, 5.24.

decorated in that style by a German 'moulder of antique', clearly a specialist.[77] It was apparently another foreign expert, 'Philip the sculptor', who with local men working under him was responsible for the one piece of interior design associated with Anne to have survived, the screen at King's College, Cambridge (plate 28), which we have already noticed.[78] The earliest major timber construction in the country entirely in Renaissance style, the screen is a paean of praise to Henry VIII and particularly to his marriage with Anne. The three bays of blind arcading on each side of the double doors have round heads, with carving in high relief on each tympanum. One bay has a remarkable treatment of the 'Fall of the Rebel Angels', but the other seven carry shields with royal arms and symbols, two of which refer specifically to Anne. One is a shield supported by cherubs with the cipher 'RA', and the other the shield of Henry's arms, impaling those of Anne.[79] Over the blind arcade is a continuous coving to accommodate the wider gallery above. In two of the eight sections of this coving, the central boss is surrounded by four ciphers of 'HA', each crowned, with a crowned falcon on the roses in profile on the left, another on the right and a third falcon in relief at the base, visible down to its wings as it displays towards the nave. Two more sections have the monogram 'HR' for Henricus Rex, balanced by another for Anne which is essentially 'RA', Regina Anna, but adds the letters 'F', 'X' and 'S'.

Antique taste can also be detected in Anne's furnishings. When her vice-chamberlain Edward Baynton visited Baynards Castle (in the city of London), which she had taken over from Katherine of Aragon, he selected for her from her predecessor's belongings 'a cup of horn with a cover, garnished with antique work, the knop of the cover and the foot of the cup of ivory'.[80] On an earlier occasion, the plate she received from the estate of Henry Guildford included six bowls with 'the feet wrought with antique work and faces'.[81] When Anne 'took her chamber' before

[77] Colvin, *King's Works*, iv.133.

[78] Ibid., iii.194; cf. Royal Commission on Historical Monuments, *City of Cambridge* (1959), i.128–30. The emphasis on the marriage of Anne and Henry is explained by Edward Fox being provost of King's.

[79] The form of the 'A' is distinctive, but whether significant is not clear.

[80] 'Inventory of the wardrobe of Katherine of Aragon', in *Camden Miscellany* iii. Camden Society, 61 (1855), p. 39 [*LP*, viii.209].

[81] *LP*, v.1063.

Elizabeth was born, her rooms were equipped with two specially made folding tables, one 'for a breakfast table' and the other 'for her grace to play upon' – that is, at cards. Each of these was made 'with tiles entailed [patterned] with antique work'.[82]

No doubt the searcher for Anne Boleyn must be aware that what has survived of her imposes its own kind of distortion. What impression would we have received if the balance of the data were reversed and only one illuminated manuscript had survived, but several sets of, say, fire dogs?[83] And what of the ephemeral life of the court, the banquets, celebrations and entertainments, at which Anne's splendid wardrobe was displayed but on which the chroniclers and letter-writers are silent after she has become queen? It is only the accident of her trial which lets us see her dancing with her ladies and the gentlemen of the court in her bedchamber.[84] It would, therefore, be unsafe to conclude from what does survive that art was dominant in her life. The fine objects that she was interested in were in many ways simply adjuncts of monarchy. Nor do we know in our present state of scholarship how unusual Anne was. Indeed, that question may never be satisfactorily answered, for only Katherine Parr among her successors had much time to show what her interests were, and thereafter the next queens consort were James I's wife, Anne of Denmark, and his son's wife, Henrietta Maria, each of whom did certainly exhibit considerable artistic interest, but, of course, in the quite different cultural climate of the seventeenth century. Yet when all allowance is made for proper caution, the cultured reality still comes through. Whatever else Anne was, she was a woman of some aesthetic commitment and discrimination. Without distorting her into a major Renaissance patron in the mould of her contemporary, Isabella d'Este, we must allow Anne Boleyn a small place in the cultural story of sixteenth-century England.

[82] Colvin, *King's Works*, iv.105.
[83] *Archaeologia Cantiana*, 9 (1874), p. xliv.
[84] See below, p. 398.

14

Anne Boleyn and the
Advent of Reform

━━━◆━━━

THE MOST haunting description of Anne Boleyn is 'Anna of the Thousand Days'. The brevity of her marriage, the gradient of catastrophe from the coronation to Tower Green, the final total vulnerability, is all there, and above all the transience – gone, almost as though she had never been. The image is arresting, but the Protestant leaders in her daughter's reign would have decisively rejected it. John Foxe declared of Anne: 'What a zealous defender she was of Christ's gospel all the world doth know, and her acts do and will declare to the world's end.'[1] Of course from 1558, although Elizabeth the new queen was committed to restoring and defending her father's supremacy over the English Church, she needed (the reformers believed) every possible stiffening to persuade her to adhere to a clearly Protestant position, so remarks like this are what we would expect of Foxe and the rest. Yet the evidence is on their side; Anne Boleyn was not a catalyst in the English Reformation; she was an element in the equation.[2]

We have seen how Anne played a major part in pushing Henry into asserting his headship of the Church. That headship was not just a constitutional rejection of the primacy of Rome. It was, as Thomas More and others at the time were well aware, a change with profound religious implications, revolutionizing the ethos of organized Christianity in England. More than this, Anne was a strong supporter of reform – defined as we shall see

[1] Foxe, *Acts and Monuments*, v.175.
[2] The following is informed, as all discussions must now be, by the seminal exposition of M. Dowling, 'Anne Boleyn and reform', in *Journal of Ecclesiastical History*, 35 (1984), 30–46.

later – and she was the first to demonstrate the potential there was in the royal supremacy for that distinctive English element in the Reformation, the ability of the king to take the initiative in religious change. Whatever the chances might have been of any grass-roots movement for reform on this side of the Channel, that the impetus towards movement came from the highest level in the land made all the difference to the outcome. Brief though Anne's influence was, it was a thousand days of support for reform from the throne itself. And hindsight can say more. The breach in the dyke of tradition which she encouraged and protected made the flood of first reformed, and later of more specifically Protestant Christianity, unstoppable. Catholic hatred of Anne damned her for the break with Rome and for the entrance of heresy into England. It was right on both counts.

The most striking evidence of Anne Boleyn's influence in the Church is what Alexander Ales described to Elizabeth as 'the evangelical bishops whom your most holy mother had appointed from among those scholars who favoured the purer doctrine of the gospel'.[3] William Latimer listed them as Cranmer, Hugh Latimer, Nicholas Shaxton, Thomas Goodrich and her almoner John Skip, although the latter was not elected a bishop until three years after Anne's death. The actual list is somewhat longer. Chapuys noted the partisan appointment of John Salcot alias Capon to Bangor, while William Barlow, elected to St Asaph's and St David's in quick succession in 1536, was a staunch Boleyn supporter.[4] Indeed, of the ten elections to the episcopate between 1532 and Anne's death in 1536, seven were reformers who were her clients. Another, Edward Fox, was clearly being rewarded for his sterling support for Anne during the divorce, and the list also included John Hilsey who, though not directly linked to Anne, was a protégé of Cranmer.[5] Alexander Ales was, of course, exaggerating when he wrote of Anne 'appointing' these men – William Latimer was more correct to talk of her 'continual mediations' with the king 'for

---

[3] RO, SP70/7 ff. 1–11 [*Cal. S. P. For., 1558–59*, 1303 at p. 532] – hereafter: Ales, 'Letter'; Oxford, Bodl. MS Don. C. 42 f. 30 – hereafter: Latimer, 'Treatyse'.
[4] *Cal. S. P. Span., 1531–33*, p. 866 [*LP*, vi.1460].
[5] Fox was very much of Anne's religious temper [see below, pp. 325–6]. He supported the Ten Articles and the *rapprochement* with the German reformers, but resisted sacramentarian heresy: Ridley, *Cranmer*, pp. 119, 121, 163; *LP*, viii.823 *D.N.B.*, vii.553–5. Fox helped Ales.

their preferment' – but the point is clear. And the influence of this spate of appointments was crucial to the future of the Reformation. At the end of the reign, the reforming bishops in office were still, predominantly, those patronized by Anne Boleyn.[6]

Anne's religious patronage extended also to lesser positions in the Church. When Henry Gold, Archbishop Warham's former chaplain, was executed for complicity with the Nun of Kent, Anne secured his benefice of St Mary Aldermanbury for Dr Edward Crome, but found that fashionable London cleric some-what slow in obeying his royal patron. She thereupon wrote him a stinging rebuke, linking the neglect of his own best interests with neglect for the advancement of godly doctrine.[7] She had been exercising an influence on appointments long before this. In the summer of 1528 she was pressing Wolsey to change his mistaken nomination of William Barlow to the living of Tonbridge into the living of Sundridge, which was what her father had originally asked for.[8] Nor, as the letter to Crome shows, was her interest just in securing rewards for favourite clerics, but in using them to promote reform. It was no accident that when she wanted to place a 'friend' in the hospital of St John Redcliffe, she couched her letter to the corporation of Bristol as a request to grant the next appointment to two reformers in her entourage, Baynton and Shaxton, and David Hutton, a local reformist leader.[9]

We know, indeed, a little of the way in which William Barlow exploited the promotion Anne secured for him to the priory of Haverfordwest in Pembroke, a year or so before his appointment as a bishop.[10] Cromwell wanted him to take over as suffragan as well, but the bishop of St David's would have nothing to do with this incomer and his contentious preaching of 'God's Word'. Considerable friction developed between the conservatives and

---

[6] Note the role of Goodrich, Skip and Capon in saving John Merbeck: Foxe, *Acts and Monuments*, v.482–4, 486, 490–2.

[7] Wood, *Letters*, ii.188–9 [*LP*, vii.693].

[8] *LP*, iv.4647, App.197.

[9] Ibid., vii.89; ix.189. Chapuys refers to the protection of 'Lutheran' clerics by Anne and her father in Mar. 1531 and May 1532, possibly Latimer in each case: *Cal. S. P. Span., 1531–33*, pp. 96, 445 [*LP*, v.148, 1013].

[10] For the following see *LP*, v.333; viii.412, 466; ix.1091; x.19, 1182; cf. E. G. Rupp, *Studies in the Making of the English Protestant Tradition* (Cambridge, 1947), pp. 62–72.

the prior, who was supported by his brother John, another Boleyn protégé who knew Anne well and was reckoned to owe to her his position as dean of Westbury. The in-fighting grew so bad that at one point William was forced to leave Pembroke. The correspondence between London and West Wales that the quarrel produced gives tantalizing glimpses of the network of conservative resistance to reform at the centre and in the provinces, at one point even touching Dr John Incent of St Paul's, who was to be accused of the murder in 1536 of the anticlerical London member of parliament, Robert Pakington.[11] Be that as it may, Anne was certainly engaged against Incent in another battle – to wrest control of the cathedral chapter from him and his fellow conservatives.[12] When Anne was arrested, John Barlow's commitment to her nearly led him to disaster. Apparently deciding that the first news of this was a malicious conservative rumour, he descended on Pembrokeshire only to have the informant, who was, as he suspected, one of the leading anti-reformers, threaten him and declare that one as close to Anne as Barlow, must have been privy to her treason and should be arrested in case he made an escape by sea from Milford Haven! Fortunately for the dean, he kept his head and arrested the informant instead, making dark threats about papist sympathizers.

As the involvement of Thomas Cromwell in the Pembroke quarrels demonstrates, Anne Boleyn was not alone in her support for reform. She was one of a group of powerfully placed individuals whose loss was lamented in the early 1540s by Richard Hilles, a London merchant of reformist leanings who found England increasingly hot for him after the death of the queen: that group comprised Anne herself, Rochford, Cromwell (all dead), Latimer (resigned), and he could have added Shaxton too.[13] Other names were added in a later remark by John Foxe, who wrote of Henry VIII: 'So long as Queen Anne, Thomas Cromwell, Archbishop Cranmer, Master Denny, Doctor Butts, with such like were about him, and could prevail with him, what organ of Christ's glory did more good in the church than he?'[14] Rochford's support for reform had been particularly open;

[11] Foxe, *Acts and Monuments*, v.250.
[12] *LP*, viii.722.
[13] *The Zurich Letters*, ed. H. Robinson (Parker Society, 1842, 1845), i.200.
[14] Foxe, *Acts and Monuments*, v.605.

Chapuys hated being entertained by him because of his insistence on starting religious debates.[15] Anne's brother referred to this love in his speech on the scaffold, which was widely reported in England and abroad:

> I was a great reader and a mighty debater of the word of God, and one of those who most favoured the gospel of Jesus Christ. Wherefore, lest the word of God should be brought into reproach on my account, I now tell you all, Sirs, that if I had, in very deed, kept his holy word, even as I read and reasoned about it with all the strength of my wit, certain am I that I should not be in the piteous condition wherein I now stand. Truly and diligently did I read the gospel of Christ Jesus, but I turned not to profit that which I did read; the which, had I done, of a surety I had not fallen into so great errors. Wherefore I do beseech you all, for the love of our Lord God, that ye do at all seasons, hold by the truth, and speak it, and embrace it; for beyond all peradventure, better profiteth he who readeth not and yet doeth well, than he who readeth much and yet liveth in sin.

The final sentence has lost its freshness and part of its point in the course of translation. Constantine remembered Rochford's words 'to the effect' that 'I had rather had a good liver according to the gospel than ten babblers.'[16]

There is even a possibility that the Boleyns sought, or maintained, private links with reformers abroad. In 1535 and 1536 Master Thomas Tebold, later known as one of Cromwell's continental agents, was travelling in Europe supported by the earl of Wiltshire, with some assistance from Cranmer.[17] Very few of the regular letters he sent home have survived, but in July 1535 he was in Antwerp, reporting to Cranmer on his enquiries into the arrest of the translator William Tyndale. We may note, here, that Tyndale's landlord and principal supporter was

---

[15] *Cal. S. P. Span., 1536–38*, p. 91 [*LP*, x.699].

[16] Bentley, *Excerpta Historica*, p. 263; Constantine, in *Archaeologia*, 23.65; for the various versions of this speech see below, p. 391[20].

[17] Elton, *Reform and Renewal*, p. 23. The Tebold letters should be ordered: 31 July 1535 from Antwerp, dated by the return to England of Gabriel Donne; 9 Jan. 1536 from Orleans, dated by the reference to 'last Lent' and the new pope; 4 Apr. from Frankfurt, dated by the reference to Wolfe and the location of Charles V; post 12 Mar. from Frankfurt or Tübingen (?), dated by the enclosure and the reference to the invasion of Savoy: *LP*, viii.1151; ix.522; viii.33; iv.6304; x.458.

Thomas Poinz, the brother of John, one of Anne's receivers, who was used to pass to Cromwell appeals for Henry to intervene to save Tyndale, before Poinz too was arrested by the authorities at Brussels.[18] Tebold meanwhile had intended to go into Germany, but no doubt the Tyndale furore decided him on a detour to Orleans, unless, that is, he went there with the intention of reporting to the Boleyns, as he did on 9 January, on the current state of religious persecution in France where an impudent reformist propaganda campaign – the Affair of the Placards – had created a massive conservative backlash. His cover, if that is not too strong a term, was scholarship and a desire to study languages, and by the spring of 1536 he was travelling in southern and central Germany, including Wittenberg, meeting everyone who was anyone – amongst them, it seems, the Strassburg reformer, Martin Bucer – spreading the idea that Thomas Boleyn was a promising patron of works, theological and other, keeping up a flow of diplomatic news, and enlivening his hosts with suggestions about the advantages of dissolving monastic houses! He was also in touch with French reformers in flight from the Placards persecution, and was able to send back to Anne's father a piece published by Clément Marot.

The reforming group was, thus, wider than Anne alone, but it is clear that the queen was a key figure. Ales went so far as to say to Elizabeth I, 'True religion in England had its commencement and its end with your mother.'[19] This explains why both Cranmer and Shaxton were terrified in 1536 that she would bring down the cause of reform with her.[20] Already in 1532, Dr John London, one of the secretary's unlovelier clerical agents, was showing great anxiety to stand in her good books; in 1534 Cranmer asked an unknown correspondent to accelerate an appointment as a personal favour, but carefully hinted that he could provide letters from Henry and from Anne if forced to do so; when the archbishop wrote to Cromwell in 1535 of the need to plant reform in Calais, he reported that he had already written to Anne to secure the next two benefices that became vacant in the town.[21]

[18] For Poinz see ibid., ix.182, 405; Foxe, *Acts and Monuments*, v.121–7; *House of Commons*, iii.147.

[19] Ales, 'Letter', p. 532.

[20] See below, p. 372 and *LP*, x.942.

[21] See above, p. 193[31]; Cranmer, *Letters*, pp. 290–1; *LP*, ix.561.

The queen's concern for religion is especially well documented in the case of monastic houses. Soon after her coronation, one of the rival factions in the abbey at Burton-on-Trent was apparently expecting that Cromwell, under pressure from Henry and Anne, would countermand the orders he had already given for the election of a new abbot.[22] In 1533 she took action to get Cromwell to investigate conditions at Thetford Priory, and later that summer she was communicating with him about the abbey of Vale Royal in Cheshire.[23] All this certainly gives credibility to the stories told by her chaplain, William Latimer. If we accept his testimony, Anne was fully behind the campaign to impose new injunctions on the monastic houses, which Cromwell began in the summer of 1535.[24] One of these injunctions prohibited the display of 'relics or feigned miracles'. When, in the third week in July, Anne and Henry arrived on progress at Winchcombe in Gloucestershire, close to the famous pilgrim centre of Hailes Abbey, she sent a posse of her chaplains to the monastery to 'view, search and examine by all possible means' the bona fides of the house's greatest attraction, 'the blood of Hailes', which was supposed never to have congealed since Christ's crucifixion. They reported that it was duck's blood or wax, whereupon Anne went to the king, and the relic was removed – to the comfort, Latimer says, of ignorant and weak Christians, but one might rather suppose their bewilderment at a raid by such exalted sceptics. Unfortunately for Latimer's story, the relic was still there in 1538 when a more thorough inspection removed the contents and decided it was some kind of resin. It may still, however, be true that Anne did intervene at Hailes Abbey in 1535.[25] A visit to the house by Henry and Anne was undoubtedly intended, and that may have led to the abbot being interviewed

[22] *LP*, vi.700.

[23] Ibid., viii.834, 1056. The Vale Royal episode is confusing. According to Anne's letter (and others) the abbot was dead, but John Harware, abbot from 1529 and an abject creature of William Brereton, was still in post when the house was dissolved. One suspects some factional conflict: *LP*, vii.868, 1094 (*recte* 1535); viii.1056; x.1187; William Dugdale, *Monasticon* (1825), v.701–2, 711; Brereton, *Letters and Accounts*, pp. 31, 40–1, 103; Ives, in *Trans. Hist. Soc. Lancs. & Ches.*, 123. 24.

[24] For the following see Latimer, 'Treatyse', ff. 30v–31; Burnet, *History*, iv.221; *LP*, viii.989.

[25] For the following see Wriothesley, *Chronicle*, i.90; *LP*, vii.App.35; viii.989; ix.747, 1118; x.192; Knowles, *Religious Orders*, iii.352–3.

by Cromwell; certainly the secretary was involved with the community. There is even support for the possibility that Anne did achieve some temporary removal of the relic. When preaching about the deception in 1538 and announcing the latest findings, John Hilsey apologized for spreading the story that the material was duck's blood, which clearly implies an earlier questioning of the relic, and agrees exactly with one of the explanations William Latimer gives of what Anne was told.

One episode for which Latimer is the sole authority is the visit that Anne Boleyn paid to the nuns of Syon, that remarkable flower of English monasticism which combined aristocratic exclusiveness with genuine piety and serious learning.[26] The detail Latimer gives, however, does allow us to date the visit as in early December, at the end of the 1535 progress when the queen was at nearby Richmond, and so to establish the authenticity of the story, for at that time a major effort was being made to compel this prestigious community to accept the new order.[27] As well as lesser agents, Cromwell himself went down; and a day or so later, on Tuesday 14 December, John Skip, Anne's almoner, and Dr William Butts, the king's physician (of whom more anon), formed the first wave of a concentrated assault. The next day the king himself sent four high-powered academics, and Lord Windsor whose sister was a nun at Syon did what he could; on the Thursday the bishop of London arrived. On the Saturday a full report was given to the king, and it seems likely that Anne's visit was the outcome. Perhaps a woman, the queen herself, would have more success. She arrived when the nuns were in choir, to be refused entry on the ground that she was married and so excluded by the rule of the order. Anne declined to accept the answer and waited, with her attendants. Eventually the choir doors were opened and her party came in, only to discover all sixty or so nuns prostrate, with their faces fixedly 'downward to the ground'. Thereupon, if we are to believe Latimer, Anne addressed this unpromising audience with 'a brief exhortation' about the moral decline of the congregation – all sorts of slanders were being reported back to the court – and she also rebuked them for persisting with Latin primers which they could not

[26] Latimer, 'Treatyse', f. 31.
[27] For the following see Knowles, *Religious Orders*, iii.218–20; *LP*, ix.954, 906. Knowles [p. 216] is misled as to date: *LP*, ix.639, 850, 897.

understand, offering them English primers instead which, after some resistance, the nuns accepted. Throughout his memoir Latimer makes Anne appear painfully stilted, and the absurd pomposity of this speech invites disbelief; it is hardly effective to admonish the backs of an audience's heads and Anne, of all people, must have known that these daughters of the best families and of the most scholarly religious house in England were better Latinists than she! But whatever really happened, Anne's visit did not effect the desired conversion. We do not know that the nuns ever promised to accept the king's headship of the Church.

Anne Boleyn was even, if we follow Latimer's reminiscences, involved in the policy debate over the dissolution of the monasteries. He reports that her response to the news of the proposal to close the smaller houses was to send for Hugh Latimer and instruct him to suggest in his next sermon before the king that monasteries should not be dissolved but converted to better uses. Latimer chose to preach on Luke chapter 20, the parable of the vineyard, from which he drew the point that when the unsatisfactory tenants in the Gospel had been evicted, the vineyard was not destroyed but better tenants put in instead; the monasteries should be converted to 'places of study and good letters'. Other court preachers, too, received the same instructions.[28] This would fit very well with the known discussions which took place over the winter of 1535–6 on the nature and extent of monastic reform in England, and the reformers certainly did argue the case for conversion, not dissolution. Alexander Ales, who left England in 1539, did not know the story about Hugh Latimer, but he too was convinced that Anne had led the opposition to the total secularization of Church property.[29]

According to William Latimer, the sequel to Anne's intervention through these sermons was an appeal to the queen by a delegation of abbots and priors to seek her support against all dissolution. She read them instead a stern lecture on their notorious corruptions (parliament may well just have been treated to the more unfavourable reports which Cromwell's visitors had sent back), attacked them for their connections with

[28] Latimer, 'Treatyse', ff. 28v–30.
[29] J. Youings, *The Dissolution of the Monasteries* (1971), pp. 40–6; Ales, 'Letter', p. 526. Cf. Cranmer, *Letters*, p. 16; *Narratives of the Reformation*, p. 224.

Rome, for their refusal to admit the preachers of 'God's Word' and for the inadequate support they gave to scholars at the universities. The religious responded by attempting to remedy the last two matters, placing cash sums at Anne's disposal and transferring to her the right to present to the best Church livings in their gift – only for the whole programme to be aborted by her death. Whether matters were quite as clear or advanced as Latimer suggests we may doubt, not least because of the timing. The news of the proposed dissolution was out by 3 March 1536, only eight weeks before her arrest; the royal assent to the bill was given on 14 April.[30] On the other hand, it does seem that from the outset the crown expected that it would grant a number of exemptions, and it is certainly the case that immediately the royal assent was known, application was made to Anne through one of her servants for the preservation of the convent of Nun Monkton in Yorkshire.[31] One may note, too, that it was when Jane Seymour pleaded for the preservation of the religious houses that she was roughly warned by the king not to interfere in his affairs as her predecessor had done.[32] It is perfectly possible, therefore, that Anne was involved in initial discussions at the time of her death, which could have significantly reduced the waste of the country's charitable capital which was about to take place.

The particular agents of Anne's religious influence were unquestionably her chaplains whom she chose with care from the most promising young reformist scholars, particularly from Cambridge.[33] Her talent-spotter was Dr William Butts, who combined his privileged position as a medical man with an interest in reform and a concern for his former university, especially his old college, Gonville Hall. It was Butts who brought Latimer to court, where he became a chaplain to Anne and was on very good terms with her vice-chamberlain, Edward Baynton. Shaxton and Skip were Gonville men and so was Crome, whom we have already noticed. Sometimes Butts went direct to the king, as he did when he recommended for promotion, John Cheke (Edward VI's future tutor), but when Cheke

---

[30] *Lisle Letters*, iii.646 [*LP*, x.406].
[31] G. W. O. Woodward, 'The exemption from suppression of certain Yorkshire priories', in *EHR*, 76 (1961). 385–401; *LP*, xii(1). 786.
[32] Ibid., xi.1250.
[33] On this see especially Dowling, in *JEH*, 35. 35, 38–41.

sought support for the up-and-coming William Bill, later her daughter's almoner, Anne was the person he approached, via another of her chaplains, Matthew Parker.[34]

The queen's pursuit of Parker, who would end his career as Elizabeth's first archbishop of Canterbury, is particularly well documented. William Betts, another Gonville Hall man had moved to Corpus Christi and later became Anne's chaplain. Parker, also a Corpus man, was evidently commended to Anne by Betts, and on the latter's death she decided that Parker should succeed him. No time was lost. Her almoner John Skip wrote two letters on the same day, urging him to come at once without bothering to collect much baggage – a long gown would do.[35] Six months demonstrated how well she had chosen. The king sent Parker, 'chaplain to our dearest wife', a doe to enjoy; and Anne gave him something more permanent, the post of dean of the collegiate church of Stoke by Clare in Suffolk.[36] He preached to the household of the princess Elizabeth, and then before Henry on the third Sunday in Lent 1536.[37] Whether Cranmer gave him the advice about preaching that he gave to Latimer is not known – not to grind any axes, not to get at individuals, and not to go on too long: 'an hour, or an hour and a half at the most, for by long expense of time the king and the queen shall peradventure wax so weary at the beginning [of the series of sermons] that they shall have small delight to continue throughout with you to the end.'[38] Probably Parker had sense enough to tell how much Anne could stand, for their relationship of patron and client, laywoman and Christian pastor, was evidently sympathetic. As we have seen, less than six days before her arrest, Anne seems to have laid a particular responsibility on him to watch over her daughter. That charge, and the debt he felt he owed to Anne, stayed with him for the rest of his life.[39]

Cranmer's advice to be cautious in sermons was wise, for Anne's clerical favourites were very much marked men. Even when they kept away from contentious religious matters, any slip would be pounced on, as John Skip discovered when preaching

---

[34] *House of Commons*, i.626–9; Parker. *Correspondence*, pp. 2–3.
[35] Ibid., pp. 1–2.
[36] Ibid., pp. 4–5.
[37] Ibid., p. ix.
[38] Cranmer, *Letters*, p. 308.
[39] Parker, *Correspondence*, pp. 59, 391, 400; see above, p. 272.

in the Chapel Royal almost a fortnight before the end of the Reformation Parliament. A sermon which apparently contained a good deal in defence of tradition in the Church and the insistence that all the clergy must not be condemned for the fault of individuals got him into hot water nevertheless when it moved on to deal with the morality and integrity of parliament, the council and the leaders of society.[40] Several of Anne's men were, indeed, men with a past. William Betts had been associated with the scandal at Wolsey's college in Oxford in 1528 over the circulation of prohibited books; at the time Anne herself had interceded with Wolsey for one of the others involved, who may have been Thomas Garret who was burned at the stake in 1540. A number were also associated with the martyr Thomas Bilney: notably Latimer, and Parker, who saw Bilney die.[41]

Yet it would be wrong to picture Anne as a patron of a tight and unified caucus. The clergy she supported differed among themselves – Edward Fox, Hilsey and possibly Cranmer found Latimer far too extreme at times – and although some would end their lives as martyrs for 'Protestantism', others such as Shaxton would find their place among the upholders of 'Catholic' ways.[42] Such confessional labels are, in fact, quite inappropriate to England in the 1520s and 1530s. When Anne first began to patronize the more innovative clergy of the day, Luther's ninety-five theses were hardly more than a decade old; the very episode which led to the coining of the name 'Protestant' only occurred two months before the opening by Wolsey and Campeggio of the legatine court at Blackfriars. Even on the continent, lines were in the course of being drawn – among reformers, as well as between reformers and conservatives – for within nine months of the Protestant 'protestation', reform had been disrupted by a disagreement about the nature of the eucharist which would produce permanent division. There would henceforth be Catholics, Lutherans and sacramentaries, as well as 'anabaptists', that inchoate religious self-help minority which added withdrawal from established society and its obligations to the sacramentarian belief that the bread and wine at the eucharist were a symbol of

---

[40] Lehmberg, *Reformation Parliament*, pp. 244–5; *LP*, x.615.

[41] Dowling, in *JEH*, 35. 36–7.

[42] For Hilsey see *LP*, vi.433(iii). Shaxton, having resigned his bishopric in 1539 because of the apparently reactionary Statute of Six Articles, recanted heretical opinions in 1546 and died in 1556 as a suffragan bishop reconciled to Rome. Latimer also resigned in 1539 and was burned as a heretic in 1555.

Christ's death and not, in some real sense, Christ's own body and blood. With London being four hundred and fifty miles and two languages away from this turmoil of definition, to say nothing of an admittedly imperfect but nevertheless highly active English censorship, it is appropriate to see still only two general positions in England – that the Church needed to be supported as it was, and that the Church as it was needed to be reformed – around which and between which most individuals ranged with varying levels of commitment.

What then did reform mean to Anne Boleyn? Chapuys damned her, her father and her brother as Lutherans, but he was probably not implying any direct link, merely a similarity in error. There is no hint, either, that Anne had links with previous English heresy, although Latimer was accused of being a Lollard, and there were certainly congruences between the new critics of the Church and the persecuted underground which looked back to John Wycliffe. Anne's central conviction was of the overwhelming importance of the Bible. For that reason, if her brand of reform needs to be given a label, that label is 'evangelical' – 'pertaining to the gospel, and especially to the written gospel'.

First of all, Anne talked about the Bible, just like her brother. William Latimer describes her habit of discussing some scriptural problem whenever she dined with Henry, and said that this was copied at the tables of her chamberlain and vice-chamberlain.[43] From time to time Henry would join in, and Latimer had himself seen the correspondence which arose out of one debate between the king and Sir James Boleyn on one side and Hugh Latimer and Nicholas Shaxton on the other. Scriptural debate at table is hardly in favour today, but it was certainly the thing among sixteenth-century evangelical hostesses. Katherine Parr, Henry's last wife, also encouraged the king's taste for this latest in intellectual stimulus.

Anne helped to disseminate the Bible. According to Latimer, she kept an English version on a lectern in her suite for anyone to read who wished.[44] If strictly true, this must refer to the final months of her life, since Coverdale's Bible did not appear until 1535 in Zurich. On the other hand, Anne's copy of Tyndale's

[43] Latimer, 'Treatyse', f. 31v.
[44] Ibid., f. 31v.

1534 edition of the New Testament is still extant (plate 32).[45] On vellum, with the capital letters hand-coloured in red and many of the woodcuts in full colour, it looks very like a presentation copy. The exiled Bible translators did certainly try to secure royal patronage; George Joye, a former associate of Tyndale, printed a sample sheet from Genesis and sent a copy to Henry and one to Anne.[46] The significant point about the Tyndale is that it was a banned book in England; one conservative cleric had declared soon after the first edition that no one who received it could be a true son of the Church.[47] Coverdale's work, too, would be banned when it appeared, despite the unofficial dedication to Henry.

Evidently the queen was confident enough of herself to defy established ecclesiastical authority in her own household. And not just there, for Anne was perfectly ready to protect the illegal trade in Bibles. It was probably as early as the end of 1530 that one Thomas Alwaye prepared to approach her in the hope that she would get the bishops off his back, following his arrest and imprisonment for possessing an English testament and other prohibited books.[48] A year after she became queen she put in hand the restoration of the Antwerp merchant, Richard Herman, to membership of the English society of merchants there, from which he had been expelled in Wolsey's time, 'only for that that he [still like a good Christian man] did both with his goods and policy, to his great hurt and hinderance in this world, help the setting forth of the New Testament in English.'[49] It has also been suggested that Anne may have been behind the licensing of a Southwark printer from the Low Countries to produce the Coverdale text in England, and therefore free of the dangerous glosses which foreign books so often carried. Add to that the possibility that the drafts of the injunctions to the clergy issued in 1536 had included, so long as she was alive, a clause requiring every parish to set up a Latin and an English Bible in its church, 'for every man that will to look and read thereon'.[50]

---

[45] *The newe Testament* (Antwerp, 1534) [BL, C23 a8].

[46] *LP*, vi.458.

[47] Ibid., iv.3960.

[48] BL, Sloane MS 1207 ff. iv, 3. The petition is only in draft, mixed up among other jottings. That it was actually presented can only be assumed.

[49] Ellis, *Letters*, 1 ii.46.

[50] A. G. Dickens, *The English Reformation* (1964), p. 131. A tradition exists that Anne Boleyn presented to her ladies miniature psalters or prayer books,

So Anne Boleyn talked about the Bible and disseminated the Bible. She also read it. Here, as Latimer says quite correctly, her private preference was for the French text:

> Her highness was very expert in the French tongue, exercising herself continually in reading the French Bible and other French books of like effect and conceived great pleasure in the same, wherefore her highness charged her chaplains to be furnished of all kind of French books that reverently treated of the holy scripture.[51]

A vivid picture of this was drawn by Louis de Brun, author of 'Vng Petit Traicte en Francoys', a treatise on letter-writing, which he dedicated to Anne at New Year 1530:

> When I consider the great affection and real passion which you have for the French tongue, I am not surprised that you are never found, if circumstances permit, without your having some book in French in your hand which is of use and value in pointing out and finding the true and narrow way to all virtues, as, for example, translations of the Holy Scriptures, reliable and full of all sound doctrines, or, equally, of other good books by learned men who give healthy advice for this mortal life and consolation for the immortal soul. And most of all, last Lent and the Lent before, when I was attending this magnificent, excellent and triumphant court, I have seen you continually reading those helpful letters of

---

and that one of these was given by her on the scaffold to a member of the Wyatt family. There is nothing impossible in this – tiny religious books were the height of female fashion – but the tradition is only identifiable from the early eighteenth century and was not known to George Wyatt. Two such have been identified with this story: (1) BL, Stowe MS 956, formerly in the collection of the earl of Ashburnham, a metrical version of thirteen penitential psalms translated into English by John Croke. The frontispiece is a miniature of Henry VIII after the Holbein privy chamber pattern (i.e. post-1537). Hist. Mss. Comm. *Eighth Report*, iii (1881) suggested that the miniature was an addition; this is not taken up by BL, *Catalogue of Stowe Mss*, and H. Tait, 'Historiate Tudor jewellery', in *Antiquaries Journal* 42 (1962), 234–5 accepts dating by the image of the king. (2) A MS owned by the earl of Romney in 1873, edited and described by his brother, Robert Marsham, in *Archaeologia* 44 (1873), 259–72, English prayers and psalms in prose. Item 10 [pp. 270–1] is the prayer attributed to Thomas Cromwell on the scaffold [Foxe, *Acts and Monuments*, v.403]. Neither book, therefore, can have been owned by Anne. Marsham, in a letter now pasted in Alnwick, Percy MS 465 (see above, p. 289), claimed that the Ashburnham MS [now Stowe 956] was the same described by R. Triphook in his edition of George Wyatt, *Life of Anne Boleigne* (1817).

[51] Latimer, 'Treatyse', f. 32.

St. Paul which contain all the fashion and rule to live righteously, in every good manner of behaviour, which you know well and practise, thanks to your continual reading of them.[52]

A number of individuals were involved in the search for books. We have seen Thomas Tebold. William Lok the mercer ran errands for her on his trips to the Low Countries, and his daughter remembered in her eighties how 'Queen Anne Boleyn that was mother to our late Queen Elizabeth caused him to get her the gospels and epistles written in parchment in French, together with the psalms.'[53] William Latimer himself was on such a book-buying trip when Anne was arrested.[54] No doubt it was Lok, Latimer or another agent who brought the French Bible owned by Henry and Anne which is part of the collection of the British Library.[55] It is a copy of the 1534 Antwerp edition of the translation by the French reformer Jacques Lefèvre d'Etaples, and still has part of the binding which was put on when it first reached England (see plate 33). There are 'HA' ciphers and Tudor roses, and a decidedly evangelical choice of texts for the front and back of each of its two volumes:

AINSI + QUE + TOVS + MEVRENT + PAR + ADAM:
AVSSY + TOVS + SERONT + VIVIFIES + PAR +CHRIST.

LA + LOY + A + ESTE + DONNEE + PAR + MOYSSE:
LA + GRACE + ET + LA + VERITE + PAR + IESV +CHRIST.

The full-page frontispiece of the creation is coloured.

Two of what Latimer called 'French books of like effect' have already caught our attention among Anne's illuminated manuscripts: 'The Ecclesiaste' and 'The Pistellis and Gospelles for the LII Sondayes in the Yere'. Each offers a scriptural text in French and a commentary in English, but in both cases the commentary is a translation from a French original. 'The Ecclesiaste' is known in an edition published at Alençon, with a conjectural date of *c*.1530 but with the author still to be identified.[56] 'The

---

[52] BL, Roy. MS 20.B xvii f. 1.
[53] J. Shakespeare and M. Dowling, 'Religion and politics in mid-Tudor England', in *BIHR*, 55 (1982), 97; cf. *LP*, viii.197.
[54] Ibid., x.827.
[55] *La Saincte Bible en Francoys* (Antwerp, 1534) [BL, C18 c9].
[56] *Lecclesiaste Preschant que toutes chose sans dieu sont vanite* (Alençon, 1530?).

Pistellis and Gospelles', however, can again be firmly attributed to the premier figure in French evangelical circles, Lefèvre d'Etaples, who had published it in Paris around 1525.[57] The translator of the commentary into English is also known: Henry Parker, Lord Morley, George Boleyn's father-in-law, who was later to side with tradition but at this time was aligned with evangelical reform.[58] Indeed, the dedication to Anne claims not only a blood relationship but also that his work had been commissioned specially by her.[59] Why, since Anne was fluent in French, she should want such hybrids can only be guessed at. It may simply be that she had become accustomed to the French text while abroad, and continued to use it in England where English translations of the Bible were banned. Beyond this, the retention of the French text could, perhaps, suggest some intention to evade that prohibition. Yet we have seen this was ignored by Anne as far as she herself was concerned, and the possibility that she had in mind letting these books circulate outside her immediate protection is ruled out by the elite quality of the manuscripts, especially 'The Ecclesiaste'. An explanation, however, is suggested by that high quality. This required a professional scriptorium and an illuminators' studio, and it might well be that neither was prepared to handle an English biblical text for fear of prosecution.

To recognize the dominant place in life which Anne Boleyn gave to the Bible is to locate her faith firmly in the world of Christian humanism. For a man like Erasmus, the premier Christian humanist of all, the Bible, in as reliable a form as scholarship could produce, was central to all good living:

> If you approach the scriptures in all humility and with regulated caution, you will perceive that you have been breathed upon by the Holy Will of God. It will bring about a transformation that is impossible to describe . . . Man may lie and make mistakes; the truth of God neither deceives nor is deceived.[60]

---

[57] *Les Choses contenu en ce present livre* (Paris, 1525?).

[58] McConica, *English Humanists*, pp. 152–8.

[59] BL, Harl. MS 6561, ff. 2, 2v. For the tradition identifying Morley as the translator see Add. MS 20768, f. 4.

[60] Erasmus, *Enchiridion Militis Christiani* (1503), quoted from *The Essential Erasmus*, ed. J. P. Dolan (New York, 1964), p. 37.

Erasmus, indeed, was aware of Anne. Already he had translated the Twenty-second Psalm for her father, but when in 1533 he wrote two more pieces dedicated to the earl, *A Preparation to Death* and *A Plain and Godly Exposition or Declaration of the Common Creed*, he began the latter:

> To the right excellent and most honourable lord, Thomas earl of Wiltshire and of Ormonde, father to the most gracious and virtuous Queen Anne, wife to the most gracious sovereign lord, King Henry the VIIIth, Erasmus of Rotterdam, Greeting![61]

Yet Anne's particular religious affinity was with the Christian humanists of France. The version of the Bible and 'The Pistellis and Gospelles' by the first great evangelical figure in France, Jacques Lefèvre d'Etaples; 'The Ecclesiaste' also from a French evangelical original; the copy of *Le Pasteur Evangélique* by the poet Clément Marot, one of the enduring lights of the movement – all put this beyond question. The verses added to the presentation copy of Marot's poem celebrated Henry as Francis I's constant friend, endowed with the virtue of true riches, one of the great Christian kings of the day, a true reforming Hezekiah; as for Anne, she would be given by the Good Shepherd [Christ] a son in Henry's image, whom they would live to see grow into manhood.[62] If Marot was the author of the additions, then we can date the text between Anne's coronation and the poet's flight from France late in 1534, pursued by name as a leading 'Lutheran' – the pejorative label the conservatives gave to all reform.[63] And this tells us how Anne's crown appeared to the Christian humanists of her adopted country. With her beside him, Henry was now a figure of evangelical hope for Europe.

There was reality in this. Latimer tells of Anne coming to the immediate rescue of a French refugee, Mistress Mary, who had fled to England to escape persecution, and of her efforts to get John Sturm, the future Strassburg educator, out of Paris on a safe-conduct.[64] Most notable of all, however, were her efforts on

---

[61] *Enarratio in Psalmum xxii* (Freiburg, 1530); *De praeparatione ad mortem* (Freiburg, 1533), translated as *A preparation to deathe* (Berthelet, 1538) [the quotation is from sig.Aiv.]; *Explanatio Symboli* (Freiburg, 1533), translated as *A playne and godly exposytion or declaration of the commune crede* (Redman, 1533).
[62] BL Roy. MS 16 E 13, ff. 15, 15v.
[63] Knecht, *Francis I*, p. 251.
[64] Latimer, 'Treatyse', ff. 28–9.

behalf of Nicholas Bourbon. Borbonius, as he called himself in suitable humanist fashion, was the son of an ironmaster from Champagne, a noted neo-Latin poet and schoolmaster, and a man prominent among that first generation of French evangelical reformers who from the 1520s had as their patroness the king's sister, Marguerite of Navarre.[65] He was in touch with Erasmus, enjoyed an old acquaintance with Guillaume Bude, the premier Greek scholar in France, knew Clément Marot intimately, and also Gérard Roussel, one of the original members of that early evangelical preaching team, the Cercle de Meaux, and later Marguerite's almoner. Bourbon joined Marguerite's household himself in 1529 as tutor to her infant daughter Jeanne d'Albret, the future mother of Henry IV.

Despite or, rather, only because of the protection of the king's sister, this group lived dangerously, watched for every false move by the die-hard conservatives of the Sorbonne and its ally, the *parlement* of Paris; and while the Affair of the Placards saw Marot scamper abroad, Bourbon was slower or less lucky. His first book of epigrams, the *Nugae*, published at Paris in 1533, had contained a scathing attack on the enemies of the humanist 'new learning', and this was quite enough to get him arrested and gaoled – during which time he lost all his possessions, including his pet nightingale.[66] News of his plight reached England, conveyed to William Butts possibly by Jean de Dinteville, a patron of French reform and a former French ambassador in England.[67] Bourbon may even have sent an appeal for transmission to Anne:

> A poor man, I lie shut up in this dark prison:
> There is no one who would be able or who would dare to bring
>   help:
> You alone, Oh Queen: you, Oh noble nymph, both can and
>   dare:
> As one whom the king and whom God himself loves.[68]

[65] M. M. Philips, 'The *Paedagogion* of Nicolas Bourbon', in *Neo-Latin and the Vernacular in Sixteenth-Century France*, ed. T. Cave (1983), pp. 71–82.

[66] Bourbon produced two best-sellers: *Nicolai Borbonii Vanderoperani Nugae* (Paris, 1533) and *Nugarum Libri Octo* (Lyons, 1538).

[67] Butts was the contact and Dinteville was Bourbon's patron [*Nugarum*, v.21, pp. 284–5, vii.113, p. 409] but the link was by letter if at all, for the poet was in England by May 1535 and the ambassador did not arrive until the autumn.

[68] *Nugarum*, vii.90, p. 402.

Butts informed Anne, and Henry intervened in France on Bourbon's behalf. The poet then found himself having to travel to England, an experience which he did not enjoy, but once here, he lodged with Butts at Anne's expense.[69] His verses show how quickly he became part of the evangelical scene: Cromwell, 'aflame with the love of Christ'; Cranmer, a gift from God, 'a head to his people'; Butts, 'my Maecenas and my father'; Holbein, 'the incomparable painter'; Latimer, 'the best of preachers', and above all, Anne.

> For no crime, but through a false charge
> Brought by certain people and their hatred, I was shut up in
>   prison.
> I was praying for all good fortune for those who afflicted me:.
> Why? I kept unshaken hope and faith.
> Then your pity lighted upon me from the ends of the earth,
> Snatching me in my affliction, Anna, away from all my troubles.
> If this had not happened, I should be chained in that darkness,
> Unhappily languishing, still under restraint.
> Express my thanks, still less, Oh Queen, repay you,
> How can I? I confess I have not the resources.
> But the Spirit of Jesus which enflames you wholly with his fire,
> He has enough to give you satisfaction.[70]

One might even speculate that Bourbon might have had something to do with the presentation of *Le Pasteur Evangélique*.

Anne's tastes were formed in France, but France before the evangelical movement got under way; Anne knew Marguerite of Navarre, but before the latter's religious enthusiasm had been roused. How then did she come to an involvement with French evangelicals? Even more elusive, how does the Anne whom Bourbon saw as 'a divine helper' whom God used to feed the afflicted, relate to the 'haughty' Anne of the 1520s, described by Cavendish? If we are to believe Latimer, Madge Shelton, one of the maids of honour, got into the hottest of hot water with Anne when it was discovered that her prayer book had 'idle poesies' written in it, and yet this scandalized queen, when herself a lady-

---

[69] Latimer. 'Treatyse', ff. 28, 28v. For Butts, see also *Nugarum*, ii.pp. 86–8.
[70] Ibid., iv.81, p. 251; viii.19, p. 377; vii.113, p. 409; vi.13, p. 338; vii.36, p. 384; vii.119, p. 411.

in-waiting, had exchanged love notes with the king on the pages of her (or his) book of hours![71]

Circumstances and ages do alter cases. We must recognize also that William Latimer is committed to portraying Anne as the archetypal 'godly matron'. We must remember too that self-interest and ambition – and Anne had both – forced her to align herself against traditional Christianity. Nevertheless there is the possibility that there was a religious side to Anne that does not come out in the early evidence, or that her experience of Christianity underwent a change. Her earliest-known religious book is a traditional Latin work of devotion; all the later ones are works of evangelical faith in French and English.[72] Anne had, after all, a grounding in French culture and an awareness of the new learning; she was attended by the most winning of spiritual directors, such as Latimer and Parker; she was close to her brother, who had the same kind of evangelical interests and plenty of opportunity to meet French Christian humanism at the court of Francis I during his diplomatic visits; she had a brain, and the burning intellectual issue of the day was the nature of religious experience; her personal confrontation was with the power of traditional ecclesiastical authority to frustrate her own private convictions. Why should we not allow her some true religious experience?

The works which Anne read – apart from the Bible where we know she had, significantly, an interest in Paul's epistles – are certainly redolent of a Christianity of faith and not of routine observance. The comment of 'The Ecclesiaste' on the final injunction in the text, 'Fear God and keep his commandments for this is the whole duty of man', is worth quotation at length.[73] The order of priorities in the text is, the *annotation* says, crucial; the fear of God is the necessary precondition for all obedience:

For faith which giveth the true fear of God, is it that doth prepare us for to keep the commandments well, and maketh us good workmen, for to make good works; and maketh us good trees for to bear [f.147v] good fruit. Then if we be not first well prepared, made good workmen, and made good trees we may not look to do

[71] Latimer, 'Treatyse', ff. 31v, 32; see above, pp. 7–8.
[72] See above, pp. 292–3; if the Book of Hours [BL, King's MS 9] was hers and not Henry's, then there are two early traditional books.
[73] Alnwick, Percy MS 465, ff. 147–8.

the least of the commandments. Therefore Moses giving the commandments for the beginning said: 'Harken Israel, thy God is one god', which is as much as to say as, believe, have faith, for without faith God doth not profit us, nor we can accomplish nothing: but the faith in God, and in our Lord Jesuchrist is it which chiefly doth relieve us from the transgressions that be passed of the sentence of the law, and yieldeth us innocents, and in such manner that none can demand of us anything, for because that faith hath gotten us Jesuchrist, and maketh him our own, he having accomplished the law, and satisfied unto all transgressions. Then faith having reconciled us unto the Father, doth get us also the Holy Ghost. Which yieldeth witness in our hearts that we be the sons of God. Whereby engendereth in us true childerly fear, and putteth away all servile and hired fear. And then it sheddeth in our hearts the fire of love and dilection, by the means whereof we be well prepared for to keep the law of God, which is but love: and [f.148] without the which it is aswell possible for us to keep the said commandments, as unto the ice to abide warming and burning in the fire. For our hearts (without this fire of the Holy Ghost) be over hard frozen and cooled, and overmuch founded and rooted in the love of ourselves.

For a man who would avoid eternal damnation, 'there is nothing better than by true faith to take Jesuchrist of our side for pledge, mediator, advocate and intercessor. For who that believeth in him and doth come with him to this judgment, shall not be confused.'[74] If this was Anne Boleyn's understanding of faith, if this was her experience of faith, then she was an evangelical by conviction and not just by policy.

For a writer to be able to turn the book of Ecclesiastes, with its refrain 'Vanity, vanity, all is vanity', into a paean to faith is a remarkable testimony to evangelical determination. The other great concerns of Christian humanism are to be found here also. First, concern for the Bible and its proper scholarly interpretation. 'We have been too long without all the Holy Scripture', so that the 'doctrines of men' have been embraced.[75] Before 'the books of men' are read, one 'must have read the true rule of the great architector or master workman', that is, the Bible.[76] Too many books by the unwise have led to 'pernicious sermons'.[77]

[74] Ibid., f. 148.
[75] Ibid., f. 146v
[76] Ibid., f. 146.
[77] Ibid., f. 145v.

The true wisdom of God is given irrespective of age, status or wealth: 'Say not then: "he is a pope, he is an emperor, he is a king, he is ancient, wilt not thou believe and follow him?"'[78] Nevertheless it is the responsibility of kings and princes, one they have neglected, to govern their realms not only by 'iron and sword' (which by themselves produce 'subjects like bondmen') but by 'good doctrine':

> If it had been so in times past, the holy Word of God should not have been so long hid, nor out of use and in the stead of the same so many superfluous and unprofitable books and curious vain questions brought forth which serve not only to lose time but they be clean contrary from the true and pure truth.[79]

There is, too, the message of the Renaissance that life is good, and fulfilment a grace of God: 'Worldly goods, honour, puissance, joy, voluptuousness, health and all the other things . . . be good and gifts of God.'[80] Certainly to abandon oneself 'unto all voluptuousness and delights' is 'to be out of the wit [crazy]', but the world of ascetic renunciation is far away:

> Should I say for all this that it is prohibited for to be merry and that Jesuchrist hath only chosen sturdy people: seeing that he himself hath helped at feasts: specially that in the law was promised the rejoicing under the fig tree? No surely. But at such joys we may not bring forth Adam but Jesuchrist that is to say we should rejoice in the Lord which we find merciful and from whose hand we receiveth his gifts and blessings.[81]

One is reminded in this of Anne's evident delight in fine things and in pomp and pageantry, and of the tone of the remarks attributed to her by William Latimer about the glory of princes.

We also find the Christian humanist concern to exploit rhetoric for effective communication; classical allusions as illustrations; popular sayings; homely illustrations like the parallel between the endless thirst of the diabetic and the vain pursuit of wordly reason ('there is no means for to have the perfectness and

[78] Ibid., f. 40.
[79] Ibid., ff. 144v–45.
[80] Ibid., f. 3.
[81] Ibid., f. 13.

certainty in all things but by true faith'); even an attempt to translate Solomon's revenue into contemporary coinage.[82] Practical application is there too – an application which Anne could accept for herself. She could well reflect after her coronation on the rightness of this sentiment about marriage, based on Ecclesiastes chapter 3, verses 1–8:

> Then it is unto God that we must lift up our eyes when one goeth about to be married. If it be ordained that thou shalt have her, she shall be thine without thy care; if it be not ordained thou losest thy pain. And this place here is to put aside the foolish love with all the hard anguish and cares thereof. When it is time for to seek, truly without doubt thou shalt find, or else thou losest thy pain. Wherefore we may attribute nothing unto ourselves but we must put all in to the hands of God.[83]

Whether she would have felt the same about an earlier section on the subject, if it had arrived during her long courtship, one cannot know: 'When God joineth then it is time to embrace and to use the fruit of marriage; and if he do not join, neither care nor labour shall not prevail.'[84] Or after marriage, about the arrival of children: 'Sara with great desire did as much as to her was possible for to have children, but she lost her time for that time was determined by God. In likewise Rachel was frustrate of her desire unto the time determined by God.'[85]

In all this there is no word of the role of the Church, of the priest, of the whole structure of sacraments, which command our attention when we look at established Christianity at the time. This does not mean that a woman like Anne who entertained such writings was hostile to matters of that kind. It was a question of priorities. Sometimes, it is true, a passage may have critical implications, as in the commentary in 'The Pistellis and Gospelles' on Hebrews chapter 9, which deals with the sacrificial death of Christ, re-presented every time a priest consecrated the host (that is, sacrifice) at mass. Anne's book says: 'The true host

---

[82] E.g. ibid., ff. 34 [Hydra], 38 ['the hand washeth the hand'], 7 [dropsy = diabetes], 15 ['crowns of the sun']. BL, Harl. MS 6561 'Pistellis and Gospelles' has a scholarly note at f. 13: 'some read Bethania, but the word is corrupt, said for Betharia.'

[83] Alnwick, Percy MS 465, f. 25v.

[84] Ibid., f. 25v.

[85] Ibid., f. 24.

is Jesu Christ which hath suffered death and passion for to save us, the which in shedding his precious blood upon us all, hath given unto us life and hath wholly purged us of sin.'[86] But this is intended as a corrective, not as a denial of the established Christian teaching on the mass, which Anne continued to revere.

The evangelical position in England in these years was one which saw itself winning the Church back to the inwardness of true religion and to the spiritual realities which underlay its fossilized formality; its task was breathing life into dead bones, not burying them. Hence it was that when Tristram Revell early in 1536 tried to dedicate to the queen a translation of a work by the renegade friar, François Lambert of Avignon, which denied the sacrifice of the mass, Anne refused the request.[87] Her attitude would be characteristic of all shades of English evangelical reform for at least a decade more: real spiritual experience, yes; the priority of faith, yes; access to the Bible, yes; reform of abuses and superstition, yes; but heretical views on the miracle of the altar, no.[88] In contrast to Revell whom she rejected, she patronized Richard Tracy, whose father's body had been exhumed and burned in 1531 because his will had implied disbelief in the Church's ability to serve the needs of departed souls – a 'superstition' which was increasingly coming under reformist questioning.[89] In the same way she was willing to intervene for Thomas Patmore, who had been imprisoned following his recantation of heresies, principally about that other issue of contemporary debate, clerical marriage.[90]

Anne Boleyn was held up by future generations of Protestants as a model in another of the concerns of Christian humanists: response to the poor. 'The Ecclesiaste' touched particularly on the responsibility of the elite:

The court of kings, princes, chancellors, judging places and audiences be the places where one ought to find equity and

[86] BL, Harl. MS 6561, f. 74.

[87] *LP*, x.371; Dowling, in *JEH*, 35. 44.

[88] Cf. BL, Harl. MS 6561: f. 15, which has no reference to Mary in the exhortation for Christmas Day; ff. 16v–17, St Stephen's Day, stresses that Stephen is not honoured, but 'the Lord for the grace he gave Stephen' and 'the wisdom and spirit of God that did speak in him'. 'It is God and our Lord Jesuchrist that we ought to call upon and not angels or any other creatures, and it is he to whom we ought to commend our souls.'

[89] *LP*, xii(2). 1304.

[90] Ibid., viii.1063.

justice. But, oh good Lord, where is there more injustice, more exactions, more oppressions of poor widows and orphans, where is there more disorder in all manners and more greater company of unjust men than there, whereas should be but all good order and just people of good and holy example of life.[91]

Again it is Latimer who provides the detail, with some corroboration from elsewhere.[92] He tells of Anne giving standing orders for the relief of the deserving poor – needy and impotent householders with large families – and for the prompt handling of petitioners, under threat of her personal intervention. The purses at the royal maundy were substantially increased. The ladies of her household spent considerable amounts of time sewing clothes which were taken on progress and distributed to the poor at each stopping place, with a shilling a head, by arrangement with the local priest and two parishioners; pregnant women received a pair of sheets and two shillings. Individual cases of misfortune might be reported by a chaplain, especially if the person concerned was of the right religious emphasis; one specific story concerns a parishioner of Hugh Latimer who was brought to Anne's attention after the death of most of his cattle. When the queen arrived at Sir Edward Baynton's house nearby – which dates the episode to about the end of August in the progress of 1535 – she interviewed the man's wife and gave an initial gift of £20.[93]

John Foxe appears to be responsible for the elaboration of this charity into the fantastic suggestion that in three quarters of a year Anne distributed £14,000 or £15,000 in poor relief.[94] Such a sum is twelve times larger than the annual surplus on Anne's expenditure. He does, however, also suggest that she was involved in a scheme to establish stocks of materials in various places to enable the poor to be given work, and this is by no means so far-fetched. In 1536 parliament passed a bill which attempted to tackle the pressing problem of poverty.[95] It was an

[91] Alnwick, Percy MS 465, f. 30.
[92] Latimer, 'Treatyse', ff. 25–7.
[93] Ibid., ff. 27v–28; *LP*, ix.186.
[94] Foxe, *Acts and Monuments*, v.135; George Wyatt, in *Wolsey*, ed. Singer, p. 443, repeats this, but also says that Anne's 'ordinary' disposed on the poor came to £1,500 p.a. This is exaggerated, but within the bounds of possibility, and suggests that Foxe elaborated an elaboration by adding a zero.
[95] 27 Henry VIII, *c*.25.

important measure, but by no means as innovative as original drafts and plans which were worked up for Cromwell by one of his assistants, William Marshall.[96] Marshall was associated with Anne, and it was he who translated the *Plain and Godly Exposition of the Common Creed* which Erasmus had written for Thomas Boleyn, with the special intention of making it suitable for circulation among the less educated.[97] In 1535, the same year as the poor law drafts, he dedicated to Anne a practical work on the treatment of poverty in Flanders, *The Form and manner of subvention or helping for poor people, devised and practised in the city of Ypres.*[98] The dedication deliberately invited Anne to persuade Henry to set up relief of a similar sort, and we may note that Marshall's drafts include the specific statement that the king had offered to make £3,000 available for poor relief. The origin of Foxe's story?

If there was one hope that buoyed up all Christian humanists, swept along as they were by events towards the rocks of the establishment and the reefs of worldly realities which would eventually break them, it was that education would rescue them and society together. It is no surprise, therefore, to find Anne Boleyn active in education and scholarship, as well as in the other concerns we have seen. Comparatively few literary dedications to Anne are so far known, other than those already noted, which probably reflects the shortness of her period as marchioness and queen, rather than anything else.[99] She did, however, appear under her father's name at the head of a work by Robert Wakefield, one of the older generation of humanists. The *Kotser Codicis R. Wakfeldi* was an impressive demolition of the validity of Henry's first marriage by a scholar of some reputation, who as early as 1519 had been professor of Hebrew at Busleiden's College at Louvain. The dedication makes clear Wakefield's move from earlier conservative patronage to reliance on the whole Boleyn family: Thomas, his wife, 'the daughter of each of you, our Queen Anne in whose happiness I rejoice exceedingly', and her uncle James, and there are dark references to a former benefactor, 'ungrateful, harsh, inhuman and unfair', who owed nearly £100 in lost payments of an annuity, a sum

---

[96] Elton, *Reform and Renewal*, pp. 71–6.
[97] McConica, *English Humanists*, p. 137; see above, p. 319.
[98] Dowling in *JEH*, 35. 41.
[99] For Anne as a subject for courtly verse see above, pp. 83–97, 173–5.

which he hints the Boleyns might enforce.[100] Perhaps the earliest author who gambled on Anne in her own right was de Brun, whose dedication is to 'Madame Anne de Rochfort', Anne's title after her father became an earl in December 1529. The manuscript is prepared for the illuminator but never begun, which is strange considering how long it remained in Anne's hands. Why it should have been left incomplete is not known. Apart from the religious appeal we have seen already, the book stresses its practical utility, explaining how various individuals should be addressed, depending on the status of the writer. It is a neat compliment that the examples of addressing a superior range from the Holy Father the pope, to the king, the bishop of London and Monsieur de Rochfort![101]

If the weight of literary dedications to Anne Boleyn is comparatively light, the evidence of her involvement elsewhere in the world of learning is quite the opposite. She was remembered for years as a generous patron of students, and several cases can be cited to warrant the tradition. As early as 1530, when John Eldmer lost the contest to become abbot of St Mary's, York, Anne persuaded the successful candidate to permit and support his return to Cambridge to study. After some years the new abbot called him back to the community and ruined his chance to study by loading him with administrative chores – clearly fellow monks resented his prolonged skiving – only to have Anne intervene again to secure Eldmer's return to the university.[102] Not only did William Barker benefit from being one of those Anne maintained at Cambridge – which opened the way to quite a literary output – but he was able to use the connection to secure favour from Elizabeth in 1559, and mercy in 1571 following his involvement in the treason of the duke of Norfolk whose secretary he had become.[103] Anne also backed scholars studying abroad, and when Thomas Winter, Wolsey's bastard son, found the money running out and returned from Padua to make what he could of Cromwell's affection for his father, the

---

[100] Robert Wakefield, *Kotser Codicis* (Berthelet, 1532). McConica, *English Humanists*, pp. 133–4.

[101] BL, Roy. MS 20 B xvii [see above, pp. 316–17]. There may have been an element of professional and courtly competition here, for in 1530, Palsgrave, Mary Tudor's protégé, produced a guide to French, and in 1532 Giles du Guez dedicated another to Princess Mary: Russell, *Cloth of Gold*, p. 126n.1.

[102] *LP*, iv.6768; Wood, *Letters*, ii.191 [*LP*, viii.710].

[103] Dowling, in *JEH*, 35. 34.

secretary pointed him in the direction of Henry and Anne. The king was too busy shooting to give him the attention he (and possibly the king) felt he deserved, but all was well the next day when Anne assured him that 'I am aware, my dear Winter, that you are beloved by the king and have many friends who wish you well. Reckon me among the number.' Whether the Latin periods represent Anne's actual words hardly matters – or mattered to Winter; it was her assurance to do what she could for him that counted.[104]

Anne also supported learned institutions, perhaps with annual subventions to Oxford and Cambridge (over and above the poor scholars) of as much as £80 each. More enduring, she interceded with the king to secure the exemption of both universities from the new clerical tax, the tenth, and from clerical subsidies.[105] At a humbler level there is her interest in Matthew Parker's reform of the collegiate church of Stoke by Clare near Sudbury to which Anne had appointed him.[106] The reforms included, as well as regular preaching, the appointment of a lecturer on the Bible to teach four days a week in English and Latin, a new grammar school with a well paid master and facilities for fee-paying as well as for free pupils, and finally eight or ten choral scholarships which could lead to a six-year bursary at Cambridge. Anne Boleyn was designated the new founder of the college. Here was the model of what the redeployment of Church endowments might have achieved. There is circumstantial evidence that she intervened in the headship of Eton, and when Nicholas Bourbon arrived, he too was put to work at his profession of teaching, but this time the sons of courtiers – Thomas, the son of Sir Nicholas Harvey, Anne's old friend and fellow evangelical, Henry Norris's son and her own nephew, Henry Carey:

> You, Oh queen, gave me the boys to educate,
> I try to keep each one faithful to his duty.
> May Christ grant that I may be equal to the task,
> Shaping vessels worthy of a heavenly house.[107]

---

[104] *LP*, vii.964.
[105] Latimer, 'Treatyse', f. 28v; Dowling, in *JEH*, 35. 34.
[106] John Strype, *Life and Acts of Matthew Parker* (Oxford, 1821), pp. 16–18. Anne's patronage of Parker's efforts at Stoke strengthens the case that she supported the redistribution of monastic wealth, not its dispersal.
[107] *Nugarum*, vii.15, p. 378.

It is fitting, perhaps, that a discussion of Anne Boleyn's religious and intellectual life should end with a French humanist evangelical. That was her milieu, and in it she mattered. Bourbon wrote the dedication to book seven of the *Nugarum*, which was to appear in 1538, soon after his arrival in London – the date is the Ides of May, 1535. Addressing 'the benevolent reader', he remarked that he had two great patrons, 'the Most Christian King, our Francis' and 'the brilliant Henry VIII, king of the Britons', who between them exhibited the greatest piety and encouragement of the arts in that age.[108] Every good humanist had to be a flatterer and a beggar. He was, perhaps, nearer the truth in the dedication of the previous book which he apparently added when he was back in France; the reference there was to 'the liberality of Henry VIII that most humane of princes and of his wife the queen' – a remarkable piece of honesty, for by that time Anne was disgraced and dead.[109]

[108] Ibid., vii.p. 368.
[109] Ibid., vi.p. 330.

IV

A Marriage Destroyed

15

The Challenge, 1535–36

$\thicksim\!\!\!\!\prec\!\!\!\!\thicksim$

THE STORY of the events which led to the disgrace and death of Anne Boleyn needs to begin almost a year before the tragedy itself. Henry VIII spent the summer of 1535 on a progress to the Severn and then down to Hampshire for most of September and October. The sport was good, particularly the hawking. The king had not hunted the area for some years, and after a few weeks away from the stress and blood of recent events, he was in tremendous form. So was Anne, who accompanied him throughout, and when the couple returned to Windsor in late October she was pregnant, though she did not yet know it.[1] The spectacular public occasion of the progress was the consecration of three favoured clerics as bishops at Winchester on 19 September, apparently in the presence of the king, and given that the three were Edward Fox, Hugh Latimer and John Hilsey, Anne's presence can be taken for granted.[2] Henry had been so enjoying himself that he had signed very few documents during the progress, and there was something of a panic to get the formalities for the new bishops completed in time, with Anne herself advising Latimer to leave it to Cromwell.[3]

In the end, several documents were signed at Wolf Hall near Marlborough, where the king stopped for a week in early September on his way to the New Forest, for a visit to which hindsight has given enormous significance.[4] Wolf Hall was the

---

[1] *LP*, ix.310, 555, 571, 579, 639.
[2] *Lisle Letters*, ii.451. The consecration dates in *Handbook of British Chronology*, ed. F. M. Powicke & E. B. Fryde (1961), differ from this, but since the Lisle letter is the earlier, it must be correct.
[3] *LP*, ix.121, 203, 252, 272–3, 342.
[4] Ibid., ix.729(6), (7), (8); W. Seymour, *Ordeal by Ambition* (1972), pp. 41–2.

home of Sir John Seymour and his large family: among them, his eldest daughter Jane. At the time, however, it is very unlikely that anyone, including Anne and Henry, saw anything momentous about the visit. Jane may or may not have been present, Anne must have been, and myth and legend are all that suggest that this was the start of the king's pursuit of the woman who would be his third and, as the mother of Edward VI, in Henry's terms his only truly successful wife.[5] Jane Seymour had, in fact, a long association with the court, where she had been one of Katherine of Aragon's ladies.[6] If she left court at all when the latter's household was reduced in the summer of 1533, she was back in Anne Boleyn's entourage by the New Year, when she received a gift from the king along with others of the queen's ladies such as Anne Zouche, Madge Shelton and Bessie Holland.[7]

The real significance of the royal visit to Wolf Hall was that it marked one further stage in the rise of Jane's eldest brother, Edward. A protégé of Wolsey, with some genuine military talent (he had been knighted on the 1522 campaign while still in his teens), Edward reached the rank at court of esquire of the body in 1530, and had accompanied Henry and Anne to Calais in 1532.[8] Now, after helping to host a successful royal visit, he went up a notch in his master's esteem – and we know that the week was successful because in October Henry toyed with the idea of staying at Edward Seymour's Hampshire house, Elvetham, although in the end he changed his mind.[9] Seymour's position – and his father, too, was of good standing in court circles – would alone make nonsense of the legend that it was by catching Henry's eye at Wolf Hall that Jane secured a place in Anne's household; the family had quite enough weight to place a daughter at court, if she had not been there already. The alternative tale comes from Jane Dormer who married a Spanish nobleman and died in 1612, the revered patroness of English Catholic exiles. Her story is that Jane was taken to court by Sir Francis Bryan and placed with Anne. The most that this could

---

[5] For the progress, see *LP*, viii.989; ix.460, 525, 620. The visit to Wolf Hall lasted from at least 4 to 10 Sept. inclusive (not the three days of tradition), and as it was a main stop for the progress (not a by-progress), Anne would have been there: *LP*, ix.271, 326.

[6] Wriothesley, *Chronicle*, i.43.

[7] *LP*, vii.9(ii).

[8] Hamy, *Entrevue*, p. liv.

[9] *LP*, ix.620, 639.

be based on is a recommendation back in 1533 that Anne should take Jane over from Katherine, but there is no corroborating evidence for this. Bryan was certainly not, as Jane Dormer said, Jane Seymour's uncle, and the story that he was acting in response to a refusal by the Dormers to accept Jane as a bride for William, the heir of the family, is an invention; the abrupt marriage of William to Mary Sidney, which supposedly defeated Bryan, did not take place until January 1535.[10] The tale seems an attempt to illustrate the family sanctity of Jane Dormer's grandmother, who had turned her back on a glittering match for her son with a relative of the wicked Francis Bryan, Henry VIII's 'vicar of hell'.

So Henry had known Jane Seymour long before the visit to Wolf Hall in September 1535, but it is a reasonable certainty that the king's interest in her only became serious in January 1536. The then French ambassador, the bishop of Tarbes, did inform Francis I in the first days of October 1535 that Henry's feelings for Anne were cooling steadily because he had 'new amours', but his opinion is contradicted by reports from various English correspondents at court, dated 2, 6 and 9 October, that Henry and Anne Boleyn were 'merry'.[11] Jane Seymour is not named as having been singled out for the king's attentions until a Chapuys letter of 10 February 1536.[12] He had heard the rumour of a third marriage by 29 January, but as he then had no name and dismissed the tale even though from 'a good authority', the natural conclusion is that the matter was of fairly recent origin – indeed, he termed it 'une nouvelle amour'.[13] The late Protestant tradition, for what it is worth, suggests much the same – that 'the time was taken to steal the king's affection' from Anne when she was well into her pregnancy 'and not so fit for dalliance'.[14] A Chapuys letter of late February contains the story that Henry had been ignoring Anne for three months, which suggests that by then observers hostile to Anne thought that the king had become seriously interested in Jane during December.[15] That, however, was backdating, for it is clear that the relationship

---

[10] Clifford, *Dormer*, pp. 40–1; *House of Commons*, i.53.
[11] *LP*, ix.566 [dated by 594], 525, 555, 571.
[12] *Cal. S. P. Span., 1536–38*, pp. 39–40 [*LP*, x.282].
[13] Ibid., p. 28 [*LP*, x.199]; *LP*, x.495; Friedmann, *Anne Boleyn*, ii.202.
[14] George Wyatt, in *Wolsey*, ed. Singer, p. 443.
[15] *Cal. S. P. Span., 1536–38*, p. 59 [*LP*, x.351].

started as yet another exercise in courtly love: as late as 1 April, Chapuys is still describing Jane by the significant phrase 'the lady whom he serves' – and who can tell if and when convention takes on real human content?[16]

Jane is generally supposed to have attracted Henry on the strength of the contrast she presented to Anne: fair, not dark; younger by seven or eight years; gentle rather than abrasive; of no great wit, against a mistress of repartee; a model of female self-effacement, against a self-made woman.[17] Perhaps. Yet we must be aware that this appearance was to a degree deliberate, and concealed a personality which it is more than kind to describe as 'pliable'. That such a woman should destroy Anne may to some appear a kind of justice, but in fairness one must say that: Henry's first marriage was over before Anne came on the scene; her sexuality challenged Henry, but she was no tease; Anne offered Henry marriage or nothing, Jane went for marriage because it was a chance for the big prize; Anne was no man's creature, Jane was a willing tool. As Agnes Strickland pointed out even more vigorously, the picture of Jane preparing for marriage to Henry while Anne was under sentence of death in the Tower 'is repulsive enough, but it becomes tenfold more abhorrent when the woman who caused the whole tragedy is loaded with panegyric.'[18] To say that she caused the tragedy is an over-harsh Victorian judgement. Chapuys considered that the guilt was primarily Henry's; Londoners watching at the time blamed Henry and Jane both, and the king had to write to his new inamorata:

> there is a ballad made lately of great derision against us, which if it go abroad and is seen by you, I pray you to pay no manner of regard to it. I am not at present informed who is the setter forth of this malignant writing; but if he is found, he shall be straitly punished for it.

There is some satisfaction in the fact that Henry never did find him.[19]

---

[16] Ibid., p. 84 [*LP*, x.601].
[17] *LP*, x.901.
[18] Strickland, *Queens of England*, ii.273.
[19] *LP*, x.909; Strickland, *Queens of England*, ii.274–5.

No such disasters were in any mind as the 1535 progress came to an end. Anne, indeed, soon began to hope that her ultimate fear was groundless; come the spring, there would be a prince. The other difficulties that she and Henry faced were, nevertheless, still there, and some as serious as ever. The French and imperial ambassadors commented independently on the prevailing mood of so-far sullen resentment at the king, his wife and his policies.[20] Support for Mary was as strong as ever, or stronger. While the small summer court had been in Hampshire, there had been a public demonstration at Greenwich in support of Mary by the wives of a number of London citizens and some ladies of the royal household not on duty. Among the ringleaders who ended in the Tower were Lady Rochford, Anne's sister-in-law, and another of the queen's ladies, her aunt Lady William Howard.[21] The matter was hushed up, but the king, encouraged by Anne's condition, began to talk in a way that suggested that if Mary persisted in her resistance she would soon find herself in the Tower too.[22] Katherine, also, had at last decided that submission was not enough; unknown to Henry, in October she wrote to Charles, inviting him to intervene.[23]

In the country at large fear of religious change was now widespread. Stories of heretical preaching abounded; royal commissioners were surveying the Church estates, down to the poorest parish; at the same time Cromwell's deputies were visiting the monasteries to enforce disturbing royal injunctions and confiscate many long-venerated relics; the new impositions on the clergy were beginning to bite; 1 December was the date for paying the new tax of 10 per cent per annum on all clerical incomes, and some small religious houses were already giving up the struggle to survive. The London merchant community was full of rumour that war with the emperor was imminent, with the consequence of the loss of England's vital markets in the Low Countries and Germany. Friction between the king and the Hanse merchants already threatened the closure of the Baltic, with its grain reserves, and this appeared all the more ominous as at home the vital weeks of fine harvest weather obstinately refused to arrive. Half the crops, it was said, had been lost, and

[20] *LP*, ix.566; *Cal. S. P. Span., 1534–35*, p. 550 [*LP*, ix.594].
[21] *LP*, ix.566.
[22] *LP*, ix.862 and p. xxxii.
[23] Mattingly, *Catherine of Aragon*, pp. 302–4.

the threat of famine after what turned out to be the worst season
for eight years and the fourth worst since Henry's accession
made it impossible to levy the taxes granted by parliament.
Plague, too, was rampant. And it was no use the king's preachers
exploiting the text, 'whom the Lord loveth he chasteneth';
ordinary Englishmen knew that the king's behaviour was to
blame, and even more the woman whom he had done everything
for and who egged him on to his godlessness.[24]

Abroad, the situation was more fluid even than it had been
earlier in the year. First, Charles V's great victory at Tunis had
freed him from Mediterranean distractions to intervene against
Henry if he wished, while the pope had responded to the death of
Fisher by excommunicating the king. The French, seeing increased danger to England, had upped the price of their support,
making it clear also that it was the marriage between the
dauphin and Mary which really interested them. Then on 1
November the situation changed, when the death without heirs
of the duke of Milan threw open again the issue over which
Francis and Charles had been quarrelling since 1515. That
might seem to tip the balance of need in Henry's favour, but
Francis might now call for the financial support which Henry
had hinted at, so dragging England, if not into direct hostilities
with Charles, at least into increasing difficulties in its relations
with the Low Countries. The pope, however, was anxious to put
together a coalition to punish Henry, so there was a good deal of
talk about an alternative scenario – a negotiated settlement
between the Empire and France and a joint descent on England.

From the disinterest of the twentieth century it is hard to
believe that England was in any real danger of isolation and
invasion, or that Henry would be unable to avoid the entangle-
ments of Francis I. Yet at the time the confusions, and the
readiness of each power to take opportunist advantage of every
other, did produce real anxiety. Matters were made more
opaque by the universal passion for disinformation and by the
existence within each country of divided counsels. In France
there was a war party and a peace party, and in England two
policies competed – either to rely on France or to seek an
accommodation with the emperor. Henry, with Anne's strong
support, believed that he ought to be able to depend on French

[24] Friedmann, *Anne Boleyn*, ii.121.

self-interest, though so long as Francis insisted on maintaining close relations with the pope and refused English advice to follow down the road of royal supremacy, he never felt he could quite trust his 'brother' as he once had. This doubt about France explains why Anne was anxious in October to interest the French envoys in Elizabeth, why Francis I's recovery from a severe illness in November was marked in London by an ostentatious show of relief, and why Anne's overture to Marguerite of Navarre in September was followed up in November and December by exploration from both sides.[25] Cromwell, by contrast, seems to have been much readier to consider doing a deal with the emperor, even though he was aware of imperial protests at the treatment of Katherine and Mary, and probably guessed at Charles' reluctance to come to terms while Anne Boleyn usurped his aunt's place as queen.[26] It was, perhaps, a half-truth that Cromwell was inviting Chapuys to believe, when in June 1535 he suggested that if Anne knew how close his relations were with the ambassador, she would have his head.[27] Henry, for the same reasons, found it hard to discuss the emperor with Chapuys without losing his temper.[28]

The opening of the New Year, however, brought further dramatic developments. On 7 January, Katherine of Aragon died of cancer at Kimbolton Castle, on the edge of the Fens. She had suddenly and somewhat unexpectedly gone downhill at the end of December, and her death was greeted at court by an outburst of relief and enthusiasm for the Boleyn marriage which put the amour with Jane Seymour in true perspective and gives the lie to later historians who suggest that Anne was already living on borrowed time. She gave the messenger who brought the news to Greenwich a handsome present; her father and brother made it clear that only one more thing was needed – for Mary to go the way of her mother. Henry cried, 'God be praised that we are free from all suspicion of war!'; he would now have the advantage over the French, who would have to toe his line or risk an English alliance with Charles, 'now that the real cause of our enmity no longer exists'. The next day, Sunday, the king and

<hr>

[25] *Cal. S. P. Span.*, *1534–35*, p. 551 [*LP*, ix.594]; Wriothesley, *Chronicle*, i.32; *LP*, ix.378, 838, 964, 965, 969, 980, 987. See above, p. 41.
[26] Ibid., ix.674.
[27] *Cal. Ss. P. Span.*, *1534–35*, p. 484 [*LP*, viii.826].
[28] Ibid., *1536–8*, p. 97 [*LP*, x.699].

queen appeared in joyful yellow from top to toe, and Elizabeth was triumphantly paraded to church. After dinner Henry went down into the Great Hall, where the ladies of the court were dancing, with his sixteen-month old daughter in his arms, showing her off to one and another. After several days of such paternal enthusiasm, he evidently decided that something more masculine was called for, and the tiltyard was soon busy with his favourite form of self-exhibition.[29] Even though, as seems probable, he paid public court there to Jane Seymour, Anne knew that Elizabeth and her unborn child were the true centre of Henry's interest, while she was herself now, for the first time, sole queen of England.

Eustace Chapuys took all this as a personal insult. His grief for Katherine was genuine and his sympathy for Mary all the more real because of instructions which had recently arrived from Charles dampening all prospects of imperial support for a rising against Henry and Anne.[30] In January Francis I had intervened in the duchy of Savoy, which had been quickly overrun in what was an obvious preliminary to renewed hostilities over the old bone of Franco-imperial contention, the duchy of Milan. For the foreseeable future, Italy would be the imperial priority and England even more of a sideshow than usual. The end of the month, however, brought the ambassador comfort. Rumours began to reach him of Anne exhibiting signs of distress, afraid that she might go the same way as Katherine.[31] Chapuys was clearly right, though, to be cautious about a story that only made sense if Anne believed the nonsense that Henry would abandon not only her but the child in her womb.

The likeliest explanation for the tale is that once again Anne's pregnancy was proving difficult, and it was death, not divorce, that she feared. And death came very near. On 24 January the king's horse fell heavily in the tiltyard at Greenwich, knocking Henry unconscious for two hours.[32] For a big man wearing nearly a hundredweight of armour, to be thrown from a galloping horse of, perhaps, seventeen hands high, was no laughing matter – still less if the horse, as it may have done, also fell on top

[29] Ibid., *1536–8*, pp. 19, 28 [*LP*, x.141, 199]. Hall, *Chronicle*, p. 818, says that Anne wore yellow, Chapuys that Henry did.
[30] *Cal. S. P. Span.*, *1534–35*, p. 595 [*LP*, ix.1035].
[31] Ibid., p. 28 [*LP*, ix.199].
[32] *LP*, x.200; *Cal. S. P. Span.*, *1536–38*, p. 67 [*LP*, x.427].

of him. Henry did not joust again, and there is no way of knowing how the fall influenced his conduct over the next few months.

The king can hardly have been out of convalescence when death came again, for real. On 29 January Anne miscarried, and to make the blow worse, the baby had been a son. To those persuaded by hindsight that Henry had already tired of his second wife, the loss of the child has seemed the turning-point to tragedy: Anne 'had miscarried of her saviour'.[33] The evidence suggests something less decisive. Anne's own resilience soon had her comforting her attendants with the confidence that she would conceive again, and that no one this time would be able to claim that her son was illegitimate.[34] Henry's response was quite different. The disaster was to him the horribly familiar and totally convincing voice of God. He said to one of his intimates in the secrecy of the privy chamber that God was again denying him a son; he had been seduced into marriage with Anne by witchcraft – the marriage was null and void, and he would take a new wife. The story reached Chapuys by a messenger sent from the Exeters, but it arrived on the morning of the miscarriage and rings all too true.[35] Divine judgement had demonstrated the wrongfulness of Henry's marriage to Katherine; had that same judgement now condemned Anne? What the comment about witchcraft referred to is not clear; perhaps the king had in mind the flood of encouraging auguries which had greeted Anne's pregnancy in 1533.[36] Be that as it may, all Henry's old fears were now out in full force, and when he saw Anne for the first time after the miscarriage, they were in the forefront of his mind.

The only contemporary account of what took place at that meeting is to be found in the letters of Chapuys. His first report was that Anne was blaming Norfolk for frightening her with the

[33] Ibid., p. 39 [LP, x.282]. The foetus was said to be three and a half months old. The quotation is from Neale, *Queen Elizabeth*, p. 17.

[34] LP, x.352.

[35] Cal. S. P. Span., 1536–38, p. 28 [LP, x.199]. Chapuys' report is dated 29 Jan., but he does not mention the miscarriage until his next letter. Henry's comment on his failure to have sons must have been made after the miscarriage, so the Exeters must have heard of the king's remark and passed it on before its cause was known by them.

[36] This would be the more probable if, as seems canonically the safer course, Henry had had his second marriage formally solemnized between the declaration of the divorce from Katherine on 23 May 1533 and the judicial ratification of the marriage with Anne on 28 May [see above, p. 204[73]].

news of the king's accident, but that the real reason for the miscarriage was either her inability to bear children or fear of her fate now that the king was paying so much attention to Jane Seymour. Just over a fortnight later he amplified the story. Henry had had very little to do with Anne for three months. His only remark to her about the miscarriage was, 'I see that God will not give me male children', and when he left her he said, as if in spite, 'When you are up I will speak to you.' Anne's recriminations during his visit upset the king for a long time, and at Shrovetide he went to stay at Whitehall by himself instead of celebrating with Anne at Greenwich, whereas previously he could not leave her for an hour.[37]

Not all of this is true. The point about Henry ignoring Anne for three months cannot be correct. Chapuys had forgotten his own report of the king's behaviour after Katherine's death, and his final comment on Shrovetide also contradicts it; either that separation was, as he claimed, significant, or the couple had not been speaking for months – it is hard to believe both. The gloss put on the king's departure to Whitehall can in any case be queried. Shrovetide 1536 coincided with the final session of the Reformation Parliament, and Henry could be expected to be on hand to monitor progress; in particular, his long-cherished attempt to recover his feudal rights was due to be approved after five years of bitter resistance. If Anne was, as is likely, still convalescent Henry would have had to go alone. We must, too, remember that Chapuys was equally ready to tell the absurd story, which was also spread by Francis I, that there had never been a pregnancy to miscarry![38] It was simply an attempt by Anne (with the help of her sister Mary) to deceive Henry into believing that she could conceive. Women prisoners did try to cheat the gallows by claiming to be *enceinte*, but Anne could only have hastened disaster by such a trick; it would have invited exactly the reaction the king had had in 1534, and did now have again. And why want to end the deception while the king was still interested in Jane Seymour?

So, as always, Chapuys tells a loaded tale, gleaned from a distance. But we may take the remark, 'I see that God will not give me male children', as genuine, confirmed as it is by the

[37] *Cal. S. P. Span.*, *1536–38*, pp. 39–40, 59 [*LP*, x.282, 351].
[38] *LP*, x.283, 450.

Exeters' earlier report of what was clearly the same remark, and by emphasis on the will of God rather than the failure of Anne. It stands in contrast to the later versions of the episode. George Wyatt has Henry say, 'he would have no more boys by *her!*'[39] Recusant sources opt for sarcasm. Sander has Henry answer Anne's complaints 'by saying, "Be of good cheer, sweetheart, you will have no reason to complain of me again", and [he] went away sorrowing.'[40] Jane Dormer, half a century later, had Anne 'betwitting' the king with his unkindness: 'who willed her to pardon him, and he would not displeasure her in that kind hereafter.'[41] As for Anne Boleyn's reply, there is good reason to believe that she did meet this complaint against God with some complaint against Henry. George Wyatt's tedious prose probably preserves for us the tradition from her ladies in waiting: 'Being thus a woman full of sorrow, it was reported that the king came to her, and bewailing and complaining unto her the loss of his boy, some words were heard to break out of the inward feeling of her heart's dolours, laying the fault upon unkindness.'[42] Sander was more specific and refers to Anne 'bewailing her mishap, and angry at the transference to another of the king's affections, cried out to him, "See, how well I must be since the day I caught that abandoned woman Jane sitting on your knees."'[43] The Dormer version is that 'there was often much scratching and bye-blows between the queen and her maid', and that 'anger and disdain' at finding Jane on Henry's lap produced the miscarriage.[44]

We may credit this plausible though late embroidery if we choose, but Chapuys at the time heard no more than the story that later reached Wyatt. Anne had told the king first that she had been upset by the news of his fall in the tiltyard, but secondly that because her personal feelings for him were so much stronger than Katherine's had been, she was broken-hearted whenever he paid attention to another woman. And it is easy to believe that in the immediate aftermath of the miscarriage Anne might have been forceful on the point that her personal involve-

[39] George Wyatt, in *Wolsey*, ed. Singer, p. 444.
[40] Sander, *Schism*, p. 132.
[41] Clifford, *Dormer*, p. 79.
[42] George Wyatt, in *Wolsey*, ed. Singer, p. 443.
[43] Sander, *Schism*, p. 132.
[44] Clifford, *Dormer*, p. 79.

ment with Henry made it impossible to treat his philandering with conventional detachment. The opinion of her ladies, preserved by Wyatt, was that if she had, like Katherine, been more tolerant of peccadilloes, she would have risked less. 'Her too great love' prevented what 'she might the rather have done respecting the general liberty and custom then that way'.[45] The king, wrapped up in his own disappointment, guilty at his flirtations with Jane and making too little allowance for Anne's state, may well have resented what she said, as Wyatt records. However, his final remark, 'When you are up I will speak with you', suggests not the spite assumed by Chapuys or the contemptuous rejection of a woman now destined to disaster, but a husband retreating from an emotional scene he cannot cope with.

Anne Boleyn's miscarriage in January 1536 was, therefore, not the knell of doom. What it did mean, however, was that she was exposed once more, and to an even greater degree, to attack from the partisans of Mary, resentful at the dominance of the Boleyns and their heretical policies. The position was in some ways, a repetition in a heightened form of the autumn of 1534, after her first miscarriage, but there were significant differences. Mary on her own was a much more formidable opponent than Katherine had been. Anne's daughter was no longer protected by the difficulty that to admit Mary's legitimacy meant defying the king and asserting the validity of the Aragon marriage. Now that Katherine was dead, all that was needed was for their father to accept that the elder girl was '*bona fide parentum* gotten, conceived and born' – as was the case – and Elizabeth was no longer the heir presumptive.[46] This was a far more attractive object for conservative critics of Henry and Anne to pursue than the treason which had been discussed with Chapuys, and one which could be advanced by all the familiar methods of court intrigue. And the omens were good. With the end to all immediate hope of a son, Henry's intention to exact the succession oath from Mary evaporated, and a relieved princess found her treatment somewhat improved.

The death of Katherine also threw into relief the hitherto unnoticed disadvantages of the Boleyn match. It was no longer

---

[45] George Wyatt, in *Wolsey*, ed. Singer, p. 444.
[46] *LP*, x.670 at p. 269.

the case that the only alternative was a return to an aged and
barren first wife and, by implication, submission to papal
authority. Now, to reject Anne offered the prize of a third and
wholly uncontested match and offspring, recognized at home
and abroad. The shock of the executions of Fisher, More and the
Carthusians also served to rally support against Anne, and there
were signs of increasing willingness to challenge her. Already
Nicholas Carewe had sheltered Henry VIII's fool from his
master's wrath when he had unwisely praised Katherine and
Mary and denigrated Anne and Elizabeth, while Richard Pate,
archdeacon of Lincoln and a career diplomat, wrote in agonized
support of Mary, well aware, even at Rome, of the risk that he was
taking.[47]

Not only was the opposition to Anne in 1536 more formidable
than in 1534, but there was now more danger from Jane
Seymour than from the unknown 'lady' the king had served for
those few months after Anne's first miscarriage. One reason was
that after two such disasters, Henry was that much more
vulnerable. The possibility of discarding Anne had already
entered his mind, if only briefly. Another reason was that Jane
was being pushed by her brother Edward, who was using his
new standing with the king in the certainty that for her to
become anything more than the king's latest flirt had to be to his
advantage. And it was.[48] At the beginning of March, Edward
Seymour was appointed to the privy chamber, and found it an
ever better place in which to act as his sister's ponce. He may
already have wondered whether Jane might end as more than a
royal mistress, but Mary's supporters in the privy chamber
realized that here was a heaven-sent opportunity to supplant
Anne and bring the princess back to her rightful place. The
alliance was made. Jane was firmly told that her price must be
marriage and nothing less, and she was coached to behave
accordingly. Thus when

> the king was [in London] and the lady Mistress Semel [Seymour]
> whom he serves was in Greenwich, he sent her a purse full of
> sovereigns and a letter. The young lady, having kissed the letter

[47] *Cal. S. P. Span.*, *1534–35*, p. 520 [*LP*, viii.1106]; *LP*, x.670 at p. 269.
[48] For the following see *Cal. S. P. Span.*, *1536–38*, pp. 81, 84–5, 106–7 [*LP*,
x.601, 752]; *LP*, x.495.

returned it to the messenger unopened and falling on her knees besought him to ask the king on her behalf, to consider carefully that she was a gentlewoman, born of good and honourable parents and with an unsullied reputation. She had no greater treasure in the world than her honour which she would rather die a thousand times than tarnish, and if he wanted to give her money she begged that he would do so once God had sent her a good match.

As we have seen, a somewhat similar story is told about Anne, but with the telling difference that Jane was using the occasion to dangle her virtue as a public bait, a ploy which, according to the marchioness of Exeter, had exactly the intended result. Henry announced that he would have no more private tête-à-têtes with Jane, but would see her in the company of her relations. He thereupon turned Cromwell out of his room at Greenwich and put in Edward Seymour and his wife instead, because it had a private passage to the king's own apartments!

Jane was also told to poison Henry's mind against Anne whenever possible, stressing particularly the illegitimacy of his second marriage, and to do so especially when others of the faction were in attendance to chorus their agreement. The Exeters also recruited Chapuys to add his contribution, which he agreed to with alacrity. Indeed, the thought of the merit in thereby serving Mary's interests, striking a blow against heresy and helping to save Henry from mortal sin, quite made him forget to mention the advantage it would bring to Charles v! The overall manager of the plot seems to have been Nicholas Carewe, but he was backed by the rest of the privy chamber staff opposed to Anne. Exeter, Rochford's opposite number as nobleman of the privy chamber, continued as the link with Chapuys, and other courtiers involved included Lord Montagu and his brother Geoffrey, Sir Thomas Elyot, and the king's cousin, the dowager countess of Kildare. About the time of the purse episode, several of the conspirators were dining with Chapuys and debating the talk of a new bride for the king. By the end of April they were even seeking ecclesiastical opinion on the validity of any divorce.[49] And all this pressure does seem to have fuelled Henry's bout of uncertainty. If hostile tales are to be believed, he did begin to

[49] *Cal. S. P. Span.*, *1536–38*, p. 106 [*LP*, x.752].

speculate with Jane about the possibility of marriage, and certainly an atmosphere of doubt was created about the long-term future of his marriage to Anne.[50]

The response of Anne Boleyn and her supporters was to fight. Chapuys reported only that Anne was raging against Jane, but the signs of more serious resistance are plain. George Boleyn maintained a high profile. He was much in evidence at court, and when the king had to choose a peer to cast the proxy vote of Lord Delaware for the session of parliament which began on 4 February, it was to George that it went.[51] The Boleyns continued to enjoy noted royal favour. Early in March they obtained letters patent reconstructing Thomas's lease of the crown honour of Rayleigh in Essex, so as to extend the term and bring George in as joint tenant, and at the same time secure a 20 per cent rebate on the rent.[52] Among the acts of parliament which received the royal assent on 14 April was one which stripped the bishopric of Norwich of the town of Lynn and other properties; a week later Chapuys had discovered that the beneficiary was to be the earl of Wiltshire, and that a couple of abbeys were earmarked for him as well.[53] It is true that on St George's Day Sir Nicholas Carewe was elected to fill up a vacancy among the Knights of the Garter, and that Chapuys interpreted this as a defeat for Rochford and a sign of Anne's weakened influence, but the choice was at least in part dictated by the king's earlier half-promise to Francis that Carewe was next in line.[54] Anne retained her influence almost to the last, and may, indeed, have been exploiting her position to disarm the opposition. Certainly she was exerting herself at the request of the earl of Westmorland to secure favours for his brother-in-law, Henry Lord Stafford – an unlikely connection, for Stafford was the son of Katherine's favourite, the last duke of Buckingham, and his wife was sister to Lord Montagu who

[50] Ibid., p. 124 [*LP*, x.908].
[51] Lehmberg, *Reformation Parliament*, pp. 57, 218.
[52] *LP*, x.597(3), (4).
[53] Lehmberg, *Reformation Parliament*, p. 230; *Cal. S. P. Span., 1536–38*, p. 102 [*LP*, x.699].
[54] *LP*, x.715. Chapuys' letter to Granvelle [ibid., 753] attributes Carewe's success to the support of Francis I; his letter of the same date to Charles portrays the election as a defeat for Anne and her brother: *Cal. S. P. Span., 1536–38*, p. 106 [*LP*, x.752]. The letter to Granvelle is correct; Francis had requested the order for Carewe in 1533 and had been promised it in 1535: *LP*, vi.555, 707; viii.174.

even then was plotting against the queen.[55] Anne did not lightly surrender her husband to Jane Seymour.

The Boleyn faction also made an important and defensive shift in its attitude to foreign affairs. With the threat to the imperial position in Italy and the death of his aunt, Charles was becoming rapidly more conciliatory. Anne's relations with Henry were now less of an offence to his family, and he had intervened early in the year to block the publication of the papal sentence depriving Henry of his throne. The emperor's great concern now was to exploit the claim of his cousin Mary to be heir presumptive to the English crown, which meant that he had somehow to deal with the obstacle of Elizabeth, who by statute stood in the way. Assuming, as he always did, that Anne was the king's mistress, Charles decided to behave accordingly and buy her out. Instructions were sent to Chapuys to do a deal with 'the Concubine' and, if necessary, to use Cromwell as an intermediary to get the best possible terms, with either Mary recognized as the heir or the succession left in suspense.[56] There were now even advantages for Charles in keeping Anne and Henry together: it would bar a French marriage. And so at Rome in March 1536 he offered the English ambassador, in return for the legitimation of Mary, his support for 'the continuance of this last matrimony or otherwise' as Henry wished.[57] Anne and her supporters, meantime, decided that they would abandon France and join with all the factions at court in backing an imperial alliance.[58] No doubt the reasons for this differed from group to group. For Anne the switch offered an end to the now damaging reputation of being wholly in the pocket of the French, and a means to undercut support for Mary. For Carewe and his cronies, no doubt, the change promised to be the first step in reversing the policies and removing the personalities of recent years. Yet whatever the motive the approach was agreed, and after a series of detailed discussions between Cromwell and Chapuys, negotiations reached their climax at a meeting at Greenwich between the ambassador and the king himself on 18 April, the Tuesday after Easter.[59]

[55] Ibid., x.741, 749. Stafford was, however, close to Edward Fox, D.N.B., vii.555.
[56] Cal. S. P. Span., 1536–38, p. 75 [LP, x.575].
[57] LP, x.670 at p. 269.
[58] Cal. S. P. Span., 1536–38, pp. 54, 89, 91, 93 [LP, x.351, 699].
[59] Ibid., pp. 91–8 [LP, x.699].

On arrival at court that day, Chapuys was effusively welcomed by George Boleyn, and Cromwell brought a message from Henry inviting him to visit Anne and kiss her hand. The ambasador excused himself – that was going too far, too fast – but Rochford conducted him to mass and to a far more public encounter with the queen. Anne accompanied Henry from the royal pew down into the chapel to make her offering, and knowing that Chapuys was placed behind the door through which she entered, she stopped, turned and bowed to this representative of the Empire, as he did to her. After mass, Chapuys was careful not to go with the king and the other ambassadors to dine with Anne, but again it was her brother Rochford who entertained him in the presence chamber, while Anne, having asked after Chapuys, gave deliberate vent to a series of remarks which were highly critical of France. These were duly carried back to the envoy. After dinner, Henry took Chapuys to his own room for a lengthy personal conversation in the privacy of a window embrasure, observed from a distance only by Cromwell and Audley.

At this stage, however, the ambassador sensed that something was wrong. His negotiations with Cromwell had been on an imperial proposal which envisaged the possibility of a restoration of some relations between England and Rome, the inclusion of Mary in the line of succession and military support for Charles V in the expected war over Milan. The king, however, now showed himself distinctly cool to the package, and Chapuys' suspicion that Henry and his ministers were out of step grew stronger when he withdrew and watched the king in deep debate with Cromwell and Audley. By now Edward Seymour was in the room, and as the ambassador made polite conversation with him, he saw Henry and Cromwell beginning to dispute angrily, to the point where Cromwell had to excuse himself, claiming he needed a drink, and sit on a chest out of the king's sight in order to control his feelings. Henry then moved out into the room to see what had happened to Cromwell and to tell Chapuys that he had to have everything in writing. When the ambassador followed Charles' instructions and demurred, the king became increasingly angry and started to imitate someone calling to a child, declaring that he was not an infant to be alternately whipped, then petted; it was for the emperor first to apologize to him for his past ill-treatment. He then began to rake up grievances against Charles which were ten years old and more, until he talked himself to a standstill. All Henry would in the end agree to was to look at the texts of existing treaties between England and the Empire, and Chapuys left the court to lick his wounds with Cromwell who, like Audley, had listened to the king's tirade in silence.

Cromwell professed himself completely baffled by the king's behaviour, but one thing stands out clearly.[60] Despite the agreement between all factions to back an imperial alliance, Henry himself remained prepared to haggle. Cromwell told Chapuys that at a council meeting the day after the king's exhibition, every councillor had gone on his knees to persuade him to continue negotiations.[61] It was in vain, for Henry's suspicion of Charles v had deep roots. Already at Christmas he had expressed his reservations to Chapuys and warned that Cromwell was exceeding his authority, a point which Cromwell himself admitted later (although subsequently he did try to claim that he had had the king's approval for his overtures).[62] Henry was certainly interested in a deal with the Empire, but he wanted to use the threat that he might ally with Francis to compel Charles to accept the new authority of kingship in England by recognizing the Boleyn marriage. He had offered the possibility of an imperial marriage for Elizabeth late in 1535, and when feelers put out by Cromwell brought no response, had broached the matter himself to the ambassador.[63] Chapuys' visit to court on 18 April was clearly stage-managed to compel the ambassador to recognize Anne, and his bow to her did cause great annoyance and apprehension among Mary's supporters.[64] Hence also the king's insistence that Charles should apologize. Far from the one issue of April 1536 being 'When will Anne go, and how?', the alternative of continuing his second marriage offered Henry the chance, in the new international situation, to demand that Europe accept that he had been right all along.

Astute as he was in foreign affairs, Henry knew very well that he would not, in the end, get this acceptance through a public apology, or even a private one. The realistic possibility was to

[60] Ibid., p. 98 [*LP*, x.699].
[61] Ibid., p. 98 [*LP*, x.699].
[62] Ibid., pp. 53, 99 [*LP*, x.351, 699], *LP*, x.308.
[63] Ibid., x.308; *Cal. S. P. Span., 1536–38*, p. 80 [*LP*, x.601].
[64] *LP*, x.720.

have Charles accept an alliance without conditions – and such a treaty would be enough. It would proclaim to the world the emperor's tacit admission that Henry had the right to settle his affairs himself – religious, matrimonial and parental. And to achieve this, Anne must remain his wife. The treatment of the French was all of a piece with this. They were urged into war with Charles, but at the same time the maximum concessions were demanded if they wished to guarantee English support, which in turn allowed an upping of the price asked of Charles for Henry's neutrality.[65] Francis I, however, was hard to handle; the English learned that he had in his possession a copy of the papal decree depriving Henry of the throne, which Charles had been holding back, but which it might now suit French interests in Italy to publish in order to secure the support of the pope.[66] By the last week of April the council was sitting every day to decide what to do – whether to call the French bluff and hold out for complete victory over Charles, or whether to clinch the imperial alliance on somewhat lower terms.[67]

According to Chapuys, Cromwell was hard-hit by the king's obstinacy and took to his bed, and there is no denying the difficulty the minister was in.[68] He had built his career on support for Anne, but it was he who had engineered the break with Rome and who was even then organizing the spoliation of the smaller monasteries. There was no way, if Anne were to be rejected in favour of Jane Seymour and the victorious conservative faction secured some reversal of policies, that he could remain in office, or even, perhaps, keep his head on his shoulders. The alternative, and at that moment the more likely outcome, the triumph of the Boleyn faction, offered almost as cold comfort, for he had begun to lose Anne's confidence. The reason is not clear. Cromwell had for some months been aware that his independent initiative in foreign affairs risked the queen's hostility, and in the atmosphere of early 1536 it could have been natural for her to fear that his negotiations with Chapuys were disloyal and would lead to the questioning of her position – especially as Cromwell was being careful to treat Mary with

[65] Ibid., x.54, 410, 688.
[66] Ibid., x.887.
[67] Ibid., x.688, 752; *Lisle Letters*, iii.686 [*LP*, x.748]; *Cal. S. P. Span., 1536–38*, pp. 99–102, 105 [*LP*, x.699, 752].
[68] *LP*, x.700.

respect and courtesy.[69] Yet Chapuys learned of the breach between the queen and the minister in late March as if it was something new, and confirmed it to his satisfaction at a subsequent meeting with Cromwell on 1 April.[70]

The most likely cause of Anne's displeasure at that date was the surrender of his room to the Seymours some days earlier – something which Cromwell may well have been unable to prevent, but which, equally, the queen was bound to blame him for. The business of the room, with its private corridor to Henry, may well explain the famous concealed smile which Chapuys noticed when Cromwell assured him that Henry, though given to entertaining and serving the ladies, was henceforth going to live chastely with his second wife. And with the loss of Anne's support, the minister could no longer rely on the rest of the faction and his contacts in the privy chamber, good though his relations with them had been. No minister under threat could expect staff there to risk their own careers for him – as he himself was to prove when he too fell from royal favour in 1540. In any case, despite his mastery of government policy and administration, in terms of the personal favour and private influence wielded by a man like Henry Norris, Cromwell was in the second division. Contrary to what is sometimes said, he was still from the point of view of Norris, Rochford and the senior members of the privy chamber circle a functionary who might from time to time be awkward and drag his feet, a man whose command over the bureaucratic machine made him important to cultivate, but who in their world of patronage, intrigue and profit would in the end do whatever they could persuade the king to order.[71]

---

[69] *Cal. S. P. Span., 1534–35*, p. 484 [*LP*, viii.826]; ibid., *1536–38*, p. 35.

[70] Ibid., pp. 81–2 [*LP*, x.601].

[71] M. St. Clare Byrne [*Lisle Letters*, i.161; ii.170–1, 333–43] and D. R. Starkey [thesis, pp. 321–3] have argued that Cromwell set out to cut down 'the effective interference' of the privy chamber circle, and that he asserted full control over the signature of bills by the king. A close reading of the fifty and more Lisle Letters between Oct. 1533 and Apr. 1536 which are concerned with patronage, suggests a different conclusion. Cromwell was important as the administrator whose workload might impose delay on the processing of grants, or who might (as duty bound) raise queries about the king's interests. In his initial months as secretary he used such possibilities to establish his claim to a share of the gratuities paid by applicants: *Lisle Letters*, ii.148, 151–2, 159–60, 168, 171, 183–5, 191 [*LP*, vii.350, 385, 386, 461, 474, 502, 522, 614, 620, 627, 652]. He also responded to the competitive pressure of factions at court: ibid., ii.259, 260a, 264 [*LP*, vii.1165, 1182, 1224]. His delay in paying out monies in his

To Cromwell, faced with the possibility that he might be damned by Anne and damned by those hostile to Anne, the king's rebuff on 18 April was the last straw. His conviction that England had to switch to an imperial alliance was deep and of long standing. He had put a deal of work into the negotiations with Chapuys, and there is no doubt what his position had been in the long series of council debates on the value of the French alliance. Yet the alternative the king was now demanding involved a climb-down by Charles v over Anne Boleyn, and the minister did not believe he could possibly secure such a humiliation. He would fail in the one task at which he must never fail – giving the king what he wanted. Already, or so he had told Chapuys, his negotiations for an imperial alliance had raised suspicions in Henry's mind.[72] He would even lose the chance of building credit with those who wanted that alliance as much as he did, if he had to frustrate matters in an attempt to force from Charles the concessions the king sought.

How long Cromwell deliberated we do not know, but as he later told Chapuys, he decided that he must act.[73] Anne's continued presence beside Henry encouraged the king to demand the impossible. He must be brought to want something or someone else. Despite Anne's public support for an imperial alliance, despite all Cromwell had achieved with and for Anne, despite all the beliefs, ideals, even the faith he had in common with her, his interests, his very safety, no longer coincided with hers. She must go.

Cromwell set out to plan the removal of Anne Boleyn with the caution the exercise demanded; the risk involved was a measure of his desperation. Simply to remove the queen would be to invite his own ruin. He had to come to terms with the con-

---

charge on the king's verbal orders via Norris may have been similarly motivated: ibid., ii.202, 202a [*LP*, vii.734, 844] and pp. 164–71. The privy chamber, and especially Norris in his capacity as groom of the stool, continued throughout this period to exercise an independent role; court experts thought Sir Henry still the man to go to, and he did continue to promote bills for the king to sign [e.g. the affair of Leonard Mell: ibid., ii.379, 412, 415, 451, 463, 467, 473, 496; iv.836 [*LP*, viii.663, 1002, 1027, 1028; ix.642, 682, 767, 905]]. For the influence of Rochford, see ibid., i.104, 104b; ii.155a, 182, 207, 283, 411; iii.556, 677 [*LP*, vi.1515; vii.436, 613, 795, 1273, 1396; viii.977; ix.87; x.675]].
[72] Ibid., p. 130 [*LP*, x.908].
[73] Ibid., p. 137 [*LP*, x.1069].

servatives first. The respect he had recently shown to Mary and the kindnesses he had done her, such as returning a cross which her mother had left her, might secure his safety, but there was no profit in a mere exchange of masters.[74] More than that, there was the danger that a complete defeat of the radicals would involve the repudiation of the policies he himself was most closely associated with and, as we have seen, place him in real jeopardy. Somehow he must achieve the gymnastic feat of a double reversed twist, ridding himself of Anne first, with the support of Mary and her allies, and then ditching them too.

The secretary's first step was to gain the confidence of Carewe, Seymour and the others supporting Jane and Mary. How he achieved this, and achieved it within a matter of days, we do not know; but Chapuys was probably the broker, for the ambassador certainly secured the guarded approval of Mary.[75] Cromwell's switch also tells us much about his convincing personality, for it would be two months before these new allies realized that, unlike them, Cromwell did not see the destruction of Anne and the restoration of Mary as two sides of the same coin. Knowing his monarch in a way which his intimate attendants did not, possessed of a wider, more analytical experience than they with their minds formed by the ideals of *The Courtier* and the *Roman de la Rose,* being a statesman and politician where they were bred in the court and conspiracy, Cromwell knew – as they did not – Henry's commitment to the royal supremacy. Already the king had been warned that to divorce Anne could imply acceptance of the papal decision in favour of Katherine of Aragon.[76] Henry, thus, could be counted on to accept the advice that the show of obedience and contrition, which convention and the king's amour propre must demand before Mary was restored to favour, had to include her acceptance of his title as supreme head and the invalidity of her mother's marriage. The princess, in effect, could be compelled to offer an equivalent of the oath she appeared to have escaped. That would cut the ground from under her supporters and force them to acquiesce, at least in public, in the policies that Cromwell had carried through since 1532. The victory of that year would be confirmed, and there

[74] Ibid., pp. 16, 60, 70 [*LP*, x.141, 351, 494].
[75] Ibid., pp. 85–6, 107 [*LP*, x.601, 699, 782].
[76] Ibid., p. 108 [*LP*, x.782].

would now be only one victor, Thomas Cromwell. What is more, any indiscreet euphoria at the rejection of Anne might well draw the conservatives within the provisions of the new treason law. If they were given enough rope they could hang themselves – or at least allow Cromwell to truss them up.

What to do about Anne was more difficult. Until Cromwell's change of sides, the opponents of the queen seem to have thought in naive terms of the king being persuaded to repudiate her – that is, to admit what they had believed all along, that Anne was only 'an affaire' – and this despite the time, effort and, most significantly, money that Henry had expended over almost a decade to convince everyone, at home and abroad, that the opposite was the case.[77] Alternatively their talk was of 'divorce', yet with Henry having, despite their pressure, publicly endorsed Anne's position at Easter, how could any separation be achieved, still less one convincing enough to quiet English and European opinion?[78]

In any case, the problem was not simply Anne. Cromwell might wish to disengage from the Boleyn faction, but he could not ignore it. Norris, Rochford and their associates had rallied to the queen and would undoubtedly seek to keep her in power; if Jane did replace her, the Seymour faction would then become the 'ins' and they would become the 'outs', forced to smile as Carewe and the others had been at promotions and policies they did not like. And if Anne were ousted and the Seymours let in, and if the Boleyn faction were still there, Cromwell would have no chance of 'dishing' the conservatives and coming out on top. Removing Anne from Henry's bed was, thus, no answer by itself. Her faction had to be destroyed at the same time. Otherwise any change which left Thomas and George Boleyn in place, Norris as groom of the stool, Anne as marchioness of Pembroke and Elizabeth begotten in as 'good faith' as Mary ever was would be no more safe or final than the defeat of Wolsey had been in the autumn of 1529. When, late in Easter Week 1536, Cromwell put his mind to, as he said, 'think up and plan' the coup against Anne, he faced the biggest challenge of his life.[79]

---

[77] Ibid., p. 106 [*LP*, x.752].
[78] Ibid., p. 108 [*LP*, x.782].
[79] '*à fantasier et conspirer le dict affaire*': ibid., p. 137 [*LP*, x.1069].

16

The Coup, April–May 1536

IF WE are to believe Thomas Cromwell – and there is no good
reason not to – he moved against Anne Boleyn only when the
king's behaviour on Easter Tuesday 1536 had convinced him
that so long as she was queen, Henry would obstruct what was
safest both for his kingdom and for his secretary. From that point
it took almost twelve days to turn decision into action, and on
Sunday 30 April the first suspect was under arrest. Less than
three weeks later Anne was dead. A month and a day – from
Chapuys' acknowledging her in the Chapel Royal at Greenwich
on Tuesday 18 April to her burial in the Tower on Friday 19
May – this is all the time it took for the most romantic, the most
scandalous tragedy in English history. A tragedy which took the
life of a queen; her brother George; Henry Norris, groom of the
stool, the closest friend King Henry had; Francis Weston,
William Brereton and Mark Smeton, all of the privy chamber;
leaving yet another of the privy chamber staff, Sir Richard Page,
ruined and in prison in the Tower, along with Sir Thomas
Wyatt. It was Wyatt who wrote the epitaph to it all:

> These bloody days have broken my heart:
> My lust, my youth did them depart,
> And blind desire of estate.
> Who hastes to climb seeks to revert:
> Of truth, *circa Regna tonat*.[1]

'About the throne the thunder rolls' – here was a sentiment
from the classics, of exact application in sixteenth-century

[1] Wyatt, *Poems*, CXLIII: 'Who list his wealth and ease retain'.

England, and it has guided discussion after discussion of the repudiation of Anne Boleyn by Henry VIII. The decision to destroy her by a charge of high treason was made, so the story goes, by 24 April, when the king approved the setting up of a commission of oyer and terminer, that is, a commission to investigate and dispose of a catch-all selection of treasons and other offences in Middlesex and Kent.[2] On the 27th, writs went out to summon a parliament. This was clearly an emergency measure – the Reformation Parliament had only been dissolved on 14 April and the calling of new elections so soon was unique in parliamentary history – and when the Lords and Commons met on 8 June the summons was explained by the need to settle the succession and to repeal statutes favouring Anne.[3] Historians have uniformly accepted this explanation and have regarded other measures in that parliament as of no importance.

Mark Smeton, the first of the arrests, was detained at Cromwell's house in Stepney on 30 April, accused of adultery with the queen. The May Day jousts at Greenwich nevertheless went ahead as planned. Anne's brother Rochford led the challengers and Henry Norris the answerers, and nothing untoward was noticed by the spectators. Indeed, if we may trust the French verse account of 2 June 1536, the king was very affable; and when Sir Henry's renowned charger began to play up, he was lent the king's own mount – although we may be sceptical of the suggestion that the first animal had been aware of the fate awaiting its master.[4] Suddenly, at the end of the joust, Henry left Greenwich for Whitehall, travelling on horseback instead of by barge and with only six attendants, one of whom was Norris whom he had, throughout the journey, 'in examination and promised him his pardon in case he would utter the truth' about his relations with Anne.[5] Norris insisted on his innocence, but was sent to the Tower at dawn on Tuesday 2 May.[6] The queen was interrogated later that morning by three of the council who were on the oyer and terminer commission (Norfolk, Fitzwilliam and Paulet), accused of adultery with Norris, Smeton and a third

---

[2] Wriothesley, *Chronicle*, i.189–91.
[3] Lehmberg, *Later Parliaments of Henry VIII*, pp. 15–16.
[4] De Carles, in Ascoli, *L'Opinion*, lines 495–508.
[5] Constantine, in *Archaeologia*, 23.64.
[6] Oxford, Bodl. Ashmole MS 861 f. 332.

(unnamed) man, and told that she would be taken to the Tower.[7]

Thus much the facts and the traditional interpretation, but tradition bristles with difficulties. If the decision to destroy Anne had been taken on 24 April, why was there a delay of eight days before her arrest? Delay spelled danger, particularly for Thomas Cromwell. There was no constraint about waiting for evidence; the Tudor rule was arrest first, interrogate later. Why did the arrests take place piecemeal? Suspects were still being discovered a week later. Why did the king, so careful of his majesty, invite public gossip by his departure after the tournament? Such events were open to the public and, in Hall's words, 'many men mused' at his behaviour.[8] Perhaps the tide dictated a journey to London by road not river, but why with so few attendants, one of whom was the chief suspect? Why did he confront Norris with the accusation, when the uniform practice of the day was to keep suspects away from the king and the chance to influence him? In the highly personalized society of the Tudor elite it was vital to isolate immediately anyone accused, and reduce them to the status of a 'non-person'. Only distance made royal justice possible, not a ride together which would have taken an hour or so. Above all there is the contradiction of a scrambling and drawn-out climax to a coup which had been lined up for a week in detail and had even considered that there would be a subsequent requirement for parliamentary legislation. The resolution often advanced is that Henry had willed the end but had kept aloof from any advance knowledge about the means. Yet to suppose this is to suppose that Cromwell chose a remarkably risky course when he decided to accuse Norris. The man was renowned for his influence with Henry, and supposing he had been able to convince the king of his innocence during that fateful ride?

Where such traditional assessment has gone wrong is in failing to recognize the difficulty Cromwell had in finding a way to separate Henry and Anne. In spite of all the influence exerted by the Seymours and their allies, Henry had openly committed himself to Anne during the Easter celebrations, and he was not likely to reverse this merely because Cromwell added his voice to

---

[7] *Wolsey*, ed. Singer, pp. 451, 456.
[8] Hall, *Chronicle*, p. 819.

the chorus against the queen. Only one way was there any hope: the technique which the minister had used so brilliantly in 1532 to bring Anne and the radicals to power. 'Bounce' the king into decision! Henry must be tipped by a crisis into rejecting Anne. Yet what crisis was on offer? All that Chapuys could pick up at the end of April was a plan to annul the marriage between Henry and Anne on the grounds that she had married the earl of Northumberland 'nine years before' – whatever that meant – and had consummated the match.[9] That was hardly a spectre to frighten Henry into the arms of Jane Seymour. The king knew all about the 1532 investigation of the relationship between Anne and Northumberland, and it is hard to have much faith in the witnesses which Chapuys said were now available! Cromwell certainly was finding it hard, closeted for four days on end with Richard Sampson, the king's adviser on canon law.[10]

That Henry was sticking to his policy of vindicating the Boleyn marriage, pressured though he may have been, was made crystal-clear on 25 April, a week after the débâcle with Chapuys, when he wrote to Richard Pate, the ambassador at Rome.[11] In the letter the king rehearsed very fairly the altercation with the imperial envoy, and instructed Pate to press the line of policy taken on that occasion when he came to negotiate with the emperor, who was then in Italy. The letter also referred to 'the likelihood and appearance that God will send us heirs male', and described Anne as 'our most dear and most entirely beloved wife, the queen'.

What then of the patent of oyer and terminer of 24 April? Had the king forgotten his signature of the day before? Not at all, because in spite of what is universally assumed, he had never signed any instruction for such a commission. The document was a routine judicial initiative taken within the chancery on the authority of the chancellor, and did not need the personal authorization of the monarch. There was nothing in it to attract any attention – the more so because Thomas Boleyn was one of the twenty peers, judges and officials to whom it was addressed (any four of whom could act), and those named would not necessarily know that they had been nominated until called upon

[9] *Cal. S. P. Span.*, *1536–38*, p. 108, [*LP*, x.782]; see above, p. 207.
[10] *LP*, x.753.
[11] *St. Pap.*, vii.683–8; *LP*, x.726.

to attend a meeting of the commission.[12] Given that Lord Chancellor Audley was so close to Cromwell, we may suspect that he had an inkling of the possible use, but even he may only have been responding to the secretary's warning to have matters ready because there was trouble afoot. It remains true, of course, that Cromwell could have been responding to secret word-of-mouth instructions from the king to get such a commission prepared, but that seems to be negated by the letter to Pate on the 25th. Not only might such a despatch appear difficult to construct if Henry had already put in train the rejection of his wife, but it would have been an entire waste of time – all would have to be done again within days. Henry VIII was capable of considerable self-deception, but self-deception which involved a great deal of hard work on two drafts and a final version of an eleven-page letter seems out of character, and the more so since he sent on the same day a further twelve pages to Gardiner and Wallop in France, effectively repeating the instructions to Pate![13]

One stage in the story which we must suppose the king did sanction was the issue of writs summoning the new parliament and it may be that we should see this as the earliest move against Anne that we can identify. On the other hand, the reason that the chancellor gave to parliament on 8 June for its assembly need not be the reason it was summoned on 27 April. For that to be the case, something must have happened to cause the king to act on Thursday against his 'entirely beloved wife' of Tuesday, and the question of what that was presses even more, since it must be presumed that some time for discussion was needed before orders could be given to start work on the parliamentary writs on the 27th. It also seems unlikely that the requirement for a parliament could have been officially explained at that time by a need to reopen the question of the succession. That would appear to promise the return of Mary, and although we might accept that Cromwell could have been glad to demonstate his

----

[12] It is similar to the commission to try Lord Dacre, June 1535, except for the added words: 'misprisions of treason, rebellions, felonies': RO, C193/3 f. 77. The clerk saw no reason to enter it in the record of chancery precedents, in contrast to later warrants in the Boleyn affair. It was witnessed at Westminster, not at Greenwich where Henry was, which could only be if, *per impossible*, the king made a special journey to sign the document. Cf. H. C. Maxwell-Lyte, *Historical Notes on the Great Seal of England* (1926), p. 222. I am grateful for the assistance of Dr J. A. Guy on this point.

[13] *LP*, x.725.

support for her to his new allies, the king was not likely to wish to encourage such speculation. It is also difficult to understand what was gained by moving on parliament in advance of Anne's arrest, if her repudiation were the only issue. The succession was a difficult matter to legislate on, and when parliament did meet it had to wait for three weeks before the relevant bill was ready.

An alternative possibility is that Cromwell explained the need for a parliament on grounds which Henry and his advisers could accept, keeping in his own mind the secret possibility of using it against the queen, as opportunity allowed. If that were the case then the legislation which was presented as so imperative as to necessitate a new parliament, must have been 'the act extinguishing the authority of the bishop of Rome', a statute usually assumed to be a mere tidying-up operation, but which only passed the parliament of June–July 1536 after some difficulty.[14] It closed the loophole in earlier statutes which had made it treason to deny the king's supremacy, but had left defence of the pope's authority no crime at all. Henceforth it would not be sufficient to go through the motions of loyalty; any murmur of even respect for the head of the Western Church was now a penal offence. Henry might well have agreed on the need for such a bill, assailed as he was at home by the Seymours and their many allies, and abroad by the efforts of Charles V to persuade him to put the royal supremacy on the negotiating table in an effort to reach a settlement with the pope. A law to strike at the 'imps of the said bishop of Rome and his see, and in heart members of his pretended monarchy' that also imposed an oath on everyone who mattered, which it was treason to refuse (no second Sir Thomas More), went a long way towards satisfying the king's obsession about the inward thoughts of his people. Even more necessary would such an act seem to Cromwell, now faced with the need to disavow in due course the supporters of Mary, who were clearly in the impish category. One may note that even as the bill was being readied for the Commons, Mary was forced 'for the perfect declaration of the bottom of her 'heart and stomach' to repudiate 'the bishop of Rome's pretended authority'.[15] Although the possibility that the issue of the parlia-

---

[14] 28 Henry VIII, c.10; Lehmberg, *Later Parliaments of Henry VIII*, pp. 25–8.
[15] Prescott, *Mary Tudor*, pp. 82–3.

mentary writs on 27 April was a first official move against Anne must remain, it is by no means probable.

So as the end of April 1536 approached, Cromwell had probably not yet found his crisis. He had the weapons of oyer and terminer and parliament ready, but no occasion to use them. And then on Sunday 30 April Anne herself presented the opening he was looking for. It is rare in Tudor history to be able to date an episode so exactly, but the evidence is plain to see. Henry had planned to go with the queen and the court to Calais that spring, and preparations had been in hand for some time.[16] May Day was to be celebrated at Greenwich, and then the journey would begin, with the first night, Tuesday 2 May, being spent at Rochester. Suddenly, at eleven o'clock on the Sunday night the arrangements were cancelled and instructions given that the king would be travelling a week later.[17] We have, indeed, a tantalizing glimpse of what had been going on that Sunday in the recollections of Anne which were sent to her daughter in September 1559 by the Scottish Lutheran divine, Alexander Ales. He claimed to have been at court that day, seeking from Cromwell the payment of a gift Henry had promised him:

> Never shall I forget the sorrow which I felt when I saw the most serene queen, your most religious mother, carrying you, still a little baby, in her arms and entreating the most serene king your father, in Greenwich Palace, from the open window of which he was looking into the courtyard, when she brought you to him. I did not perfectly understand what had been going on, but the faces and gestures of the speakers plainly showed that the king was angry, although he could conceal his anger wonderfully well. Yet from the protracted conference of the council (for whom the crowd was waiting until it was quite dark, expecting that they would return to London), it was most obvious to everyone that some deep and difficult question was being discussed.[18]

Evidently something had happened to produce open friction between Henry and Anne, serious enough to cause the king to change his plans at the last minute so as to stay in England to sort it out. Cromwell now had his crisis, and he set out to exploit it to the full.

[16] *Lisle Letters*, iii.677, 684, 687, 689 [*LP*, x.675, 738, 748, 779].
[17] Ibid., iii.690 [*LP*, x.789].
[18] Ales, 'Letter', at p. 527.

To understand what had happened, we need to read back from a group of letters which tell of the queen's behaviour and conversation after her arrest. Unfortunately these were damaged in the great fire which spoiled the Cottonian Collection in 1731, but a good deal can be reconstructed from the work of John Strype who had used them prior to that.[19] In particular, they reveal two episodes. One, which came to a head on Sunday 30 April, is almost certainly the explanation of the public altercation between Anne and Henry which Ales observed. What happened was that Henry Norris went to the queen's almoner to volunteer the statement that he would take his oath that the queen 'was a good woman', and what is more he did so acting on her instructions! This incredible step – and we have Anne's word for it – must mean that something had thrown her conduct into question, and again it was she who explained what this was. Either that day or fairly soon before, while talking with Norris she had asked him why he was postponing his proposed marriage to Margaret Shelton, the king's old flame; he had already been a widower for five years. Her obvious suspicion was that he was reluctant to complete such a match in view of the current campaign against Anne, and so his non-commital reply, coming from one who had been a close supporter, provoked the queen into a shocking imprudence. Flinging away the safety of courtly convention, she said, 'You look for dead men's shoes; for if ought came to the king but good you would look to have me.'

Norris's horrified response to this totally unfair and improper shift in the basis of their relationship was to stammer that if he had any such thought 'he would his head were off', but the queen would not let him escape. She could, she said, undo him if she wanted to. A right royal quarrel about their relationship then ensued, before witnesses, and when calm restored common sense, there was nothing left to do but try to stop the rumours of what had occurred doing damage; hence the message to the almoner. But such a fracas was impossible to hide, and it was soon all over the court.[20]

[19] BL, Cott. MS Otho Cx ff. 209v, 222, 223, 224v, 225 [*Wolsey*, ed. Singer, pp. 458–9, 453–5, 460–1, 456–7, 451–3]. One undamaged letter in the series remains in Harl. MS 283 f. 134 [*Wolsey*, ed. Singer, pp. 459–60] and another in RO, SP1/103 ff. 313–14. [*LP*, x.902]. Singer supplies some of the lacunae from Strype.

[20] *Wolsey*, ed. Singer, p. 452. The suggestion that news of the quarrel was widely known at court is based on Edward Baynton knowing of it at Greenwich

Of itself, the pretence that Norris loved his sovereign's wife was harmless and the common currency of courtly dalliance. More than a year before, Francis Weston had been taken to task by the queen for neglecting his own wife and flirting with Madge Shelton, instead of leaving the field clear for Norris.[21] His reply had been that Norris came to the queen's chamber more for Anne than for his intended bride. He then capped that by saying that he himself loved someone in her household better than either his wife or Madge; knowing well the answer, the queen asked, 'Who is that?', but when Weston replied, 'It is yourself', 'she defied him' – slapped him down. All this was evidently part of a cheeky game. What made the Norris episode so dangerous was the current tension at court and the fact that the queen was the aggressor. The rules said that the courtier should make the proposition and the great lady reject him gently or with scorn, as she willed; but Anne had reversed the roles. At once that put Norris's reply on a different level of significance. Anne was making an effort to force the response from Norris which would, because of her flesh and blood challenge, have been a personal commitment, far beyond convention. No more caution about supporting her; he would then truly have been in her power.

If we assume that gossip about Anne and Norris explains Sunday 30 April – the king's anger, Anne's desperate defence even to the point of appealing to him through Elizabeth, and the postponement of the journey to Calais – there was clearly not enough of substance in it yet to provide the jolt Cromwell was looking for. Uncorroborated, the suggestion that there was something illicit between Anne and Norris denied all past behaviour and all probability. Even if the two of them did not remove the king's suspicions, they must have quietened his mind, for Norris remained in attendance and the May Day celebrations went ahead as planned.[22] But the charge against

---

– 'the communication that was last between the queen and Master Norris' – on what must be Wednesday morning, since he makes no mention of accused other than Smeton, Norris and Rochford: ibid., 458–9. Kingston's letter to Cromwell at Westminster must be Wednesday morning also, hence the news was known independently.

[21] Ibid., p. 452.

[22] Ibid., pp. 456–7 does not, as is often supposed, support the idea that Anne knew of Smeton's arrest on the Sunday night. At most it establishes that she learned he was in the Tower 'that night', i.e. Monday, but the mutilated passage may refer to Kingston, and not to Anne.

them would revive if something more serious could be alleged involving Anne and someone else. A second story would make the first plausible, and the attempts of Anne and Norris to pacify the king would then seem like a conspiracy to deceive. Such an opportunity, or rather the raw material to manufacture one, was already in Cromwell's hands, presented by Anne's conduct in the second of the crucial episodes of that last weekend in April.[23] It had taken place on Saturday 29 April and showed Anne acting not in the 'unfeminine' way she had to Norris (which commentator after commentator has censured as evidence either of guilt or of immodesty), but as a queen in charge of her household, exercising authority in a way that must be described as kind and considerate. The scene was the queen's presence chamber at Greenwich where Anne saw Mark Smeton standing in a window embrasure. Smeton is variously described as a musician, a player of the virginals or the spinet, or an organist; he was possibly not much over twenty. Seeing that the young man appeared downcast, Anne asked why.[24] Smeton replied that it did not matter, at which the queen said, 'You may not look to have me speak to you as I should do to a noble man, because you be an inferior person.' 'No, no, Madam,' he answered, 'A look sufficed me, and thus fare you well.'

This interchange is revealing. Smeton was a skilled and valued member of the privy chamber, in fact something of a pet. According to Cavendish he was the son of a carpenter, but perhaps better evidence suggests that he was a Fleming, as other of the king's leading musicians were.[25] He had been recruited as a lad, five years or more before, and had been brought up by the king alongside Francis Weston, in the same way as, earlier, the marquis of Exeter had been. But unlike them he was not a gentleman. His court upbringing thus made him *déclassé*: he now belonged nowhere.[26] In particular he was excluded from the

[23] Ibid., p. 455.

[24] Nicolas, *Privy Purse, passim*, implies he was of an age with Weston.

[25] Cavendish, *Metrical Vissions*, pp. 36–7; Lowinsky, in *Florilegium*, pp. 192–200. The assumption [p. 199] that one of the proverbs entered in BL, Roy. MS 20 Bxxi refers to Anne is pure conjecture.

[26] Lowinsky, in *Florilegium*, pp. 193–4, 233–4, takes the critical verses of Borbonius entitled '*In Marcum*' to apply to Smeton, thus suggesting a slight figure, a good dancer, avarice and a good opinion of his own capacity. Some of these verses antedate the author's visit to England: e.g. the verse quoted ibid., p. 193 was first published in *Nicolai Borbonii Vandoperani Nugae* (Paris, 1533) at

game of courtly love around the queen and her ladies, and one
may suggest that Anne's remark to him had been triggered by
some trouble on that account. Most of the comments on the
affair imply that Smeton was trying to compete above his
station. The poem attributed to Wyatt clearly portrays the
musician as an outsider:

> A time thou haddest above thy poor degree,
> The fall whereof thy friends may well bemoan:
> A rotten twig upon so high a tree
> Hath slipped thy hold, and thou art dead and gone.[27]

At the trials, a separate count in the indictment alleged friction
and competition between Anne's alleged 'lovers'.[28] Alternatively,
Smeton may have genuinely failed to distinguish between being
a servant in the menial sense, which he was – 'an inferior person'
– and being a servant in the chivalric sense, which he was not. If,
as has been suggested, he was preparing for Anne the book of
motets which is now in the Royal College of Music, he may well
have found the idea of such a gift from a person of his status
greeted with scorn.[29] Most poignant of all is the third possibility
that the young man had failed to realize that courtly love and
true love were different coin.

Either the interchange between Anne and Smeton or, more
likely, the exhibition he had been making of himself had come to
Cromwell's attention, but the opportunity to exploit Smeton's
obvious weakness only arose when the king's annoyance had
been roused by the confrontation with Norris. On the Sunday,
therefore, Cromwell proceeded to have Smeton taken to his
house at Stepney and interrogated. The young man seems to
have held out for nearly twenty-four hours, but in the end he
confessed to adultery with the queen and was committed to the
Tower about six o'clock on the Monday afternoon.[30] As soon as

---

sig.g1v. The poems relating to Borbonius' visit are concentrated in *Nugarum*
Books iv–viii, which appeared for the first time in 1538, and the only two of these
which are addressed to a 'Mark' are to an incompetent doctor: *Nugarum*, v.84,
85, p. 302; *Florilegium*, p. 234.

[27] Wyatt, *Poems*, CXLIX, lines 49–56.

[28] See below, p. 394.

[29] MS 1070; see above, pp. 295–7.

[30] Constantine, in *Archaeologia*, 23. 64 says 'May Day in the morning', but
Antony Antony gives 6 pm [p. 359 above]. The latter is more likely since the
king was clearly not told until the end of the joust.

he had the confession, Cromwell must have informed Henry, who thereupon left Greenwich and, with his previous day's suspicions of Anne and Norris seemingly all confirmed, proceeded to face Sir Henry with the accusation. There is, in fact, a hint that the first charge was that of concealing Smeton's offence, and that only when Norris denied that he knew anything of the musician's adultery was the conclusion drawn that the groom of the stool must have been involved too.[31] The denials of Anne, Norris, and later Rochford were turned by Smeton's confession into evidence of guilt. Sir Edward Baynton wrote on the Wednesday morning to William Fitzwilliam, one of those who had interrogated Anne:

> here is much communication that no man will confess anything against her, but all-only Mark of any actual thing. Whereof (in my foolish conceit) it should much touch the king's honour if it should no farther appear. And I cannot believe but that the other two [Norris and Rochford] be as fully culpable as ever was he. And I think assuredly the one keepeth the other's counsel ... I hear farther that the queen standeth stiffly in her opinion ... which I think is in the trust that she [hath of the] other two.[32]

What is not known about Smeton's confession is the way it was obtained. George Constantine, at the time one of Norris's servants, reported some years later that although Smeton did confess, 'the saying was that he was first grievously racked, which I never could know of a truth.'[33] His caution is in contrast to the *Cronica del Rey Enrico*, which tells a story of Cromwell enticing Smeton to his house, where he was seized by six men while the secretary forced him to confess by tightening a knotted rope around his head.[34] Such a course would have been illegal, and in any case is totally at variance with what Constantine suspected. He was very clearly thinking of interrogation on the rack in the Tower in the usual way, which could not have taken place before Smeton had been admitted there, and by that time or very soon after the king had already received the information

---

[31] *Cal. S. P. Span., 1536–38*, pp. 107–8 [*LP*, x.782]. Roland Bulkeley reported the same day that Norris was the principal and Wiltshire, Rochford, Smeton and sundry ladies were accessories: RO, SP1/103 f. 218 [*LP*, x.785].

[32] *Wolsey*, ed. Singer, pp. 458–9.

[33] Constantine, in *Archaeologia*, 23. 64.

[34] *Cronica del Rey Enrico*, pp. 80–1 [*Chronicle*, ed. Hume, pp. 60–1].

which drove him from Greenwich and into the confrontation with Sir Henry Norris.[35] What, undoubtedly, was used against the musician was psychological pressure. It is possible that Smeton, like Norris, was promised pardon if he confessed, although he may only have been promised royal favour, which might mean life or, failing that, at least a quick and decent death – not the agony of being dragged through the streets on a hurdle, half-strangled, castrated and then disembowelled while still conscious. However, although Thomas Cromwell had Smeton's confession, it remained necessary to hold him to it, so the musician was kept in irons (the only one of those arrested with Anne to be so treated), an earnest of what might worse befall if he changed his story.[36]

Read in this way the coup against Anne Boleyn was a piece of inspired improvisation. But there was more to it than grabbing a chance to remove the queen at the cost of a few unfortunates who had given grounds which might be thought suspicious. Cromwell may well have liked to see it that way. He did have principles and genuine religious feeling, and may well have rationalized his actions as simply his duty in the face of what he had learned. Yet the fact that it was Norris who had become vulnerable meant that the most influential man in the Boleyn faction could be neutralized at the same time as the queen. As has been pointed out by Dr David Starkey, that did mean that Cromwell could henceforth expect to have greater control over the privy chamber, but it is doubtful whether that prospect was yet a main concern.[37] The immediate gain was that he had been able by a single pre-emptive strike to take out both the queen and the groom of the stool. He had, at least in part, solved the problem of how to neutralize Anne and her faction at the same time. It remained to see whether the Boleyns and their supporters possessed a second-strike capacity.

Cromwell, therefore, could not relax. The first need was to

---

[35] If the evidence of Antony Antony who was possibly in the Tower at the time is rejected in favour of Constantine [see above, p. 368[30]], then Smeton could not have confessed at Stepney, but this would have allowed time for torture to be applied, as Constantine suspected, before his confession, which reached the king at Greenwich at the end of the joust.

[36] Burnet, *History,* iv.570; *Wolsey,* ed. Singer, p. 454.

[37] See below, pp. 414–15.

manage the king. This he left to Carewe and the Seymours, to the exploitation of the king's capacity for self-pity and the seductive promise of Jane. A maudlin readiness to feel sorry for himself was one of the least endearing features of Henry VIII's unendearing personality, and it was now indulged to the full.[38] If Chapuys had the story right, the king in the end even poured his sense of ill-usage into a tragedy which he carried in his pocket and tried to get people to read. On the very night of Anne's arrest, when the duke of Richmond had come to say goodnight to his father, the king had begun 'to weep and say that he and his sister [Mary] owed God a great debt for having escaped the hands of that cursed and poisoning whore who had planned to poison them.' As well as self-pity, the exchange with Richmond shows how quickly the Seymour alliance had got to work, for the story that Anne intended to poison Mary and actually had poisoned Katherine had been a fixation with them for months. Jane was removed to Sir Nicholas Carewe's house at Beddington, near Croydon, ostensibly for propriety but actually to encourage the king's ardour and make necessary a series of romantic night-time assignations and river trips which actually began to win popular sympathy for Anne. No man, Chapuys reported, ever paraded with such regularity the fact that his wife had cuckolded him, and with so little sign that he minded![39]

Cromwell, meanwhile, had more serious things to attend to. It was essential that the Boleyn faction should not recover its balance and mount a counter-coup. That alone would have necessitated the arrest of Rochford, and it may be that he did make some such attempt. Rochford was not detained at Greenwich where he had been on May Day, but at Whitehall after dinner on the Tuesday, reaching the Tower at two o'clock.[40] Since he evidently had not accompanied the king the night before and since he could perfectly well have been held and interrogated at Greenwich as his sister was, it is reasonable to suspect that he went to London of his own volition with the

---

[38] On the following see *Cal. S. P. Span.*, *1536–38*, pp. 124–5, 127 [*LP*, x.908]. This reads as though Henry had composed his tragedy before Anne's arrest, which seems hardly likely. But the ambassador was clearly puzzled, for he suggested that the king was referring to poems which Anne and George Boleyn had laughed at. For the full text: Friedmann, *Anne Boleyn*, ii.176 n.1, 267 n.2.

[39] *Cal. S. P. Span.*, *1536–38*, p. 121 [*LP*, x.909].

[40] *Wolsey*, ed. Singer, p. 451 and p. 359" above.

intention of intervening with Henry. That he failed was probably due to Cromwell's care in blocking access to the king. Boleyn supporters were simply unable to get through; Henry remained incommunicado, venturing out only 'in the garden and in his boat at night, at which times it may become no man to prevent him'.[41]

This certainly killed Cranmer's attempt to speak up for Anne. Letters had been despatched immediately Anne was sent to the Tower, ordering the archbishop to come to Lambeth but by no means to attempt to see the king, so that he was reduced on Wednesday to writing the most difficult letter of his life, pleading for Anne but in no way impugning either the king's actions or motives, while at the same time (since he did not know the strength of the evidence) trying to distance Anne from the reformed cause she had favoured.[42] That some writers have stigmatized his efforts as sycophantic or cowardly is a measure of their failure to appreciate Cranmer's dilemma. He was then summoned to appear in star chamber, where the council presented as fact the accusations against Anne. In a postscript to his letter he allowed himself one final vibration of doubt before rehearsing the inevitable royal credo: 'I am exceedingly sorry that such faults can be proved by the queen, as I heard of their relation. But I am, and ever shall be, your faithful subject.'

Sir Francis Bryan was similarly treated. He was away from court but was 'sent for in all haste on his allegiance', and only admitted to the king's presence after an interview with Cromwell.[43] A man with either a greater loyalty or perhaps a less well developed sense of self-preservation was Sir Richard Page. He, like Bryan, was away from court at the time and, no doubt,

---

[41] *Lisle Letters*, iii.698 [*LP*, x.919].

[42] Cranmer, *Letters*, pp. 323–4.

[43] BL, Cott. MS Cleo. E iv ff. 109v–110 [*LP*, xiii(1).981(2) at pp. 362–3]. Retha M. Warnicke, 'The fall of Anne Boleyn: a reassessment', in *History* 70 (1985), 4–6, has argued (apparently following D. R. Starkey) that Bryan was a key figure in the alliance against Anne. The evidence presented to link him with the Seymours is suspect [see above, pp. 336–7]; in Jan. 1536 French sources say that Bryan was hostile to Katherine [*LP*, x.175]; there is the difficulty that Bryan only returned to court in early April, having been 'long absent', but left again after 14 and before 28 April: *Lisle Letters*, iii.671, 673, 686 [*LP*, x.635, 669, 748]; there is the need to explain his sudden recall. The fact that Bryan became the alternate chief gentleman of the privy chamber *after* the fall of Norris [Starkey, thesis, pp. 240–3] cannot be used to establish his factional alignment *before* that event.

called back by another 'marvellous peremptory commandment', but on Monday 8 May he was in the Tower.[44] Sir Thomas Wyatt was another supporter taken there that day, though we have no details.[45] It would be all of a piece with his character for Wyatt to have shown open contempt for the servile rush to vilify Anne and the other unfortunates; even the Tower would only keep him quiet briefly. On the other hand, Wyatt himself believed that his imprisonment was Suffolk's contribution to the disaster of May 1536.[46] Other Boleyn men seemed lucky to have escaped. Harry Webbe, sewer of the chamber, was suspected by some; George Taylor, Anne's receiver-general, was reported to be showing visible signs of relief after the executions were over.[47]

The arrest of Rochford and the others and the blocking of access to the king drew the teeth of the remaining Boleyn supporters. The earl of Wiltshire himself bought safety by a willingness to condemn his daughter's alleged lovers, while others, like Bryan, began to think more about adapting to the new situation and coming away with a share of the inevitable spoils. Yet Cromwell still had to demonstrate that 'such faults can be proved', and as Edward Baynton admitted on 3 May, that had not yet been convincingly done.

It was then that Thomas Cromwell found an unwitting ally in Anne herself. The suddenness of her arrest seems to have produced a temporary nervous collapse in the queen.[48] She managed the ignominious daylight journey from Greenwich – not yet three years since her coronation triumph along the same stretch of river – with a hostile escort of men like Cromwell whom she had trusted, in through the Tower gates as far as the inner ward; and when the counsellors left her at the Court Gate she was able to go on her knees to declare her innocence and ask them to intercede with the king for her. When, however, she realized that Kingston, the constable of the Tower, was taking her to the royal apartments, the relief broke her. He reported to Cromwell what happened:

[44] *Lisle Letters*, iii.684, 694 [*LP*, x.738, 855] and p. 359⁰ above.
[45] Antony says at 9.00 am: above, p. 359⁰.
[46] Muir, *Life and Letters of Wyatt*, p. 201.
[47] *Lisle Letters*, iii.695; iv.846 [*LP*, x.865, 920]; *LP*, iv.895; Nicolas, *Privy Purse*, pp. 97, 112, 168.
[48] See the letters at p. 365¹⁹.

'Master Kingston, shall I go in to a dungeon?'
'No, Madam you shall go into your lodging that you lay in at
your coronation'.
'It is too good for me. Jesu, have mercy on me!' and she kneeled
down weeping a great pace, and in the same sorrow fell into a
great laughing, and she hath done so many times since.

Put with four unsympathetic attendants, she began to babble
incriminating material, and Kingston, whose original instructions had been to prevent conversation with the queen, seized
the chance to inform Cromwell of this flood of talk. The full story
of the Norris encounter came out, so too the exchange with
Smeton and the year-old impudence of Weston whom, she said,
she feared most. Sir Francis was immediately arrested and taken
to the Tower with the rest – a valuable bonus for the secretary,
for his affinities were with those hostile to Anne. She had clearly
thought of the damage Weston could do if he deposed that for
more than a year Norris had had a personal interest in her, but
Cromwell realized that Weston was more effective as a victim
than as a witness; his arrest disproved the allegation that the
whole affair was a sordid factional putsch.[49] It remained true,
however that this is what it was, and about the same time as
Weston yet another of the Boleyn faction was taken to the
Tower, William Brereton, groom of the privy chamber.[50]
   As the original instructions to keep her in isolation show,
Cromwell had not initally counted on getting anything out of
Anne after her arrest.[51] What other sources, then, were available
to the secretary as he built the case against the queen and the
five men? That question seemed even more pressing at the time
and later in the century than it does today, for the existence of
Kingston's reports of the Tower conversations remained a state
secret, but even now it can be only partly answered. Alexander
Ales would have it that Anne had persuaded Henry to ally with
the German Protestants, and that to frustrate this, Stephen
Gardiner, that *bête noire* of the reformers, sent reports from
France, where he was ambassador, to the effect that stories were

[49] Antony says 5 May, no time stated: above, p. 359⁶.
[50] Antony says Friday 5 May [above, p. 359⁶] but Constantine, who spoke to
Brereton before his arrest, says Thursday before 2.00 pm [*Archaeologia*, 23,
p. 65.
[51] *Wolsey*, ed. Singer, pp. 452–3.

circulating at the court there (based on certain letters) that Anne
was guilty of adultery. This was disclosed to Henry by Cromwell
and his allies, who were opposed to Anne because she was trying
to block their schemes to pocket the profits of the spoliation of
the Church. Spying, bribery and invention did the rest.[52]

Lancelot de Carles told a different tale.[53] When the sister of
one of the most strait-laced of the king's counsellors was taken to
task by her brother for loose behaviour, she hit back by
suggesting that she was not as great an offender as the queen, who
was guilty with both Mark Smeton and her own brother. The
counsellor told two others, and together they went to the king. A
slightly different version appears in a French prose account in
the Lansdowne MSS, dating from Elizabeth's reign.[54] In this the
sister has become one of the king's former mistresses who had
been exiled from court for taking another lover, while the brother
is now a doctor named 'Antoine Brun', clearly a confused
memory of Sir Anthony Browne of the privy chamber. This time,
too, Henry himself demands to know the details, and the girl
gives him the names of Mark the musician and one of the
queen's ladies named Marguerite. A second, anonymous,
French poem tells of a plot by Rochford, Anne Boleyn and their
supporters to poison the king, who intends to abandon Anne and
return to Katherine, a plan that is overtaken by two counsellors
who strike at Anne by accusing her of adultery with Brereton,
Weston, Smeton, Norris and Rochford himself.[55] Marguerite, or
rather Marguerita, turns up again in the Spanish *Cronica del Rey
Enrico*, this time as an old woman and an archetypal bawd who
hides Smeton in the sweetmeat closet in the anteroom to the
queen's bedchamber, and produces him when Anne calls for
marmalade. The queen has also to sleep with her former lovers
to assuage their jealousy, and the dénouement comes via a
Thomas Percy, who envies the material prosperity that has
followed Mark's nightly services and informs Cromwell of the
musician's activities.[56]

These and later stories, such as Sander's tale of the queen
finally convincing Henry of her guilt by dropping a handkerchief

[52] Ales, 'Letter', pp. 525–7.
[53] De Carles, in Ascoli, *L'Opinion*, lines 339–458.
[54] Pocock, *Records*, ii.574–5.
[55] Ascoli, *L'Opinion*, pp. 274–8.
[56] *Cronica del Rey Enrico*, pp. 68–76 [*Chronicle*, ed. Hume, pp. 55–9].

to one of her lovers to mop his face after the exertions of the May Day tilt, have enlivened many accounts of Anne Boleyn's fall, but though they may contain occasional vestiges of truth amongst the obvious error, they preserve what was essentially popular gossip and speculation.[57] There are only two informed contemporary sources: accounts of the trial, and the versions which circulated in the royal household. Eustace Chapuys took good care to have an informant present in the Tower for the trials of Anne and Rochford, and his report provides valuable details, but the envoy was more interested in the substance of the allegations than in their source. His, however, is the report which identifies Rochford's wife as the source of the story that Henry's sexual capacities had been a matter of discussion in the queen's household.[58] The lost journal of Antony Antony also referred to the role of Lady Rochford, and probably included words to the effect that 'the wife of Lord Rochford was a particular instrument in the death of Queen Anne.'[59] Bishop Burnet was more specific, suggesting that she provided particularly damaging evidence, 'that there was a familiarity between the queen and her brother beyond what so near a relationship could justify.'[60] The bishop did not have Chapuys' letter, so we can perhaps assume that he was relying on evidence now missing – possibly Antony Antony, possibly someone else. According to de Carles, Rochford said to his judges, 'On the evidence of only one woman you are willing to believe this great evil of me.'[61]

Why Jane, Lady Rochford provided the information is another question. Burnet's suggestion that she was motivated by jealousy at whatever relationship did exist between Anne and George could be correct. A second foreign visitor to London in May 1536 wrote of 'that person who more out of envy and jealousy than out

[57] Sander, *Schism*, p. 133.
[58] *Cal. S. P. Span., 1536–38*, p. 126 [*LP*, x.908].
[59] Oxford, Bodl. Fol. Δ 624, Herbert of Cherbury, *Henry VIII* (1679), contains jottings by Thomas Tourneur from the journal of Antony Antony [facing p. 384]. I am indebted to Mr Gary Hill for this and other references to Antony Antony, and to the argument that Antony did not expand his comment with any mention of Lady Rochford's jealousy or later fate.
[60] Burnet, *History*, i.316.
[61] De Carles, in Ascoli, *L'Opinion*, lines 861–4. In this poem the initial accusations included Rochford, so that the remark applies to the initial informant. If, however, the sequence above is correct, Rochford was not an original suspect and if he made any such remark at the trial it must refer to whoever accused him of incest.

of love towards the king did betray this accursed secret and together with it the names of those who had joined in the evil doings of the unchaste queen'.[62] There is, however, the fact that, whatever her earlier stance, by the end of 1535 Jane had come over to support Mary, with whom her family had had a long association, so that she may have been acting as part of the plot against Anne.[63] Burnet certainly concluded from his evidence that 'she carried many stories to the king or some about him', and Cromwell carefully looked after her interests once she was a widow.[64] Jane did, it is true, send to ask after her husband in the Tower and promised to intercede with the king, apparently to get him the hearing before the commissioners of oyer and terminer which he seems never to have had. We may, if we choose, smell malice, for the message was brought with Henry's express permission and by Carewe and Bryan in his newly turned coat.[65]

Chapuys was relying on his observer, but a first-hand report of the trial was kept by Justice John Spelman, who was officially present. This concludes: 'And note that this matter was disclosed by a woman called Lady Wingfield who was a servant of the said queen and shared the same tendencies. And suddenly the said Wingfield became ill and a little time before her death she showed the matter to one of those etc.'[66] The final 'etc.' is only a lawyer's abbreviation for any matter that is self-evident,

---

[62] This exists in an Italian version [Hamy, *Entrevue*, p. ccccxxxi] but is quoted here from the Portugese version [Bentley, *Excerpta Historica*, pp. 261–2].

[63] Warnicke, in *History* 70. 6–7, argues for the association of the Parkers with Katherine and Mary. On the other hand, Lord Morley was on close terms with Anne: see above, p. 318.

[64] Ellis, *Letters*, 1 ii.67 [*LP*, x.1010]; *LP*, xi.17. One may also wonder whether the incrimination of Lady Rochford in the crimes of Katherine Howard may not have owed something to revenge.

[65] *Wolsey*, ed. Singer, pp. 453–4.

[66] Spelman, *Reports*, i.71. Bishop Burnet, who saw Spelman's original (now lost), noted that the rest of the page was torn off, which has given rise to the belief that part of the report has been lost [Burnet, *History*, i.316]. Any loss must have happened before the Yelverton MS copy [BL, Hargrave MS 388], which is now the only authority, was written early in Elizabeth's reign, for this shows no sign of any awareness of missing material at the relevant point: f. 187v. The Yelverton MS rearranged the original alphabetical order of topics into a chronological one [*Reports*, i.xxiii–iv, xxxii–iii], with the Boleyn material having originally appeared under the heading *Corone*. But there is no sign of lost or defective material in any of the sections which could have appeared on the other side of the torn page. Therefore either the half-page torn off coincided

not a sign that something is missing, and in this case it means: 'who reported the story'. Lady Wingfield was born Bridget Wiltshire, daughter of Sir John, of Stone Castle in Kent, and had married Richard, one of the twelve Wingfield brothers, a KG and prominent in diplomatic circles until his death in 1525. She took as her second husband Sir Nicholas Harvey, again an ambassador and a strong supporter of Anne Boleyn, but he died in 1532. She then married another courtier, Robert Tyrwhitt, but must herself have died fairly soon afterwards, for she is last noticed receiving a New Year's gift from the king in 1534.[67]

Chapuys implies that Lady Wingfield was deliberately recruited for Anne's service, and this could well be explained by the Kent connection, for Stone is only twenty miles north of Hever; but when he first noticed her in 1530, she was in no way a newcomer to the court itself. She was in Katherine's retinue as far back as the Field of Cloth of Gold.[68] And she was close to Anne, or was so at one time: a letter to Lady Wingfield from Anne, undated but possibly written between December 1529 and August 1532, tantalizes with its questions:

> I pray you as you love me, to give credence to my servant this bearer, touching your removing and any thing else that he shall tell you on my behalf; for I will desire you to do nothing but that shall be for your wealth. And, madam, though at all time I have not showed the love that I bear you as much as it was in deed, yet now I trust that you shall well prove that I loved you a great deal more than I fair for. And assuredly, next mine own mother I know no woman alive that I love better, and at length, with God's grace, you shall prove that it is unfeigned. And I trust you do know me for such a one that I will write nothing to comfort you in your trouble but I will abide by it as long as I live. And therefore I pray you leave your indiscreet trouble, both for displeasing of

---

exactly with a complete report on the opposite side, or one side was blank (neither probabilities), or both sides were blank – hence the removal. To end a report 'etc.' is standard legal practice, and there are numerous examples in Spelman.

[67] There are too many Lady Wingfields for comfort. The identification is made on the evidence of Chapuys that Sir Richard's widow, who had married Harvey, 'came to court in attendance on' Anne: *Cal. S. P. Span., 1529–30*, p. 586; *House of Commons*, ii.310; iii.501, 645; RO, E101/421/13 [*LP*, vii.9]; *LP*, vii.1672. Anne and Henry stayed at Stone Castle in Nov. 1532: Nicolas, *Privy Purse*, p. 274.

[68] Russell, *Cloth of Gold*, p. 203.

God and also for displeasing of me, that doth love you so entirely. And trusting in God that you will thus do, I make an end. With the ill hand of

Your own assured friend during my life,

Anne Rochford[69]

The most plausible explanation of this letter is to tie it to Chapuys' report in 1530, and to an invitation from Anne to Lady Wingfield to come to court. That first request had evidently been denied for two reasons: first, a sense that Anne, in her new-found prosperity, had been neglecting an old friend (something that is freely admitted and amendment promised), and second, a hint of some 'indiscreet trouble'. What that was we do not know, but 'indiscreet' carries the sense that it is Lady Wingfield's reaction that is being questioned as excessive, and since it also fails to 'please' God we can assume some natural mishap such as the loss of a close relative or child. It was also a 'trouble', for which 'removing' and the promise of Anne's favour would be a 'comfort' – the offer of a prominent place in the service of the king's intended wife as, one may presume, an opportunity to dispel grief.[70]

This is by no means the only construction that can be put on this letter – there may be far more in Lady Wingfield's grievance than it allows for – but what is more important is that the letter itself establishes her as a bona fide source: she was in a position to know. But how did whatever she knew reach Cromwell? One possibility is suggested by Wyatt's involvement in May 1536, provided we do not take the 'death-bed revelation' story too literally. Wyatt, as we have seen, placed the blame for his arrest on Suffolk, and there is no doubt of the duke's hostility to Anne, which, if anything, was even greater after the death of Henry's sister Mary and his own remarriage to the daughter of one of Katherine of Aragon's Spanish ladies-in-waiting.[71] The Wingfields, the family of Bridget Wiltshire's first husband, were

---

[69] Wood, *Letters*, ii.74–5 [*LP*, v.12]. The dating depends on the fact that Anne was called Lady Rochford after her father became earl of Wiltshire, 8 Dec. 1529, until she became marchioness of Pembroke, 1 Sept. 1532.

[70] If the 'trouble' refers to the death of Harvey, it would place the letter between 5 and 30 Aug. 1532 and divorce it from the Chapuys reference.

[71] J. E. Paul, *Catherine of Aragon and her Friends* (1966), pp. 34–47, 126–8, 131–3. For the Wingfields and Brandon, see *House of Commons*, iii.638–41.

clients of Suffolk, and it is easy to see how any of her reminiscences – say, of Anne's early passage with Wyatt – could have
reached the duke from the Wingfields. A more direct line for
stories is through the family of Bridget's third husband, the
Tyrwhitts of Kettleby in Lincolnshire who, unlike the Wingfields,
would have heard any actual death-bed revelation. Sir Robert
Tyrwhitt, her father-in-law, was prominent in the Lincolnshire
rebellion later in the year as one of the leading gentlemen of the
shire who wished to manipulate the rising to force changes in
government policy; he was in touch with Lord Hussey and was
the brother-in-law of Sir Robert Constable, the captain of the
Pilgrimage of Grace in Yorkshire.[72] In other words, he may well
have sympathized with the faction which in April 1536 had
supported Mary, and have made what he knew available.

The account of the evidence against Anne which was current
in the royal household exists in both an official and an unofficial
form. The first is found in a letter from Cromwell to Wallop and
Gardiner in France, which is dated 14 May and may be felt to be
congruent with the de Carles version: after ladies of the privy
chamber had informed certain counsellors, there followed an
interrogation of some of the privy chamber and a number of the
queen's staff.[73] When, however, Gardiner asked for more
specifics, Cromwell evaded the request, saying that he had gone
as far as he could without sending the confessions, which were
'so abhominable' that a good part was not even given in evidence
at the trial![74] For what circulated amongst the courtiers themselves we are indebted to the letters of the indefatigable John
Hussey to his employer Lord Lisle, starved of news at his post in
Calais.

According to Hussey, three court ladies gave information
against Anne – one unnamed, another Anne Cobham, and the
third and principal source, 'my Lady Worcester'.[75] The significance of what Mrs Cobham said we do not know, but the
identity of the anonymous lady can be guessed at. In his letter of
3 May about the need to find more evidence, Edward Baynton,

[72] E.g. *LP*, xi.533–4, 539.
[73] Ibid., x.873.
[74] Ibid., xi.29.
[75] *Lisle Letters*, iii.703a; iv.847 [*LP*, x.953, 964].

Anne's vice-chamberlain of the household, gave Fitzwilliam what was obviously intended as a nudge to the commission of enquiry: 'I have mused much at [the behaviour] of Mistress Margery which hath used her [self most] strangely toward me of late, being her friend as I have been. But no doubt it cannot be but that she must be of council therewith; there hath been great friendship between the queen and her of late.'[76] 'Mistress Margery' could be Margaret Shelton the queen's cousin, but is more likely to have been Margery Horsman, who was well known and useful to Hussey, and whose identity he therefore had reason to keep close.[77] Her involvement may explain the 'Marguerite' or 'Marguerita' of the European accounts, but these clearly magnify and blacken her role out of all reason. Despite what Baynton says as to her obstinate support of her mistress, Margery Horsman passed smoothly, on Anne's death, into the service of her successor, Jane Seymour.[78]

A more important thread to follow is Lady Worcester. She was Elizabeth Browne, daughter of Sir Anthony of the privy chamber and niece of Sir William Fitzwilliam, treasurer of the household – and this leads straight back to the French prose account and the de Carles poem. Browne was a staunch supporter of Mary, and Baynton's letter alone would establish how prominently Fitzwilliam was engaged on the Boleyn affair in that first fortnight in May.[79] On the other hand it does well to be cautious, as over 'Mistress Margery' and 'Marguerita'. Elizabeth Browne was not the king's ex-mistress, nor was she Browne's sister, nor one of the bright young things at court. She had been married to Henry earl of Worcester for nine years and more, and was currently expecting a child. She was certainly close to Anne. Her husband's sister was William Brereton's wife, and in the Tower the queen showed considerable distress on her account: '[she] much lamented my lady of Worcester for because her child did not stir in her body, and [Lady Kingston] said, "What should be the cause?" She said,

---

[76] *Wolsey*, ed. Singer, p. 458.

[77] See above, pp. 266–8.

[78] *Lisle Letters*, iv.863 [*LP*, x.1165].

[79] *Wolsey*, ed. Singer, p. 458. It was Fitzwilliam who obtained Norris's (withdrawn) confession, who helped to interrogate Anne, and who was noted as not having the time to read correspondence 'since these matters begun': Constantine, in *Archaeologia*, 23.64; *Wolsey*, ed. Singer, p. 456; *Lisle Letters*, iii.695 [*LP*, x.865].

"For sorrow she took for me."[80]

What Anne meant is not clear. It seems unlikely that she would have known of any reaction to the shock of her arrest (though that is not impossible), but if she was referring to some earlier failure of the baby to quicken, then 'sorrow she took for me' must refer to the loss of Anne's own child or to her recent struggle to preserve her marriage, or both, and it certainly indicated Lady Worcester as a Boleyn supporter worth interrogating. Thus she may have come into the business, not as an ally of Fitzwilliam and Browne or because, as their relative, she was vulnerable to pressure, but as another illustration of Cromwell's methodical pursuit of all the leads Anne presented to him. We must also note Hussey's caution – 'Lady Worcester beareth the name to be the principal' – which could mean no more than that contemporary gossip had put daughter and father together as historians have done since, or that her interrogation was known to have been protracted, or both.

The Lady Wingfield trail and the Lady Worcester trail do, therefore, both lead directly to Anne. So, too, Lady Rochford and Mistress Margery. And then there was Anne's own conversation. As Cromwell sat down to whip into shape a case against Anne and the rest, he certainly had material to work on. How substantial it was is another question, and one which first would have to be decided by two grand juries and then by two trial juries, one for the four commoners and the other of peers, presided over by the lord steward of England, for the trial of Anne herself and her brother, George Viscount Rochford. When the queen had been taken into custody by Sir William Kingston she had asked, 'Master Kingston, shall I die without justice?', and he had replied, 'The poorest subject the king hath, had justice', whereupon she laughed.[81] It remained to be seen whether her laughter was justified.

[80] *Wolsey*, ed. Singer, p.452.
[81] Ibid., p. 452.

17

Judgement

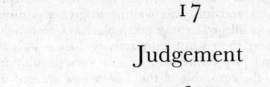

BY THE end of the first week of May Cromwell's sources had given him enough for his purpose. The judicial machine was then put to work with an unaccustomed despatch, which was eloquent of the need to end matters speedily.[1] On Tuesday 9 May a writ went out to the sheriffs of London, to assemble the next day a grand jury of 'discreet and sufficient persons' to decide whether there was prima facie evidence of the offences alleged at Whitehall and Hampton Court. Despite the short notice the sheriffs produced a list of forty-eight men, three quarters of whom turned up at Westminster, as instructed, before John Baldwin, chief justice of the common pleas, and six of his judicial colleagues.

Why Chief Justice Baldwin was chosen is a minor puzzle. John Fitzjames, chief justice of the king's bench, would have been the expected choice, and Baldwin had the disadvantage of being Norris's brother-in-law. Whether Baldwin was selected so that, having presided over a routine scrutiny of the charges, he would be inhibited from later obstruction, or whether it was because Fitzjames had publicly shown his distaste for the prosecution of Thomas More, it is impossible to say.[2] The jury, in any case, had no real choice but to send such serious allegations for trial, and any doubts would have been borne down by the foreman, who was none other than More's son-in-law, Giles Heron; just to make matters doubly sure, another

---

[1] For the following see Wriothesley, *Chronicle*, i.189–226 and the letters listed above, p. 365[19]; RO, C193/3 f. 80.

[2] R. Marius, *Thomas More* (1985), p. 510.

juryman was a senior officer of the royal household. The next day, Thursday, Baldwin and three of the judges went to Deptford, where a Kent grand jury was waiting to give a positive verdict on the offences alleged to have taken place at Greenwich. Meanwhile in London, there was frantic activity. Just as soon as the Middlesex grand jury return was in – or very possibly in anticipation of it – the constable of the Tower was ordered to have Weston, Norris, Brereton and Smeton at Westminster Hall on the Friday. At the same time private summonses clearly went out to the trial jury; formal instructions to the sheriffs did not go out until the day itself, by which time thirty-six knights and esquires were already on the way to do their duty.

Westminster Hall that day was a grim contrast to the scene three years before. By an irony, the prisoners found themselves not more than twenty feet from where Queen Anne had sat, but instead of the blue carpet, the golden tapestries and the laden tables, there were the timber scaffoldings of the law courts. Where the king's musicians had filled the air with noise, there was now the silence of his guard and the brooding presence of the great axe, its edge for the present turned away from the prisoners, but ready to swing towards them at the moment judgement was given against them.[3] As the jurymen were called one by one into the court, Norris and the others knew their fate was sealed. Everyone who was sworn was a knight – a more prestigious jury could not be imagined – but everyone was known to be a royal servant or hostile to Anne or committed to Cromwell. Even before the sheriffs had received the formal orders to send up jurors independent of the prisoners, Cromwell had pre-selected as hostile a panel as could be imagined. The foreman was Edward Willoughby, who owed Brereton money. Next came William Askew, a welcome guest in Mary's household; then Walter Hungerford, a scape-grace dependant of Cromwell's and a homosexual. Giles Alington was married to More's stepdaughter; Sir John Hampden's daughter was sister-in-law to William Paulet, controller of the royal household; William Musgrave, as the star government witness who had failed to make treason charges stick against Lord Dacre, was desperate to cling to Cromwell's favour; Thomas Palmer was one of the king's

---

[3] De Carles was much impressed by this feature of English criminal procedure: in Ascoli, *L'Opinion*, lines 717–32, 774–6.

gambling cronies and a client of William Fitzwilliam. Robert Dormer was a known opponent of the breach with the pope; Richard Tempest was related to and an ally of another conservative, Lord Darcy (and on good terms with Cromwell); Thomas Wharton was a leech clinging to the earl of Northumberland, who was desperately afraid that his earlier courtship of Anne would drag him down too.

Whether the accused challenged any of the jurymen is not clear. Under the normal rules the four defendants could have refused twenty (or possibly thirty-five) each, which would have prevented the trial that day and for several days to come. But there was doubt about such challenges in treason trials, and nobody before had tried the tactic. It is possible that Norris or one of the others did refuse the ex-lord mayor John Champnes, who was probably going blind, and Antony Hungerford who was related to Jane Seymour, but instead they only got William Sidney, who was an old colleague of Lord Darcy and close to the duke of Suffolk as well. And behind Sidney were many more of that same ilk.[4] In any case there was, to such lifelong courtiers, only one hope – that the king would relent. It was a faint hope, but one that would be entirely extinguished by too much obstinacy and obstruction. And it was, of course, entirely in the king's hands to mitigate the full rigour of any sentence for treason – or to refuse to do so.

The trial ground through its established procedures. Smeton confessed to adultery, but pleaded not guilty to the rest of the charge; Norris, Weston and Brereton pleaded not guilty to all. Even where the jury was not loaded in advance, defendants in a Tudor criminal trial – even more, a state trial – were at an enormous disadvantage. They did not have advance warning of the detailed charges, and since they were not allowed defence counsel, they were reduced to trying to answer on the spot what was in effect a public interrogation by hostile and well prepared crown prosecutors determined not so much to present the government case as to secure a conviction by fair questions or foul. The expected verdict came – guilty. And the judgement –

---

[4] The remaining member of the jury was William Drury, esquire of the body and an associate of Russell. For the jury see *House of Commons*, i.307–8, 342–3; ii.52–3, 60–1, 409–10, 646–8; iii.54–6, 430–1, 597–9; *LP*, iv.1136(16); 1939(8), 5623(10), 6187(12); G.E.C., *Peerage*, vi.624–7; Brereton, *Letters and Accounts*, p.105; John Stow, *Survey of London*, ed. C. L. Kingsford (Oxford, 1908), i.133.

drawing, hanging and quartering in all its horror. The edge of the axe was turned to the prisoners, and they were returned to the Tower to await execution at Tyburn.

Anne and her brother had a weekend to wait. They were not to be tried at Westminster Hall but in the Great Hall of the Tower. This was a matter of propriety, not privacy; Chapuys estimated the number attending that Monday at two thousand, and the special stands erected to hold them could still be seen in 1778.[5] They watched a scene of the utmost solemnity, with the duke of Norfolk sitting as lord steward under a cloth of estate, and his son at his feet, deputizing for his father as earl marshal, plus a jury of twenty-six peers assisted by the chancellor and the royal justices.[6] Anne was brought in by the constable and the lieutenant of the Tower to be tried first, accompanied by Lady Kingston and her aunt, Lady Boleyn. After formal courtesies on both sides, Anne sat in the chair provided, raised her right hand when called, and pleaded 'not guilty' to the indictment.

The queen was once more in command of herself and clearly of the situation, and her sparing and effective answers quietly dominated the court.[7] From the moment of her arrest, Anne had realized the difficulty of establishing her innocence. As she had said to Kingston: 'I can say no more but "nay", without I should open my body;' and, 'If any man accuse me, I can say but "nay", and they can bring no witnesses.'[8] Yet when the time came, her manner did carry conviction. No, she had not been unfaithful; no, she had not promised to marry Norris; no, she had not hoped for the king's death; no, she had not given secret tokens to Norris; no, she had neither poisoned Katherine nor

---

[5] *Cal. S. P. Span.*, *1536–38*, p. 125 [*LP*, x.908]; E. O. Benger, *Memoirs of the Life of Anne Boleyn* (1827), p. 404.

[6] Given the small number of available peers, the crown was in no position to attempt much 'packing'. It had to rely on the peculiar loyalty peers were expected to give the king – or on their personal respect and fear of him. For the trial of Anne and Rochford see p. 383[1] above and also Wriothesley, *Chronicle*, i.37–9; de Carles, in Ascoli, *L'Opinion*, lines 821–1046; Friedmann, *Anne Boleyn*, ii.238; *Cal. S. P. Span.*, *1536–38*, pp. 125–7 [*LP*, x.908]; Ales, 'Letter'; Antony Antony in Herbert, *Henry VIII* (1679) [see above, p. 376[59]], facing p. 385; Spelman, *Reports*, i.59, 70–1.

[7] Ales goes too far in presenting Anne as a silent martyr. He does, however, suggest that Richard Pollard ['Master Polwarck'] led for the crown, not Christopher Hales A.G. Pollard was later in the forefront of government prosecution of rebels after the Pilgrimage of Grace.

[8] *Wolsey*, ed. Singer, pp. 451, 457.

planned to poison Mary; yes, she had given money to Francis
Weston, but she had done the same to many of the always
penurious young courtiers; and so it went on. Charles Wriothesley,
who was temperamentally inclined to Katherine and Mary,
expressed the common view: 'She made so wise and discreet
answers to all things laid against her, excusing herself with her
words so clearly as though she had never been faulty to the
same.'[9] If de Carles is correct and Anne was in some way
formally deprived of her honours before being sentenced, even
then she kept up her plea and the sympathy of the onlookers. But
not of the jury, as it deliberated under the watchful eye of the
duke of Suffolk. The peers returned to their seats and in
traditional form gave their verdicts one by one, from the most
junior upwards, as the lord steward summoned them by name:
'Guilty, guilty, guilty . . .' Norfolk pronounced sentence, weeping
as he did so – and is it cynical to wonder whether they were more
tears of relief than sympathy?

> Because thou has offended our sovereign the king's grace in
> committing treason against his person and here attainted of the
> same, the law of the realm is this, that thou hast deserved death,
> and thy judgement is this: that thou shalt be burned here within
> the Tower of London, on the Green, else to have thy head smitten
> off, as the king's pleasure shall be further known of the same.[10]

Burning or beheading? An angry rustle went round the judges;
such an either/or judgement was most improper![11] Anne, however, did not hesitate as she addressed the court. Speeches at
such a moment are notoriously subject to later embellishment,
and de Carles puts into the queen's mouth an eloquent excul-
pation which is the less credible because delivered after and not,
as procedure dictated with that sort of plea, before judgement.[12]
Parts do, however, agree with Chapuys' report that Anne said in
mitigation that she was ready to die but regretful for the lives of
those innocent and loyal men who were to die because of her.
There may also be a ring of truth in the words:

[9] Wriothesley, *Chronicle*, i.37–8.
[10] Ibid., i.38.
[11] Spelman, *Reports*, i.71.
[12] De Carles has Anne presenting a mixture of defence, rebuttal of judgement
and defiance, plus a plea for those condemned with her. This last, and a request
for time to prepare her soul, is found in Chapuys: *Cal. S. P. Span.*, *1536–38*,
p. 127 [*LP*, x.908].

> I do not say that I have always borne towards the king the humility which I owed him, considering his kindness and the great honour he showed me and the great respect he always paid me; I admit, too, that often I have taken it into my head to be jealous of him . . . But may God be my witness if I have done him any other wrong.[13]

She knew that she had not been the waxen wife of conventional expectation, to be moulded or impressed at her husband's will. What she did not say was that the king had pursued her because of her steel, that he had needed her steel and was only where he was because of it. Instead she asked for time, time to make her peace with God. And then she was gone.

A minor flurry caught the attention for a moment, after Anne had left. The earl of Northumberland, who had given his verdict along with the rest against the woman he had once courted, collapsed and had to be helped out. Then the second trial began, as Rochford was brought to the bar of the court. Again the plea was not guilty, and again a Boleyn used intellect and wit to crumble the royal case to dust. The performance of Anne and George that day is a clear indication of the calibre of each and of why they had to die; they were certainly not upstarts or pasteboard figures, enjoying favour only because and for as long as Henry lusted after Anne's body. The questions about the king's sexual performance were asked, and Rochford showed his contempt by reading out what Cromwell wanted kept secret. Again the audience was with him – not even More had been so effective – and the odds, Chapuys said, ran ten to one for an acquittal. Again, not so among the peers. 'Guilty' . . . and the duke of Norfolk found himself again condemning one of his sister's children to death, the full butchery of the male sentence for treason, to be carried out at Tyburn. For the second time there was no collapse. Rochford made a conventional acceptance of death – was not every man a sinner and deserving of death every day? – but his main thought was for the many to whom he owed money, and who faced ruin if the king, who was now entitled to all his property, did not choose to pay them. According to Chapuys he actually read out a list of his debts before leaving the court, and he certainly continued to be troubled about them in the little time that was left to him.

[13] De Carles, in Ascoli, *L'Opinion*, lines 1002–12.

When the duke of Suffolk's 'Guilty' completed the verdict against Rochford, it was the ninety-fifth consecutive voice against the Boleyns and those accused with them.[14] The peers, knights and gentry of two grand juries, a petty jury, and a jury of peers sitting twice had all decided against them. It is an impressive total and at first sight suggests that even granted the demonstrable hostility of some jurors, the government must have had a strong case. We have seen that Cromwell's investigations did lead directly to Anne. What had he unearthed to persuade so many? By far the largest part of the indictments concerned the allegation of adultery. Anne was accused, with dates and with locations in the county of Middlesex, of one offence of soliciting and one of illicit intercourse with each of the men, and the same in the county of Kent, twenty offences in all. Each allegation was protected by the catch-all addition, 'and on divers other days and places, before and after', so that even if the specific charge was rebutted, the force of the indictment would remain. Yet as far as testing the truth of the charge is concerned, the dates stated are all that we have to go on.[15]

The first accusation of misconduct was with Henry Norris at Westminster on 6 and 12 October 1533, followed by Norris and William Brereton at Greenwich in November. May and June 1534 saw offences by Weston at Whitehall and Greenwich and by Smeton at Greenwich only; the latter's Middlesex offence was at Whitehall in April 1535, while Rochford appears in November 1535 at Whitehall and in December at Eltham. Where Anne and the others actually were on these occasions cannot always be established, and since the king and queen did not always keep household together it is only of partial help to know where the king was. However, a considerable coverage of data can be obtained.

The first point that is glaringly obvious is the near-exclusive concentration of offences at Whitehall and Greenwich. Only Brereton 'obliged' the queen at Hampton Court, only Rochford at Eltham and nobody at all at Richmond, while unsullied

[14] Two grand juries of sixteen, a petty jury of twelve, a jury of twenty-six peers for Anne and twenty-five for Rochford.
[15] The 'divers other days and places' are always limited to the location alleged in the main charge, e.g. Norris accused of intercourse at Westminster on specific days is accused also of 'divers . . . at Westminster', never elsewhere in Middlesex. Brereton is the exception, with the original offence at Hampton Court and 'divers . . . at Westminster'.

morality reigned in all the counties visited by the court except for Middlesex and Kent. Perhaps it was the air of those two counties, or perhaps the cost of mobilizing the evidence from further afield. Eleven of the twenty offences definitely could not have happened, since either Anne or the man involved was somewhere else, and two others could be ruled out if we presume that Anne was in the same palace as the king at the relevant time. The solicitation of Smeton at Greenwich on 13 May 1535 can also be ruled out as it was linked to intercourse there on 19 May, by which time Anne was actually at Richmond. The alleged dates and places of the offences only coincide with the possible location of the parties in November 1533 and at Christmas 1535–6. Why this should be is readily explicable. Everybody knew (and could be expected to remember) that Anne had spent the autumn of 1533 at Greenwich recovering from the birth of Elizabeth on 7 September. Admittedly, to claim that the solicitation of Norris took place at Westminster on 6 October, and intercourse there on 12 October, was careless, as well as medically improbable; Anne was likely still to have been in purdah at Greenwich, pending being churched after the birth of the baby. Nevertheless, the November charges could be true. Similarly with Christmas 1535–6. Everyone, prisoners included, might be expected to remember where they had spent the previous Christmas. Such obvious memory-points apart, the charges against Anne and her fellow accused are rebutted by alibis, and the care taken to inject probability where it might be noticed brings the whole section of the indictment into disrepute. Only the 'divers other days and places' trap remains, and to rebut this Anne would have needed to show that she had spent her married life in a closed nunnery.

Against the implausibility of the charges it may seem hardly necessary to deploy the positive indications of innocence. Anne, at the damnation of her immortal soul, swore on the sacrament twice – before and after receiving the consecrated wafer – that she had never been unfaithful to the king.[16] Her oath convinced Chapuys, and it certainly deserves as much credence as history has usually allowed to Sir Thomas More's denial of the evidence Richard Rich gave against him; if More, then Anne. Rochford, too, asked for the exceptional privilege of access to the eucharist

[16] *Cal. S. P. Span., 1536–38*, p. 131 [*LP*, x.908]; *Wolsey*, ed. Singer, p. 461.

before he died.[17] More impressive, perhaps, to modern minds ignorant of the prospect of Hell is Norris's choice to face death rather than admit to Anne's dishonour. He did make some sort of statement, supposedly at the persuasion of Fitzwilliam, but he quickly withdrew it.[18] William Brereton, too, insisted on his innocence. Before he was arrested his old school companion George Constantine 'did ask him and was bold upon him', and the answer Brereton gave was 'that there was no way but one with any matter [alleged against him].' His wife certainly believed him; in her will, nine years later, she bequeathed to her son 'one bracelet of gold, the which was the last token his father sent me'.[19]

On the scaffold, the men's conduct was of a piece with this. Royal mercy had exchanged Tyburn for Tower Hill and had remitted all the sentence except beheading. They had each been given a warning by the constable of the Tower early on the day after Anne's trial that they were to die on the Wednesday morning, and they used that last twenty-four hours in trying to clear their obligations and their consciences.[20] Rochford continued to worry about the financial ruin his death would bring

---

[17] Ibid., p. 460.

[18] Constantine, in *Archaeologia*, 23.64. The badly mutilated conclusion to one letter [*Wolsey*, ed. Singer, p. 455] may suggest that Norris confessed the facts of his conversation with Anne but denied the alleged implication. It can be reconstructed as '[whoever tries to take advantage of] anything of my confession, he is worthy to have [my place here; and if he stand to] it, I defy him.'

[19] Constantine, in *Archaeologia*, 23.65; Ives, in *Trans. Hist. Soc. Lancs. & Ches.*, 123.31–2. We may note Chapuys' opinion: 'condemned on presumption and circumstances, not by proof or valid confession' [*'ont este condampnez par presumption et aucuns indices, sans preuve ne confession valid'*]. He did, however, have civil law procedure in mind, which required witnesses or the confessions of the accused: *Cal. S. P. Span., 1536–38*, p. 125 [*LP*, x.908].

[20] Work still needs to be done on the accounts of the executions of May 1536. The following can be identified: (1a) An Italian account by 'P. A.', possibly a Venetian diplomat in England, dated 1 June 1536: in Hamy, *Entrevue*, pp. ccccxxxi–ccccxxxvi, also printed version, Bologna (1536); (1b) A Portugese translation of (1a), dated 1 June, in Bentley, *Excerpta Historica*, pp. 261–5. (2a) An imperial account, printed in Thomas, *The Pilgrim*, pp. 116–17; (2b) A Spanish version of (2a) at Vienna: *LP*, x.911(1). (3) A French account, printed partially in Ascoli, *L'Opinion*, p. 273 and partially in Hamy, *Entrevue*, pp. ccccxxxvii–ccccxxxviii, possibly derived from (2a). (4) De Carles [see above, p. 70[31]]. (5) *Les regretz de Millort de Rocheffort*, printed in Ascoli, *L'Opinion*, pp. 274–8. (6) Constantine, in *Archaeologia*, 23. 64–6. (7) Wriothesley, *Chronicle*, 1.39–40. (8) *Chronicle of Calais*, pp. 46–7.

on others – so much so that the hardened Kingston wrote to Cromwell, 'you must help my lord of Rochford's conscience'; he was also upset when his favourite priest failed to turn up to hear his confession.

The behaviour of state prisoners at the time of execution was almost predictable in Tudor England. As men about to face divine judgement, they were expected to forgive and ask for forgiveness and prayers, and as those condemned by due process of law it was proper to accept the system which had condemned them. No railing against injustice was compatible with this, to say nothing of the unspoken threat that royal mercy could be withdrawn and friends and family might suffer for any final indulgence. Thus Rochford began: 'I was born under the law, I am judged under the law and I must die under the law, for the law has condemned me.' He then went on to confess that he was a sinner whose sins had deserved death twenty (or a thousand) times; and declaring that his fate was a warning to his fellow courtiers not to trust in the vanity of fortune, he asked anyone whom he had offended to forgive him. What he did not say was that he deserved death for the crimes alleged against him. Only Smeton said that: 'Masters I pray you all pray for me for I have deserved the death.' Norris said almost nothing; Weston said that his fate was a warning to others not to presume on life, for 'I had thought to have lived in abhomination yet this twenty or thirty years and then to have made amends.' Brereton came the nearest to implying his innocence: 'I have deserved to die if it were a thousand deaths. But the cause whereof I die, judge not. But if ye judge, judge the best.' And he repeated the last phrase several times. Their remarks and general demeanour were sufficient to convince the average onlooker that they died 'charitably' – they confessed 'in a manner', so Constantine said.[21] Yet he picked up also the significance of what was not said, particularly in the case of Brereton: 'By my troth, if any of them were innocent it was he. For either he was innocent or else he died worst of all.' According to de Carles, Anne's only reaction to the story of the executions was when told that Mark had persisted in his confession: 'Alas! I fear that his soul will suffer punishment for his false confession.' He also noticed that Rochford avoided confessing any offence against the king.

[21] Cf. the opinion of John Hussey: *Lisle Letters*, iii.698 [*LP*, x.919].

The allegations of adultery took up the largest part of the indictments of May 1536, but there were half a dozen other counts as well. Indeed, it is arguable that the adultery charges, implausible as they are to us and were to at least some observers at the time, were primarily there to prejudice opinion against the accused. To rape a queen was a treasonable offence under the statute of 1352. Yet although the adultery of Anne and the rest is time after time so described, sleeping with the king's wife with her consent was not high treason – ill advised, to be sure but not a crime known to the common law or statute, and only punishable in the Church courts as an affront to morality.[22] Of the later charges, several had a similar propaganda purpose or were self-evidently spurious. The implication was made that Anne had somehow stolen the allegiance of Henry's servants. At the trial, though not in the indictment, the rumours about the poisoning of Katherine and the intention to poison Mary were dragged in.[23] The indictment did suggest that the king's life had been endangered by the impact of the revelations; yet not only did the noisy, public pursuit of Jane Seymour show that this supposedly enfeebled monarch was decidedly in rut, but nothing was made at the trial of a construction which would have opened every adulterer to a charge of causing grievous bodily harm!

The charge that all this farrago was designed to embellish, and the one that mattered, was treasonable conspiracy to procure the king's death. The key element in this was the allegation that the queen had many times promised to marry one of her lovers, once the king was dead, and had often said that the king never had her heart. It was a general charge, and Weston's behaviour could easily be inverted and presented so as to support it, but Chapuys makes it clear that Norris was the particular target and that gifts by Anne to him were interpreted as tokens of this contract. Very evidently this accusation is based on the exchange when Anne accused Norris of waiting for dead men's shoes. On her own admission she had discussed with the

[22] That the Treasons Act of 1352 was found not to cover adultery by a queen is indicated by subsequent legislation: 28 Henry VIII, c.7; 33 Henry VIII, c.21.

[23] The suggestion [*LP*, x.908 at pp. 377–8] that the poisoning charge was supported by Anne's gift to Norris of certain *médailles* is based on a wrong punctuation and conflates two separate items [*Cal. S. P. Span., 1536–38*, p. 126; Friedmann, *Anne Boleyn*, ii.277n.1].

groom of the stool what would happen 'if the king dies' – or was it 'when the king dies', or 'as soon as the king is dead', or even, 'if only the king were dead'? To speculate about, and to wish for, may be a wafer apart. Imagining the king's death was treason by the original treason law of 1352, but it had recently been restated to make it clear that words alone were also covered, and though no statute was cited in the indictment, the drafting clearly brought the charge within the latest 1534 act.[24] Also included to indicate conspiracy, or so one must presume, was the allegation that her lovers were quarrelling and vying amongst themselves for her favour – disputes which were made to seem worse by hints of sexual excess and competition, which, as we have seen, derived from Smeton. The inference that the prosecution intended should be drawn from all this even reached France, where one rumour was that Henry was to be poisoned, after which one of the men would marry Anne and take the throne!

What is important for the argument about guilt or innocence is that the events on which the conspiracy charge was principally based occurred on 29 and 30 April, and that the details were revealed by Anne's frenzied disclosures in the Tower on and after 2 May. In other words, the apparent sequence of suspicion, investigation, evidence and arrest, which Cromwell described to Chapuys and to the English ambassador abroad, is an illusion. Anne and the others were not arrested and charged on the basis of known evidence; they were arrested, and the evidence (so-called) then came to light. In the case of one of the accused, William Brereton, we have not the slightest information as to what that evidence was. Anne showed little reaction to the news of his late arrest, and despite his efforts, George Constantine never managed to discover the grounds for the charge against his old schoolfellow.

The appearance of Brereton amongst the queen's 'lovers' does, indeed, seem odd. He was not as prominent as Rochford, Norris and Weston; Wyatt described him as 'one that least I knew', and he was, as the king's contemporary, one of the older

---

[24] Spelman [*Reports*, i.71] reported a charge of slandering the royal issue 'which is made treason by the statute of the twenty-sixth year of the present king'. There is some doubt about what statute was intended. The suggestion adopted above is that he conflated two separate charges: imagining the king's death (restated as treason by 26 Henry VIII, c.13, Dec. 1534) and slandering the royal issue (treason by 25 Henry VIII, c.22, Mar. 1534).

men in the background of the Boleyn faction.[25] He was very much a dependant of Norris and, as we have seen, may well have been in on the secret of Anne's wedding. He had, however, wider links at court, with the duke of Norfolk and especially with the latter's son-in-law, Richmond, so that when Norfolk and Anne fell out, Brereton was pulled two ways. All this might suggest that Brereton was unlucky to be singled out in May 1536 – a small fish caught up with the main catch. In fact his arrest is very revealing of the brutal pragmatism behind the choice of victims. He was picked out from the Boleyn faction as an act of gratuitous malice (or perhaps rough justice), following an earlier and quite separate altercation with Cromwell.

This had arisen from the fact that Brereton had secured, as well as his place at court, a virtual monopoly of royal appointments in Cheshire and North Wales, some of the most important as deputy to Richmond, and that he exploited his authority independent of Cromwell, with the one object of furthering the interests of the Brereton faction in the area. In particular, and with Anne Boleyn's help, he had had a Flintshire gentleman he was quarrelling with, one John ap Gryffith Eyton, arrested in London in 1534, returned to Wales and hanged, in defiance of the minister who had done everything he could to save him.[26] Such a man was a serious obstacle to the minister's plans for settling the problem of the Welsh border, but as much in Cromwell's mind must have been the feeling for just retribution. George Cavendish still echoed it in his *Metrical Visions* twenty years later.

> Furnished with rooms I was by the king,
> The best I am sure he had in my country.
> Steward of the Holt, a room of great winning
> In the Marches of Wales, the which he gave to me,
> Where of tall men I had sure great plenty
> The king for to serve, both in town and field,
> Readily furnished with horse, spear and shield.
>
> God of his justice, foreseeing my malice,
> For my busy rigour would punish me of right,
> Ministered unto Eyton, by colour of justice –

---

[25] Wyatt, *Poems*, CXLIX. For Brereton, see Brereton, *Letters and Accounts*, and Ives, in *Trans. Hist. Soc. Lancs. & Ches.*, 123.1–38.
[26] Ibid., pp. 28–30.

> A shame to speak, more shame it is to write:
> A gentleman born, that through my might
> So shamefully was hanged upon a gallows tree,
> Only of old rancour that rooted was in me.
>
> Lo, here is th'end of murder and tyranny!
> Lo, here is th'end of envious affection!
> Lo, here is th'end of false conspiracy!
> Lo, here is th'end of false detection
> Done to the innocent by cruel correction!
> Although in office I thought myself strong,
> Yet here is mine end for ministering wrong.[27]

The irony of a Brereton hanging an enemy on a flimsy charge of felony, then being himself executed on a flimsy charge of high treason, was a moral too good to forget. For Cromwell it was a chance to weaken the Boleyn faction, pay back old scores and get rid of a real nuisance.

So Cromwell was provided with the essential material against Norris, Weston, Smeton and Anne herself as a result of the queen's ramblings, while charging Brereton similarly but for quite different reasons. Rochford, too, appears to have been a special case. Anne seems to have been unaware at first that she was to be charged with incest, and the early rumours spoke of her brother only as an accessory. The minister also deployed a number of other charges in corroboration of the conspiracy allegations, of which the origin is in doubt. These included the story that the queen had given gifts to her alleged lovers, and that she had become incensed every time she saw one of them paying attention to another woman.

Over and above those stories that were included in the indictment, a mass of scandal as well was produced in court. What John Hussey picked up, even though he could recognize the exaggeration, seems to have shocked him deeply:

Madam, I think verily, if all the books and chronicles were totally revolved, and to the uttermost persecuted [prosecuted] and tried, which against women hath been penned, contrived, and written since Adam and Eve, those same were, I think, verily nothing in comparison of that which hath been done and committed by

---

[27] Cavendish, *Metrical Visions*, pp. 33–5; the first and penultimate stanzas are omitted here.

Anne the Queen; which though I presume be not all thing as it is now rumoured, yet that which hath been by her confessed, and others, offenders with her, by her own alluring, procurement and instigation, is so abhominable and detestable that I am ashamed that any good woman should give ear thereunto. I pray God give her grace to repent while she now liveth. I think not the contrary but she and all they shall suffer.[28]

His letter should not be read as indicating that there were confessions revealed which we now know nothing of. He was writing on 13 May, and clearly in the light of the trials of Norris and the others the day before, where undoubtedly Anne's Tower revelations had been put in against the accused, and in the worst possible light. Indeed, the government had reaped a great advantage by dropping any thought of indicting a principal and accessories. It then became possible to proceed against the four commoners at once, on the basis of 'a confession' consisting of Anne's revelations, presented in the most damning fashion and before she had had the opportunity to challenge them. The judgement against Norris and the rest then disqualified their testimony in law from being cited in her defence, as well as making it virtually impossible to acquit Anne on charges already 'proved'; adulterers necessarily come in pairs!

In the accusations that so impressed Hussey, we can see the information that Cromwell had been able to pick up from the court ladies. That it amounted to no more than what Spelman, perhaps sceptically, described as 'bawdy and lechery, so that there was never such a whore in the realm', is no surprise. In the case of the deceased Lady Wingfield, given the perennial watch kept by Anne's enemies for material to use against the queen, it is certain that anything she said of substance on her death-bed would have been seized on immediately, and not left to gather dust until Cromwell started to ask questions. As for Lady Worcester, again nothing of significance can have been found, for it is a feature of Anne Boleyn's fall that no lady of the court was accused with her. If Anne was a traitor, then anyone who had concealed knowledge of her crimes was, if not an accessory, certainly guilty of misprision of treason.[29]

What seems to have come out from the interrogations was no

---

[28] *Lisle Letters*, iv.845a [*LP*, x.866].
[29] This virtually conclusive point was put by George Wyatt, in *Wolsey*, ed. Singer, pp. 445–6, and powerfully demonstrated in the charge against Lady

more than the trivia of 'pastime in the queen's chamber'. As well
as her jealousy of any rivals and her liberal gifts to her admirers
– neither out of place in the convention of courtly love – she was
accused of dancing with her ladies and the king's gentlemen in
her bedchamber (again, something that was perfectly usual),
and much was made of her being handed from partner to partner
in the course of the dance![30] If the parade of such stories by the
prosecution had any point beyond darkening the atmosphere, it
was in order to make out the most difficult case of all, that
against Rochford. He, in particular, was accused of leading
Anne into the dance – and so of handing her to the next man in
the set! Anne was reported to have kissed him – but English
ladies were famed Europe-wide for their custom of greeting even
strangers with an embrace. This turns up as the accusation that
Anne and George indulged in public in what would now be called
'deep kissing'. She was accused of writing to tell him she was
pregnant – another innocuous practice given a sinister twist. He
was also asked about a suspiciously long stay alone with his sister
in her room. Deliberately misrepresented, conventions of the
court and courtly love could be made damning.

There are, however, one or two items amongst all the rest
which do give pause. There was the accusation that the king had
been held up to ridicule, that his clothes had been laughed at,
and so too his attempts at poetry. Anne's ramblings about
Weston show that the licence in conversations around her
sometimes went quite far, while her own probing of the private
emotions of the courtiers suggests an inability to keep a safe
distance. She could not break herself of that even when in the
Tower, wanting to know how the other accused were housed and
who made their beds, and when told that nobody did, joking that
if they could not make their pallets they might be able to make
ballets [ballads]. There was a good deal in the comment on that
occasion of one of her attendants (the not very favourite aunt),
that 'Such desire as you have had to such tales has brought you
to this.'[31] 'Pastime in the queen's chamber' seems, in fact, to

---

Rochford of being involved in the offences of Katherine Howard. Any
alteration of the routines of attendance on a great lady (e.g., if she insisted on
sleeping alone) would raise immediate comment. Hence it was only possible for
her to commit misconduct if she had an accomplice among her attendants.
[30] For the following see Ales, 'Letter', pp. 528–9.
[31] *Wolsey*, ed. Singer, pp. 454–5.

have got somewhat out of hand, and excessive high spirits never do sound good in a court of law. Perhaps Anne was even hoping to make Henry jealous, or perhaps the feverish atmosphere was an instinctive retort to the emergence of an alternative court around Jane Seymour.

The most dangerous part of this courtly brinkmanship was, of course, tolerating the discussion of how good – or bad – the king was in bed. When, as we have seen, Rochford was asked at his trial whether Anne had talked about that to his wife, he made the clever reply, refusing the question as likely to impugn the royal issue – a response dictated as much by propriety and loyalty as by the Succession Act of 1534. He was, however, silenced by a supplementary question: 'Had he at any time spread the story that Elizabeth was not Henry's child?' Very clearly something of the kind had been said, and apparently more than once. We can imagine it as a joke – 'With his problems, it's hard to see how the king ever got Elizabeth!' – but could anything be more foolish to joke about or for Anne to overlook? It is no doubt this that was the ground for the charge, under the 1534 statute, of slandering the royal issue, which is not in the indictment but which Judge Spelman reported as having been made during the trials. Strange though it is – and we may put it down to ageing, to stress, to overconfidence, to what we will – Anne had allowed herself to relax at the point of her greatest strength, her court-craft. Perhaps she now remembered with bitter regret the advice of Margaret of Austria over twenty years before: 'Trust in those who offer you service, and in the end, my maidens, you will find yourselves in the ranks of those who have been deceived.'[32]

Folly, however, is no crime, nor was it justice to punish with death what at most deserved the rustication from court which Henry had imposed on Carewe, Bryan and his other 'minions' long before. The ninety-five voices which had cried 'guilty' were lying, were deceived, or chose to be deceived. A case sufficient to quiet the general public and satisfy pliant consciences had been manufactured by innuendo and implication, but those in the know were aware how flimsy it was. Chapuys did not believe it – 'condemned on presumption and not evidence, without any witnesses or valid confession' was his conclusion – and Mary of

[32] See above, p. 26.

Hungary, regent of the Low Countries, that niece of Margaret of Austria whom Anne had known as a seven-year-old in Mechelen, was completely cynical about it. The king had

> paid considerable attention to [Jane] before her predecessor was dead which, along with the fact that none of those executed with her except for the organist admitted the deed, any more than she had, made people think he invented the ploy to get rid of her. Nevertheless the woman herself suffered no great injustice by this for she was well known to be a worthless character ... I think that women will not be all that happy if such ways of going on become the custom – and with good reason. And although I do not intend to take the risk myself, yet for the sake of the female sex I will pray like the rest that God will protect us![33]

Thomas Cromwell made a more informed assessment of Anne in which we may detect at least a hint of posthumous amends. When discussing her with Chapuys early in June, he went out of his way to praise the intelligence, spirit and courage of the queen and her brother.[34] Worthy adversaries.

Henry VIII, by contrast, was faced with the fact that in permitting the arrest and, still more, the trial of his wife and friends, he had taken a step which he could not reverse, even if the rage and suspicion which had tipped him over the edge were to seem more questionable in the cold light of reflection. He admitted to Cranmer nearly ten years later that, once a victim was in the Tower and open to every trick of false evidence, there was little to be done.[35] In the case of Anne, the Seymour faction kept up the pressure of enticement, while Cromwell fed him 'facts' about Anne's guilt which he could hide behind. The king responded by whipping up a prurient self-righteousness which anaesthetized all doubt. He declared that his wife had been unfaithful with more than a hundred men, and was morbidly concerned about the plans for the executions, even to the making of the scaffolds.[36] He was at his most judicious in refusing the very considerable persuasions and inducements he was offered to reprieve Francis Weston, so unhappily caught on the wrong side

[33] *Cal. S. P. Span.*, *1536–38*, p. 125; RO, PRO31/8 f. 85 [*LP*, x.908, 965].
[34] *Cal. S. P. Span.*, *1536–38*, pp. 137–8 [*LP*, x.1069].
[35] *Narratives of the Reformation*, p. 255.
[36] *Cal. S. P. Span.*, *1536–38*, p. 121 [*LP*, x.909]; *Wolsey*, ed. Singer, p. 459.

of the factional battle.[37] Since Francis's father was still alive, his death would bring the crown little profit, and Henry would not normally have turned down the chance to trade blood for cash. But not so this time; justice must be done! The king was at his most nauseous in making arrangements – even perhaps in advance of the trial – to bring over the executioner of Calais to kill Anne.[38] He was an expert in the use of the heavy continental executioner's sword which could cut the head off a prisoner who was kneeling upright, in place of the clumsier English axe necessitating the prisoner's neck on the block. A death in the French style may have been requested by Anne herself; it was certainly intended as an act of grace towards her, to add to the kindness of a death by beheading, instead of the accustomed fire of the female traitor. The warrant for Anne's execution actually states that the king, moved by pity, was unwilling to commit her to the flames.[39] One can only wonder at a psychology which transmutes doubt about the guilt of a loved one into a loving concern about the way to kill her.

James Anthony Froude, that great nineteenth-century historian of English nationalism, laboured mightily to exonerate both Henry and his ministers from the charge of judicial murder.

> Though we stretch our belief in the complacency of statesmen to the furthest limit of credulity, can we believe that Cromwell would have invented that dark indictment – Cromwell ... the dearest friend of Latimer? Or ... Norfolk ... who had won his spurs at Flodden? Or ... Suffolk and ... Fitzwilliam, the Wellington and the Nelson of the sixteenth century? Scarcely among the picked scoundrels of Newgate could men be found for such work; and shall we believe it of men like these?

As for the king himself:

> I believe history will be ransacked vainly to find a parallel for conduct at once so dastardly, so audacious, and so foolishly

---

[37] *Cal. S. P. Span.*, *1536–38*, p. 128 [*LP*, x.908]; de Carles, in Ascoli, *L'Opinion*, lines 788–808; *Lisle Letters*, iii.695 [*LP*, x.865].

[38] *LP*, x.902, xi.381. Not from St Omer: RO, PRO31/8 f. 85 [*LP*, x.965]. That the executioner was at the Tower for the Friday morning implies either that any messenger who left after the sentence on Monday had a quick journey to Calais and the executioner an equally prompt crossing, or that advance warning had been given.

[39] RO, C193/3 f. 80.

wicked as that which the popular hypothesis attributes to Henry VIII.[40]

A. F. Pollard, too, found uxoricide hard to square with his vision of 'Henry the Lion':

> it is not credible that the juries should have found her accomplices guilty, that twenty-six peers should have condemned Anne herself, without some colourable justification. If the charges were merely invented to ruin the queen, one culprit besides herself would have been enough. To assume that Henry sent four needless victims to the block is to accuse him of a lust for superfluous butchery, of which even he, in his most bloodthirsty moments, was not capable.[41]

In the very different atmosphere of recent years the thought has been that Anne was justified in being unfaithful:

> Anne, realising that her survival depended on her production of a son, may have hoped that other men would succeed where the king had failed. The king, moreover, was being unfaithful to her, and she may have tried to get her own back. Above all, perhaps, she was losing her beauty and was anxious to reasure herself by the admiration of others – an admiration which would always be forthcoming from an ambitious courtier.[42]

The evidence, however, justifies nothing of this. If we are to believe Chapuys, Henry had told Jane on the morning of the trial that Anne would be condemned by 3.00 pm.[43] Anne was the victim of a struggle for power, and Henry at his rare moments of honesty admitted it. When later in 1536 Jane Seymour tried to persuade the king to restore the abbeys, he reminded her brusquely of his frequent advice not to meddle in affairs of state and warned her to take Anne as her object lesson.[44]

[40] J. A. Froude, *History of England from the Fall of Wolsey* (1912), ii.161–2, 167. Froude [p. 161] rejected all parallels between Henry VIII and Leontes in Shakespeare, *A Winter's Tale*, but the parallels are there: E. W. Ives, 'Shakespeare and History: divergencies and agreements', in *Shakespeare Survey*, 38 (1985), 24–5.
[41] A. F. Pollard, *Henry VIII* (1951), pp. 276–7.
[42] Muir, *Life and Letters of Wyatt*, p. 28.
[43] *Cal. S. P. Span., 1536–38*, p. 129 [*LP*, x.908].
[44] Du Bellay, *Correspondance*, ii.453 at p. 506 [*LP*, xi.860]; cf. *LP*, xi.1250.

Innocent but a prisoner, guiltless but condemned, Anne awaited her fate. We need not believe that she was forced to watch the execution of her brother and the other men, as Chapuys suggests.[45] The queen would have had to be moved specially right across the Tower, to one of the few vantage points in the Bell Tower from which the scaffold on Tower Hill could be seen two hundred yards away. Wyatt, we know, did watch from there:

> The Bell Tower showed me such a sight
> That in my head sticks day and night:
> There did I learn out of a grate,
> For all favour, glory or might,
> That yet *circa Regna tonat*.[46]

Excused such horrors, and after the hysteria of the first few days, Anne showed some signs of adjustment, but all the time she was battered by the demoralization and fragmentation of the prisoner under constant and unsympathetic scrutiny. What we learn of her then is certainly revealing. Strangely, nothing has come down to us of anything Anne said about her daughter of two years and eight months. From the start, her family was uppermost in her mind, not only her 'sweet brother' but her mother and the father we think of as deserting her. Perhaps he did, but Anne was evidently concerned that the whole Boleyn family would be destroyed with her – as effectively it was.[47] Sir Thomas, in fact, had not much to show for his lifetime of service to Henry VIII except for his earldom, and the grants he did have were held jointly with his son; the great days of the monastic bonanza had not yet come. The only hope for the Boleyn line now appeared to be the unsuccessful sister, Mary!

Disoriented in terms of time, Anne became avid for news of the outside. She called for supper far too soon after dinner, built great castles of imagination – that it would not rain until she was released, that the evangelical bishops would intervene on her behalf, that most English people were praying for her and a disaster from heaven would follow her execution. Sometimes her

---

[45] *Cal. S. P. Span., 1536–38*, p. 128 [*LP*, x.908].

[46] Wyatt, *Poems*, CXLIII 'grate' = grating.

[47] For this see the letters above, p. 365[19]; the reference to George is from *Wolsey*, ed. Singer, p. 461.

hope ran high – the king was doing it all to test her, she would be sent to a nunnery – or again she would be determined to die, and would discuss the technical details with Kingston as if it was the most amusing subject in the world. There would, she said, be no difficulty in finding a nickname for her: it would be 'Queen Anne the Headless'. Then her mind would run over details of her treatment at the hands of the commissioners, or she would recall a promising bet on the game of tennis she had been watching when first summoned before them – 'if it [the chase] had been laid she had won.' With the completion of the trial, preparation for death loomed ever larger in Anne's mind, hours spent with her almoner and before the blessed sacrament until her spirit reached the exaltation of the martyr. Kingston wrote towards the end: 'I have seen many men and also women executed and that they have been in great sorrow, and to my knowledge this lady hath much joy and pleasure in death.'[48]

Yet before Anne could be allowed to die there was to be one final twist in the story, and the nastiest of all. Her marriage to Henry was declared null and void and Elizabeth her daughter bastardized. The formal declaration was made by Cranmer at Lambeth on Wednesday 17 May – the afternoon of the day on which Rochford and the others were executed – but as the detailed grounds on which such a judgement was given were never included in it and as all the cause papers have disappeared, we do not know the reason which was alleged.[49] The notion of a divorce had been under consideration for some days, for the previous Saturday (that is, before Anne was tried), the earl of Northumberland had written to Thomas Cromwell because news had reached him that the old story of the supposed pre-contract between himself and Anne had been resurrected. He reminded the secretary of his denials in 1532, and insisted that he would stick by that 'to his damnation'. As well as showing that to divorce Anne was not, as if often said, a last-minute idea, this letter seems to dispose of one of the rumours which circulated explaining the grounds for it.[50] Chapuys picked up two more – that Elizabeth had been ruled to be the daughter of

[48] *Wolsey*, ed. Singer, p. 461.
[49] *LP*, x.896; Kelly, *Matrimonial Trials*, pp. 250–9 considers a whole range of possible reasons, without being able to reach a firm conclusion.
[50] *Wolsey*, ed. Singer, pp. 464–5; Wriothesley, *Chronicle*, i.41.

Norris and that Henry's relations with Anne's sister Mary had been summoned up again.[51] The first we can dismiss, and the second is at first sight hard to square with the legislation which was passed by parliament in July, explaining that the marriage with Anne was void because of 'certain just, true and lawful impediments unknown at the making' of the legislation protecting it. That Anne's sister had been Henry's mistress was certainly not 'unknown'.

Some writers have seen a sinister twist to all this in the appointment by Henry on 16 May of Cranmer to hear Anne's confession.[52] Did he hint at life in return for compliance? Did Anne confess to a consummated relationship with Percy or a third party, although her bare word would hardly seem adequate? There is no way of knowing what passed that Tuesday between the client, now archbishop, and the queen his patron, now a condemned traitor. In all probability the meeting was what it purported to be, a spiritual exercise. Now that the verdict had been given against Anne, it was safe to let Cranmer back on the scene to do what he was best at, pastoral care. The suggestion that Cranmer secured information from her on the Tuesday, either elicited voluntarily or by deceit, which enabled him to rush all the necessary documents and legal processes through in time to pronounce a sentence of nullity within twenty-four hours, asks a great deal. In any case there was no reason to rush; the court at Lambeth could as easily have sat on the Thursday. That it sat when it did implies that the business was largely complete when Cranmer visited Anne.

The riddle cannot be finally solved, and it may simply be that Cranmer's policy was pragmatic – 'least said, soonest mended' – relying on the sword to end all speculation as to the reasons for his decision. Tudor minds, however, set great store on due process, and one answer is suggested by looking back at the legislation of 1534, which had explained the position of existing papal dispensations, now that any that might be issued by Rome in future had been declared both illegal and invalid.[53] Those that had been granted were still to be valid and new ones issued by application to the archbishop of Canterbury, except where

[51] *Cal. S. P. Span., 1536–38*, p. 121 [*LP*, x.909].
[52] *Wolsey*, ed. Singer, p. 459.
[53] 25 Henry VIII, c.21.

contrary to 'the Holy Scriptures and laws of God'. The impediment presented by the previous relationship between Henry VIII and Mary Boleyn had been removed by a dispensation granted by Clement VII. If, however, the law of God said otherwise, then, according to the 1534 act, that dispensation was worthless. It could never be validated, and the impediments would still exist. This could also have fairly been held to be 'unknown' at the time of the marriage with Anne, not in the sense that the facts were unknown, but that it was not realized that the previous intercourse between Henry and Mary could never be dispensed against. That this is the right answer is strongly suggested by the Succession Act of July 1536 which specifically stated:

> it is to be understood that if it chance any man to know carnally any woman, that then all and singular persons being in any degree of consanguinity or affinity ... to any of the parties so carnally offending shall be deemed and adjudged to be within the cases and limits of the said prohibition of marriage.[54]

This was divine law and could not be dispensed; marriages already made were invalid and all children begotten were illegitimate, like Elizabeth.

The decision to annul Anne's marriage to Henry and at the same time to proceed against her on a charge of high treason was, of course, schizoid. If Anne Boleyn was not the king's wife, then she could not have committed adultery against him, and to plan to marry Norris would not have been at all improper. The point, so glaringly obvious to us, does not seem to have been made at the time, probably because it was recognized (as it was recognized by Chapuys) that the divorce was not directed at Anne herself.[55] She was already doomed; the target of the annulment was Elizabeth. Henry was determined not to admit the legitimacy of his elder daughter – Cromwell was secretly counting on that. With the younger bastardized also, he would now have no legitimate children at all, and it would become possible to make a serious case for the only boy, the duke of Richmond, as the heir presumptive. Of course Henry hoped that

[54] 28 Henry VIII, c.7.
[55] *Cal. S. P. Span.*, *1536–38*, p. 121 [*LP*, x.909]. For Anne to be divorced because married in defiance of the immutable law of God did, however, preserve Henry's confidence in his guidance by God.

Jane Seymour would give him a healthy son, but he was wise enough not to bank on it as he had with Anne. This line of thinking clearly influenced the Succession Act of July 1536. The statute switched the legitimate line from Elizabeth to the off-spring of Henry and Jane Seymour, or any future wives, but it also provided that if Henry had no legitimate heirs, then he could by letters patent or his last will declare who the next ruler would be. Richmond, therefore, could be held in reserve should Jane fail to produce the heir, *sans reproche*.[56] In the end, however, all this planning went for nothing. Consumption had taken its final grip on the young duke, and four days after the Succession Act received the royal assent, he was dead.

Anne Boleyn was not at Lambeth that Wednesday to watch the twists and turns of Cranmer and the lawyers in their attempt to give the king what he wanted. Instead she was facing what she expected to be the last night of her life, and by 2.00 a.m. the next morning the sleepless queen was closeted with her almoner. Her preparation for the sacrament complete, she called Kingston to hear mass with her soon after dawn on the Thursday. It was then that she swore twice, on the consecrated bread and wine, that she was innocent, and the constable duly passed her oath on, as she knew he would. Then there was only the waiting. Later that day Kingston was summoned again. Anne had heard that she was not to die until noon:

> Master Kingston, I hear say I shall not die afore noon, and I am very sorry there for, for I thought to be dead by this time and past my pain.[57]

In fact, as Kingston knew, she had never been intended for the scaffold that day. He had just received a letter from Cromwell instructing him to clear the Tower of foreigners, and this may have included the warrant for Anne's execution, but he had still

[56] 28 Henry VIII, c.7.

[57] *Wolsey*, ed. Singer, pp. 460–1. This letter is usually read to indicate that Anne's execution was postponed from Thursday to Friday, as Chapuys reported: *Cal. S. P. Span., 1536–38*, p. 131 [*LP*, x.908]. Kingston's letter shows that final arrangements had still to be made, and it reads more naturally to take Anne's complaint as an indication that she and her ladies (and from one of the latter, Chapuys) had misunderstood procedures. De Carles, in Ascoli, *L'Opinion*, lines 1150–65, also believed the execution was delayed.

to be told the hour the sentence was to be carried out on the Friday morning.[58] Where Anne got her mistaken expectation is not clear, and some have suspected deliberate unkindness. More likely, she had jumped to the conclusion that she would follow her brother to death as soon as the divorce was through, and had not realized that it was Kingston's custom – or so it was in this series of executions – to give the victims warning early on the morning of the day they were to die. The constable avoided revealing his ignorance of the timetable by seizing on Anne's last remark. The execution, he explained, would not be painful; the blow was 'so subtle'. Anne replied:

I heard say the executor was very good, and I have a little neck

– and she put her hands round her throat and burst out laughing.

---

[58] RO, C193/3 f. 80, dated 18 May.

18

Finale

IT WAS a short journey. Out of the Queen's Lodgings, past the
Great Hall where she had dined on the night before the
coronation, through the Cole Harbour Gate and the first sight of
the scaffold.[1] It stood three or four feet high, draped in black,
surrounded by a large crowd: the lord mayor and aldermen
come to see the king's justice done, and behind them hundreds of
ordinary Londoners – no foreigners – Englishmen and women
come to see the first English queen die. And around the scaffold
itself the faces she knew so well: Thomas Audley, the lord
chancellor, whom she had last seen at her trial; Charles Brandon,
duke of Suffolk, whose life had been so entwined with her own,
ever since her journey to France as a thirteen-year-old attendant
on the king's sister Mary, who had married Brandon, had hated
her and was now dead; Henry Fitzroy, her seventeen-year-old
stepson, white-faced with the mark of consumption upon him;
and Thomas Cromwell who had climbed to power behind Anne,
and now had to destroy her in order to retain that power.[2] How
Anne and Thomas reacted at this last meeting we can only
guess. Pride on her part, and on his, the formal last deference
due even to a fallen queen, and the relief that it was Anne, and
not himself, at the centre of the drama.

Escorted by Sir William Kingston, followed by her four ladies
– no longer, it seems, the 'wardresses' she had disliked, but her
own women restored for one last time – Anne walked the final

---

[1] For the execution of Anne see p. 391[20] above.
[2] *Wolsey*, ed. Singer, p. 461; *Cal. S. P. Span., 1536–38*, pp. 130–1 [*LP*, x.908];
Wriothesley, *Chronicle*, i.41; *Lisle Letters*, iii.697 [*LP*, x.918] says that the crowd
numbered 1,000; Antony Antony in Herbert, *Henry VIII* (1679), facing p. 385.

fifty yards. Over a grey damask gown lined with fur she wore an ermine mantle with an English gable hood.[3] The constable saw her safely up the steps (no Thomas More jokes this time), and following the etiquette of state executions, Anne moved to the edge of the scaffold to make the expected address to the crowd.[4] It was simple and brief:

> Good Christian people, I have not come here to preach a sermon; I have come here to die.

Did she know that she was echoing the words of her brother two days earlier?

> for according to the law and by the law I am judged to die, and therefore I will speak nothing against it. I am come hither to accuse no man, nor to speak of that whereof I am accused and condemned to die, but I pray God save the king and send him long to reign over you, for a gentler nor a more merciful prince was there never, and to me he was ever a good, a gentle, and sovereign lord. And if any person will meddle of my cause, I require them to judge the best [shades of William Brereton]. And thus I take my leave of the world and of you all, and I heartily desire you all to pray for me.

Again it was the sort of speech the crowd expected, and one which reveals the enormous gulf between the sixteenth-century mind and our own. Once more we feel compelled to ask, 'How could she not protest her innocence, how acquiesce in such injustice?' Convention demanded it; religion demanded it; as for practical considerations, it would be Elizabeth who would suffer from the luxury of defying the king and his supposed justice. But the crowd, far more attuned to nuances than we are, got the point nevertheless. There was no public admission of sin, even of a general kind, and still less any confession that she had wronged Henry. Anne spoke firmly, 'with a goodly smiling countenance', and soon the news would be all round London that she had died 'boldly', without the acceptance of the morality of the sentence which a truly penitent adulteress should show.[5]

---

[3] See the imperial account (2a), above p. 391[20].

[4] For Anne's speech see also George Wyatt, *Papers*, p. 189; *Wolsey*, ed. Singer, p. 448; Hall, *Chronicle*, p. 819; Foxe, *Acts and monuments*, v.134; Antony Antony, in Herbert, *Henry VIII* (1679), facing p. 385.

[5] *Lisle Letters*, iii.698 [*LP*, x.920].

The speech done, the ermine mantle was removed, revealing the proud neck Sanuto the Venetian had noted years before, and a low collar which would present no obstacle to the sword. Then Anne herself lifted off her head-dress, and the crowd saw for the last time the brief glory of her hair as she tucked it into a cap one of the ladies had ready. The only sign of nervousness was her trick of continually glancing behind her; like many similar victims, her fear was that the executioner would strike when she was not ready. She had no chaplain with her, no one to repeat a prayer, and no psalm was said, but we can guess what she tried desperately to hold in her mind. In the happy days of 1535 Erasmus of Rotterdam had written for her father *A Preparation to Death*: 'In peril of death, man's infirmity is overpowered unless instant by instant, unless with a pure affection, unless with an unvanquished trust he crieth for the help of him which only reviveth the dead.'[6]

A brief farewell to her weeping servants, perhaps the last gift of a tiny prayer book, a request for prayer, and Anne kneeled down, saying all the while, 'Jesu receive my soul; O Lord God have pity on my soul.' Continentals who heard the story were amazed that she was not bound or restrained in any way: only a blindfold, tied for her by one of the maids of honour. 'To Christ I commend my soul!' And while her lips were still moving, it was suddenly over.[7]

Almost, it seemed, in slow motion, the ladies-in-waiting covered Anne. Then one with the head in a white cloth, quickly red, and the other three with the body wrapped in a sheet, they carried the queen unaided the thirty yards or so into the chapel of St Peter, past the two newly filled graves, Norris with Weston, Brereton with Smeton. There the clothes were removed – the Tower claimed its perquisites even from a queen – and the corpse was placed in an elm chest earmarked to carry a consignment of bow-staves to Ireland, but now to go no further than the chancel of the chapel.[8] There Anne Boleyn was buried

[6] Erasmus, *A Preparation to Death* (Redman, 1543), sig. fvij [see above, p. 319]. The text above is modified to read 'overpowered' for 'overcome' and 'instant by instant' for 'instantly'.

[7] Source after source stresses the suddenness and speed of the execution; the headsman 'did his office very well': Spelman, *Reports*, i.59. A French report was 'before you could say a paternoster': Hamy, *Entrevue*, p. ccccxxxvii.

[8] *LP*, xi.381. Thus Antony Antony and the imperial account; the Italian account suggests that the box was by the scaffold.

near her brother, three years and thirty-seven days after she had 'first dined abroad as queen' on Easter Sunday 1533.

She had been a remarkable woman. She would remain a remarkable woman even in a century which would produce many of great note. There were few others who rose from such beginnings to a crown, and none who on the way had contributed to a revolution as far-reaching as the English Reformation. To use a description no longer in fashion, Anne Boleyn was one of the 'makers of history'. Yet historians see through a glass darkly; they know in part and they pronounce in part. What Anne really was, as distinct from what Anne did, comes over very much less clearly. To us she appears inconsistent – religious yet aggressive, calculating yet emotional, with the light touch of the courtier yet the strong grip of the politician – but is this what she was, or merely what we strain to see through the opacity of the evidence? As for her inner life, short of a miraculous cache of new material, we shall never know. Yet what does come to us across the centuries is the impression of a person who is strangely appealing to the later twentieth century. A woman in her own right – taken on her own terms in a man's world; a woman who mobilized her education, her style and her presence to outweigh the disadvantages of her sex; of only moderate good looks, but taking a court and a king by storm. Perhaps, in the end, it is Thomas Cromwell's assessment that comes nearest: intelligence, spirit and courage.

Life is cruel to the dead, the more so where guilt and fear combine to censor the memory. Francis Bryan had carried the news of Anne's condemnation to Jane Seymour; and the rest of the courtiers, with equal resolution, turned their backs on the past.[9] For the first time since the execution of Buckingham in 1521, there was the chance for a bonanza in forfeited property, and competition started as soon as news of the first arrests was out. Rochford had two large annuities, but apart from the Cinque Ports he had only just over £100 a year gross in royal offices, farms and grants, and the Boleyn lands remained in the hands of his father. Weston, too, was probably worth relatively little. Brereton, however, had over £1000 a year gross from the crown, and Norris over £1200.[10] On 2 May, the very day of Anne's arrest, a Gray's Inn lawyer, Roland Bulkeley, had written to his

   [9] Cal. S. P. Span., 1536–38, p. 129 [LP, x.908].
   [10] LP, x.878.

brother Sir Richard in North Wales, sending news of the early
victims and urging a swift journey to London to press his suits in
person; Roland evidently saw this as an inside tip – 'when it is
once known that they shall die, all will be too late.' His
messenger talked too much and ended up in Shrewsbury town
gaol, but Sir Richard, who had been Norris's deputy in North
Wales, still got in quickly enough to secure and apparently
advance his interests.[11] Gardiner, not for the last time, risked his
credit with the king by expressing dissatisfation with his share;
£200 of the £300 per annum he had previously paid to Rochford
and Norris was cancelled, but he resented the remainder going
to Bryan.[12] Viscount Lisle came too late, and seems never to
have found satisfactory replacements for the court contacts he
had lost in 1536. When, after fifteen months of solicitation, his
stepdaughter was admitted as maid of honour to the new queen,
her first and last duty was to take part in Jane Seymour's
funeral.[13]

Unaware of what the future held, the victorious faction exuded
satisfaction at the destruction of Anne Boleyn. Sir John Russell
wrote: 'The king hath come out of hell into heaven for the
gentleness in this [Jane] and the cursedness and the unhappiness
in the other.'[14] Even before Anne had faced her judges, Henry
had sent Carewe to bring her successor to a house on the river a
mile from Whitehall, and as soon as news of the execution
reached him he set off to meet Jane.[15] The following day they
were betrothed, and on Tuesday 30 May the marriage ceremony
took place in the queen's closet at Whitehall.[16] A week later
Edward Seymour was elevated to the peerage, and soon after,
Henry Seymour, probably his younger brother, took the place of
groom of the privy chamber made vacant by Smeton's death.[17]
And always comparison was made to Anne's disadvantage,
although we may not today draw quite the pejorative implication intended by another John Russell remark, made after
attending the marriage of Henry and Jane, that 'the richer she
[Jane] was in apparel, the fairer and goodly lady she was and

11 Ibid., vii.611; x.785, 820, 870.
12 Ibid., x.873; xi.29.
13 *Lisle Letters*, iii.698, 702 [*LP*, x.919, 943], p. 173.
14 Ibid., iii.713 [*LP*, x.1047].
15 *LP*, x.926.
16 *Lisle Letters*, iv.848a [*LP*, x.1000].
17 *LP*, x.g.1256(4); BL, Roy. MS 7F xiv f. 100.

appeared; and the other [Anne] he said was the contrary, for the richer she was apparelled, the worse she looked.'[18] Anyone familiar with Holbein's portrait of Jane Seymour might be forgiven for feeling that she needed all the help she could get.[19]

For Thomas Cromwell, intent on being free of these troublesome courtiers, the death of Anne, Rochford, Norris and the rest was only the end of the first act. The Seymour family had been paid off for the moment – and he would have to work with them anyway – but Carewe and the other supporters of Mary were in a high state of excitement, daily expecting her return to favour and a place in the succession.[20] London was buzzing with rumours. Cromwell appeared to countenance their expectations, but from the start he knew the price he would exact from Mary: a full acceptance of the supremacy and of her own illegitimacy. There was to be no conservative reaction or return to the traditional powers and status of the Church, as the princess and her allies fondly believed. Poor Mary, it was so obvious to her that everything was the fault of Anne, 'nobody dared speak for me' – and we may add 'or the Church' – 'as long as that woman lived, which is now gone.'[21]

For a while Mary's comeback seemed to be only a formality, but it was not long before the secretary revealed the terms.[22] The princess's moral toughness held out, and Cromwell, who had clearly promised Henry that he would secure her submission, began (or so he said) to feel for the head on his own shoulders; there are indeed signs of the king's own distinctive sledgehammer intervention in the commencement of judicial moves against his daughter. The secretary, however, by now had enough on Mary's supporters at court to proceed against them; he convinced Henry that they were behind her obstinacy, thereby facing the princess with isolation and the loss of her

---

[18] Oxford, Bodl. MS Jesus College, 73 f. 249. The original for this appears to be the now mutilated BL, Cott. MS Otho C x [*LP*, x.1134]. Cf. Herbert, *Henry VIII*, p. 573. I owe this Bodleian reference to the kindness of Mr Richard Hoyle.

[19] Cf. E. O. Benger, *Memoirs of the Life of Anne Boleyn*, p. 377, suggesting that Jane must have been attractive 'since we hear of no other fascination she possessed'.

[20] *LP*, x.1212.

[21] Ibid., x.968. Cf. Reginald Pole, 2 Oct. 1553: 'the misery of that period, and all that ensued subsequently, came through a woman': *Cal. S. P. Ven.*, *1534–54*, p. 424.

[22] For the following see Prescott, *Mary Tudor*, pp. 76–83; *Cal. S. P. Span.*, *1536–38*, pp. 183–5; *LP*, vii.1036; x.1134, 1150.

friends. Fitzwilliam, the treasurer, was excluded from the council, and his half-brother Anthony Browne subjected to a series of interrogations. How serious the matter was is indicated by the preparation of a list of the treasurer's grants and offices, just like the one drawn up at the start of May for Rochford and his father.[23] Exeter, also, was banned from the council, Lady Hussey was put in the Tower, and other court ladies found themselves being questioned by Cromwell and Audley along with several more of the privy chamber staff; and there was a burst of activity in the royal households, demanding that suspects should swear allegiance to the established succession.

At this point, very fortunately for her supporters, Mary succumbed both to the king's pressure and to their frightened cries to her to sign whatever her father wanted. She admitted all that was asked of her, and thereby cut the ground from under the feet of her friends. Even so, Cromwell continued to press the interrogations; and despite denials to a man – and woman – of any disloyalty, and especially of any discussion of the bona fide argument about Mary's legitimacy, there was soon ample evidence for a charge of conspiracy far more convincing than that against Anne. Lady Hussey was still being held in the Tower under investigation as late as August.[24] This time, however, there was no need to press matters to the scaffold on Tower Green. The court, led by Mary, surrendered abjectly to the will of the king and his minister. Cromwell's triumph was complete. At the start of July Anne's father, Wiltshire, was required to hand over to him the office of lord privy seal, and a week later Cromwell was raised to the peerage, though he did not take his seat in the Lords until the final day of the parliamentary session, 18 July.[25]

The relegation of Mary and her supporters to the periphery of power had a number of consequences. The fear Rochford had expressed on the scaffold and which Cranmer certainly had shared, that the destruction of Anne would mean the end of religious reform, would not now materialize. Instead, the clients she had promoted would remain to hold and consolidate a bridgehead for the Protestant religion in England. The defeated conservatives had nowhere to go but to violence, and one

[23] Ibid., x.1268.
[24] Ibid., xi.222; cf. vii.1036.
[25] Ibid., xi.202(3), (14).

element in the Lincolnshire Rising and the Pilgrimage of Grace, which in the following autumn would lose Henry control of one third of the country, was the leadership of Mary's discredited supporters, who now attempted to achieve by outside pressure the victory denied them by Cromwell's subtlety.[26] Hussey and Darcy would die by the executioner's axe for their part in this, and although a number of Mary's friends chickened out of supporting the rebels in the field, an attitude of continued disaffection marked them out for suspicion. Several of Anne's conservative enemies thereby followed her to the scaffold – Exeter, Lord Montagu and Sir Edward Neville in December 1538, Carewe in the following March; Lady Exeter was in the Tower for eighteen months and her son for nearly fifteen years. Richard Tempest, one of the petty jury which condemned Norris and the other commoners, caught typhus and died in the Fleet Prison in August 1537; Giles Heron, foreman of the Middlesex grand jury which endorsed the original indictment, was drawn, hanged and quartered at Tyburn in August 1540.[27]

In the narrower confines of the royal court, the check to the Marian faction allowed some recovery among those associated with Anne. Richard Page was released from the Tower and restored to favour, but decided to give up being 'a daily courtier'.[28] Wyatt, who seems to have been protected from whatever innuendos were spread about him by none other than Cromwell, celebrated his release by telling the truth in circumspect but suggestive verse.[29] One poem attributed to him is almost an elegy on May 1536:

> In mourning wise since daily I increase,
> Thus should I cloak the cause of all my grief;
> So pensive mind with tongue to hold his peace
> My reason sayeth there can be no relief:
> Wherefore give ear, I humbly you require,
> The affect to know that thus doth make me moan.
> The cause is great of all my doleful cheer
> For those that were, and now be dead and gone.

[26] G. R. Elton, 'Politics and the Pilgrimage of Grace', in *After the Reformation*, ed. B. Malament (New Haven, Conn., 1980), pp. 25–56.
[27] For Heron and Tempest see *House of Commons*, ii.350; iii.430–1.
[28] *Lisle Letters*, iii.748 [*LP*, xi.107].
[29] That Cromwell was Wyatt's patron is clear from *Poems*, CLX. Cf. *House of Commons*, iii.669–70.

What though to death desert be now their call,
As by their faults it doth appear right plain?
Of force I must lament that such a fall
Should light on those so wealthily did reign,
Though some perchance will say, of cruel heart,
A traitor's death why should we thus bemoan?
But I alas, set this offence apart,
Must needs bewail the death of some be gone.

As for them all I do not thus lament,
But as of right my reason doth me bind;
But as the most doth all their deaths repent,
Even so do I by force of mourning mind.
Some say, 'Rochford, haddest thou been not so proud,
For thy great wit each man would thee bemoan,
Since as it is so, many cry aloud
It is great loss that thou art dead and gone'.

Ah! Norris, Norris, my tears begin to run
To think what hap did thee so lead or guide
Whereby thou hast both thee and thine undone
That is bewailed in court of every side;
In place also where thou hast never been
Both man and child doth piteously thee moan.
They say, 'Alas, thou art far overseen
By thine offences to be thus dead and gone'.

Ah! Weston, Weston, that pleasant was and young,
In active things who might with thee compare?
All words accept that thou diddest speak with tongue,
So well esteemed with each where thou diddest fare.
And we that now in court doth lead our life
Most part in mind doth thee lament and moan;
But that thy faults we daily hear so rife,
All we should weep that thou art dead and gone.

Brereton farewell, as one that least I knew.
Great was thy love with divers as I hear,
But common voice doth not so sore thee rue
As other twain that doth before appear;
But yet no doubt but thy friends thee lament
And other hear their piteous cry and moan.
So doth each heart for thee likewise relent
That thou givest cause thus to be dead and gone.

Ah! Mark, what moan should I for thee make more,
Since that thy death thou hast deserved best,
Save only that mine eye is forced sore
With piteous plaint to moan thee with the rest?
A time thou haddest above thy poor degree,
The fall whereof thy friends may well bemoan:
A rotten twig upon so high a tree
Hath slipped thy hold, and thou art dead and gone.

And thus farewell each one in hearty wise!
The axe is home, your heads be in the street;
The trickling tears doth fall so from my eyes
I scarce may write, my paper is so wet.
But what can hope when death hath played his part,
Though nature's course will thus lament and moan?
Leave sobs therefore, and every Christian heart
Pray for the souls of those be dead and gone.[30]

Of the victims, only one is missing in Wyatt's lament – Anne herself. For some years yet, few voices would be raised in her favour, though the king's rapid remarriage made suspicions about the official story widespread.[31] For her the most poignant memorial was in the Tower of London, where it remains to this day on the wall of one of the cells in the Beauchamp Tower (plate 40). There crudely and hastily scratched by a man who knew he had little time, is Anne Boleyn's falcon.[32] Which of her 'lovers' made it we do not know but the image is unmistakable. The tree stump is there – the barren Henry – the Tudor rosebush bursting into life, the perching bird whose touch wrought the miracle. But there is one change to the badge which Anne had proudly flourished in the face of the world. This falcon is no longer a royal bird. It has no crown, no sceptre; it stands bareheaded, as did Anne in those last moments on Tower Green.

---

[30] Wyatt, *Poems*, CXLIX.
[31] Constantine, in *Archaeologia*, 23.64; *LP*, x.926; Ales, 'Letter', pp. 530–1.
[32] The inscription is unnumbered but can be found at the bottom right of no. 31 on the west wall of the main chamber of the first floor. It was first identified by Mr B. A. Harrison, a yeoman warder and an authority on the Tower inscriptions. The Martin Tower contains a fire-damaged carving which has been read as 'boullen', in which case it could refer to George Boleyn; alternatively, and on inspection more probably, it can be read as 'bouttell': Royal Commission on Historical Monuments, *London* (1924–30), v.83. I am indebted to Mr Peter Hammond for drawing my attention to these inscriptions, and for a rubbing of that in the Martin Tower, and to Mr Harrison.

Epilogue

~~~~~~~~~~~~~~~~~~~~~~~

FOR TWENTY years after May 1536, Anne Boleyn was a non-person. People who had known her said nothing, while the king, who knew most, grew old, obese and bad-tempered. When he had allowed Cromwell to strike Anne down, Henry had been at the height of his magnificence. By the time he allowed Cromwell himself to be struck down four years later, the physical deterioration was obvious. Four more attempts at marriage brought him little joy. Jane Seymour's death from puerperal fever left him with the son he had done so much evil to get, but his remaining wives remained barren. Number four was divorced; number five, Katherine Howard, died by the axe on Tower Green and is buried in St Peter's, near her cousin Anne; but the luck of the sixth held out, despite the risks of mothering a sick and irascible old man. And all the while there was little said of Anne, and little left of her but her child, the young Elizabeth, who had been declared a bastard but who was nevertheless acknowledged as the king's daughter and in 1544 was restored to the succession. A bright and intelligent girl, prematurely cautious. When her elder sister Mary came to the throne in 1553, the twenty-year-old Elizabeth found she needed this caution as never before. On Palm Sunday 1554 Anne Boleyn's daughter was brought by river to the Tower of London, just as her mother had been almost eighteen years earlier. Suspected of plotting rebellion, she spent the next two months in the Bell Tower, followed by almost a year under house arrest in Oxfordshire.

In 1558, however, the miracle happened. On Monday 28 November, to the cheers of the London crowd and the roar of the Tower artillery, Elizabeth came through the gates to take possession of the fortress as queen. The bastardized daughter of the disgraced Anne Boleyn, with her father's complexion but her mother's face, splendidly dressed in purple velvet: Elizabeth, by the grace of God, queen of England, France and Ireland, defender of the faith. Is it fanciful to feel that after twenty years, the mother in the nearby grave in the chapel of St. Peter was at last vindicated?

Bibliographical Abbreviations

The following lists the abbreviated and full titles of works etc. referred to. Unless otherwise stated, both here and in the footnotes the place of publication is London.

ABBREVIATION	EXPLANATION
Actes de François Ier	*Catalogue des Actes de François Ier* (Paris, 1887–1910).
Ales, 'Letter'	Alexander Ales, letter to Queen Elizabeth, 1 Sept. 1559, in RO, SP70/7 ff. 1–11, translated and calendared in *Calendar of State Papers Foreign, 1558–59*, 1303.
Ambassades de du Bellay	*Ambassades en Angleterre de Jean du Bellay*, ed. V. L. Bourilly & P. de Vassière (Paris, 1905).
Ascoli, *L'Opinion*	G. Ascoli, *La Grande-Bretagne devant L'Opinion Française* (Paris, 1927).
Anglo, *Great Tournament Roll*	S. Anglo, *The Great Tournament Roll of Westminster* (Oxford, 1968).
Anglo, *Spectacle*	S. Anglo, *Spectacle, Pageantry and Early Tudor Policy* (Oxford, 1969).
Ballads	*Ballads from Manuscript*, ed. F. J. Furnivall. Ballad Society (1868–72).
du Bellay, *Correspondance*	*Correspondance du Cardinal Jean du Bellay*, ed. R. Scheurer (Paris, 1969).

Bentley, *Excerpta Historica*   S. Bentley, *Excerpta Historica* (1831).

BIHR   *Bulletin of the Institute of Historical Research.*

BL   British Library.

BM   British Museum.

Bodl.   Oxford, Bodleian Library.

de Boom, *Marguerite d'Autriche*   G. de Boom, *Marguerite d'Autriche – Savoie et la Pré-Renaissance* (Paris & Brussels, 1935).

Brereton, *Letters and Accounts*   *Letters and Accounts of William Brereton*, ed. E. W. Ives. Record Society of Lancashire and Cheshire, 116 (1976).

Brewer, *Henry VIII*   J. S. Brewer, *The Reign of Henry VIII* (1884).

'Building work', in *Transactions of the Greenwich and Lewisham Antiquarian Society*, 5   J. W. Kirby, 'Building work at Placentia, 1532–33', in *Transactions of the Greenwich and Lewisham Antiquarian Society*, 5 (1954–61), 22–50.

Burnet, *History*   Gilbert Burnet, *History of the Reformation*, ed. Nicolas Pocock (Oxford, 1865).

Cal. S. P. For.   *Calendar of State Papers, Foreign Series, Elizabeth I*, ed. J. Stevenson et al. (1863–1950).

Cal. S. P. Milan.   *Calendar of State Papers . . . in . . . Milan*, ed. A. B. Hinds (1912).

Cal. S. P. Span.   *Calendar of Letters . . . and State Papers . . . between England and Spain*, ed. G. A. Bergenroth et al. (1862–1954).

Cal. S. P. Ven.   *Calendar of State Papers . . . in . . . Venice*, ed. Rawdon Brown et al. (1864–1940).

de Carles, in Ascoli, *L'Opinion*   Lancelot de Carles, *'De la royne d'Angleterre'*, in G. Ascoli, *La Grande-Bretagne devant L'Opinion Française* (Paris, 1927).

Cavendish, *Metrical Visions*	George Cavendish, 'Metrical Visions', in *The Life of Cardinal Wolsey and Metrical Visions*, ed. S. W. Singer (1825).
Cavendish, *Wolsey*	George Cavendish, *The Life and Death of Cardinal Wolsey*, ed. R. S. Sylvester. Early English Text Society, 243 (1959).
Chronicle, ed. Hume	*Chronicle of King Henry VIII of England* (see below, *Cronica del Rey Enrico*), ed. M. A. S. Hume (1889).
Chronicle of Calais	*Chronicle of Calais*, ed. J. G. Nichols. Camden Society, 35 (1846).
Clifford, *Dormer*	Henry Clifford, *Life of Jane Dormer* (1887).
Colvin, *King's Works*	H. M. Colvin, *The History of the King's Works* (1963–82).
Constantine, in *Archaeologia*, 23	'A memorial from George Constantine', ed. T. Amyot, in *Archaeologia*, 23 (1831).
Cranmer, *Letters*	*Miscellaneous Writings and Letters of Thomas Cranmer*, ed. J. E. Cox. Parker Society (1846).
Cronica del Rey Enrico	*Cronica del Rey Enrico Otava de Inglaterra*, ed. Marquis de Molins (Madrid, 1874).
Dewhurst, in *Medical History*, 28	J. Dewhurst, 'The alleged miscarriages of Catherine of Aragon and Anne Boleyn', in *Medical History* 28 (1984), 49–56.
Dowling, in *JEH*, 35	M. Dowling, 'Anne Boleyn and reform', in *Journal of Ecclesiastical History*, 35 (1984), 30–46.
EHR	*English Historical Review*.
Ellis, *Letters*	H. Ellis, *Original Letters Illustrative of English History* (1824–46).
Elton, *Reform and Renewal*	G. R. Elton, *Reform and Renewal* (Cambridge, 1973).
Foxe, *Acts and Monuments*	John Foxe, *Acts and monuments*, ed. S. R. Cattley (1837).

Friedmann, *Anne Boleyn*   P. Friedmann, *Anne Boleyn: a Chapter of English History, 1527–1536* (1884).

Gairdner, in *EHR*   J. Gairdner, 'Mary and Anne Boleyn', and 'The Age of Anne Boleyn', in *EHR*, 8 (1893), 53–60; 10 (1895), 104.

Ganz, *Die Handzeichnungen*   P. Ganz, *Die Handzeichnungen Hans Holbein des Jungeren* (Berlin, 1911).

G. E. C., *Peerage*   G. E. Cockayne, *Complete Peerage*, ed. V. Gibbs (1910–49).

Giustinian, *Four Years at the Court of Henry VIII*   Sebastian Giustinian, *Four Years at the Court of Henry VIII*, ed. R. Brown (1854).

Guy, in *EHR*, 97   J. A. Guy, 'Henry VIII and the *praemunire* manoeuvres of 1530–31', in *EHR*, 97 (1982), 481–503.

Guy, in *Moreana*, 21   J. A. Guy, 'Thomas More and Christopher St German', in *Moreana*, 21 (1984), 5–25.

Guy, *Public Career of More*   J. A. Guy, *The Public Career of Sir Thomas More* (Brighton, 1980).

Hall, *Chronicle*   Edward Hall, *The Union of the Two Noble and Illustre Famelies of York and Lancaster*, ed. H. Ellis (1809).

Hamy, *Entrevue*   P. A. Hamy, *Entrevue de François Premier avec Henri VIIIᵉ à Boulogne* (Paris, 1898).

Harpsfield, *More*   Nicolas Harpsfield, *The Life and Death of Sir Thomas More*, ed. E. V. Hitchcock and R. W. Chambers. Early English Text Society, 186 (1932).

Harpsfield, *Pretended Divorce*   Nicholas Harpsfield, *A Treatise on the Pretended Divorce between Henry VIII and Catherine of Aragon*, ed. N. Pocock. Camden Society, 2nd series, 21 (1878).

Harrier, *Canon*   R. C. Harrier, *The Canon of Sir Thomas Wyatt's Poetry* (Cambridge, Mass., 1975).

Herbert, *Henry VIII* (1679)   Edward Herbert, *The Life and Raigne of King Henry the eighth* (1679).

Herbert, *Henry VIII*   Edward Herbert, *The History of England under Henry VIII* [ed. White Kennett] (1870).

Hist. Mss. Comm.   Historical Manuscripts Commission.

House of Commons   *The House of Commons, 1509–58*, ed. S. T. Bindoff (1982).

de Iongh, *Margaret of Austria*   Jane de Iongh, *Margaret of Austria* (1954).

Ives, in *Trans. Hist. Soc.*   E. W. Ives, 'Court and county
Lancs. & Ches., 123   palatine in the reign of Henry VIII', in *Transactions of the Historic Society of Lancashire and Cheshire*, 123 (1972), 1–38.

Kelly, *Matrimonial Trials*   H. A. Kelly, *The Matrimonial Trials of Henry VIII* (Palo Alto, California, 1975).

Kipling, *Triumph of Honour*   G. Kipling, *The Triumph of Honour* (The Hague, 1977).

Knecht, *Francis I*   R. J. Knecht, *Francis I* (1983).

Knowles, *Religious Orders*   D. Knowles, *Religious Orders in England*, iii (1959).

Latimer, 'Treatyse'   William Latimer, 'Treatyse' on Anne Boleyn, in Oxford, Bodleian Library, MS Don. C.42.

Lehmberg, *Later Parliaments*   S. E. Lehmberg, *The Later Parliaments
of Henry VIII*   of Henry VIII* (Cambridge, 1977).

Lehmberg, *Reformation*   S. E. Lehmberg, *The Reformation
Parliament*   Parliament, 1529–36* (Cambridge, 1970).

Lisle Letters   *The Lisle Letters*, ed. M. St. Clare Byrne (Chicago & London, 1981).

Love Letters	*Love Letters of Henry VIII*, ed. H. Savage (1949).
Lowinsky, in *Florilegium*	E. E. Lowinsky, 'A music book for Anne Boleyn', in *Florilegium Historiale*, ed. J. G. Rowe & W. H. Stockdale (Toronto, 1971), pp. 160–235.
LP	*Letters and Papers, Foreign and Domestic, of the Reign of Henry VIII*, ed. J. S. Brewer et al. (1862–1932).
The Maner of the Tryumphe	*The Maner of the Tryumphe at Caleys and Bulleyn*, Wynkyn de Worde (1532), ed. A. F. Pollard, in *Tudor Tracts* (1903).
Mattingly, *Catherine of Aragon*	G. Mattingly, *Catherine of Aragon* (1950).
McConica, *English Humanists*	J. K. McConica, *English Humanists and Reformation Politics* (Oxford, 1965).
Muir, *Life and Letters of Wyatt*	K. Muir, *The Life and Letters of Sir Thomas Wyatt* (Liverpool, 1963).
Muller, *Gardiner*	J. A. Muller, *Stephen Gardiner and the Tudor Reaction* (1926).
Murdoch, *English Portrait Miniature*	J. Murdoch et al., *The English Portrait Miniature*.
Narratives of the Reformation	*Narratives of the Days of the Reformation*, ed. J. G. Nichols. Camden Society, 77 (1859).
Neale, *Queen Elizabeth*	J. E. Neale, *Queen Elizabeth* (1934).
Nicolas, *Privy Purse*	*Privy Purse Expenses of King Henry VIII*, ed. N. H. Nicolas (1827).
The noble tryumphant coronacyon	*The noble tryumphant coronacyon of Quene Anne*, Wynkyn de Worde (1533), ed. A. F. Pollard, in *Tudor Tracts* (1903).
NPG, *Portraits*	National Portrait Gallery, *Catalogue of Tudor and Jacobean Portraits*, ed. R. Strong (1969).

Nugarum

Ogle, *Lollards' Tower*

Ordinances for the Household

Original Letters

Paget, in *BIHR*, 54

Parker, *Correspondence*

Parker, *Drawings*

Pocock, *Records*

Prescott, *Mary Tudor*

Quinn in *Irish Historical Studies*

Ridley, *Cranmer*

RO

Rowlands, in *British Museum Yearbook*

Russell, *Cloth of Gold*

Sander, *Schism*

Scarisbrick, *Henry VIII*

Borbonius [Nicholas Bourbon], *Nugarum Libri Octo* (Lyons, 1538).

A. Ogle, *The Tragedy of the Lollards' Tower* (1949).

Ordinances and Regulations for the Royal Household, ed. Sort, Gough, Topham and Brand (Society of Antiquaries, 1790).

Original Letters relative to the English Reformation, ed. H. Robinson. Parker Society (1846–7).

Hugh Paget, 'The youth of Anne Boleyn', in *BIHR*, 54 (1981).

Correspondence of Matthew Parker, ed. J. Bruce and T. T. Perowne. Parker Society (1853).

K. T. Parker, *The Drawings of Hans Holbein . . . at Windsor Castle* (1945).

Records of the Reformation: the Divorce, 1527–33, ed. N. Pocock (Oxford, 1870).

H. F. M. Prescott, *Mary Tudor* (1952).

D. B. Quinn, 'Henry VIII and Ireland, 1509–34', in *Irish Historical Studies*, 12 (1961), 318–44.

J. Ridley, *Thomas Cranmer* (Oxford, 1962).

London, Public Record Office.

J. Rowlands, 'A portrait drawing by Hans Holbein the younger', in *British Museum Yearbook*, 2 (1977).

J. G. Russell, *The Field of Cloth of Gold* (1969).

Nicolas Sander, *The Rise and Growth of the Anglican Schism*, ed. D. Lewis (1877).

J. J. Scarisbrick, *Henry VIII* (1968).

Sergeant, *Anne Boleyn*   P. W. Sergeant, *Anne Boleyn: a Study* (revised ed., n.d.).

Southall, *Courtly Maker*   R. Southall, *The Courtly Maker* (Oxford, 1964).

Spelman, *Reports*   *The Reports of Sir John Spelman*, ed. J. A. Baker. Selden Society, 93, 94 (1977–8).

Starkey, thesis   D. R. Starkey, 'The King's Privy Chamber, 1485–1547' (unpublished Ph.D. thesis, University of Cambridge, 1973).

Sterling, *Master of Claude*   Charles Sterling, *The Master of Claude, Queen of France* (New York, 1975).

St German, *Doctor and Student*   Christopher St German, *Doctor and Student*, ed. T. F. T. Plucknett & J. J. Barton (Selden Society, 91, 1974), pp. 315–40.

St. Pap.   *State Papers, King Henry VIII*, (1830–52).

Stickland, *Queens of England*   Agnes Strickland, *Lives of the Queens of England* (1868).

Thomas, *The Pilgrim*   William Thomas, *The Pilgrim*, ed. J. A. Froude (1861).

Thomson, *Wyatt and his Background*   P. Thomson, *Sir Thomas Wyatt and his Background* (Stanford, California, 1964).

Tudor Royal Proclamations   *Tudor Royal Proclamations*, ed. P. L. Hughes & J. F. Larkin, i(1964).

Warnicke, in *History*, 70   Retha M. Warnicke, 'The fall of Anne Boleyn: a reassessment', in *History* 70 (1985) 1–15.

Wolsey, ed. Singer   *The Life of Cardinal Wolsey by George Cavendish*, ed. S. W. Singer (2nd edn 1827).

Wood, *Letters*   *Letters of Royal and Illustrious Ladies*, ed. M. A. E. Wood (1846).

Wriothesley, *Chronicle*   Charles Wriothesley, *A Chronicle of England, 1485–1559*, ed. W. D. Hamilton. Camden Society, 2nd series, 11 & 20 (1875, 1877).

George Wyatt, *Papers*   *The Papers of George Wyatt*, ed. D. M. Loades. Camden Society, 4th series, 5 (1968).

George Wyatt, in *Wolsey*, ed. Singer   George Wyatt, 'The Life of Queen Anne Boleigne', in *The Life of Cardinal Wolsey by George Cavendish*, ed. S. W. Singer (1827).

Wyatt, *Poems*   Sir Thomas Wyatt, *Collected Poems*, ed. J. Daalder (Oxford, 1975).

Yates, *Astraea*   F. A. Yates, *Astraea: The Imperial Theme in the Sixteenth Century* (1975).

Index